Afrocentricity and the Academy

Dedicated to the memory of our beloved brother, teacher, friend, husband, and father, Dr. Lorenza Jelani Williams (June 19, 1955–July 8, 2002).

Afrocentricity and the Academy

Essays on Theory and Practice

Edited by JAMES L. CONYERS, JR.

McFarland & Company, Inc., Publishers
Jefferson, North Carolina, and London

ALSO BY JAMES L. CONYERS, JR.

African American Jazz and Rap:
Social and Philosophical Examinations of Black Expressive Behavior
(McFarland, 2001)

Africana Studies:
A Disciplinary Quest for Both Theory and Method
(McFarland, 1997)

Library of Congress Cataloguing-in-Publication Data

Afrocentricity and the academy : essays on theory and practice /
edited by James L. Conyers, Jr.
    p.   cm.
    Includes bibliographical references and index.

    ISBN 0-7864-1542-8 (softcover : 50# alkaline paper)

    1. African-Americans — Study and teaching. 2. Afrocentrism —
United States. 3. African-Americans — Ethnic identity. 4. African
Americans — Education (Higher) — Philosophy. 5. Africa —
Civilization — Study and teaching. 6. Pan-Africanism. I. Conyers,
James L.
E184.7.A35   2003
973'.0496073 — dc21   2002156433

British Library cataloguing data are available

©2003 James L. Conyers, Jr. All rights reserved

No part of this book may be reproduced or transmitted in any form
or by any means, electronic or mechanical, including photocopying
or recording, or by any information storage and retrieval system,
without permission in writing from the publisher.

On the cover: ©2000 Artville

Manufactured in the United States of America

McFarland & Company, Inc., Publishers
  Box 611, Jefferson, North Carolina 28640
  www.mcfarlandpub.com

Table of Contents

Preface   1

Part 1: Pedagogy and Implementation

African American Achievement: Using Critical Pedagogy to Critique a Plan Intending to Address Educational Disparities
  Carol Lloyd   5

The Black Studies Paradigm: The Making of Scholar Activists
  Terry Kershaw   27

The Afrocentric Idea in Education
  Molefi Kete Asante   37

Afrocentricity and the Arrangement of Knowledge
  Kathleen E. Bethel   50

Part 2: Theoretical Assessment

W.E.B. Du Bois and/as Africana Critical Theory: Pan-Africanism, Critical Marxism, and Male Feminism
  Reiland Rabaka   67

A Theoretical Analysis of Persuasive Tactics Used by Frederick Douglass in "The Meaning of July Fourth for the Negro"
  Jason J. Thompson and *Reynaldo Anderson*   113

The Philosophy of the Black Power Movement Using Ntu as a Theoretical Construct
  Paul Easterling   123

African American Intellectual History: Philosophy and Ethos
  Malachi Crawford   129

Part 3: Critical Analysis

Afrocentricity and African Psychology
    Kevin Cokely   141

The Black Male Narrative: An Afrocentric Assessment
    James L. Conyers, Jr.   163

What Is Afrocentric? Applying Afrocentric Analysis to a Non-Fiction Text
    Sandy Van Dyk   176

Part 4: Pan-Africanist Thought

The Return: Slave Castles and the African Diaspora
    Tanya Y. Price   187

The Shebanization of Knowledge
    Miriam Ma'at-Ka-Re Monges   199

Why Write "Black"? Reclaiming African Culture Resource Knowledges in Diasporic Contexts
    George J. Sefa Dei   211

"There Was No Better Place to Go"? Quintard Taylor, Afrikancentricity, and the Historiography of the Afrikan Experience in the American West
    Ahati N.N. Toure   231

Mulattos, Freejacks, Cape Verdeans, Black Seminoles, and Others: Afrocentrisim and Mixed-Race Persons
    Rhett Jones   257

The Interaction Sphere of Nubia and Egypt: From the Old Kingdom to the Meroitic Period
    Larry Ross   286

About the Contributors   309
Index   311

Preface

This study seeks to closely question the theoretical framework of Afrocentricity. It is organized into four parts, each of which provides descriptive and evaluative analyses centered on agency, humanism, common sense, and the quest for Africana autonomy. The parts are titled "Pedagogy and Implementation," "Theoretical Assessment," "Critical Analysis," and "Pan-Africanist Thought." Readers will have an opportunity to study the theoretical accounting for the Afrocentric Idea.

The first part focuses on pedagogy and implementation in regard to Afrocentricity. Carol Lloyd's article, "African American Achievement: Using Critical Pedagogy to Critique a Plan Intending to Address Educational Disparities," is a survey and analysis with emphasis on the Omaha Public School System. Lloyd uses the Paulo Freire theory of pedagogy of the oppressed as a framework to establish what she refers to as "critical pedagogy." Her hypothesis is that student education and success depend on mastery of knowledge, rather than rote memory of names, dates, and events. She discusses the problems with measuring achievement in school districts focusing on standardized test scores rather than conceptual knowledge of information and technology. Lloyd raises many thought-provoking points regarding the importance of critical reflection in developing educational plans for low-achieving African American students.

Terry Kershaw's essay, "The Black Studies Paradigm: The Making of Scholar Activists," is a critical analysis of Black Studies, with emphasis on theory and methods. Recognized nationally for his cutting edge work on research methodology, Kershaw offers an innovative critique in which he outlines the boundaries of traditional academic disciplines in mediating Africana phenomena. Kershaw also provides a systematic approach to validate theory and methods in the social and humanistic aspects of Africana culture and history. The "assumptions that guide research and theory in Black/Africana Studies" use multiple variables of measurement, such as the nature of human beings (ontology); the role of common sense; theory as an orientation to data; and place and value. The approach Kershaw offers is insightful and presents opportunities for scientific advancement in the discipline of Africana Studies.

Molefi Kete Asante's article, titled "The Afrocentric Idea in Education," considers the reasons and the techniques for infusing Afrocentricity into general education curricula. He discusses the nature and scope of a truly Afrocentric approach and suggests ways to promote Afrocentricity in educational systems. As Asante points out, the Afrocentric view in education encourages viewing Africans as ordinary humans but with a heightened sense of awareness and autonomy. Profferring the thesis established by Carter G. Woodson in the *Mis-education of the Negro*, published in 1933, Asante considers the social goals of education and what they mean for African Americans. The article includes a powerful discussion of Afrocentricity and history.

Kathleen E. Bethel's "Afrocentricity and the Arrangement of Knowledge" limns the epistemological boundaries of Africana studies. In a discussion of how the concepts and teaching of Africana Studies are based on a system of knowledge and not on the social construction of race, she concentrates on cataloging information with emphasis on the professionalism of librarianship and the topic area of ancient Kemet. Bethel offers suggestions for Afrocentric cataloging and emphasizes the important role of Black Studies professionals as "culture keepers."

Part 2, "Theoretical Assessment," begins with Reiland Rabaka's article "W.E.B. Du Bois and/as Africana Critical Theory: Pan-Africanism, Critical Marxism, and Male Feminism." It uses critical theory to review the philosophical and historical ideas of Du Bois. Rabaka places his discussion within the context of Africana social philosophy—borrowing from Lucius Outlaw, Lewis Gordon, and other Black existentialists. His thesis is to "appropriate the thought and texts of W.E.B. Du Bois as an instance and tradition of philosophizing." The second part of his article examines the unequal treatment of black and white students and the institutional racism which permeates education from a Eurocentric hegemonic perspective.

Jason J. Thompson and Reynaldo Anderson's study, "A Theoretical Analysis of Persuasive Tactics Used by Frederick Douglass in 'The Meaning of July Fourth for the Negro'," highlights Douglass' lecture given at Corinthian Hall on July 5, 1852. The authors provide an historical context and discuss the rhetorical strategies Douglass employed to make his points to a predominantly white audience. Thompson and Anderson also cover lynchings in the Deep South. A brief biography of Douglass is offered.

Paul Easterling's essay discusses "The Philosophy of the Black Power Movement Using Ntu as a Theoretical Construct." Ntu is "the universal force" manifested as humans, things, time and place, and modality. Easterling discusses the Black Power Movement in the context of each of these manifestations.

Malachi Crawford's essay, "African American Intellectual History: Philosophy and Ethos," considers three systems of thought as represented in the works of Frederick Douglass, Alexander Crummel, and W.E.B. Du Bois. Crawford shows how all these systems address the vital need for African Americans to realize their humanity.

Part 3, "Critical Analysis," begins with Kevin Cokely's "Afrocentricity and African Psychology," which concentrates on Black psychology and Afrocentricity. The author's ideas advance the body of literature on Africa-centered psychology. Cokely explores the concept of psychology and the limitations it has in the study and evaluation of Africana phenomena. Additionally, the author offers his hypotheses about Africa-centered psychologists and the continued use of Afrocentric paradigms in psychological studies.

James L. Conyers, Jr.'s, essay titled "The Black Male Narrative: An Afrocentric Assessment" examines selected texts and sources on African American males. What are the commonalities among different narratives? Can we use such narratives to construct a framework for understanding problems in the African American community? This essay considers these questions and the possible answers suggested by biographies of John Henrik Clarke, Nat Turner, Malcolm X, and others.

Sandy Van Dyk's article, "What Is Afrocentric? Applying Afrocentric Analysis to a Non-Fiction Text," uses systematic Africology as a theoretical construct to examine texts related to African people and subjects. Van Dyk reviews the ongoing debates within and outside of the discipline of African American studies concerning the validity of Afrocentricity. An essential feature of this article is its discussion of whether the Afrocentric idea can be used by non–African ethnic groups.

Part 4, "Pan-Africanist Thought," begins with Tanya Y. Price's essay, "The Return: Slave Castles and the African Diaspora," an ethnographic study of the relationship between slave castles at Cape Coast in Ghana and the African diaspora. Price offers an historical overview of these castles dating back to 1652, and addresses issues of colonialism and the occupation of west African states by European settlers. Within this discussion on colonization, Price points out how mineral resources were stripped from Ghana, which led to the advancement of European economic growth and expansion. Importantly, Ghana was one of the last major empires of the western Sudan. The holding of enslaved Africans in this nation state was critical to the initiation of the African diaspora.

Miriam Ma'at-Ka-Re Monges's article, "The Shebanization of Knowledge," uses an Afrocentric methodological approach to examine the Queen of Sheba and her knowledge. In Makeda, the Queen of Sheba, Monges finds a paradigm for discovery research and the writing of the biographies of people of African descent. Using biblical sources and addressing the Queen of Sheba's place of origin in Ethiopia, the author seeks a new perspective on the queen and her relationship with King Soloman. This search leads to observations about the intuitive and the feminine as aspects of knowledge.

George J. Sefa Dei's essay, "Why Write 'Black'? Reclaiming African Culture Resource Knowledge in Diasporic Contexts," looks at knowledge as a tool of liberation for oppressed people, with emphasis on Africana phenomena. Dei critiques the limitations of the Eurocentric hegemonic perspective, then demonstrates the logic of the Afrocentric idea and its flexibility in organizing, interpreting, and examining data and information. This article shows how knowledge systems are organized, produced and extrapolated for the infusion of cultural values.

Ahati N.N. Toure's article, "'There Was No Better Place to Go'? Quintard Taylor, Afrikancentricity, and the Historiography of the Afrikan Experience in the American West," is a synopsis of African American historiography, particularly in the works of Quintard Taylor, Jr. Toure notes some of the major themes Taylor has created in a body of literature, including caste (race), gender, and European ethnicity with emphasis on the American West. He studies Taylor's analysis of migration patterns and settlements in states such as California, New Mexico, and Texas. Toure analyzes Taylor's historigraphical methods and considers the author's contributions to knowledge of the African experience in United States history.

Rhett Jones's article, titled "Mulattos, Freejacks, Cape Verdeans, Black Seminoles, and Others: Afrocentrisim and Mixed-Race Persons," explores Europeans' labeling of Africans as non-humans. He reveals how European colonists created a racial hierarchy by separating blacks from Indians. Jones then examines the strategies that persons of mixed descent employed to deny their African heritage.

Larry Ross's essay, "The Interaction Sphere of Nubia and Egypt: From the Old Kingdom to the Meroitic Period," examines the historical and cultural connection between ancient Nubia and Egypt. Ross offers a chronology of Ancient Nubia and discusses the "Old Kingdom" in ancient Kemetic culture. These areas of research are critical to understanding Nile Valley civilization, as well as to studying knowledge systems and development.

Part 1: Pedagogy and Implementation

African American Achievement: Using Critical Pedagogy to Critique a Plan Intending to Address Educational Disparities
Carol Lloyd

African American students in a metropolitan school district in the Midwest display, like most other African American students across this country, lower achievement than other students in the district. The school district developed an "African American Achievement Plan" to address this discrepancy. Though created with sincere intentions, it fails to critically evaluate the complexities of schooling and related social issues in which poor educational achievement is embedded. The proposed solutions, therefore, are not likely to be effective since they fail to address the underlying issues.

I have chosen to use this Plan as a vehicle to articulate my concerns about changes in schooling that attempt to address disparate educational outcomes, intending to further the dialogue that is occurring in this district as well as similar dialogues transpiring around the country.

In this paper, I weave together my perspectives with the published work of others, anecdotes from preservice teachers in my classes, examples from my children's experiences as students in this district, and the beliefs of district teachers and administrators I have learned through conversations and interviews.

Critical Pedagogy as a Framework

To examine this Plan, I use critical pedagogy as my overarching framework, drawing heavily on work of Paulo Freire. I chose this perspective because critical pedagogy "challenges us to recognize, engage, and critique (so as to transform) any existing undemocratic social practices and institutional structures that produce and sustain inequalities and oppressive social identities and relations" (Leistyna and Woodrum, 1996, p. 2). Given that African American low achievement in schools is both historically and currently pervasive, the lens of critical pedagogy is essential if effective transformations are to occur.

The Plan aims to integrate African American students into an existing system without questioning the basic premises upon which that system operates. As Freire (1993) tells us, "The solution is not to 'integrate' them into the structure of oppression, but to transform that structure so that they can become 'beings for themselves'" (p. 55). Yet there is a glaring absence of critical reflection about the political nature of education, of the power relationships embedded in schools. Rather than attempting to democratize schools, the guiding purpose seems to be finding an answer to the question, "How can educators in this district help African American students improve their achievement (grades, scores on standardized tests, and placement in high level classes) in an existing system?"—a hegemonic perspective. If these students do not achieve at acceptable levels, the Plan requires further assessment to determine if they are learning disabled or if their cognitive ability is "high" enough to meet higher expectations.

These proposed actions indicate a belief in a deficit model in which students are described as having some deficiency which requires remediation (Ladson-Billings, 1995). This is in stark contrast to the belief that disenfranchised groups contain rich and abundant funds of knowledge in their families and communities (Moll, 1993). A deficit model to describe minorities is so often part of the ideology of educators. It ignores inner-city African American children's "learning in order to survive the cruel and stark reality of their community" (Macedo, 1994, p. 141).

The Plan does not critique what constitutes school-sanctioned knowledge. Yet knowledge is not politically neutral; those with knowledge have power (Freire and Faundez, 1989). There is also no critique of the use of standardized tests to judge the acquisition of that knowledge. When the educational system and the community define school success as above average (or better) scores on standardized tests, they appear to take a neutral stance in defining achievement. Not addressed are the ways in which existing assessment practices are based on a view of education that reflects dominant (i.e., White, middle-upper class) knowledge, values, and behaviors (Fischer *et al.*, 1996).

The construct of cultural capital provides a perspective that removes the neutrality of existing educational practices in that it represents "institutionalized, i.e., widely shared, high status cultural signals (attitudes, preferences, formal knowledge, behaviors, goods and credentials) used for social and cultural exclusion" (Lamont and Lareau, 1988, p. 156).

Exclusion through cultural capital gives power to one group over another. "[I]t is a power of legitimating the claim that specific cultural norms and practices are superior, and of institutionalizing these claims to regulate behavior and access to resources" (Lamont and Lareau, 1988, p. 159). Minority students, as a group, are likely to go through and leave school without the cultural and social capital (LaMont and Lareau, 1988) that provide access to the knowledge and resources that would allow them to reach their goals (Stanton-Salazar, 1997). In this sense, power is "the ability to gain freedom from the control of others" (Spring, 1998, p. 31). Though this Plan is designed with the intention of providing more African American students with this cultural capital, the absence of addressing the social and political structures that define cultural capital, the ways in which it is assessed, and the lack of congruence between African American culture and the cultural capital of dominant society make it difficult to achieve this goal.

One recurring theme expressed by African American parents and community members is the lack of respect shown toward students. Using knowledge from students' lives is integral and essential to teaching that shows respect for students (Freire, 1998). In other words, respect is not just about speaking politely, showing concern about students' well-being, or celebrating Black History Month, but is also about respecting the dignity of students' life experiences (Fantini and Weinstein, 1968; hooks, 1994; Thompson, 1998). A group of English as a Second Language students (Students for Cultural and Linguistic Democracy [ScaLD], 1996) in California voice this powerfully:

> Education should not be preparing us to live in an abstract, distant world, it must be living, today. Students have backgrounds, history, and most importantly, students are human beings.... For students of color, ... there is nothing in the educational system that they can identify with. Our culture, language, life history is severed, there is nothing in the content or the relations that is recognizable to our lives. If the education that is being offered to students has nothing to do with our lives, why should we consider education anything important [pp. 134, 135]?

The Plan buys into the "middle-class cultural ideal that holds out the promise of individual mobility to those who acquiesce to the curriculum" (Aronowitz, 1993, p. 10). Belief in this promise was demonstrated by an African American parent who suggested that students needed to be told that school success would get them better jobs. Though it is true that more and better education affects employment possibilities, Whites are more likely to get hired and to have better paying jobs than African Americans with similar or more education (Mickelson, Smith, and Oliver, 1993; Sable, 1998). In fact, White male high school drop-outs make more money, on average, than Black males with high school diplomas (Sable, 1998). The overrepresentation of African American males in professional (football, basketball, and baseball) and NCAA Division I (basketball and football) sports reflects the perception that this population is unlikely to succeed in mainstream America (Sailes, 1996/97).

If schools are to be "sites of social transformation where students are educated to become informed, active, and critical citizens" (Giroux and McLaren, 1996, p. 309), then the realities of the relationships between education, employment, salary, and race, as well as the other issues I have described, have to be part of the discussion. "[E]ducation, as a specifically human experience, is a form of intervention in the world" (Freire, 1998, pp. 90–91). Praxis, the reflection and action Freire (1993) describes, is the basis of transformation. It occurs through dialogues when the purpose of those dialogues is transformation out of an oppressive condition. "To exist humanly, is to *name* the world, to change it. Once named, the world in its turn reappears to the namers as a problem and requires of them a new *naming*" (Freire, 1993, p. 69). This paper attempts to name the world this achievement Plan purports to address, but has failed to name.

For example, the typical classroom perspective on multiculturalism is to show differences and similarities between races and ethnicities. This perspective does not name the world in that it is not designed to examine the nature of the oppression of marginalized people. In effect, much of multiculturalism in schools has subdued attempts at radical transformation of the education system (McCarthy, 1988). Here is an example of how this shallow, rather than transformational, perspective is played out. I recently observed a high school history class during a lesson on the 1960s civil rights movement. Students had read a chapter in their textbook which described Rosa Parks' famous bus ride, the Voting Rights Act, and Brown v. Board of Education. Classroom interaction followed a recitation model: the teacher asked text-based questions, students responded. The teacher made a brief comment about court-ordered desegregation in the district. Though no student interaction was encouraged, an African American student shared her story anyway, telling the class that she was in that school after experiencing discrimination in an adjoining district. I was looking forward to an interesting discussion about racism in schools as experienced by students, but the teacher merely acknowledged the student's story and continued with the lesson. Within a critical perspective, this was *the* teachable moment, yet an opportunity to show students that they were learning about their world because they are *in* the world (Freire, 1998) was neglected. The teacher silenced the students by cutting off any possibility of dialogue.

The district's process that developed the Plan has, on the surface, components that might lead some to see it as true dialogue. Educators, parents, and community members were on the committee that drafted the Plan. Four public meetings were held to discuss the draft. Several subsequent meetings for African American parents were held in which they were encouraged to discuss their aspirations for their children, and ways in which they could ensure their child's success in school. However, existing educational practices were not the focus of either set of meetings. The "world" was not questioned. I am referring to the world of existing curriculum, the world of standardized tests, and the world of existing teaching methodologies in which the banking model (Freire, 1993) is found more frequently than methodologies that encourage problem-solving in ways that question social, political and economic realities. Indeed, maintaining these hegemonic beliefs about schooling is not likely to "diminish the resistance of students as they refuse to read the 'chosen' word" (Macedo, 1994, p. 104).

Engaging in praxis requires a paradigm shift by educators (hooks, 1994), politicians, parents, and other community members (i.e., taxpayers) in the ways education is viewed. Spiro (Spiro *et al.*, 1987) provides a useful analogy to consider here. He describes expert learning in terms of cognitive flexibility. This type of learning requires one to move away from narrowly defined heuristics for problem solving to a different view of problem solving altogether. His analogy is that of approaching a landscape from different directions. Likewise, we need to encourage multiple perspectives as we confront the experiences of African American students in our schools.

Demographics of African American Students

This district is located in a metropolitan area in the Midwest, encompassing both urban and suburban neighborhoods. There are just over

43,000 students enrolled in pre-kindergarten through twelfth grade. African Americans comprise the largest minority group, 31.2 percent, in the district. Hispanic Americans account for almost 10 percent of the school population, with Asian Americans and Native Americans representing 1.4 percent and 1.6 percent, respectively. (See Table 1.)

African American students are overrepresented in the special education population (defined as students with any kind of handicapping condition), making up 37.8 percent of this group. In contrast, they are underrepresented in advanced placement classes—only 9.7 percent of students in these classes are African American. (See Table 1.) Though the differences in achievement between African American students and all other students is decreasing, a huge gap still exists (see Table 2).

Table 1:
Pre-K–12 Race and Class Placement Data
(1998–99 academic year)

	Total	%	Total	%	Total	%
All students	45,119		6,143		503	
By race:						
Caucasian	25,212	55.9				
African American	14,068	31.2		37.8		9.7
Hispanic American	4,469	9.9				
Native American	732	1.6				
Asian American	638	1.4				

Table 2:
Comparison of Mean Percentile Scores
for African American and Other Students
(California Achievement Tests) (1998–99)

Grade	2		3		4		5		6		8	
	AA	O	AA	O	AA	O	AA	O	AA	O	AA	O
Total Reading	40	68			38	70	35	67	37	67	39	63
Total Language	52	79	44	76	45	77	49	79	49	78	45	72
Total Math	52	82	46	79	45	77	43	73	48	77	39	65

AA = Af. Am.   O = Other

Improving African American achievement in mathematics and science has been a priority of this district for the last few years and has been supported by a federally funded project. Though these students have shown improvement, there is still a wide gap between them and their Caucasian counterparts. Table 3 shows the numbers and percentages of high school students in college preparatory math and science courses. Disparities occur at two points: a lower percentage of African American students enroll in the math or science pipeline to upper-level (and therefore college bound) classes than White students, and, of those who do enroll, a lower percentage finishes with a grade of C or better.

Table 3:
High School[1] Math[2] and Science[3] College Prep Classes:
Enrollment and Success (1997–98)

	MATH					SCIENCE				
	Total	Enrolled		Successful		Total	Enrolled		Successful	
	#	#	%	#	%	% of total enrollees	#	#	%	#	%	% of total enrollees
Caucasian	6677	4440	66	2600	39	59	6677	4468	67	2699	40	60
African American	3053	1527	50	553	18	36	3053	1863	61	613	20	33

[1]Represents 6 out of 7 high schools, grades 9–12.
[2]Math courses giving students opportunity to take precalculus or calculus as seniors.
[3]Biology, chemistry, or physics.
[4]Success = grade of C or better.

The overrepresentation of African Americans in low level classes and their underrepresentation in advanced classes is consistent with research in English (Gamoran, Nystrand, Berends, and LePore, 1995), math, and science classes (Clewell, Anderson, and Thorpe, 1992; Oakes, 1990). Nationally, students who are either African American (or Latino) or from low-income families are more likely to be placed in non-college prep classes than their White or high-income peers (The Education Trust, 1998), thus having fewer opportunities to participate in advanced courses (Secada, 1990). Additionally, African Americans are overrepresented in special education programs, accounting for 20.6 percent in those programs while their population represents 16.9 percent of the public school population (U.S. Department of Education, 1998).

Proficiency in reading, math, science, and writing, as measured by the National Assessment of Educational Progress (NAEP), is congruent with African American representation in classes: African American students continue to have significantly lower scores at ages 9, 13, and 17 in all four areas, though the gap between Blacks and Whites has been gradually narrowing (Sable, 1998). Though schools do not track students based on race, the effect of tracking is de-facto racial segregation.

The Complexity of the Issue

A major weakness of this district's plan is the absence of acknowledging, at least publicly, the complexity of African Americans' experiences in schools. Also absent is an acknowledgment of the importance of teachers' beliefs about teaching and students. Since these two issues are interrelated, I have not separated them in my discussion.

African American Support Structures

In African American culture, problem-solving often occurs within social networks that revolve around peers, family, or churches (Nelson-Legall and Jones, 1991). In schools, African Americans often use social support groups to balance the effects of racist institutional practices (Clark, 1991). The importance of these social networks is described by the construct of fictive kinship, in which unrelated peers act as if they are part of a family (Fordham, 1996). Because African Americans often assume an oppositional stance to education (Ogbu, 1995), fictive kinship typically perpetuates negative attitudes and behaviors towards schooling (Ford, 1996).

Schools can use the importance of social support prevalent in African American culture to students' educational advantage. School support, especially in the form of caring, is positively correlated to elementary students' attitudes and behaviors (Slaughter and Carlson, 1996), and somewhat positively correlated to their achievement (Battistich, Solomon, Kim, Watson, and Schaps, 1995; Clark, 1991). Involving students in teaching practices that are engaging, challenging and built around problem-solving contributes to students' sense of community in the classroom (Battistich, *et al.*, 1995). These types of classrooms improve the "goodness-of-fit" between the student's social characteristics and the expectations of school, reducing the risk of failure for African American students (Taylor, 1991).

The typical instruction for poor students, namely a focus on low-level skills and literal knowledge in classrooms that implement isolated, competitive classroom structures and tasks, is counter-productive (Battistich *et al.*, 1995; Nelson-LeGall and Jones, 1991).

Politically, African Americans have had little power in and out of school. Historically, many states in all regions of the country created multiple obstacles to education for freed slaves (Anderson, 1995). The parents and grandparents of today's children were students in 1954 when the Brown v. Board of Education decision was rendered and in 1964 when Congress passed the Voting Rights Act. This school district operated under a court-ordered desegregation plan from 1976 to 1984. Bussing continued voluntarily through the 1998–99 school year. (As a result of a successful bond issue, a return to neighborhood schools, with a commitment to equity, began in the fall of 1999.) In this district, Black children are more likely to receive Title I services and are more likely than White children to be placed in low-level classes. When my daughter was a third-grader and bussed to a Black school, she asked why the children removed from class for special help were mainly the neighborhood African American students. An assistant principal of an elementary school described the neighborhood middle school as a two-tiered school: an upper tier composed of mainly White students, and a lower tier of predominantly Black students. Even with integrated schools, racial stratification exists.

Ogbu (1995) describes African Americans (and American Indians, Mexican Americans in the Southwest, and Native Hawaiians) as involuntary minorities in a country that enslaved, conquered or colonized its ancestors. Many African Americans develop an oppositional stance to ideas, behaviors, and structures that they perceive as White to cope with their oppression and maintain a sense of cultural independence (Ogbu, 1992). These behaviors are often a major source of conflict between schools and students (Gilmore, 1985). An African American middle school assistant principal told me that she receives more referrals for African American children than White because the White teachers perceived these students' behaviors as disrespectful. My daughter frequently shared stories about one of her eighth-grade teachers who sent African American classmates to the office while White students who talked or behaved in similar ways were merely asked to stop. Simultaneously, Black children feel disrespected when their behaviors are not affirmed in schools. Also, during my daughter's bussed third-grade year, she wondered why the students sent to the principal for misbehaving were almost always Black.

Students with different ways of speaking and styles of social interaction than those of their teachers are often perceived as at-risk students and are likely to have difficulty in school (Heath, 1983). Yet these behaviors are valued within their own communities (Moll, 1993; Taylor and Dorsey-Gaines, 1988), informing children early on that the speech and styles of their parents and communities are not valued in the school setting.

Since family income can change, the poverty level of individual families does not correlate highly with academic achievement (Orland, 1994), but it does make a difference at the school level. The higher the poverty level of a school, the greater the likelihood that all students, even those from non-poor families, will experience lower academic achievement than those from non-poverty schools (The Education Trust, 1998). In poor elementary schools, there is a greater emphasis on decontextualized, skills-based instruction in reading (Allington, 1991), math, and science (The Education Trust, 1998). At the secondary level, students in poor schools are less likely to be enrolled in the math or science classes that fulfill college entrance requirements. Simultaneously, minority students are less likely to receive instruction that is challenging, engaging, and requires higher-level thinking (The Education Trust, 1998). (See Shannon, 1998, for a discussion about the relationships between poverty, politics, and education.)

Many educators believe that learning is sequential, and that higher-level thinking is not possible for students who have not mastered basic skills. This deficit (often attributed to poor parenting) and remediation (to "fix" students) perspective looks at teaching methods as ways to ameliorate this situation (Bartolomé, 1994). For example, teachers may learn that, as a group, African Americans have a different learning style than White students (e.g., Rowser and Koontz, 1995) and thus alter their teaching methods. While there are differences in how students learn, it is simplistic to think that merely altering methods will result in major changes in African American achievement (Bartolomé, 1994). In contrast, Bartolomé maintains that to effect true change in schools, educators must examine practices that have been discriminatory towards certain groups. In this altered environment, teachers are more likely to develop an effective educational ideology that guides their teaching, rather than implementing methods as if there were no political impact.

Freire (Freire and Faundez, 1989) also makes the point that if education is to be democratized, it "cannot simply undergo changes in methods" (p. 78). Rather, the people who are most affected, in this case the African American community, must participate with educators in the transformation of schools. The school district did include, and continues to include the community. These conversations, however, did not focus on school transformation. Though some parents openly criticized the school for what they saw as racist practices, the emphasis continues to be on ways to address the outcomes of schooling rather than the nature of schooling itself. As one school administrator explained,

> You don't see institutionalized racism happening. It's like a cancer and it's difficult to [show] people that they are ill.... Obviously, if you could put a finger on it, you could take care of it immediately. Instead you have to cajole and walk around the issue because nobody wants to talk about racism in America [Interview 9-2-98].

Ignoring race is one way that teachers, especially White teachers, attempt to equalize their treatment of students. It is not uncommon for White teachers to say that they are colorblind. "I don't care if kids are black, white, or purple. They're all the same." Yet African Americans take their Blackness wherever they go. Parents *want* teachers to notice their children's Blackness (Paley, 1979; Thompson, 1998). "From a Black standpoint, racist conflict is too obvious to be denied" (Thompson, 1998, p. 537). When that Blackness is ignored in schools, African American children see school as irrelevant (Thompson, 1998).

Sometimes these well-meaning teachers, in their attempts to ignore racial differences so that all children feel the same, display unintentional insensitivity to students' cultures. Willis (1997), an African American researcher, tells about her son's writing assignment which, on the surface, seemed to encourage engagement with ideas and provide an authentic writing opportunity. The class had completed reading *Across Five Aprils* (Hunt, 1991), a novel about the Civil War. The teacher told the students to write a letter to someone as if they had lived during the time of the story. Willis' son was faced with a dilemma. If he had been alive then, he would have been a slave and would not have known how to write. I recounted this anecdote to students in a graduate course, many of whom teach in the district I have been discussing. Most of the students' initial responses were about ways to make the assignment do-able. Suggestions ranged from asking this boy to pretend he could write even though he would not have been able to, to writing his paper as if he had somehow learned to write as a slave, to pretending he was White. No one suggested that the teacher re-frame the assignment to look at the political, historical, and social issues related to slavery and literacy. When I made that suggestion, some teachers asked if it was acceptable to bring up race. I wondered aloud how *not* addressing this question about racism would be acceptable. The teachers' responses reflect, to me, a reluctance to bring uncomfortable issues into the classroom. Though teachers may be concerned about political issues in education, especially as they are brought to their attention, many are averse to discussing matters that make them or their students uncomfortable. Several pre-service elementary teachers I taught were likewise reluctant to bring *Nightjohn* (Paulsen, 1993), a powerful story about slavery, into an elementary classroom.

Assessments and Race

Like the country as a whole and many other school districts, this district places much emphasis on students' standardized test scores.

"Unfortunately, the consumers of school achievement test scores have often used test results without considering the complexity of achievement and its causes, ... erroneously attributing the level of achievement test scores to the influence of a single teacher, school, or school district" (Haladyna et al., 1991, p. 4).

The results of standardized assessments are reified, which means that, though an abstraction, they are treated as if they were something concrete (Sirotnik, 1994). For example, the district assesses students' learner characteristics, using the results to infer the ways in which students learn. Math assessments are used to identify which learners are low math achievers. This assumes these students need remediation in math skills and that they cannot succeed in math classes that require higher-level thinking and problem-solving. In other words, the outcome measures are translated into student attributes: Jerome is 5'2", weighs 120 pounds, and is a low-achiever in math. The first two *are* attributes; the last is a reification of Jerome's scores on a standardized math test. At best, any test is an indicator of that student's performance on that measure at that time.

Using many types of assessment would provide expansive descriptions of relevant educational factors, such as critical thinking and problem-solving abilities in different situations, the ability to define and successfully complete complex tasks, attendance, and knowledge. Adding credibility and importance to these non-standard assessments would help to promote more equitable and excellent educational opportunities for students (Sirotnik, 1994).

Students may know more and be able to do much more than is evidenced at school. A discrepancy between teachers' low perceptions of students' knowledge and skills and their actual abilities may be a result of irrelevant, decontextualized school tasks. For example, Mahiri and Sablo (1996) describe the prolific writings of a 15-year-old African American girl who wrote poetry, songs, raps, and plays at home. A 17-year-old African American eleventh grade boy wrote raps and songs outside of school since sixth grade. Unfortunately, neither of these students had opportunities in school to develop and produce writing that demonstrated their actual abilities.

Blacks, as a group, have always scored significantly lower than Whites on all standardized tests of intelligence, general ability, and academic achievement (Haney, 1993). Standardized tests are racially biased because the constructs upon which they are based, such as vocabulary knowledge and comprehension, are ambiguous, and test items are ethnocentric to White, middle-upper class children (Ford, 1996; Hilliard, 1997).

The emphasis in this country on standardized tests has perpetuated the historical belief in African Americans' inferiority and deprived backgrounds (Fischer et al., 1996). It allows educators to see Black children from a deficit perspective (Hilliard, 1997) that costs them as being in need of compensatory education. Without a critical examination of the relationships between socio-cultural background, testing, and education, standardized tests will continue to be emphasized in this district and across the nation. Several elementary and secondary teachers told me that many of their African American students know much more than their test scores indicate.

Tests and teaching. Teachers in schools with mandated standardized tests who have high-minority classrooms tend to teach low-level knowledge in science and math since that matches the emphasis of the test. Higher-order thinking, such as problem solving, generating ideas, or justifying procedures, is rarely part of science instruction (Lomax, West, Harmon, Viator, and Madaus, 1996). Consequently, minorities are underrepresented in professions dependent on science or math (Clewell, Anderson, and Thorpe, 1992). Others have found this same situation across the curriculum: teachers are also pressured to teach low-level skills in reading and social studies, often abandoning teaching that focuses on conceptual understanding and problem solving (Cooper, E.J., 1995; Johnston, 1989; Shepard, 1991; Smith, 1991).

White (1999) found that elementary teachers in two schools in this district believed that they had independence in the ways in which they taught reading while simultaneously describing and adhering to the district policy of grouping children for skills instruction based on standardized scores from the previous year. Their primary instructional focus in reading instruction was on skills, a finding similar to Johnston's (1989).

The stakes related to test scores have been high in this district and are increasing in importance as the state explores ways in which to rate each school district, intending to post the results on the Internet. The local newspaper reports average scores for this and adjoining districts, profiling schools according to their rankings based on these tests. Principals in some of the schools in this district are supportive of their teachers, encouraging effective teaching. Others publicly ridicule teachers at faculty meetings if their test scores are lower than others.' Some elementary teachers in this district tell stories of colleagues who change students' answers on the California Achievement Test. At some schools, entire classes re-take the test when their scores are believed to be lower than what was expected. The effects of the proliferation of high-stakes testing on children, on children's learning, and on teachers are, in many schools, catastrophic (Kohn, 1999).

18 Part 1: Pedagogy and Implementation

A second grade teacher explained her frustration with the emphasis placed on the California Achievement Test.

> I honestly believe that the CAT test[s] ... we give are biased. My African American students do not use words such as "ordinarily, rare," you know, I mean it's just not in their vocabulary.... A lot of them aren't exposed to the vocabulary that's on there; not that that's wrong.... They are just not exposed to the words and the things that we [Whites] use.... So I just think it's kind of biased and, you know, if you asked one of my African American students that live around here, they could count money probably better than anybody in the world.... We assume that they have the same experiences that the rest of the population has and they don't. They have ones that make them the person they are.... When the [local newspaper] came in here and did those big articles and they were hammering away at us, they just wanted to say, "Well, they are poor, and they don't know [much]...." That's not it. Their experiences are different. They are very rich and smart in their own ways. Maybe we are not testing this; maybe we never look in and tap what they know" [Interview 5-6-98].

The public and educators' perception of standardized tests. Increases in standardized test scores have been used to provide more money to schools (an obvious irony), reported in the local news media (Sirotnik, 1994), and considered when parents purchase houses (Johnston, 1992; Sirotnik). In this state, educational standards for reading, writing, science, mathematics, and social sciences were recently developed and approved. State legislators want a single test to be given to students across the state to measure school and district success in teaching those standards. The politicians are frustrated with the recommendations from psychometricians and the state school superintendent to allow each district to determine how to assess its students. Even if a test were found or could be developed that matched the state standards, standardized measures cannot assess educational goals such as "interpersonal understandings and human relations, citizenship and civic responsibility, enculturation, intellectual development in the disciplines, critical and independent thinking, emotional and physical well-being, creativity and aesthetic expression, self-realization, moral and ethical character development, and career, vocational and life preparation" (Sirotnik, p. 164).

Access to Educational Opportunities

Students' access to educational opportunities is part of the complexity of African American achievement. In this district, some elementary students receive differential instruction, remedial or challenge, based on reading and math scores on standardized tests. In some middle schools, there are honors classes in math, science, social studies, and language arts. In the high schools, there are honors and advanced placement classes, "regular" classes, and remedial classes in academic offerings.

While tracking is predicated on the assumption that appropriate level classes will help students catch up, most students who are in low track classes in elementary and middle school remain in the low tracks in high school (Oakes and Lipton, 1994). "[A]cademic grouping, such as placement in special education classes, ability grouping, curriculum tracking, and segregated bilingual education" (Spring, 1998, p. 83) segregates students and results in inequitable access to knowledge and opportunities (Allington, 1991). Teachers tend to have lower expectations of these students (Carey, 1989), which impacts students' performance (Weinstein, Madison, and Kuklinksi, 1995). These classrooms exhibit what Freire (Freire and Faundez, 1989) called "the castration of curiosity" (p. 35). Teachers, guided by the demands of standardized tests and textbook information, perpetuate an authoritarian classroom with little, if any, room to generate ideas.

The interactions between race, tracking and achievement were evident at the awards assemblies at my son's high school and my daughter's middle school. Though over fifty percent of the students were African American at both schools, they comprised a very low minority of academic award recipients at the high school. At a recent National Junior Honor Society induction ceremony at my daughter's school, only twenty percent of the new inductees were African American.

Students' perceived academic abilities, whether based on teacher feedback, class placement, or receipt of special services, positions them on a status continuum. Since African Americans are often the students in low level classes, low ability groups, Title I, or special education, schools label and confirm their low status. This results in low expectations by teachers, other students, and the students themselves (Cohen, Kepner, and Swanson, 1995).

A high school teacher described how teachers' lack of knowledge of their students beyond typical classroom tasks often leads them to have low expectations. The teacher's comments also points out how what counts as mathematical knowledge in school often discounts the mathematical ways of knowing of disenfranchised groups (Frankenstein and Powell, 1994).

> We have kids here in the inner city that can run down those things at amazing rates to you and tell you what they're broken down for and what

percentage goes into something else, into making a block of acid or crack. And they can tell you all the ingredients right down to the smallest percentage and make it for you. And you say, "This is a chemistry lab...!" And [other teachers] tell me this kid's not smart enough to be [in your class]? I have a problem with that.... Algebra, geometry, they do it all on the street. They're just not taught to apply it in the correct way. And that's my inner city view on teachers not being teachers, teachers that conform to a society that's willing to place the kids in categories rather than give the kids the opportunity to learn [Interview 5-20-97].

In this district, placement in higher level classes in the middle school, if available, is inconsistent. Some elementary teachers say they have no input into the placement of their sixth graders into seventh grade classes; placements are determined solely by CAT scores. Other teachers indicate that their recommendations are heavily weighed when counselors make decisions about middle school placement. Parents have input also, but at a recent meeting of African American parents, one mother said that she had to convince her child's counselor that an upper-level math course would be appropriate for her daughter. Counselors do not solicit parental input; the involvement and request of this parent in her child's middle school schedule was an exception. Though parents must sign their child's proposed schedule for middle school, there is no systematic discussion about the ramifications of enrollment in courses. Rather, requiring a parent's signature gives the appearance of school-parent interaction.

More experienced teachers usually teach higher-level classes (Oakes and Lipton, 1994) and, in this district, teach at higher achieving schools. The district is committed, however, to altering at least the latter condition by no longer automatically honoring teachers' requests to transfer schools. Another problem is that teachers in this district who are responsible for the students who struggle the most (Title 1, special education, and remedial students) are not required to have any special preparation in reading and the other language arts, or math — the areas in which these students have the most difficulty.

Schools must provide the codes of power, the cultural capital of our society, to marginalized students, thus giving them the skills they need to compete in our society. Simultaneously, schools must honor the cultural codes of these students (Delpit, 1995). In math and science, areas that greatly affect college and employment opportunities, minorities have poorer attitudes and achievement (Dossey, Mullis, Lindquist, and Chambers, 1988; Mullis and Jenkins, 1988). They also have less knowledge about careers related to these subject areas (Clewell, Anderson, and Thorpe, 1992). I provide another anecdote from my daughter's school experiences to demonstrate how some of the district's actions perpetuate unequal access to educational opportunities. Recently, my daughter was invited, because of her success in honors classes, to attend a series of Saturday workshops aimed at teaching study skills and ways to learn about colleges. The irony, if not educational malpractice, seemed so obvious to me! The achievement levels at this school are very low compared to other middle schools in this district, and the student population is about half African American. The students who should have been invited to learn about study skills and think about college are the ones who needed that support (Sable, 1998), not students who were already successful!

Teachers' beliefs about students' abilities translates into educational opportunities provided or denied, sometimes in subtle ways. During a discussion about emergent literacy in my class, a preservice teacher described with dismay a kindergarten teacher she was observing who always wrote the poor, mainly Black children's names on their papers because "They can't write their names." A fifth-grade teacher I observed during a science lesson explained, after I suggested that a three-column organizer, "What I Know, What I Want to Know, What I Learned" (Ogle, 1986) might be useful in such a lesson, that she could not use that strategy because she had run out of those forms. She said that these poor, mainly Black children were unable to divide their paper into thirds, and need paper with the lines already drawn.

Moving On

At the time of this writing, Al Gore and George W. Bush were campaigning for the office of President of the United States. With typical political rhetoric, they each have a plan to improve the education (read: "to improve test scores") of American students. Regardless of the election results, the absence of a critical conversation about the purposes of education in a democratic society composed of diverse groups, and the complexities related to such purposes, will result in the continued marginalization of many of its students.

We have often heard that schools mirror society. When teachers deposit knowledge, the meaning of which is uncontested by students (or teachers, for that matter), it reflects, in Freirian pedagogy, the dominance of existing societal relationships and the subordination of others who are thus marginalized (da Silva and McLaren, 1993). Teachers are caught in the middle of this house of mirrors as states emphasize standards which are measured by standardized tests, and state legislatures mandate the ways in which reading must be taught.

On a more positive note, for this school district to have made public the need to address the unequal educational outcomes for African American students shows courage. Administrators are pursuing many avenues to address inequities, such as making costly renovations to run-down buildings and lowering class sizes in the inner-city schools. This district has just completed a 5-year program that has increased the number of African American students taking and succeeding in upper-level math and science courses (Mitchell, Nichol, and Flowers, 1998). The same program showed African American parents how to work with and be advocates for their children.

Freire (1998) tells us that we must have hope. "Hope is something shared between teachers and students. The hope that we can learn together, teach together, be curiously impatient together, produce something together, and resist the obstacles that prevent the flowering of our joy" (p. 69). He also explains that we have a responsibility to intervene in the world. "[M]y role in the world is not restricted to a process of only observing what happens but it also involves my intervention as a subject of what happens in the world ... I am equally subject and object in the historical process" (pp. 72–73).

Thus it is our obligation "to construct an educational vision in which self-development and social transformation go hand in hand in the struggle for social justice" (da Silva and McLaren, 1993, p. 52).

References

Allington, R.L. (1991). "How policy and regulation influence instruction for at-risk learners, or why poor readers rarely comprehend well and probably never will." In L. Idol and F.G. Jones (eds.). *Educational values and cognitive instruction: Implications for reform* (pp. 273–293). Hillsdale, NJ: Erlbaum.

Anderson, J.D. (1995). "Literacy and education in the African-American experience." In V.L. Gadsden and D.A. Wagner (eds.), *Literacy among African-American youth: Issues in learning, teaching, and schooling* (pp. 19–37). Hampton, NJ: Hampton Press.

Aronowitz, S. (1993). "Paulo Freire's radical democratic humanism." In P. McLaren and P. Leonard (eds.), *Paulo Freire: A critical encounter* (pp. 8–24). New York: Routledge.

Bartolomé, L.I. (1994). "Beyond the methods fetish: Toward a humanizing pedagogy." *Harvard Educational Review, 64,* 173–194.

Battistich, V., D. Solomon, D. Kim, M. Watson, and E. Schaps. (1995). Schools as communities, poverty levels of student populations, and students' attitudes, motives, and performance: A multilevel analysis. *American Educational Research Journal, 32,* 627–658.

Carey, N. (1989, July). "Instruction." In R.J. Shavelson, L.M. McDonnell, and J. Oakes (eds.), *Indicators for monitoring mathematics and science education: A sourcebook.* Santa Monica, CA: RAND.

Clark, M.L. (1991). "Social identity, peer relations, and academic competence of African-American adolescents." *Education and Urban Society*, 24, 41–52.

Clewell, B.C., B.T. Anderson, and M.E. Thorpe (1992). "Breaking the barriers: Helping female and minority students succeed in mathematics and science." San Francisco: Jossey-Bass. *American Educational Research Journal*, 32, 493–522.

Cohen, E.G., D. Kepner, and P. Swanson (1995). "Dismantling status hierarchies in heterogeneous classrooms." In J. Oakes and K.H. Quartz (eds.), *Creating new educational communities: Ninety-fourth yearbook of the National Society for the Study of Education* (pp. 16–31). Chicago: University of Chicago Press.

Cooper, E.J. (1995). "Curriculum reform and testing." In V.L. Gadsden and D.A. Wagner (eds.), *Literacy among African-American youth: Issues in learning, teaching, and schooling* (pp. 281–298). Hampton, NJ: Hampton Press.

da Silva, T.T., and P. McLaren (1993). "Knowledge under siege: the Brazilian debate." In P. McLaren and P. Leonard (eds.), *Freire: A critical encounter* (pp. 36–46). New York: Routledge.

Delpit, L. (1995). *Other people's children: Cultural conflict in the classroom*. The New Press: New York.

Dossey, J.A., I.V.S. Mullis, M.M. Lindquist, and D.L. Chambers (1988). *Mathematics: Are we measuring up? The mathematics report card*. Princeton, NJ: Educational Testing Service.

The Education Trust (1998). *Education watch 1998: The Education Trust state and national data book (Vol. II)*. Washington, DC: The Education Trust.

Fantini, M., and G. Weinstein (1968). *Making urban schools work: Social realities and the urban school*. New York: Holt, Rinehart and Winston.

Fischer, C.S., M. Hout, M.S. Jankowski, S.R. Lucas, A. Swidler, and K. Voss (1996). *Inequality by design: Cracking the bell curve myth*. Princeton, NJ: Princeton University Press.

Ford, D.Y. (1996). *Reversing underachievement among gifts Black students: Promising practices and programs*. New York: Teachers College Press.

Fordham, S. (1996). *Blacked out: Dilemmas of race, identity and success at Capital High*. Chicago: University of Chicago Press.

Frankenstein, M., and A.B. Powell (1994). "Toward liberatory mathematics: Paulo Freire's epistemology and ethnomathematics." In P.L. McLaren and C. Lankshear (eds.), *Politics of liberation: Paths from Freire* (pp. 74–99). New York: Routledge.

Freire, P. (1993). *Pedagogy of the oppressed*. New York: Continuum.

———. (1998). *Pedagogy of freedom: Ethics, democracy, and civic courage*. Lanham, MD: Rowman and Littlefield.

———, and A. Faundez (1989). *Learning to question: A pedagogy of liberation*. New York: Continuum.

Gamoran, A., M. Nystrand, M. Berends, and P.C. LePore. (1995). "An organizational analysis of the effects of ability grouping." *American Educational Research Journal*, 32, 687–715.

Gilmore, P. (1985). "'Gimme room': School resistance, attitude, and access to literacy." *Journal of Education*, 167, 111–128.

Giroux, H.A., and P. McLaren (1996). "Teacher education and the politics of engagement: The case for democratic schooling." In P. Leistyna, A. Woodrum, and S.A. Sherblom (eds.), *Breaking free: The transformative power of critical pedagogy* (pp. 301–331). Cambridge, MA: Harvard Educational Review.

Haladyna, T.M., S.B. Nolen, and N.S. Haas (1991). "Raising standardized achievement test scores and the origins of test score pollution." *Educational Researcher, 20* (5), 2–7.

Haney, W. (1993). "Testing and minorities." In L. Weis and M. Fine (eds.), *Beyond silenced voices: Class, race, and gender in United States schools* (pp. 45–73). New York: State University of New York Press.

Heath, S.B. (1983). *Ways with words.* New York: Cambridge University Press.

Hilliard III, A.G. (1997). "Language, culture and the assessment of African American children." In A. L. Goodwin (Ed.) *Assessment for equity and inclusion: Embracing all our children* (pp. 229–240). New York: Routledge.

hooks, bell (1994). *Teaching to transgress: Education as the practice of freedom.* New York: Routledge.

Hunt, I. (1991). *Across five Aprils.* Berkley Publishing Group

Johnston, P. (1989). "Constructive evaluation and the improvement of teaching and learning." *Teachers College Record, 90,* 535–549.

_____. (1992). *Constructive evaluation of literate activity.* White Plain, NY: Longman.

Kohn, A. (1999, December 9). "Tests that cheat our students" [Op-Ed]. *New York Times.*

Ladson-Billings, G. (1992). "Reading between the lines and beyond the pages: A culturally relevant approach to literacy teaching." *Theory into Practice, 31,* 312–320.

_____. (1995). "Toward a theory of culturally relevant pedagogy." American *Educational Research Journal, 32,* 465–491.

Lamont, M., and A. Lareau (1988). "Cultural capital: Allusions, gaps and glissandos in recent theoretical developments." *Sociological Theory, 6,* 153–168.

Leistyna, P., and A. Woodrum (1996). "Context and culture: What is critical pedagogy?" In *Breaking free: The transformative power of critical pedagogy.* Cambridge, MA: President and Fellows of Harvard College.

Lomax, R.G., M.M. West, M.C. Harmon, K.A. Viator, and G.F. Madaus. (1996). The impact of mandated standardized testing on minority students. *Journal of Negro Education, 64,* 171–185.

Macedo, D. (1994). *Literacies of power: What Americans are not allowed to know.* Boulder: Westview Press.

Mahiri, J., and S. Sablo (1996). "Writing for their lives: The non-school literacy of California's urban African American youth." *Journal of Negro Education,* 65, 164–180.

McCarthy, C. (1988). "Rethinking liberal and radical perspectives on racial inequality in schooling: Making the case for nonsynchrony." *Harvard Educational Review,* 58, 265–279.

Mickelson, R.A., S.S. Smith, and M.L. Oliver (1993). "Breaking through the barriers: African American job candidates and the academic hiring process." In L. Weis and M. Fine (eds.), *Beyond silenced voices: Class, race, and gender in United States schools* (pp. 9–24). New York: State University of New York Press.

Mitchell, C., R. Nichol, and M. Flowers (1998). "Pushing the drivers and getting results: The Banneker Partnership's use of data." Paper presented at the Ninth Education Trust National Conference, Washington, DC.

Moll, L. (1993). "Bilingual classroom studies and community analysis." *Educational Researcher,* 21, (2) 20–24.
Mullis, I.V.S., and L.B. Jenkins (1988). *The science report card: Elements of risk and recovery.* Princeton, NJ: Educational Testing Service.
Nelson-LeGall, S., and E. Jones (1991). "Classroom help-seeking behavior of African-American children." *Education and Urban Society,* 24, 27–40.
Oakes, J., and M. Lipton (1994). "Tracking and ability grouping: A structural barrier to access and achievement." In J.I. Goodlad and P. Keating (eds.), *Access to knowledge: The continuing agenda for our nation's schools* (pp. 187–204). New York: College Entrance Examination Board.
Ogbu, J.U. (1992). "Adaptation to minority status and impact on school success." *Theory into Practice,* 31, 287–295).
Ogbu, J. (1995). "Literacy and Black Americans: Comparative perspectives." In V.L. Gadsen and D.A. Wagner (eds.), *Literacy among African-American youth: Issues in learning, teaching, and schooling* (pp. 83–100). Cresskill, NJ: Hampton Press.
Ogle, D. (1986). "K-W-L: A teaching model that develops active reading of expository text." *The Reading Teacher,* 39, 564–570.
Orland, M.E. (1994). "Demographics of disadvantage: Intensity of childhood poverty and its relationship to educational achievement." In J.I. Goodlad and P. Keating (eds.), *Access to knowledge: The continuing agenda for our nation's schools* (pp. 43–58). New York: College Entrance Examination Board.
Paley, V.G. (1979). *White teacher.* Cambridge: Harvard University Press.
Paulsen, G. (1993). *Nightjohn.* New York: Bantam Doubleday Dell.
Rowser, J.F., and T.Y. Koontz (1995). "Inclusion of African American students in mathematics classrooms: Issues of style, curriculum, and expectations." *The Mathematics Teacher,* 88, 448–453.
Sable, J. (1998). *The educational progress of Black students.* Washington, DC: National Center for Educational Statistics.
Sailes, G.A. (1996/1997). "Betting against the odds: An overview of Black sports participation." *African American Men,* 2, 11–22.
Secada, W.G. (1991). "Student diversity and mathematics education reform." In L. Idol and B.F. Jones (eds.), *Educational values and cognitive instruction: Implications for reform* (pp. 297–332). Hillsdale, NJ: Lawrence Erlbaum.
Shannon, P. (1998). *Reading poverty.* Portsmouth, NH: Heinemann.
Shepard, L. (1991). Interview on assessment issues with Lorrie Shepard. *Educational Researcher,* 20(2), 21–23, 27).
Sirotnik, K.A. (1994). "Equal access to quality in public schooling: Issues in the assessment of equity and excellence." In J.I. Goodlad and P. Keating (eds.), *Access to knowledge: The continuing agenda for our nation's schools* (pp. 159–185). New York: College Entrance Examination Board.
Slaughter, D.T., and K.G. Carlson (1996). "Young African-American and Latino children in high-poverty urban schools: How they perceive school climate." *Journal of Negro Education,* 65, 60–70.
Smith, M.L. (1991). "Put to the test: The effects of external testing on teachers." *Educational Researcher,* 20 (5), 8–11.
Spiro, R.J., W.P. Vispoel, J.G. Schmitz, A. Samarapungavan, and A.E. Boerger. (1987). "Knowledge acquisition for application: Cognitive flexibility and transfer in complex content domains." In B.K. Britton and S.M. Glynn (eds.),

Executive control processes in reading (pp. 177–199). Hillsdale, NJ: Lawrence Erlbaum Associates.

Spring, J. (1998). *Conflict of interests: The politics of American education.* Boston, MA: McGraw Hill.

Stanton-Salazar, R.D. (1997). "A social capital framework for understanding the socialization of racial minority children and youths." *Harvard Educational Review, 67,* 1–40.

Students for Cultural and Linguistic Democracy (SCaLD) (1996). "Reclaiming our voices." In C.E. Walsh (Ed.), *Education reform and social change: Multicultural voices, struggles, and visions* (pp. 145). Mahway, NJ: Lawrence Erlbaum Associates.

Taylor, A.R. (1991). "Social competence and the early school transition: Risk and protective factors for African-American children." *Education and Urban Society, 24,* 15–26.

Taylor, D., and C. Dorsey-Gaines. (1988). *Growing up literate.* Portsmouth, NH: Heinemann.

Thompson, A. (1998). "Not the color purple: Black feminist lessons for educational change." *Harvard Educational Review, 4,* 522–554.

U.S. Department of Education, National Center for Education Statistics (February 1998). *Overview of public elementary and secondary schools and districts: School year 1995–96.* Washington, DC: U.S. Department of Education.

Weinstein, R.S., S.M. Madison, and M.R. Kuklinski. (1995). "Raising expectations in schooling: Obstacles and opportunities for change." *American Educational Research Journal, 32,* 121–159.

White, M. (1999). "The impact of norm-referenced standardized test scores on teachers and on reading instruction." Unpublished master's thesis, University of Nebraska at Omaha.

Willis, A.I. (1997). "A critical response to motivation for literacy research." Paper presented at the 47th Annual Meeting of the National Reading Conference, Scottsdale, AZ.

The Black Studies Paradigm: The Making of Scholar Activists

Terry Kershaw

History is a guide to the present, which is a guide to the future. The promises made in the past have to be kept by those in the present. The history and promise of Black Studies has put the onus on Black Studies scholars to fulfill Black people's expectations. A critical analysis of the history of Black education reveals those expectations.

With the passage of the 13th amendment to the United States Constitution in 1866, formal slavery was ended. This allowed formerly enslaved African Americans to pursue the means to provide for themselves and their families. One of the ways this was attempted was through education. Examples of this approach are the lives of Booker T. Washington and W.E.B. Du Bois. Both pursued education as vehicle for social mobility, Washington advocating primarily for vocational education and Du Bois primarily advocating a liberal arts and classical education. Both men supported their position on the basis of what was best for Black people in their continuous struggle for equality. Both men also understood that any attempt at an education for Black Americans had to empower the group.

Carter G. Woodson, in the *Mis-Education of the Negro*, states that the education of the "Negro" takes him away from solving the needs of the people to pursuits of individual self aggrandizement. This type of education perpetuates the status quo, which in a racist society does not benefit the victims of racism. African American people want an education that helps them to solve problems. For example, during the 1960s and 1970s in urban Black communities, Black parents were demanding input and sometimes control of their school boards. Also, during the 1960s the demand for Black education that would empower students reached its pinnacle with the development of the first Black Studies department at San Francisco State University. Every Black Studies program or department has the same charge. Black Studies is an interdisciplinary field of study shaped by the three paradigmatic assumptions of centeredness, critical analysis, and empowerment. These criterion help to guide research both in its purpose and the relationship between the researcher and the "community." First, let us begin with interdisciplinarity.

A discipline of study can be thought of as a compartmentalized way of looking at subject matter. Sociology, for instance, looks at phenomena in terms of its relationship to social forces. Examples of social forces include social structure, ideology, power relations, racism, sexism, and unemployment. Social forces are shaped by human interaction and have a direct effect on life chances and life experiences. When a sociologist describes and explains social phenomena he or she does so in terms of its relationship to social forces. For example, a sociological analysis of North American divorce rates could emphasize that industrialization and urbanization lead to changes in marital roles. In turn, those forces facilitate a shift in thinking about love, marriage, children, and divorce.

The content of sociology is shaped by its disciplinary boundaries. Its theories attempt to explain and predict phenomena relative to social forces in the context of behaviors, attitudes, institutions, and other aspects of culture. Most sociological works tend to be historical because of the emphasis on empirical verification and adherence to the search for natural social laws. To view the world sociologically, according to Mills (1959), is to use the sociological imagination to understand how the larger social world and the individual life chances and experiences are interconnected. It provides the individual or group a tool by which to construct the proper context to understand the conditions of the "world" that significantly impact their life chances and experiences. The emphasis for the sociologist is on group phenomena and its impact on various groups of which all individuals are members (i.e. race, gender, class). Adopting a psychological view of the world puts a lens on the individual level of description and analysis. A psychological perspective reduces the group description and analysis to the individual level in terms of individual forces (i.e. cognition, intelligence, genes, personality). Some concentrate on attitudes and values; others are especially interested in personality, mental aberration, and how individuals cope with problems. The economist studies the production and distribution of goods and services. The political scientist focuses on the distribution of power, politics and government. All of these approaches are valid and generate valuable knowledge. However, compartmentalizing knowledge can also be problematic.

If one is trying to understand a people's history and culture then one attempts to ascertain how the different parts of their world operate together to give shape and meaning to their existence. A compartmentalized approach to knowledge could miss the important links between the individual, the group, and history because the focus within each compartment is to support its ascendancy. One may omit key descriptions and analyses that serve as positive forces for social change and empowerment. Multidisciplinary refers to the housing of multiple disciplines and the multidisciplinary ways of examining particular subject matter.

A multidisciplinary view of African American families would employ, just as the term suggests, multiple disciplines in examining the phenomena. There would be a psychological analysis, a sociological analysis, a historical analysis, and so forth. Very rarely would they overlap and often times they would compete for the "best" analysis. In a Department of Black Studies characterized by a multidisciplinary approach, the major unifying force is agreement on subject matter. There tends to be little agreement on research methods, goals, and sources of evidence. This is especially true, if the department is characterized by humanities and social science disciplinary scholars. There have been few attempts to integrate these different disciplinary perspectives into an overarching perspective as is the idea behind an interdisciplinary field of study. The field of Black Studies is an attempt to study African-descended people holistically, which necessitates a movement toward a framework that does not stop with compartmentalizing knowledge.

Interdisciplinarity can serve as an organizing framework for Black Studies. It challenges disciplinarity as being too narrowly focused for some phenomena. For example, when looking at African American family structure, an interdisciplinary analysis would focus on how historical, psychological, sociological and economic forces have shaped the structure of African American family inter- and intra-relations. The subject matter would not be different from that of a disciplinary approach, however, there would be a conscious effort to discern how linking disciplinary compartments adds to our understanding of the phenomena. Black Studies family scholars would be searching for new theories and paradigms that could serve as a guide for social change. They would be willing to seek out various sources of knowledge and different ways of understanding.

In terms of research methods, both quantitative and qualitative methods are appropriate. If the problem determines the method, then there is no one way of researching Black Studies content because disciplinary approaches tend to emphasize a particular methodological approach. The goal of Black Studies research is directly related to an attempt to understand the whole by describing and analyzing linkages between the various parts that help shape life experiences and life chances. Sources of evidence can also be qualitative and quantitative with no one type preferred over another. The only criteria, is that any method used produces the best source of data to help the researcher describe, explain and empower African American people to positively effect their life experiences and chances. In general, interdisciplinary scholars search for new paradigms and theories, and have no one preferred methodological approach. Black Studies is best served by an interdisciplinary approach.

This brings us to two important questions whose answers are directly related: "What is the primary subject matter of Black Studies?" and "Who is a person of African descent?" The primary subject matter of Black Studies is the total life experiences, past and present, of people of African descent. An African is a person who is an ancestor of the Black people who originated culturally on the continent of Africa. I extend the definition further to include those people who identify themselves as members of that group and are identified by others as members, whether living or born in Africa or the African diaspora. These are the primary sources of data for the interdisciplinary field of Black Studies.

All fields of study have at least one paradigm that serves as a guide in the development of theory and research. Paradigms are shaped by a community of scholars who accept a basic set of assumptions that determine range of phenomena, concepts, theories, methods of data collection, and analysis as well as the important questions to be answered. An example of a paradigm, and one that tends to dominate the social sciences, is positivism.

Positivists see social science "as an organized method for combining deductive logic with precise empirical observations of individual behavior in order to discover and confirm a set of probalistic causal laws that can be used to predict general patterns of human activity" (Neuman, 1997 p. 63).

Positivists assume that there are natural social laws that may be discovered by studying stable, pre-existing patterns of social behavior. The only patterns that can serve as evidence of a law are based on precise measurements and observations that can be verified empirically. Also, the researcher must always maintain a scientist's objectivity.

If one examines some of the major introductory sociology textbooks, one can find the threads of positivism running throughout the analysis. For example, discussing the social sciences, James Henslin's *Sociology: A Down to Earth Approach* (1993) states:

> Just as the natural sciences are an attempt to objectively understand the world of nature, the social sciences are an attempt to objectively under-

Table 1:
Positivist Assumptions that Guide Research and Theory in the Social Sciences

1. Reason for Research	To discover natural laws so people can predict and control events
2. Nature of Social Reality	Stable, preexisting patterns or order that can be discovered
3. Nature of Human Beings	Self-interested and rational individuals who are shaped by external forces
4. Role of Common Sense	Clearly distinct from and less valid than science
5. Theory looks like	A logical, deductive system of interconnected definitions, axioms, and laws
6. An Explanation that is True	Is logically connected to laws and based on facts
7. Good Evidence	Is based on precise observations that others can repeat
8. Place for Values	Science is value-free, and values have no place except when choosing a topic

stand the social world. Just as the world of nature contains ordered (or lawful) relationships that are not obvious but must be discovered through controlled observation, so the ordered relationships of the human or social world, too, are hidden, and must be revealed by means of controlled and repeated observations [p. 4].

According to Henslin, there is only one way to study sociology and that is through the assumptions of positivism. Now, it must be said that positivism is not the only paradigm in sociology, but it is the most dominant and informs the other two major sociological paradigms, the interpretive and critical social science paradigms. I would argue that they are all part of the same overarching paradigm of positivism because each assumes that there are natural social laws to be discovered by interpretation or through dialectics. That, however, is the subject of another discussion. This discussion focuses on identifying the paradigmatic assumptions of Black Studies that can serve as a guide to the development of research and theory.

The first criteria of the Black Studies paradigm is centrism. According to Asante (1993), Afrocentricity is an orientation to data that places African people as subjects and agents in the shaping of life chances and experiences. What this means is that phenomena studied in Black Studies must be viewed from a "Black" perspective. Karenga (1988) echoes similar sentiments when he states, "An Afro-centric approach is essentially intellectual inquiry and production centered on and in the image and interest of African peoples." Keto (1991), in his discussion of an African centered perspective on history, argues that Africa must be at the center of any African centered analysis.

The Africentric psychologists also emphasize the importance of being "centered." Azibo states, when talking about Africentric theory construction, "theories from which constructs and instruments are selected must, at best, come out of the Black perspective or, at least, not be incongruous with it" (Azibo, 1990). Baldwin (1990) argues that African psychology's conceptual framework is directly related to African reality.

Other scholars, who do not identify themselves as Afrocentric, when talking about the field of Black Studies, also point to the importance of a Black perspective as the proper frame of reference (Andersen, 1990; Taylor, 1990). Anderson states that "Black Studies emanates from an African or Afrocentric ethos and background" (Anderson, 1990: 2–3), while Taylor discusses how a number of scholars in Black Studies emphasize the importance of that work coming from a Black perspective (Taylor, 1990). Therefore, assumption number one of the Black Studies paradigm is that theory and research must be centered in the life experiences and life chances and understandings of African people.

Centered means being well-grounded in the history, culture, and understandings of African people. For example, Afrocentric scholars studying African American people have to be well grounded in African and African American history as well as African American culture in order to tell the story of African peoples life experiences and life chances from the perspective of African people.

Another way of thinking about centrism, as it relates to being well-grounded in African people's understandings, is that the story tellers must be African people. That does not mean that the physical story teller must be an African person, but the story must be African in terms of the description and analysis of the subject and major characters. Consequently, when reading a piece of work or listening to a presentation concerning African people's life experiences and life chances, we should ask some or all of the following questions: Is this how African people understand these conditions? How do we know? What are the factors that they see as important? How did or do they understand certain historical or contemporary phenomena? Where are their words? When are they speaking? Where are their voices?

All of these questions have to do with evidence and sources of data.

Questions such as Are you using primary sources? If there are not primary sources available, could you have used secondary sources that rely on primary sources of data? must be raised and answered in order to assess the centeredness of the work. The story teller must provide evidence that would allow the listeners to decide whether or not African people are telling their story. Therefore, when conducting Black Studies research, a Black perspective, a centered perspective, telling the story as African people tell the story is the key ingredient.

There are three questions that can serve as a guide to being centered. The first guiding question is, How do Black people describe their lives? The is, How do they describe what their lives ought to be? and the third is, What do they see as obstacles effecting their opportunity to live the lives they ought to be living? In seeking answers to these questions using as many primary sources as possible, the researcher can meet the centered criteria.

The second major criteria that serves as a guide in the development of Black Studies theory and research is critical analysis. This criteria helps the researcher to problematize the obstacles identified within the centered research. The question, Are the obstacles, identified by the subjects, "real" obstacles? becomes the guiding question for the researcher. The notion of real obstacles is related to empirical verification. Can the obstacles be empirically verified? is the question the researcher is trying to answer. For example, if job discrimination is seen as an obstacle, the researcher will critically examine empirical data in order to determine the relationship between the obstacle(s) and what ought to be answer. Can job discrimination, by race, be empirically verified? If so, then the empirically verified obstacles are problematized as something to be solved and also affirm the group's understandings. The obstacles that can't be empirically verified are re-examined by both the researcher and the group. The possibility of the group's understanding as an obstacle is then critically examined by both the researcher and the group.

The third criteria is that the research and theory must be empowering. It is the responsibility of the researcher to move the research and theory from the problem posing to the problem solving stage. Two interrelated questions can help guide this part of the Black Studies paradigm. The questions are, What tasks have been undertaken to eliminate the obstacles? and Have those tasks been successful? This criteria allows the researcher to act as an agent in solving the problem(s) that the obstacles cause.

Table 2 identifies some key assumptions that help elucidate this discussion of the parameters of the Black Studies paradigm and the role of Black Studies scholars.

Table 2:
Assumptions that Guide Research and Theory in Black/Africana Studies

1. Reason for Research	Relocating African people to their "African" center(s).
	Describing and explaining the agency of Africans in the shaping of their life experiences.
	Empowering Africans to positively affect their life chances and experiences.
	Generating "authentic" knowledge.
2. Nature of Human Beings	All people act from a cultural center and in their own best interest.
3. Role of Common Sense	Common sense consists of intuition and individual and group understandings based on historical and cultural context.
4. Theory as an Approach and Orientation to Data	Connects African people to their common heritage.
	Rejects the agenda of any oppressor (historical and cultural specific).
	Seeks to ensure harmony throughout humanity.
	Searches for "truth."
5. Place of Values	All research begins with a value position.
	The research must reflect an understanding of the subject group's value system.

1. The Reasons for Research must fall within the parameters of the paradigm. The guiding principle of centrism is met by locating African people to their African centers and granting agency to African people through their voice and deeds. "Centers" refer to the historical and social contexts that influence the group's understandings and actions that have an effect on their life chances and experiences. A second reason for research is to meet the criteria of critical knowledge through the generating of "authentic" knowledge. Authentic knowledge refers to the knowledge that is verified by valid sources of evidence, which includes the group's understandings. Another reason is to assess the action taken by people of African descent, that have an effect on their life chances and experiences, which is directly related to the empowerment criteria.

2. The Nature of Human Beings is that all human beings act from a cultural center and in their own best interest. This assumption about the nature of human beings is tied to the centrism and empowerment criteria. Since we assume that all human beings act from a cultural center and in their own best interest, then Black Studies research should help describe and explain that center and generate knowledge that helps Black people act in their own best interest.

3. **The Role of Common Sense** in Black Studies research is valued as a valid way of understanding how the group understands its world. It consists of intuition and group understandings within a historical and cultural context. It is directly related to the criteria of centrism and can best be generated using qualitative research techniques.

4. **Theory as an Approach and Orientation to Data** is an approach and orientation to data that describes and explains the commonalities and differences of African people as they struggle with obstacles. In particular historical moments it identifies, rejects, and presents alternatives to the agenda of any oppressor. It seeks to bring about harmony through a unity of theory and practice for African people in particular and for humanity in general. It searches for "truth" assuming that truth is both objective and subjective. Some things are whether we say they are or not. Take the classic example of a tree falling in a forest. The question, Does it make a sound if no one hears it? has to do with the concepts of objective and subjective truth. The tree makes a sound whether someone is there or not. Our presence is not primary except when interpretation becomes the criteria. And interpretation is the key to explanation.

Truth, in terms of Black Studies theory, is a synthesis between precise observations and the groups understandings. This truth can be verified testing the group's understandings using quantitative research methods. Quantitative methods allow for the testing of empirical "reality" and lend favorably to the purpose of critical analysis. It allows for problematization which is necessary for empowerment.

5. **The Place of Values** in research starts from the assumption that all research starts from a value position. Black Studies research is subjective and does not deny that position by hiding under a cloak of value neutrality. Hiding under a cloak of value neutrality is not meant to suggest intentional "fudging" of data. The data falls where it lands for all ethical researchers. What it is meant to suggest is that Black Studies research must serve the best interests of African people. Black Studies researchers must be in touch with the group of African people in which they are interested. Therefore, Black Studies researchers must be willing to assess the viability of African people's values and actions toward the improvement of life

chances and experiences. This assumption, of the role of values in Black Studies research, is related to the criteria of empowerment.

The purpose of Black Studies research is to describe, explain, and empower African people to positively effect their life chances and experiences. The role of the researcher is to maintain a dialogical relationship with African people, which leads to research agendas that are both subjective and political — vis-à-vis, in the best interest of African people. The role of the researcher is to problematize and help problem solve those forces that have a negative impact on Black people's life chances and experiences.

In conclusion, the history and needs of Black people clearly illuminates the path that Black Studies scholars must follow. They must be centered, critical, and empowering. They must be scholar activists. We promised and we must fulfill that promise.

References

Anderson, T. (1990). Black Studies: Overview and Theoretical Perspectives. In T. Anderson (Ed.), *Black Studies: theory, method, and cultural perspectives.* Pullman, WA: Washington State University Press.

Asante, M. K. (1993). Afrocentric Systematics. In M.K. Asante (Ed.), *Malcolm X as a cultural hero and other afrocentric essays.* Trenton, N.J.: Africa World Press.

Azibo, D. (1990). Personality, Clinical, and Social Psychological Research: Appropriate and Inappropriate Research Frameworks in T. Anderson (Ed.), *Black Studies: theory, method, and cultural perspectives.* Pullman, WA.: Washington State University.

Badwin, J. (1990). Notes on an Afrocentric Theory of Black Personality. In T. Anderson (Ed.) *Black Studies: theory, method, and cultural perspectives.* Pullman, WA.: Washington State University.

Henslin, J. (1993). *Sociology: A Down to Earth Approach.* Boston, MA: Allyn and Bacon.

Mills, C. W. (1959). *The Power Elite.* New York: Oxford University Press.

Neuman, W. (1994). *Social Research Methods.* Boston, MA: Allyn and Bacon. New York: Harper and Row.

Taylor, R. (1990). The Study of Black People: A Survey of Empirical and Theoretical Models. In T. Anderson (Ed.), *Black Studies: theory, method, and cultural perspectives.* Pullman, WA.: Washington State University.

Woodson, C. G. (1990). *The Mis-Education of the Negro.* Trenton, NJ: Africa World Press.

The Afrocentric Idea in Education
Molefi Kete Asante

Many of the principles that govern the development of the Afrocentric idea in education were first established by Carter G. Woodson in *The Mis-Education of the Negro* (1933). Indeed, Woodson's classic reveals the fundamental problems pertaining to the education of the African person in America. As Woodson contends, African Americans have been educated away from their own culture and traditions and attached to the fringes of European culture; thus dislocated from themselves, Woodson asserts that African Americans often valorize European culture to the detriment of their own heritage (p. 7). Although Woodson does not advocate rejection of' American citizenship or nationality, he believed that assuming African Americans hold the same position as European Americans vis-à-vis the realities of America would lead to the psychological and cultural death of the African American population. Furthermore, if education is ever to be substantive and meaningful within the context of American society, Woodson argues, it must first address the African's historical experiences, both in Africa and in America (p. 7). That is why he places on education, and particularly on the traditionally African American colleges, the burden of teaching the African American to be responsive to the long traditions and history of Africa as well as America. Woodson's alert recognition, more than 50 years ago, that something is severely wrong with the way African Americans are educated, provides the principal impetus for the Afrocentric approach to American education.

In this article I will examine the nature and scope of this approach, establish its necessity, and suggest ways to develop and disseminate it throughout all levels of education. Two propositions stand in the background of the theoretical and philosophical issues I will present. These ideas represent the core presuppositions on which I have based most of my work in the field of education, and they suggest the direction of my own thinking about what education is capable of doing to and for an already politically and economically marginalized people — African Americans:

1. Education is fundamentally a social phenomenon whose ultimate purpose is to socialize the learner; to send a child to school is to prepare that child to become part of a social group.
2. Schools are reflective of the societies that develop them (i.e., a White supremacist-dominated society will develop a White supremacist educational system).

Definitions

An alternative framework suggests that other definitional assumptions can provide a new paradigm for the examination of education within the American society. For example, in education, *centricity* refers to a perspective that involves locating students within the context of their own cultural references so that they can relate socially and psychologically to other cultural perspectives. Centricity is a concept that can be applied to any culture. The centrist paradigm is supported by research showing that the most productive method of teaching any student is to place his or her group within the center of the context of knowledge (Asante, 1990). For White students in America, this is easy because almost all the experiences discussed in American classrooms are approached from the standpoint of White perspectives and history. American education, however, is not centric; it is Eurocentric. Consequently, non–White students are also made to see themselves and their groups as the "acted upon." Only rarely do they read or hear of non–White people as active participants in history. This is as true for a discussion of the American Revolution as it is for a discussion of Dante's *Inferno*; for instance, most classroom discussions of the European slave trade concentrate on the activities of Whites rather than on the resistance efforts of Africans. A person educated in a truly centric fashion comes to view all groups' contributions as significant and useful. Even a White person educated in such a system does not assume superiority based upon racist notions. Thus, a truly centric education is different from a Eurocentric, racist (that is, White supremacist) education.

Afrocentricity is a frame of reference wherein phenomena are viewed from the perspective of the African person. The Afrocentric approach seeks in every situation the appropriate centrality of the African person (Asante, 1987). In education, this means that teachers provide students the opportunity to study the world and its people, concepts, and history from an African world view. In most classrooms, whatever the subject, Whites are located in the center perspective position. How alien the African American child must feel, how like an outsider! The little African American child who sits in a classroom and is taught to accept as heroes and heroines individuals who defamed African people is being actively de-centered, dislocated, and made into a nonperson, one whose aim in life might be to one day shed that "badge of inferiority": his or her Blackness. In Afrocentric educational settings, however, teachers do not marginalize African American children by causing them to question their own self-worth because their people's story is seldom told. By seeing themselves as the subjects rather than the objects of education — be the discipline biology, medicine, literature, or social studies — African American students come to see themselves not merely as seekers of knowledge but as integral participants in it. Because all content areas are adaptable to an Afrocentric approach, African American students can be made to see themselves as centered in the reality of any discipline.

It must be emphasized that Afrocentricity is *not* a Black version of Eurocentricity (Asante, 1987). Eurocentricity is based on White supremacist notions whose purposes are to protect White privilege and advantage in education, economics, politics, and so forth. Unlike Eurocentricity, Afrocentricity does not condone ethnocentric valorization at the expense of degrading other groups' perspectives. Moreover, Eurocentricity presents the particular historical reality of Europeans as the sum total of the human experience (Asante, 1987). It imposes Eurocentric realities as "universal," i.e., that which is White is presented as applying to the human condition in general, while that which is non–White is viewed as group-specific and therefore not "human." This explains why some scholars and artists of African descent rush to deny their Blackness; they believe that to exist as a Black person is not to exist as a universal human being. They are the individuals Woodson identified as preferring European art, language, and culture over African art, language, and culture; they believe that anything of European origin is inherently better than anything produced by or issuing from their own people. Naturally, the person of African descent should be centered in his or her historical experiences as an African, but Eurocentric curricula produce such aberrations of perspective among persons of color.

Multiculturalism in education is a nonhierarchical approach that respects and celebrates a variety of cultural perspectives on world phenomena (Asante, 1991). The multicultural approach holds that although European culture is the majority culture in the United States, that is not sufficient reason for it to be imposed on diverse student populations as "universal." Multiculturalists assert that education, to have integrity, must begin with the proposition that all humans have contributed to world development and the flow of knowledge and information, and that most human achievements are the result of mutually interactive, international effort. Without a multicultural education, students remain essentially ignorant of the contributions of a major portion of the world's people. A multicultural education is thus a fundamental necessity for anyone who wishes to achieve competency in almost any subject.

The Afrocentric idea must be the stepping-stone from which the multicultural idea is launched. A truly authentic multicultural education, therefore, must be based upon the Afrocentric initiative. If this step is skipped, multicultural curricula, as they are increasingly being defined by White "resisters" (to be discussed later), will evolve without any substantive infusion of African American content, and the African American child will continue to be lost in the Eurocentric framework of education. In other words, the African American child will neither be confirmed nor affirmed in his or her own cultural information. For the mutual benefit of all Americans, this tragedy, which leads to the psychological and cultural dislocation of African American children, can and should be avoided.

The Revolutionary Challenge

Because it centers African American students inside history, culture, science, and so forth rather than outside these subjects, the Afrocentric idea presents the most revolutionary challenge to the ideology of White supremacy in education during the past decade. No other theoretical position stated by African Americans has ever captured the imagination of such a wide range of scholars and students of history, sociology, communications, anthropology, and psychology. The Afrocentric challenge has been posed in three critical ways:

1. It questions the imposition of the White supremacist view as universal and or classical (Asante, 1990).
2. It demonstrates the indefensibility of racist theories that assault multiculturalism and pluralism.
3. It projects a humanistic and pluralistic viewpoint by articulating Afrocentricity as a valid, nonhegemonic perspective.

Suppression and Distortion: Symbols of Resistance

The forces of resistance to the Afrocentric, multicultural transformation of the curriculum and teaching practices began to circle their wagons almost as quickly as word got out about the need for equality in education (Ravitch, 1990). Recently, the renowned historian Arthur Schlesinger and others formed a group called the Committee for the Defense of History. This is a paradoxical development because only lies, untruths, and inaccurate information need defending. In their arguments against the Afrocentric perspective, these proponents of Eurocentrism often clothe their arguments in false categories and fake terms (i.e., "pluralistic" and "particularistic" multiculturalism) (Keto, 1990; Asante, 1991). Besides, as the late African scholar Cheikh Anta Diop (1980) maintained, "African history and Africa need no defense." Afrocentric education is not against history. It is for correct and accurate history. If it is against anything, it is against the marginalization of African American, Hispanic American, Asian American, Native American, and other non–White children. The Committee for the Defense of History is nothing more than a futile attempt to buttress the crumbling pillars of a White supremacist system that conceals its true motives behind the cloak of American liberalism. It was created in the same spirit that generated Bloom's *The Closing of the American Mind* (1987) and Hirsch's *Cultural Literacy: What Every American Needs to Know* (1987), both of which were placed at the service of the White hegemony in education, particularly its curricular hegemony. This committee and other evidences of White backlash are a predictable challenge to the contemporary thrust for an Afrocentric, multicultural approach to education.

Naturally, different adherents to a theory will have different views on its meaning. While two discourses about multiculturalism presently are circulating, only one is relevant to the liberation of the minds of African and White people in the United States. That discourse is Afrocentricity: the acceptance of Africa as central to African people. Yet, rather than getting on board with Afrocentrists to fight against White hegemonic education, some Whites (and some Blacks as well) have opted to plead for a return to the educational plantation. Unfortunately for them, however, those days are gone, and such misinformation can never be packaged as accurate, correct education again.

Ravitch (1990), who argues that there are two kinds of multiculturalism — pluralist multiculturalism and particularist multiculturalism — is the leader of those professors whom I call "resisters" or opponents to

Afrocentricity and multiculturalism. Indeed, Ravitch advances the imaginary divisions in multicultural perspectives to conceal her true identity as a defender of White supremacy. Her tactics are the tactics of those who prefer Africans and other non–Whites to remain on the mental and psychological plantation of Western civilization. In their arrogance the resisters accuse Afrocentrists and multiculturalists of creating "fantasy history" and "bizarre theories" of non–White people's contributions to civilization. What they prove, however, is their own ignorance. Additionally, Ravitch and others (Nicholson, 1990) assert that multiculturalism will bring about the "tribalization" of America, while in reality America has always been a nation of ethnic diversity. When one reads their works on multiculturalism, one realizes that they are really advocating the imposition of a White perspective on everybody else's culture. Believing that the Eurocentric position is indisputable, they attempt to resist and impede the progressive transformation of the monoethnic curriculum. Indeed, the closets of bigotry have opened to reveal various attempts by White scholars (joined by some Blacks) to defend White privilege in the curriculum in much the same way as it has been so staunchly defended in the larger society. It was perhaps inevitable that the introduction of the Afrocentric idea would open up the discussion of the American school curriculum in a profound way.

Why has Afrocentricity created so much of a controversy in educational circles? The idea that an African American child is placed in a stronger position to learn if he or she is centered — that is, if the child sees himself or herself within the content of the curriculum rather than at its margins — is not novel (Asante, 1980). What is revolutionary is the movement from the idea (conceptual stage) to its implementation in practice, when we begin to teach teachers how to put African American youth at the center of instruction. In effect, students are shown how to see with new eyes and hear with new ears. African American children learn to interpret and center phenomena in the context of African heritage, while White students are taught to see that their own centers are not threatened by the presence or contributions of African Americans and others.

The Condition of Eurocentric Education

Institutions such as schools are conditioned by the character of the nation in which they are developed. Just as crime and politics are different in different nations, so, too, is education. In the United States, a "Whites-only" orientation has predominated in education. This has had a profound impact on the quality of education for children of all races and ethnic groups. The African American child has suffered disproportionately, but White children are also the victims of monoculturally diseased curricula.

The Tragedy of Ignorance

During the past five years, many White students and parents have approached me after presentations with tears in their eyes or expressed their anger about the absence of information about African Americans in the schools. A recent comment from a young White man at a major university in the Northeast was especially striking. He said to me, "My teacher told us that Martin Luther King was a commie and went on with the class." Because this student's teacher made no effort to discuss King's ideas, the student had maliciously been kept ignorant. The vast majority of White Americans are likewise ignorant about the bountiful reservoirs of African and African American history, culture, and contributions. For example, few Americans of any color have heard the names of Cheikh Anta Diop, Anna Julia Cooper, C. L. R. James, or J. A. Rogers. All were historians who contributed greatly to our understanding of the African world. Indeed, very few teachers have ever taken a course in African American Studies; therefore, most are unable to provide systematic information about African Americans.

Afrocentricity and History

Most of America's teaching force are victims of the same system that victimizes today's young. Thus, American children are not taught the names of the African ethnic groups from which the majority of the African American population are descended and few are taught the names of any of the sacred sites in Africa. Few teachers can discuss with their students the significance of the Middle Passage or describe what it meant or means to Africans. Little mention is made in American classrooms of either the brutality of slavery or the ex-slaves' celebration of freedom. American children have little or no understanding of the nature of the capture, transport, and enslavement of Africans. Few have been taught the true horrors of being taken, shipped naked across 25 days of ocean, broken by abuse and indignities of all kinds, and dehumanized into a beast of burden, a thing without a name. If our students only knew the truth, if they were taught the Afrocentric perspective on the Great Enslavement, and if they knew the full story about the events since slavery that have served to constantly dislocate African Americans, their behavior would perhaps be different. Among these events are the infamous constitutional compromise of 1787, which decreed that African Americans were, by law, the equivalent of but three-fifths of a person (see Franklin, 1974); the 1857 Dred Scott decision in which the Supreme Court avowed that African Americans had no rights Whites were obliged to respect (Howard, 1857); the complete dismissal and nonenforcement of Section 2 of the Fourteenth Amendment to the Constitution (this amendment, passed in 1868, stipulated as one of its provisions a penalty against any state that denied African Americans the right to vote, and called for the reduction of a state's delegates to the House of Representatives in proportion to the number of disenfranchised African American males therein); and the much-mentioned, as-yet-unreceived 40 acres and a mule as reparation for enslavement, promised to each African American family after the Civil War by Union General William T. Sherman and Secretary of War Edwin Stanton (Oubre, 1978, pp. 18–19, 182–183; see also Smith, 1987, pp. 106–107). If the curriculum were enhanced to include readings from the slave narratives, the diaries of slave ship captains, the journals of slaveowners, the abolitionist newspapers, the writings of the freedmen and freedwomen, the accounts of African American civil rights, civic, and social organizations, and numerous other such texts, African American children would be different and White children would be different. America would be a different nation today.

America's classrooms should resound with the story of the barbaric treatment of the Africans, of how their dignity was stolen and their cultures destroyed. The recorded experiences of escaped slaves provide the substance for such learning. For example, the narrative of Jacob and Ruth Weldon presents a detailed account of the Middle Passage (Feldstein, 1971). The Weldons noted that Africans, having been captured and brought onto the slave ships, were chained to the deck, made to bend over, and "branded with a red hot iron in the form of letters or signs dipped in an oily preparation and pressed against the naked flesh till it burnt a deep and ineffaceable scar, to show who was the owner" (pp. 33–37). They also recalled that those who screamed were lashed on their faces, breasts, thighs, and backs with a "cat-o'-nine tails" wielded by White sailors: "Every blow brought the returning lash pieces of grieving flesh" (p. 44). They saw "mothers with babies at their breasts basely branded and lashed, hewed and scarred, till it would seem as if the very heavens must smite the infernal tormentors with the doom they so richly merited" (p. 44). Children and infants were not spared from this terror. The Weldons tell of a nine-month-old baby on board a slave ship being flogged because it would not eat. The ship's captain ordered the child's feet placed in boiling water, which dissolved the skin and nails, then ordered the child whipped again. Still, the child refused to eat. Eventually the captain killed the baby with his own hands and commanded the child's mother to throw the dead baby overboard. When the mother refused, she, too, was beaten, then forced to the ship's side, where "with her head averted so she might not see it, she dropped the body into the sea" (p. 44). In a similar vein, a captain of a ship with 440 Africans on board noted that 132 had to be thrown overboard to save water (Feldstein, 1971, p. 47). As another wrote, the "groans and suffocating [sic] cries for air and water coming from below the deck sickened the soul of humanity" (Feldstein, 1971, p. 44).

Upon landing in America, the situation was often worse. The brutality of the slavocracy is unequalled in the psychological and spiritual destruction it wrought upon African Americans. Slave mothers were often forced to leave their children unattended while they worked in the fields. Unable to nurse their children or to properly care for them, they often returned from work at night to find their children dead (Feldstein, 1971, p. 49). The testimony of Henry Bibb also sheds light on the bleakness of the slave experience:

> I was born May 1815, of a slave mother ... and was claimed as the property of David White, Esq.... I was flogged up; for where I should have received moral, mental, and religious instructions, I received stripes without number, the object of which was to degrade and keep me in subordination. I can truly say that I drank deeply of the bitter cup of suffering and woe. I have been dragged down to the lowest depths of human degradation and wretchedness, by slaveholders [Feldstein, 1971, p. 60].

Enslavement was truly a living death. While the ontological onslaught caused some Africans to opt for suicide, the most widespread results were dislocation, disorientation, and misorientation — all of which are the consequences of the African person being actively de-centered. The "Jim Crow" period of second-class citizenship, from 1877 to 1954, saw only slight improvement in the lot of African Americans. This era was characterized by the sharecropper system, disenfranchisement, enforced segregation, internal migration, lynchings, unemployment, poor housing conditions, and separate and unequal educational facilities. Inequitable policies and practices veritably plagued the race.

No wonder many persons of African descent attempt to shed their race and become "raceless." One's basic identity is one's self-identity, which is ultimately one's cultural identity; without a strong cultural identity, one is lost. Black children do not know their people's story and White children do not know the story, but remembrance is a vital requisite for understanding and humility. This is why the Jews have campaigned (and rightly so) to have the story of the European Holocaust taught in schools and colleges. Teaching about such monstrous human brutality should forever remind the world of the ways in which humans have often violated each other. Teaching about the African Holocaust is just as important for the same reasons. Additionally, it underscores the enormity of the effects of physical, psychological, and economic dislocation on the African population in America and throughout the African diaspora. Without an understanding of the historical experiences of African people, American children cannot make any real headway in addressing the problems of the present.

Certainly, if African American children were taught to be fully aware of the struggles of their African forebears they would find a renewed sense of purpose and vision in their own lives. They would cease acting as if they have no past and no future. For instance, if they were taught about the historical relationship of Africans to the cotton industry — how African American men, women and children were forced to pick cotton from "can't see in the morning' til can't see at night," until the blood ran from the tips of their fingers where they were pricked by the hard boll, or if they were made to visualize their ancestors in the burning sun, bent double with constant stooping, and dragging rough, heavy croaker sacks behind them, or if they were made to picture them bringing those sacks trembling to the scale, fearful of a sure flogging if they did not pick enough — perhaps our African American youth would develop a stronger entrepreneurial spirit. If White children were taught the same information rather than that normally to fed them about American slavery, they would probably view our society differently and work to transform it into a better place.

Correcting Distorted Information

Hegemonic education can exist only as long as true and accurate information is withheld. Hegemonic Eurocentric education can exist only so long as Whites maintain that Africans and other non–Whites have never contributed to world civilization. It is largely upon such false ideas that invidious distinctions are made. The truth, however, gives one insight into the real reasons behind human actions, whether one chooses to follow the paths of others or not. For example, one cannot remain comfortable teaching that art and philosophy originated in Greece if one learns that the Greeks themselves taught that the study of these subjects originated in Africa, specifically ancient Kemet (Herodotus, 1987). The first philosophers were the Egyptians—Kagemni, Khun-anup, Ptahhotep, Kete, and Seti—but Eurocentric education is so disjointed that students have no way of discovering this and other knowledge of the organic relationship of Africa to the rest of human history. Not only did Africa contribute to human history, African civilizations predate all other civilizations. Indeed, the human species originated on the continent of Africa. This is true whether one looks at either archaeological or biological evidence.

Two other notions must be refuted. There are those who say that African American history should begin with the arrival of Africans as slaves in 1619, but it has been shown that Africans visited and inhabited North and South America long before European settlers "discovered" the "New World" (Van Sertima, 1976). Secondly, although America became something of a home for those Africans who survived the horrors of the Middle Passage, their experiences on the slave ships and during slavery resulted in their having an entirely different (and often tainted) perspective about America than that of the Europeans and others who came, for the most part, of their own free will seeking opportunities not available to them in their native lands. Afrocentricity therefore seeks to recognize this divergence in perspective and create centeredness for African American students.

Conclusion

The reigning initiative for total curricular change is the movement that is being proposed and led by Africans, namely, the Afrocentric idea. When I wrote the first book on Afrocentricity in 1980, now in its fifth printing, I had no idea that in 10 years the idea would both shake up and shape discussions in education, art, fashion, and politics. Since the publication of my subsequent works, *The Afrocentric Idea* (1987) and *Kemet, Afrocentricity, and Knowledge* (1990), the debate has been joined in earnest. Still, for many White Americans (and some African Americans), the most unsettling aspect of the discussion about Afrocentricity is that its intellectual source lies in the research and writings of African American scholars. Whites are accustomed to being in charge of the major ideas circulating in the American academy. Deconstructionism, Gestalt psychology, Marxism, structuralism, Piagetian theory, and so forth have all been developed, articulated, and elaborated upon at length, generally by White scholars. On the other hand, Afrocentricity is the product of scholars such as Nobles

(1986), Hilliard (1978), Karenga (1986), Keto (1990), Richards (1991), and Myers (1989). There are also increasing numbers of young, impressively credentialed African American scholars who have begun to write in the Afrocentric vein (Jean, 1991). They, and even some young White scholars, have emerged with ideas about how to change the curriculum Afrocentrically.

Afrocentricity provides all Americans an opportunity to examine the perspective of the African person in this society and in the world. The resisters claim that Afrocentricity is anti–White, yet if Afrocentricity as a theory is against anything, it is against racism, ignorance, and monoethnic hegemony in the curriculum. Afrocentricity is not anti–White; it is, however, pro-human. Further, the aim of the Afrocentric curriculum is not to divide America, it is to make America flourish as it ought to flourish. This nation has long been divided with regard to the educational opportunities afforded to children. By virtue of the protection provided by society and reinforced by the Eurocentric curriculum, the White child is already ahead of the African American child by first grade. Our efforts thus must concentrate on giving the African American child greater opportunities for learning at the kindergarten level. However, the kind of assistance the African American child needs is as much cultural as it is academic. If the proper cultural information is provided, the academic performance will surely follow suit.

When it comes to educating African American children, the American educational system does not need a tune-up — it needs an overhaul. Black children have been maligned by this system. Black teachers have been maligned. Black history has been maligned. Africa has been maligned. Nonetheless, two truisms can be stated about education in America. First, some teachers can and do effectively teach African American children; secondly, if some teachers can do it, others can too. We must learn all we can about what makes these teachers' attitudes and approaches successful, and then work diligently to see that their successes are replicated on a broad scale. By raising the same questions that Woodson posed more than 50 years ago, Afrocentric education, along with a significant reorientation of the American educational enterprise, seeks to respond to the African person's psychological and cultural dislocation. By providing philosophical and theoretical guidelines and criteria that are centered in an African perception of reality and by placing the African American child in his or her proper historical context and setting, Afrocentricity may be just the "escape hatch" African Americans so desperately need to facilitate academic success and "steal away" from the cycle of miseducation and dislocation.

References

Asante, M. K. (1980). *Afrocentricity: The theory of social change.* Buffalo, NY: Amulefi.
Asante, M. K. (1987). *The Afrocentric idea.* Philadelphia: Temple University Press.
Asante, M. K. (1990). *Kemet, Afrocentricity, and knowledge.* Trenton, NJ: Africa World Press.
Bloom, A. (1987). *The closing of the American mind.* New York: Simon & Schuster.
Feldstein, S. (1971). *Once a slave: The slave's view of slavery.* New York: William Morrow.
Franklin, J. H. (1974). *From slavery to freedom.* New York: Knopf.
Herodotus. (1987). *The history.* Chicago: University of Illinois Press.
Hilliard, A. G., III. (1978, June 20). *Anatomy and dynamics of oppression.* Speech delivered at the National Conference on Human Relations in Education, Minneapolis, MN.
Hirsch, E. D. (1987). *Cultural literacy: What every American needs to know.* New York: Houghton Mifflin.
Howard, B. C. (1857). *Report of the decision of the Supreme Court of the United States and the opinions of the justices thereof in the case of Dred Scott versus John F. A. Sandford, December term, 1856.* New York: D. Appleton & Co.
Jean, C. (1991). *Beyond the Eurocentric Veils.* Amherst, MA: University of Massachusetts Press.
Karenga, M. R. (1986). *Introduction to Black studies.* Los Angeles: University of Sankore Press.
Keto, C. T. (1990). *Africa-centered perspective of history.* Blackwood, NJ: C. A. Associates.
Nicholson, D. (1990, September 23). "Afrocentrism and the tribalization of America." *The Washington Post,* p. B-1.
Nobles, W. (1986). *African psychology.* Oakland, CA: Black Family Institute.
Oubre, C. F. (1978). *Forty acres and a mule: The Freedman's Bureau and Black land ownership.* Baton Rouge, LA: Louisiana State University Press.
Ravitch, D. (1990, Summer). Multiculturalism: E pluribus plures. *The American Scholar,* pp. 337–354.
Richards, D. (1991). *Let the circle be unbroken.* Trenton, NJ: Africa World Press.
Smith, J. O. (1987). *The politics of racial inequality: A systematic comparative macroanalysis from the colonial period to 1970.* New York: Greenwood Press.
Van Sertima, I. (1976). *They came before Columbus.* New York: Random House.
Woodson, C. G. (1915). *The education of the Negro prior to 1861: A history of the education of the colored people of the U.S. from the beginning of slavery.* New York: G. P. Putnam's Sons.
Woodson, C. G. (1933). *The Mis-Education of the Negro.* Washington, DC: Associated Publishers.
Woodson, C. G. (1936). *African background outlined.* Washington, DC: Association for the Study of Afro-American Life and History.

Afrocentricity and the Arrangement of Knowledge
Kathleen E. Bethel

This paper will explore what the theories of Afrocentricity can mean to the arrangement of knowledge and the dissemination of information. The basic premise of Afrocentricity is to study and examine phenomena from the standpoint of Africans as subjects rather than as objects. Here, I speculate on the implications of an Afrocentric approach to such technical facets of cataloging as a controlled vocabulary, computer applications and classification schemes. The inconsistencies of classification and indexing vocabulary wreak havoc for patron access to materials on Africa and the diaspora. While this criticism about various system inadequacies is often voiced by other area and ethnic subject specialists, the evolving methodologies of Afrocentricity prompt discussion of the traditional systems in regard to Black Studies.

I am a public services librarian in the reference department at Northwestern University Library and have collection management responsibilities for African-American Studies. The Northwestern University Library boasts one of the finest collections in the world on Africa, the Melville J. Herskovits Library of African Studies, with a long-running strength in diaspora studies materials. I am the fourth person to hold a position that originated twenty-five years ago with the birth of Black Studies when there was a exigency for a subject specialist. My frustration in trying to instruct researchers in Black Studies on how to approach the collection and its catalog prompts this discussion. What would our libraries be like if the materials were arranged in a non–Western format?

How comforting it must be, not to mention empowering, for some white men to enter each and every library in the Western world and find solid validation of their existence. At the same time, many librarians know how disheartening it is for people of color to enter these same institutions and find little about their lived experiences. Of that small amount of material that people of color manage to locate, a major portion deals with pathological behaviors or may be a misrepresentation of the histories and cultures of non–Western peoples. It is not simply the materials housed in libraries that empower some white men, but also the arrangement of these items and the systems used to locate them that assure these men a preeminent position in their world of learning.

My world of learning is different. In this presentation, I want to scratch the surface in discussing Afrocentricity, knowledge, libraries, and the classification and cataloging of materials. This will not be an exercise in Cataloging 101. Nor is it a call to arms to cease supporting the information colonization of African peoples. I merely want to remind my colleagues that we are either existing on our own terms or on others' terms.

I could not discuss cataloging the Afrocentric way without acknowledging early discourse, particularly the late Doris Clack's *Black Literature Resources*,[1] and the efforts of many to address problems of subject access by many culture keepers. The task before us as librarians is to advocate the refinement of library systems and indexing language in regard to Black Studies. How we gather, classify, and disseminate the documentation of Black history and culture will ensure enlightenment and empowerment.

The Afrocentric Idea

As previously stated, the basic premise of Afrocentricity is to study and examine phenomena from the standpoint of Africans as subjects, not objects. I speak of Africans in the broadest sense, including her sons and daughters dispersed throughout this Diaspora. One of the most intellectually stimulating and innovative concepts that has emerged in the scholarship on African peoples within the last decade is Afrocentricity. This concept, as articulated by its main proponents— Cheikh Anta Diop, Molefi Asante, Maulana Karenga, John Henrik Clarke, Jacob Carruthers, Linda Myers and others— holds that any meaningful and authentic study of peoples of African descent must begin and proceed with Africa as the center, not the periphery. Afrocentricity proposes a fundamental shift in one's world view. It is not a social science method, but can be applied to the unique cultural, historical and contemporary experiences of people of African descent.

> Complex and multi-disciplinary, the concept embodies a humanistic philosophy, a scholarly methodology, and a model of practical action.[2]

An Afrocentric idea has surfaced sporadically in the history and literature of African peoples. Pan-Africanist, Negritude, and Black Nationalist movements also seek an African world view. Africa-centered historiography dates back to the closing years of colonial rule in Africa.

> African methodology grounded the works of many African scholars in the early 1960s. This development of the Africa centered approach as a theory and philosophy is a product of the 1980s and of diasporan African writings.[3]

My approach to cataloging the Afrocentric way is to first shed the twentieth century look of a nineteenth century idea and envision twenty-first century possibilities for the use of libraries and information in the liberation of African peoples. An Afrocentric perspective seeks to liberate Black Studies from an Eurocentric monopoly on scholarship and thus assert a valid world view through which Africa can be studied. It also assumes that the historical and contemporary experiences of people of African descent can prove instructive about human relations. Many Afrocentrists want all cultural groups and their respective viewpoints to be treated as equally valid. The Afrocentric study of phenomena asks questions about location, place, orientation and perspective.

> The Afrocentric paradigm is predicated on traditional African philosophical assumptions that emphasize the interconnectedness and interdependency of natural phenomena.[4]

In the history of intellectual thought, the Eurocentric paradigm has often assumed a hegemonic universal character, and European culture has placed itself at the center of the social structure, becoming the reference point by which other cultures are defined. The Eurocentric world view has become so dominant in the contemporary world that it has overshadowed other world views.[5]

> Eurocentrism ... grew out of the historical process of western colonial and economic dominance and has, in turn, provided an ideological justification for that dominance. The categories and approaches used in European academia help to maintain the political and intellectual superiority of Europe. The continuing presence of such academic constructs is a by-product of a widespread Eurocentric bias in the production, dissemination and evaluation of knowledge.[6]

Afrocentricity is not without its critics. In Black Studies today, many debate the definition, scope and direction of this perspective. One may more often find a definition of what Afrocentricity is not than what it is. I will not engage in this debate. I want to stimulate librarians, scholars, and information specialists to think about what an Afrocentric perspective can mean to the arrangement of knowledge.

Let us think about what an Afrocentric collection would look like. It would be multi-disciplinary covering all areas of knowledge. There would be greater emphasis on oral literature and the shelves would be teeming with publications and materials produced by the Black community. The materials would be promoted to assist academic excellence and social responsibility. Reflecting its collective, rhythmic and spiritual character, the physical arrangement would have an easy shelving flow that meanders through flora and fauna accompanied by the beat and rituals of the community surrounding the gathering places where generations explore knowledge and culture. I get carried away, but I am trying to create a scenario that can best describe the possibilities before us.

Knowledge and Conceptual Systems

The nature of knowledge is quite subjective and is directly related to human interest.[7] What is knowledge? A variety of definitions are found in Webster's: 1) a clear and certain perception of something; 2) learning; 3) practical experience; 4) acquaintance or familiarity; 5) recognition; 6) information; 7) the body of truth, information and principals acquired by mankind. Knowledge or perception is not a passive act in which the individual is simply an observer, but an active process where the individual can, to a degree, be said to construct her or his own perception. The world and knowledge are our own perceptions of what our minds are programmed to give meaning to.

Let us examine the origin and development of knowledge within the mind in terms of conceptual systems. A conceptual system consists of those philosophical ideas one adheres to, forming the lens through which one sees the world. It has been stated that the Eurocentric view predominately assumes a material reality, with highest value placed on the acquisition of objects. External knowledge is assumed to be the basis of all knowledge, and which is acquired through counting and measuring. The logic of this conceptual system is dichotomous and the process is technology. The consequent basis for identity and self worth in this system is external criteria (i.e. how one looks, what one owns, prestige and status symbols, etc.).[8]

An Afrocentric view assumes reality is both spiritual and material, with the highest value on interpersonal relationships between women and men, people and their groups. Self knowledge is assumed to be the basis of all knowledge, which one knows through symbolic imagery and rhythm. The logic of this conceptual system is a union of opposites as it sees all sets are interrelated through human and spiritual networks. The consequent basis for identity is intrinsic in being.

> Conceptual systems as divergent as the Eurocentric and Afrocentric ... will yield very different perceptions, cognition, and experiences for their adherents. People interested in the pursuit of knowledge must be forthright in their declaration and honest in their evaluation of the conceptual system used in their work.[9]

For the Temple School,[10] as espoused by Molefi Asante, there is a moral imperative to use an Afrocentric approach to inquiry that will bring people of African descent to the center of the discourse about knowledge acquisition. The intellectual task is to re-conceptualize the social fabric and rename the world in a way that obliterates the compartmentalization of knowledge established by European studies.[11]

> The Afrocentric orientation is that its world view, normative assumptions, and frames of reference derive from the historical experiences and folk wisdom of people whose ancestral roots trace back to prehistoric Africa, the birthplace of humanity.[12]

Kemetic Collections

The most famous libraries of ancient times were the Royal Library at Thebes and the temple libraries in Kemet (Egypt). It is said that what became the Royal Library at Alexandria, established early in the third century B.C., had a copy of every existing scroll known to its administrators. Scholars have found references to Kemetic libraries at Amarna in the 1300s B.C. and Thebes in the 1200s B.C. Barely a trace of these earlier libraries remain and no one knows for certain how they originated and what became of most of them.[13] It is important to discuss Kemetic libraries because many Afrocentric scholars have increasingly drawn a link between their work and the primacy of the classical African civilizations. The Diop and Temple University school of Afrocentric thought insists that the ancient Kemetic civilization should be the classical reference point for the study of African civilization, as the Greek civilization is for analysis of European civilization.[14]

Libraries preserve a society's cultural heritage. Had these ancient libraries survived, we might well have had models for classification and cataloging that more accurately reflected African civilization. Perhaps there were archives or libraries at the academies in Timbuktu and Great Zimbabwe that could have added to this discussion. A criticism leveled at some Afrocentric scholars is this reliance on ancient Egyptian high culture. We know that much of Egyptian culture came from much further up the Nile. Perhaps we need to look to Axum, Meroe, Nubia, and other classical African civilizations. With more archaeological work and linguistic studies, future research may reveal a more accurate history of African repositories. Much of my research for this work is from texts on Africana librarianship and on libraries in the developing world. Many Asian and African librarians believe that Western librarians do not fully understand the problems that the Asian or African book poses to its cataloger, and they are concerned that current cataloging and classification practices do not take the unique properties of non–Western materials into account.[15] We have many of the same problems with classification and cataloging for Africans in the United States or the Caribbean or South America or England as African librarians and scholars on the continent have.

We have often been taught that for those things the indigenous peoples do possess to be of any value to the academic world, they must first be analyzed, classified, and "demystified" by the "objective expert academician."[16] In order to progress and develop, human societies must be able to store knowledge for future use. Librarians, or keepers of the social record, must understand the complex nature of human cognitive and communicative processes, communication technology and the supporting culture and the maze of relationship among these factors.

A Change Is Going to Come

Librarians did not always appreciate the continual change which occurred in the structure of knowledge. Libraries are not static institutions—more thought should be given to the need for relocating material which could be better used in an up-to-date classification environment. The Dewey Decimal Classification System was developed in the nineteenth century, and the Bliss Bibliographic Classification and most of the Library of Congress Classification systems were developed in the first half of this century. We are really dealing with rather recent developments. We are aware that makers of these schemes had little information on Africa with which to work. It was still very much considered the "Dark Continent" back then.

Librarianship, as a social instrument and as a service to society, has followed a process of institutionalization influenced by the organizational structures and value systems of its supporting culture. Simply put, American and European classification schemes are not expansive enough to cover Black Studies materials. There is a colonial orientation in Western classification schemes. Most African and Caribbean histories reflect the European presence and activities on the continent, not the culture and deeds of African peoples themselves. The basis of arrangement is not the events in Africa's own history or the lives and cultures of its own peoples, but European activities and influence.[17] Social research on people of color has proceeded from a white normative orientation that sees African people in particular as passive objects acted on rather than as living beings with thoughts, feelings, desires, and aspirations of their own.[18]

> The neglect of African origins and contributions to the world's intellectual history in effect misrepresents much knowledge and perpetuates a narrow scholarship.[19]

Taking an Afrocentric approach would require extensive cooperation and coordination between librarians and scholars. There would need to be decisions made about appropriate theories of design to be adopted and on which categories of analysis would be applicable to our kind of material. This is certainly not the first, fifth or fiftieth call for exploration of a new classification scheme. This is a tremendous task to undertake and it is my opinion that the evolving theory and methodology of Afrocentricity could form the basis of a new scheme.

Catalog Lessons

The catalog is the key to a library. Some catalogers get so bogged down by cataloging codes that they forget that their readers are unaware of them. Other catalogers do not bother to consider that readers may expect to find books under entries other than those laid down in those codes. If a book is not found in the catalog where the reader expects to find it the book is as good as lost and the catalogers are wasting their time. Cataloging is a job in which one must pay great attention to detail and be prepared to take endless trouble in ensuring that entries are provided in all the possible places where patrons may expect to find them, now and in the future.

My concerns, as a reference librarian trying to mediate the struggle between scholars, the collection and its catalog, were verified by an exercise I gave to incoming minority freshmen in a summer workshop in 1992 to demonstrate difficulty with subject access. I gave students book jackets from recent titles in Black Studies and asked them to list subject terms they would use to find this material in the catalog. Their terminology was right on the money, and very little of it matched the indexing language from the Library of Congress Subject Headings. They had puzzled looks on their faces when I returned the exercises with printouts from the online catalog. I was able to make my point about access difficulty to this group, which represented some 30 percent of African-American freshmen, in a vivid manner.

Students do not approach a catalog thinking "Afro-American" as a primary subject term, nor do they make the distinction between that term and the words "Blacks," "Women, Black," "African-American" or even "Negro." Moreover, patrons do not remember to search the headings, such as "minority," "race relations," "urban," "racism," "segregation," "prejudice," "discrimination," etc., that usually examine topics in Black Studies.

Example 1:

Stone, Albert E. *The Return of Nat Turner: History, Literature, and Cultural Politics in Sixties America.* (Athens: University of Georgia Press, 1992).

Student's Language:

Nat Turner, slaves, politics, Civil Rights, 1960s, racism, violence, revolution

LCSH terms:

Nat Turner, 1800?–1831, in fiction, drama, poetry, etc.
United States—Civilization—1945–
United States—Civilization—Afro-American influences.
United States—History—1961-1963—Historiography.
United States—History—1963-1969—Historiography.

Example 2:

Chalmers, David Mark. *And the Crooked Places Made Straight: The Struggle for Social Change in the 1960s.* (Baltimore: Johns Hopkins University Press, 1991).

Student's language:

Civil Rights in America 1960s, Supreme Court Civil Rights decisions, American culture in 1960s, Youth culture 1960s

LCSH terms:

Social Change — History — 20th century.
United States — History — 1961–1969.
United States — Social conditions — 1960–1980.

Example 3:

Holloway, Karla F. C. *Moorings & Metaphors: Figures of Culture and Gender in Black Women's Literature.* (New Brunswick: Rutgers University Press, 1992.)

Student's language:

Black Women's Literature, Black Language Studies, Black Culture, Black-African Traditions, Buchi Emecheta, Toni Morrison, Efua Sutherland, Gayl Jones, Ntozake Shange, Gloria Naylor, Alice Walker

LCSH Terms:

American literature — Afro-American authors — History and criticism.
West African literature (English) — Women authors — History and criticism.
Literature, Comparative — American and West African (English).
Literature, Comparative — West African (English) and American.
Women and literature — United States — History — 20th century.
American literature — Women authors — History and criticism.
Women and literature — Africa, West — History — 20th century.
American literature — 20th century — history and criticism.
Afro-American women in literature.
Women, Black, in literature.
Sex role in literature.
Myth in literature.
Metaphor.

This rough sample of some 80 titles yielded a mere handful of terms listed in LCSH. This dilemma is not unique to Black Studies, but as an African-American Studies librarian I sense its acuteness. I have often communicated my dissatisfaction with catalogers, who empathize but are bound to policy. If one is fortunate enough to work in an institution with an online catalog, with keyword and Boolean operators, this issue of poor subject access may not pose such a drastic problem.

Librarians are genuinely concerned that patrons often do not approach a service desk after searching the catalog. Their inclination is to assume that the collection does not have the information they seek. This is particularly true for research in Black Studies, where unsuccessful searches often impede the production of scholarship. I shared the exercise with my colleagues in the reference and catalog departments, who were impressed by the students' language and supportive of the challenges of my job.

Doris Clack has based much of her work on subject access on discussions of problems of specificity, relevance, structure and predictability. Her ideal catalog equalizes access to information resources.

> An effective verbal access system will (1) provide access to all relevant materials, (2) bring together materials which, conceptually, treat substantially the same subject regardless of the difference in terminology, (3) show the relationships between and among subject fields, (4) provide access to any subject field regardless of the level at which entry into the field is made, whether general or specific, and (5) provide a description of the subject content of any bibliographic item in precise terms and in a vocabulary that is common and acceptable to the users.[20]

Dr. Clack and members of the Indexing Project of the Afro-Americans Studies Librarianship Section of the Association of College and Research Libraries21 are engaged in examining index terminology in Black Studies. I am confident that a useful thesaurus will be produced in the near future. This thesaurus will take us in the direction of thinking in the terminology that looks at the Black experience from an African centered point of view.

Cataloging Methods and Computer Applications

The Library of Congress Subject Headings and Sears List are difficult to use for Black Studies. There is a tremendous need for a stable, controlled vocabulary that is continually updated and reflects the discussions in our community. While there is an awareness among librarians of their responsibility for eradicating biases and prejudices against other cultures and heritages, requests for establishing headings and eliminating individualized changes have received a less than enthusiastic reaction from the Library of Congress and catalogers and library administrators who put a price tag on these efforts.

Cataloging simplification is the call of the day. Budgetary retrenchment and reallocation makes additional funding for cataloging unlikely. Cataloging backlogs and minimal level cataloging are unsatisfactory for librarians who want to ensure that bibliographic records continue to support effective bibliographic access.

The introduction of online searching has given the powers previously enjoyed only by indexers to searchers. Keyword access and Boolean operators allow searchers to pull words out of titles or other fields and to coordinate terms into a single concept. Such functionality supports rising user expectations in other areas. Increased subject access heads the list of suggestions for enriching bibliographic records with improved vocabulary to guide users to the controlled terminology.

There is a tendency for Africana or Black Studies librarians to look to the new information technologies as a means of "leap frogging" whole development stages in cataloging and classification. The implication is that online catalogs can facilitate global thesaurus alterations. This prompts me to note that a new library and information paradigm, based on the recognition that poverty and illiteracy dictate a revision of priorities, and guided by the principle that self-reliance is all-important, has to be rooted in clear ideas about users and potential users of information. We must at all times remember who we are servicing. A new approach must meet the needs of all libraries, public and academic, rich or poor, automated or manual.

It is relatively easy for me to speak of Africana collections, new information technologies, and the like because I am working in a major academic research library that developed one of the leading online systems, NOTIS Systems, Inc.,[22] and also boasts four Africana catalogers. I do not want to fail to consider the information environment as an organic whole, with legitimate needs at all economic and educational levels requiring the provision of service either immediately or at some subsequent planning stage.

I want us to develop foresight about our roles in the profession. Our needs and demands are so great that all too often we merely react and play defense. I believe that we should be on the offensive — plan, develop and synthesize our responsibility for the discipline. Certainly, one of these tasks is taking on the controlled thesaurus, but another task is to think of how knowledge would be arranged from an Afrocentric perspective.

Cataloging the Afrocentric Way 101

In cataloging the Afrocentric way, Afrocentrism must first be recognized as a valuable system of human thought, belief and practice. The ideal is to produce a new classification scheme that is Africa-centered with a stable and controlled, but flexible, vocabulary. Afrocentricity is particular on a proper language of discourse. These days, we should not use terms like "tribes," "Third World," "Black Africa," "African slave trade," "Middle East," "minority," "disadvantaged," "ghetto," "underclass," etc., because they are considered degrading or appear as a manipulation of our reality.[23]

The ongoing work requires us to remain vigilant and insistent that the Library of Congress Subject Headings and classification systems develop some relevance to the African experience. The ideal is to contemplate the African world in its broadest sense, wherever people declare themselves as African despite their out-migration. The ideal is to utilize subheadings and not have geographic subdivisions. Imagine collections that reflected an African presence in the world, whether it is in the Pacific, Europe or the Caribbean. For most cataloging and classification practices, the European is seen at the center of all discussions in all knowledge areas. The existing geographic divisions based on European names and jurisdictions all too often divide and conquer many discussions of African phenomena. (Refer to Example 3).

We must remind Black Studies librarians of their continuing commitment to and scholarship for Africana resources. All over the globe we are dealing with many of the same issues and problems. Afrocentrists should insist on standardization that would enable a reader in one library to use with equal facility the catalogs or bibliographies of other collections. As information specialists, we are all in this together; we should work toward solutions of our common concerns. The reality of Afrocentric cataloging must also promote literacy. We cannot catalog and have books in collections if people can not read them.

In cataloging the Afrocentric way, the practical approach is to support the development of a thesaurus of relevant subject headings in Black Studies through the efforts of the AFAS Indexing Project. We also need to disseminate lists of Black Studies resources in our own collections to our colleagues and constituents. There is a need to gather together and synthesize subject or topical bibliographies that would be difficult to glean from established headings and shelf arrangements. For example, I often compile reading lists. One such list on African-American women's health pulled titles from various subject categories such as herbal medicine, fashion, psychology, mental health, family violence, cookery, and so on. This practice will assist us in conceptualizing what an Afrocentric approach would be to organizing this material.

"Nommo," or the power of the spoken word, is alive in our society. We need to promote the oramedia in our communities. Africans are an oral people, and we need to better integrate the quilts, tapestries, folklore, dance, drama, music, cuisines, sports, historic and sacred sites and monuments, film and video, exhibitions, bazaars, story telling, humor, orature,24 and such into our buildings and collections. These aspects of our culture are so much of who we are as an African people that our collections should reflect this fullness in all media and not confine it solely to the flat, printed page. The promotion of this material should be a major focus of what we do in our libraries.

Conclusion

It is important to understand the cultural dislocation often experienced by people of African descent who are educated, socialized, and acculturated in Eurocentric systems that discount their African heritage, values, and self-worth. We should also understand that there needs to be a redefinition of issues of race, gender, culture, class, language, myth, dance, music, art, value and aesthetic appeal from an African centered world view. As library professionals, we should help prepare the infrastructures of our institutions to receive new languages and categorizations. There is an immediate need for Black Studies professionals to redefine or reshape our work as "culture keepers" if we are to enlighten and empower our communities as they move toward an African center.

Notes

1. Clack, Doris, *Black Literature Resources: Analysis and Organization* (New York: Marcel Dekker, Inc., 1975).

2. Abu Shardow Abarry, "Afrocentricity Introduction," *Journal of Black Studies* 21 (December 1990): 123.

3. Oyebade, Bayo, "African Studies and the Afrocentric Paradigm," *Journal of Black Studies* 21 (December 1990): 233.

4. Schiele, Jerome H., "Organizational Theory from an Afrocentric Perspective," *Journal of Black Studies* 21 (December 1990): 146.

5. Oyebade, 234.

6. Joseph, George Gheverghese, Vasu Reddy and Mary Searle-Chatterjee, "Eurocentrism in the Social Sciences," *Race & Class* 31.4 (April-June 1990): 1. The authors note that they "use the terms Europe and Eurocentrism to refer

primarily to Britain and North America, and not to parts of Europe such as Russia and Central Europe, which have a very different history and intellectual tradition."

7. Myers, Linda J. "The Psychology of Knowledge: The Importance of World View," *New England Journal of Black Studies* 4 (1984): 9.

8. *Ibid.*, 4.

9. *Ibid.*, 4.

10. Temple University has the first Ph.D. program in African-American Studies, chaired by Molefi Asante. During his lecture at the Graduate Summer School in Black Studies, Dr. Asante made clear distinctions between the Temple School of Afrocentricity and other evolving theories. Temple scholars have the good fortune to make use of the distinguished collection assembled by African-American bibliophile Charles L. Blockson.

11. Asante, Molefi Kete, *Kemet, Afrocentricity and Knowledge* (Trenton, NJ: Africa World Press, 1990), 8.

12. King, William M., "Challenges Across the Curriculum: Broadening the Bases of How Knowledge is Produced," *American Behavioral Scientist* 34.2 (November-December 1990): 165–80.

13. James, George G. M., *Stolen Legacy*, (Newport News, VA: United Brothers Communication Systems, 1989), 45–49. James discusses the looting of libraries and temples by invading Greek armies. It is his belief that Alexander gave Aristotle and his pupils the great opportunity to carry off as many books as they wanted from the temples and convert the Royal Library into a research center.

14. Asante, 14. Dr. Asante's work is largely informed by the writings and research of noted historian and anthropologist, Cheikh Anta Diop (1923–1986).

15. Aman, Mohammed M., *Cataloging and Classification of Non-Western Materials* (Phoenix, AZ: Oryx Press, 1980), 1.

16. Frye, Charles A., *Towards a Philosophy of Black Studies* (San Francisco: R & E Research Associates, 1978), 32.

17. Aman, 64.

18. King, 165.

19. Clack, Doris, "Collection Access Through Subject Headings," in *Social Responsibility in Librarianship*, edited by Donnarae MacCann (Jefferson, NC: McFarland & Co.,1989), 56.

20. The goal of the AFAS Indexing Project is to "determine the relevant terms to more efficiently and effectively retrieve articles on the African American experience."

21. Northwestern Online Total Integrated System, designed in the late 1960s, is now owned by Ameritech.

22. Asante, 32.

23. *Ibid.*, 18. Orature is the total body of oral discourses, styles and traditions of African people

References

Abarry, Abu Shardow, ed. "Afrocentricity Introduction," *Journal of Black Studies* 21 (December 1990): 123.

Amadi, Adolphe O. *African Libraries: Western Tradition and Colonial Brainwashing*. Metuchen: Scarecrow Press, 1981.

Aman, Mohammed M., ed. *Cataloging and Classification of Non-Western Material: Concerns, Issues and Practices*. Phoenix: Oryx Press, 1980.

Amankwe, Nwozo. "Africa in the Standard Classification Schemes." *Library Resources & Technical Services* 16.2 (Spring 1972): 178–194.

Asante, Molefi K. *Afrocentricity, the Theory of Social Change*. Buffalo: Amulefi Publishing Co., 1980.

———. *The Afrocentric Idea*. Philadelphia: Temple University Press, 1987.

———. *Kemet, Afrocentricity and Knowledge*. Trenton: Africa World Press, 1990.

Berman, Sanford. *Prejudices and Antipathies: A Tract on the LC Subject Heads Concerning People*. Jefferson: McFarland & Co., 1993.

Clack, Doris H. *Black Literature Resources: Analysis and Organization*. New York: Marcel Dekker, Inc., 1975.

———. "Collection Access Through Subject Headings." In *Social Responsibility in Librarianship: Essays on Equality*, edited by Donnarae MacCann, 53–80. Jefferson: McFarland & Co., 1989.

Frye, Charles A. *Towards a Philosophy of Black Studies*. San Francisco: R and E Research Associates, 1978.

James, George G. M. *Stolen Legacy*. Newport News: United Brothers Communications Systems, 1989, c1954.

Joseph, George Gheverghese, Vasu Reddy and Mary Searle-Chatterjee. "Eurocentrism in the Social Sciences," *Race & Class* 31.4 (April–June 1990): 1–26.

Josey, E. J. *The Black Librarian in America*. Metuchen: Scarecrow Press, 1970.

———. *What Black Librarians Are Saying*. Metuchen: Scarecrow Press, 1972.

Karenga, Maulana. "Black Studies and the Problematic of Paradigm: The Philosophical Dimension." *Journal of Black Studies* 18.4 (June 1988): 395–414.

Kaungamno, E.E. and C.S. Ilomo. *Books Build Nations*. Vol. 1, of *Library Services in West and East Africa*. Dar Es Salaam: Transafrica, 1979.

King, William M. "Challenges Across the Curriculum: Broadening the Bases of How Knowledge is Produced." *American Behavioral Scientist* 34.2 (Nov.–Dec. 1990): 165–80.

Kotei, S. I. A. "Some Problems in Africana Library Classification." In *The Bibliography of Africa; Proceedings and Papers* (International Conference on African Bibliography, Nairobi, 1967), edited by J. D. Pearson and Ruth Jones, 138–154. New York: Africana Pub. Corp., 1970.

McCarthy, Constance. "The Reliability Factor in Subject Access." *College and Research Libraries* 47.1 (January 1986): 48–56.

Myers, Linda James. "The Psychology of Knowledge: The Importance of World View." *New England Journal of Black Studies* 4 (1984): 1–12.

———. "Transpersonal Psychology: the Role of the Afrocentric Para-digm." *Journal of Black Psychology* 12.1 (August 1985): 31–42.

———. *Understanding an Afrocentric World View: Introduction to an Optimal Psychology*. Dubuque, IA: Kendall/Hunt, 1988.

Nitecki, Andre, ed. *The Dewey Decimal Classification and African Studies: Selected Papers Presented at a Conference on Problems of Classification for Africana Held at the University of Ghana, 22–24 November 1973*. Legon: University of Ghana, 1974.

Oyebade, Bayo. "African Studies and the Afrocentric Paradigm: a Critique." *Journal of Black Studies* 21.2 (December 1990) 233–238.
Schiele, Jerome H. "Organizational Theory from an Afrocentric Perspective." *Journal of Black Studies* 21.2 (December 1990): 145–61.
Sturges, R.P. *The Quiet Struggle: Libraries and Information for Africa.* New York: Mansell Publishing, 1990.
Wise, Michael, comp. and ed. *Aspects of African Librarianship: A Collection of Writings.* London: Mansell Pub. Ltd., 1985.
Woodson, Carter Godwin. *The Mis-Education of the Negro.* Trenton: Africa World Press, 1990.

Part 2: Theoretical Assessment

W. E. B. Du Bois and/as Africana Critical Theory: Pan-Africanism, Critical Marxism, and Male Feminism
Reiland Rabaka

Introduction to Du Bois's Contributions to Critical Theory

The African holocaust and anti-colonial struggle, pan–Africanism and the Peace movement, Marxism and male-feminism, the African American struggle for human and civil rights, Frederick Douglass and Alexander Crummell, disputations with Booker T. Washington and Marcus Garvey — an enigmatic and eclectic combination of critical ideas and interests unfolds across the landscape of William Edward Burghardt Du Bois's life and work. For some, he was "the father of pan–Africanism," and for others, such as Cedric Robinson in *Black Marxism*, he was one of the most sophisticated Marxist theorists in American radical history, though "his work had origins independent of the impulses of Western liberal and radical thought" (2000: 186). Still others, such as Joy James, Beverly Guy-Sheftall, Cheryl Townsend Gilkes, and Nellie McKay, contend that Du Bois's name, alongside that of Frederick Douglass, belongs on that very short list of men who openly advocated gender equality and spoke out against female domination and discrimination. His work, in many senses similar to that of C.L.R. James, and due no doubt to its highly porous nature, has been critically analyzed and appropriated by scores of academics and political activists who harbor harrowingly different intellectual and ideological agendas.

Though his thought took several crucial philosophical and political twists and turns in his 80-year publishing career, it is Du Bois's pan–Africanism and anti-colonialism, critique of capitalism and critical Marxism and, most recently, his male-feminism and pro-feminist politics that have come under the greatest scholarly scrutiny and can be said to have ushered in the contemporary Du Bois renaissance. But, I should bellow from the beginning, rarely if ever have these central themes in Du Bois's work been juxtaposed and examined for their import to critical theory, theory which (1) transverses traditional academic boundaries (disciplines) by synthesizing the most emancipatory elements of philosophy, politics, art, and the social sciences; (2) provides comprehensive criticisms of a wide range of imperial impulses in social, political, and cultural phenomena and practices—from racism to religion, sexism to suicide, AIDS to advertising, and mass movements to the mass media; and (3) projects alternatives to *what is* (domination and discrimination) by arguing on ethical grounds for *what ought to be, what could be* and (human liberation). To be sure, Du Bois's thought has traveled an almost unfathomable tract of intellectual terrain, receiving commentary and criticisms from historians, political scientists, economists, philosophers, literary theorists, feminists, and psychologists, to name only a few scholarly communities. However, on no occasion to this writer's knowledge has Du Bois's thought and texts been critically engaged for their contribution to contemporary critical theory.[1] In this study, I will first engage Du Bois's pan–Africanism as an anti-colonial theory critical of both the physical and psychological forms and forces of violence unleashed by the European interruption of and intervention into African history and cultural practices, and African philosophical, spiritual and axiological systems and traditions. This section will also connect Du Bois's anti-colonialism and discourse on decolonization with his critique of capitalism and thoughts on the radical redistribution of power, radical reorganization of the global economy, and the radical restructuring of U.S. society. The second section continues with a more meticulous treatment of Du Bois's critique of capitalism and reveals that he was more a critic of Marxism than a Marxist in any dogmatic sense. Also commented upon in this section will be Du Bois's critique and concept of democracy. His discourse on radical democracy is of crucial importance in analyzing his contributions to critical theory, in so far as democracy and the critique of anti-democratic trends and traditions purportedly lies at the heart of the ever-expanding critical theory project (see Bohman 1996). The third section explicates Du Bois's male-feminism and pro-feminist politics, and discusses some of the commentary and critiques it has elicited. Finally, in the concluding section, I will briefly comment on the continuing importance of Du Bois's contributions to critical thought traditions and their relevance for developing a more multicultural and multiperspectival, anti-racist and anti-sexist critical theory in the present age. It is the ultimate task of this study to delineate and develop a concept of critical theory that highlights and accents the often overlooked and unengaged contributions of continental and diasporan African theorists to contemporary critical theory traditions.

Du Bois's Critical Theory of the Colonial World and Discourse on Decolonization

Du Bois (1986a:825) began discursively in 1897, with his essay "The Conservation of Races," to engage part of what he termed "the Negro problem." The "Negro problem," as Du Bois understood it then, revolved primarily around "race" or, more to the point, the problem of race in the modern moment, what we would call today, racism (815). He queried, "What is the real meaning of Race; what has, in the past, been the law of race development, and what lessons has the past history of race development to teach the rising Negro people?" No sooner than he poses the question does Du Bois provide an answer, and one, as was his custom, based upon the most contemporary scientific research. With regard to the "essential differences of races," proclaims Du Bois, science found it "hard to come at once to any definite conclusions" (815). As he understood this to be the case, Du Bois sought an historical answer to the "Negro problem" in which he claimed that "the history of the world is the history, not of individuals, but of groups, not of nations, but of races, and he who ignores or seeks to override the race idea in human history ignores and overrides the central thought of all history" (815).[2]

The "race idea," being "the central thought of all history," was precisely the "idea" that Du Bois advocated "the Negroes of Africa and America" organize around and act on (817). In language prefiguring Fanon's, Du Bois asserted that "the black" was bound to the "darker races" not because of "physical race lines," but on account of "deeper differences," which were "spiritual" and "psychical" differences (818). In consequence of their "differences" in comparison to the peoples of "the Romance nations of Southern and Western Europe," "the darker races" were held by persons of the European nations to be inferior, and subsequently dominated, denuded, and degraded (816–817). It was on this account that Du Bois developed and promoted his first major contribution to the discourse of Africana critical theory, "Pan-Negroism" or, as he would later term it, "pan–Africanism" (820).

Pan-Africanism, according to Du Bois in "Pan-Africa and New Radical Philosophy," means "intellectual understanding and co-operation among all groups of Negro descent in order to bring about at the earliest possible time the industrial and spiritual emancipation of the Negro peoples" (1971a: 208). Hence, it is essentially a "movement" for the physical ("industrial") and metaphysical ("spiritual") freedom of persons of African descent. It is, as Tsenay Serequeberhan (1996: 244) contends of contemporary continental African philosophy, an "emancipatory project," a project geared toward self-determination and social transformation, human freedom and African cultural flourishing. However, in order to bring about the "industrial and spiritual emancipation" of "all groups of Negro descent ... at the earliest possible time," Du Bois (1971a: 207) argued, as Frantz Fanon and Amilcar Cabral would later, that "[i]t may be that in the end nothing but force will break down the injustice of the color line."[3]

The "color line," or the "color bar," was not an exclusively black/white or African/ European, Manichean affair, but as Du Bois (1985a: 231–232) acknowledged in "Colonialism, Democracy, and Peace After the War," it affected and was applicable to all human groups existing under "the modern colonial system." For Du Bois, "the colonies proper" were "the countries of America, Africa and Asia." And, "a colony, strictly speaking, is a country which belongs to another country, forms a part of the mother country's industrial organization, and exercises such powers of government, and such civic and cultural freedom, as the dominant country allows" (230, 229). In his critical theory of "the colonial world," Du Bois included persons which he understood to be enduring and experiencing a "semicolonial world," stating that "beyond the narrower definition" of a colony and a colonized people, "there are manifestly groups of people, countries and nations, which while not colonies in the strict sense of the word, yet so approach the colonial status as to merit the designation semicolonial" (229–230). Among the peoples he considered "semicolonial," Du Bois lists the "classic example" of the Chinese, and "the Negroes of the United States, who do not form a separate nation and yet who resemble in their economic and political condition a distinctly colonial status" (229). These peoples, "colonial and quasi-colonial peoples," are as a mass "poverty-stricken, with the lowest standard of living; they are for the most part illiterate and unacquainted with systematized knowledge of modern science; and they have little or no voice in their own government, with a consequent lack of freedom of [and for] development" (230).

A pervasive and "common characteristic" of "colonial countries" is the seldom discussed fact that the great "mass of people, predominantly of direct African descent," or clearly of color, "illiterate largely, and making a decent living with difficulty; subject to disease, with high infant mortality, and having for the most part no voice in government, and with restricted personal freedom," form, according to Du Bois, a "dark" and or "native proletariat[s]" (1985a: 230, 181, 232). The "native proletariat," similar to the proletariat in classical Marxist theory, "...nothing to lose but their chains," and they fight against the exploitation and alienation of a global imperial system (Marx & Engels 1978: 500). However, unlike "white labor," "the native proletariat" revolts against not only the ravaging effects of capitalism, but also the "colonial exploitation," "racial exclusion," "color caste," and "white supremacy" of the "colonial system" (Du Bois 1985a: 238, 175, 179, 181, 238). It was the combined experience and endurance of capitalism and colonialism by "colonial and semicolonial peoples" that led Du Bois (1995a: 649) to prophesy, in "The African Roots of the War:" that "war will come from the revolutionary revolt of the lowest workers." These workers, en mass, "colored peoples," according to Du Bois, "will not always submit passively to foreign domination" (649–650). They will not submit because

> [w]hen a people deserve liberty they fight for it and get it, say such philosophers; thus making war a regular, necessary step to liberty. Colored people are familiar with this complacent judgment. They endure the contemptuous treatment meted out by whites to those not "strong" enough to be free. These nations and races, composing as they do a vast majority of humanity, are going to endure this treatment just as long as they must and not a moment longer. Then they are going to fight and the War of the Color Line will outdo in savage inhumanity any war this world has yet seen. For colored folk have much to remember and they will not forget [650].

It was Du Bois's deep commitment to "the earth's disinherited" and "the disinherited of modern culture" that led him to the Left, and to develop "a more critical historical method" insofar as the "colonial problem" was concerned (1985a: 238, 240, 235). His thought-system can be conceived as critical theory when and where it is understood to be "informed by multidisciplinary research, combined with the attempt to construct a systematic, comprehensive social theory that can confront the key social and political problems of the day" (Kellner 1989: 1).[4] For Du Bois the "colonial problem" was indeed a "key social and political problem," but "traditional" or mainstream political theory, philosophy, and social science — and especially as they were taught to him at Harvard and the University of Berlin — proved inadequate for the task of engaging both the "crisis of capitalism" and the "colonial problem" (Du Bois 1995a: 622; 1985a: 235). Therefore, Du Bois (1985a: 216), perhaps the first major critical theorist of capitalism and colonialism, asserted that "if there is to be set up in the world a hierarchy of people some of whom rule and receive large income while others work and live in poverty, then the future of the world is going to be a future of war and struggle." He knew, as Fanon (1968: 36–37) would come to know, that in the final analysis just as the "first encounter" between "the colonizer" and "the colonized"—"the two protagonists"—was "marked by violence," so too would "decolonization," that is, the end of "the exploitation of the native by the settler," call for and be "carried on by dint of a great array of bayonets and cannons." For "decolonization," according to Fanon, is nothing other than "the veritable creation of new men," new human beings who speak a "new language," to bring about and express their "new humanity" (36). As a precursor to Fanon's dialectic of decolonization, Du Bois's critical theory of the colonial world maintained a non-dogmatic multi-perspective that was sustained by an interest, ultimately, in "emancipation from all forms of oppression, as well as by a commitment to freedom, happiness, and a rational ordering of society" (Bronner & Kellner 1989: 2). His critical theory, homologous to Habermas's critical theory, does at certain moments follow the Marxian model. That is, Du Bois's theory is "critical both of contemporary social sciences and of the social reality they are supposed to grasp. It is critical of the reality of developed societies inasmuch as they do not make full use of the learning potential culturally available to them, but deliver themselves over to an uncontrolled growth of complexity" (Habermas 1984: 375). However, Du Bois's critical theory focuses not only on "the reality of developed societies," as Habermas contends his does, but also on the reality of underdeveloped societies. This is also to say that Du Bois's critical theory has a different point of departure than that of Habermas and the host of Frankfurt School and Institute of Social Research theorists: the historico-cultural and socio-political lived-experiences, thought-systems and practice-traditions, and concrete actualities of continental and diasporan Africa and Africans.

Critical theory is not merely critical thought, but "critical activity" (praxis) that seeks to confront the major cultural contradictions and social and political problems of the present age. It provides criticisms and accessible alternatives to "traditional" and or academically popular social philosophy, political theory and social science, along with critiques of a wide range of ideologies from popular culture to organized religion. A primary aim of critical theory is to relate theory to praxis with the intent to emancipate those who are oppressed and dominated. Thus, critical theory at its very core is dialectical in that it is "informed by a critique of domination and a theory of liberation" (Kellner 1989: 1). Hence, with his supra-disciplinary synthesis of history, sociology, philosophy, politics, economics, radical journalism and creative writing (novels, poems, pageants and plays), Du Bois developed a dialectical and materialist critical social theory of the "colonial and semicolonial world" that was simultaneously a socio-political theory which aimed to describe and criticize the capitalist and colonial organization of the world, and a historico-cultural theory concerned with cultural and social change.

As a critical theory, pan–Africanism provides a potent and powerful anti-racist and counter-colonial discursive space where Africans the world over can communicate and come into cultural contact. However, as a movement and or critical praxis under the auspices of Du Bois, pan–Africanism mutated, moving from a discursive formation to a set of discursive practices which initiated in the modern moment the daunting and dogged work of engaging the existential question: What does it mean to be African in "the Age of Europe" (1492–1945), to build on the work of Cornel West (1993a: 7) and Lewis Gordon (1997: 1–10; 2000: 1–21)?

Describing and criticizing "the colonial world" and "the wretched people who inhabit" it, two decades prior to Fanon in *The Wretched of the Earth*, Du Bois (1995a: 676) revealed in his characteristic critical fashion the dialectic of Europe's "Enlightenment." He understood, as Fanon did, that "[t]he seizing of the land and dividing it is looked upon not only as a policy which puts unused acreage into remunerative use, but also as one that compels folk to work who otherwise would sing and dance and sit in the sun" (Du Bois 1995a: 682). According to Fanon (1968: 37, 38, 41), "[t]he colonial world is a world divided into compartments," it "is a world cut in two," it "is a Manichean world." Further, Cabral (1973: 39, 41) claims that "the colonial world" is purely a world of "foreign domination," and that as a result it negates "the historical process of the dominated people" (Cabral's emphasis). With the "negation" of their "historical process," "the dominated people," their lives and their lands become, Du Bois argues, "the slums of the world." In "The Disenfranchised Colonies," he succinctly states:

> Colonies are the slums of the world. They are today the places of greatest concentration of poverty, disease, and ignorance of what the human mind has come to know. They are centers of helplessness, of discouragement of initiative, of forced labor, and of legal suppression of all activities or thoughts which the master country fears or dislikes....

> For the most part, today the colonial peoples are colored of skin; this was not true of the colonies in other days, but it is mainly true today. And to most minds, this is of fatal significance; coupled with Negro slavery, Chinese coolies, and doctrines of race inferiority, it proves to most white folk the logic of the modern colonial system: Colonies are filled with peoples who never were abreast with civilization and never can be [1995a: 676–677].

In Du Bois's critical theory of the colonial world there are two antagonistic classes, "the conquerors" and "the conquered" and they, in their "colonial areas," "lie inert or sullenly resentful or seething with hate and unrest" (677). As Fanon (1968: 39) contended two decades later, "[t]he colonized man is an envious man." Why? Because "the invaders" made him and his people, says Du Bois (1995a: 677), "slaves to industry and servants to white men's ease." "The colonial world," being "a world cut in two," being "a world divided into compartments," being "a Manichean world," is for the forementioned facts an unnatural world, "a world without spaciousness," where "men live ... on top of each other, and their huts are built one on top of the other" (Fanon 1968: 38–39). And, it is for this reason that "[t]he look the native turns on the settler's town is a look of lust, a look of envy; it expresses his dreams of possession — all manner of possession: to sit at the settler's table, to sleep in the settler's bed, with his wife if possible" (39). Prefiguring Fanon's critique of the colonial world, Du Bois's critical theory of colonialism understands that "colonial peoples are living abnormally, save those of the untouched or inert mass of natives." He also believes that

> Their normal and traditional life has been more or less disrupted and changed in work, property, family life, recreation, health habits, food, religion, and other cultural matters. Their initiative, education, freedom of action, have been interfered with to a greater or less extent. Authority has been almost entirely withdrawn from their control and the white man's word is law in most cases. Their native standards of life have been destroyed and the new standards cannot be met by a poverty that is the worst in the world. The mass of natives sink into careless, inert, or sullen indifference, making their contact with whites as rare as possible, and incurring repeated punishment for laziness and infraction of arbitrary or inexplicable rules [Du Bois 1995a: 679–680].

It is the violent interruption of and intervention into "the darker world" that unleashes the very "counter-violence" that both Du Bois (1995a: 647; 1985: 181) and Fanon (1968: 88) understand "the dark proletariat['s]" decolonization and liberation to depend on. To be sure, many progressive scholars and political activists are familiar with Fanon's infamous first chapter of *The Wretched of the Earth*, "Concerning Violence," but what is less known and discussed is Du Bois's concept of violence. As noted above, Du Bois (1995a: 649) believed that "war will come from the revolutionary revolt of the lowest workers." And, "colored peoples," he thundered, composing a large constituency of "the lowest workers," "will not always submit passively to foreign domination" (650). In fact, when it came right down to it, Du Bois, understanding African Americans to be a "semicolonial people," stated:

> There is no moral question facing America of greater and more pressing importance than this question of racial tolerance in the Western Hemisphere. We are only deceiving ourselves if we try to think that the solution of the problem of these millions of black folk in America is going to cost us nothing....
> If we want to realize humanity and world peace, this can only be done at the cost of so thorough and drastic an overturning of our inherited fixations and cultural patterns as will shake the Western world....
> It has never been a democratic organization and does not today propose to be one, because its white minority is supporting itself in luxury from the depressed wage and cheap raw material which they are extracting from colored folk through their organized and dominant military power and industrial technique [1985a: 184].

Advocating a "thorough and drastic ... overturning of our [read: 'the conquerors' and 'the conquered'] inherited fixations and cultural patterns," Du Bois reveals, as Fanon's "Concerning Violence" does, that "[d]ecolonization is the veritable creation of new men," new human beings who speak "a new language" in order to bring about and express their "new humanity" (Fanon 1968: 36). The whole notion of democracy in a colonial world is an impossibility so long as human beings are reduced to and or rendered "human beasts" (Du Bois 1995a: 606) or "human things" (Fanon 1968: 37) in compliance with the "white supremacy" of Western European "race philosophy" (Du Bois 1985a: 179; 1995a: 616). Democracy in a colonial world is a "sham," a dream that every colonized person knows can never come true, at least not without a rude, violent awakening (Du Bois 1995a: 314). Violence, and violence alone, keeps the colonized in check. According to Du Bois, "only by war can China, Africa, Southeast Asia and the Middle East be kept in their [European] control, as the source of the greatest profit for industrial enterprise" (619). However, as Du Bois (1985a: 216) stated sternly above, "if there is to be set up in the world a hierarchy of people some of whom rule and receive large income while others work and live in poverty, then the future of the world is going to be a future of war and struggle." The "future of the world is going to be a future of war and struggle," if, and perhaps only if, it is a world of "a hierarchy of people some of whom rule and receive large income while others work and live in poverty." In Du Bois's worldview,

> The majority of human beings do not ... have enough to eat and wear or sufficient shelter for decent existence; the majority of the world's peoples do not understand what the world is, what it has been and what the laws of its growth and development are; and they are unable to read the record of this history. Most human beings suffer and die years before this is necessary and most babies die before they ever really live. And the human mind with all its visions and possibilities is ... deliberately distorted and denied freedom of development by people who actually imagine that such freedom would endanger civilization. Most of these disinherited folk are colored, not because there is any essential significance in skin color, but because most people in the world are colored" [1985a: 235–236].

Understanding the vast majority of humanity to be "colored," it was Du Bois's contention that "colored peoples" have a special stake in the rapid radical transformation of the world and their respective societies. He promoted both "world peace" and "world democracy," but knew, as will be discussed in the succeeding section, that neither could be brought into being so long as "the spirit of man [remained] in chains" (Du Bois 1985a: 240, 209, 198).

Du Bois's Critical Marxism, Critique of Capitalism, and Development of Radical Democracy

Du Bois's second major contribution to the Africana critical theory project involves his critical engagement of Marxism from perspectives that previously had not been considered by either Marxist or non–Marxist radical theorists. Which, in other words, is to say that when he critically questioned Marxist theory from an African historical and cultural standpoint and from the position of colonized people, as early as his 1907 essay, "The Negro and Socialism," Du Bois detected deficiencies in the Marxist tradition which included, among other things, a silence on and an inattention to: race, racism, and anti-racist struggle; colonialism and anti-colonial struggle; and the ways in which *both* capitalism and colonialism exacerbate not simply the economic exploitation of non–European peoples, but continue colonization and violation (both physical and psychological) beyond the realm of political economy. Du Bois, therefore, laboring long and critically with Marxist theory and methodology, deconstructed it and developed his own original radical democratic socialist theory that simultaneously built on his pioneering work as a race theorist and pan-Africanist; called for the radical transformation of U.S. society and the power relations of the world; was deeply concerned about world peace and demanded disarmament; and advocated the liberation of all colonized, politically oppressed, and economically exploited human beings. This section of my study, consequently, will be devoted to reconstructing and, in many senses, *developing* Du Bois's democratic socialist theory. The primary objective here is to identify and analyze those aspects of Du Bois's democratic socialism that continue to be relevant with regard to contemporary critical social theory and radical politics, and isolate those aspects of his socialist theory that are now obsolete or in need of revision and further development due to the new social and political problems of the present age.

As Du Bois (2000: 418) understood it, "the salvation" of persons of color, and people of African descent in particular, "lies in socialism." He was, however, extremely adamant in stating that continental and diasporan Africans should not graft Eurocentric (Marxist-Leninist) and or Asiocentric (Maoist) communism or socialism onto African life-worlds, but that they should "study socialism, its rise in Europe and Asia, and its peculiar suitability for the emancipation of Africa" and her peoples (416). Du Bois maintained that the "question of the method by which the socialist state can be achieved must be worked out by experiment and reason and not by dogma. Whether or not methods which were right and clear in Russia and China fit our circumstances is for our intelligence to decide" (418).[5]

In its broadest sense, "socialism," according to Du Bois (1985a: 295), "means the ownership of capital by the state; the regulation of all industry in the interests of citizens and not for private profit of the few; and the building of a welfare state where all men work according to ability and share income according to need." However, he is quick to point out that "[t]he complete socialism called communism has been reached by no nation," and he included the socio-political economic experiments of the "Soviet Union" (Russia) and China in his analysis (295). In attempting to understand Du Bois's connections and contributions to contemporary critical theory, it is important to point out — as Cedric Robinson (2000: 207) has in *Black Marxism*—that "Du Bois was one of the first American theorists to sympathetically confront Marxist thought in critical and independent terms." Because of the brevity of his tenure in the Socialist Party, which he felt betrayed African Americans on account of its internal racial hierarchy (which replicated U.S. society and the European imperial impulse) and the Socialist's non-existent external critique and confrontation of racism, and considering his longstanding distrust of the Communist Party, the Party which drove him to unflinchingly state "American Negroes do not propose to be the shock troops of the Communist Revolution, driven out in front to death, cruelty and humiliation in order to win victories for whites workers," it is not hard to understand *how* or *why* I, following Robinson, read Du Bois as more of a critic of Marxism than a Marxist in any dogmatic or orthodox sense (Du Bois 1995a: 591; Robinson 2000: 228).

Du Bois is easily understood to be a contributor to the critical theory tradition when and where the critique of *both* capitalism and Marxism are acknowledged as basic characteristics of critical theory (see Agger 1992; Aronson 1995; Kellner 1989, 1995). And, when his critiques of capitalism and Marxism are coupled with his pioneering work as a pan–Africanist and anti-colonial theorist, as discussed in the previous section, Du Bois immediately emerges as an innovator in the critical theory tradition, one who broadened its base by using Africana philosophy as his foundation and grounding point of departure. As I have discussed Du Bois's pan–Africanism and anti-colonial theory in relation to critical theory above, I will forego a recollection of it here and very briefly delineate some of the central ideas involved in his critique of capitalism and Marxism before focusing exclusively and extensively on his version of democratic socialism.

On the issue of Du Bois's critique of capitalism, one need look no further than his classic essays, "The Economic Future of the Negro" (1906), "The Economics of Negro Emancipation" (1911), "The Denial of Economic Justice to Negroes" (1929), and "Negroes and the Crisis of Capitalism in the United States" (1953), among other texts, in which he puts forward critiques of capitalism that synthesize class theory with anti-racist, anti-colonial, and pan–African perspectives. Moreover, concerning his critique of Marxism, Du Bois not only criticizes it, but also revises and reconstructs the Marxian tradition by providing new theories, concepts, and categories of analysis (such as race, racism, and anti-racist theory and praxis, and colonialism and anti-colonial theory and praxis) that extend and expand its original intellectual arena and political program. Robinson's remarks in this regard are extremely insightful: "Du Bois committed himself to the development of a theory of history, which by its emphasis on mass action was both a critique of the ideologies of American socialist movements and a revision of Marx's theory of revolution and class struggle" (2000: 196). Further, he "possessed no obligation to Marxist or Leninist dogma, nor to the vagaries of historical analysis and interpretation that characterized American communist thought" (228).

This means, then, that when Du Bois advances democratic socialism, or communism, as he did at the end of his life, he does so from a position independent of mainstream Marxism and Marxist party politics, and often from an optic that stands outside the Marxist tradition all together. For instance, Wilson Jeremiah Moses (1978: 140) maintains that "[e]ven when he urged Communism, the aging Du Bois did so on black nationalistic rather than on Marxist grounds." Du Bois's concept of democratic socialism highlights and accents several aspects of classical and contemporary social reality which Marx, his disciples, and the members of the Frankfurt School and Institute of Social Research neglected or downplayed in their discourse. These assertions are given greater weight and gravity when we turn to Du Bois's discourse on democratic socialism.

A socialist society, says Du Bois (2000: 410), is a society where there exists "the central idea that men must work for a living, but that the result of their work must not mainly be to support privileged persons," persons who as a result of the labor and economic exploitation of the "colored" masses and working classes have an exponential amount of power and privilege. It is a society where "the welfare of the mass of people should be the main object of government" (410). At bottom, a socialist society is a society where the government is "controlled by the governed," which is to say it is a democratic society (410). In such a society, "the mass of people, increasing in intelligence, with incomes sufficient to live a good and healthy life, should control all government, and ... they would be able to do this by the spread of science and scientific technique, access to truth, the use of reason, and freedom of thought and of creative impulse in art and literature" (410).

Du Bois (1985a: 230), calculating "seventy-five to ninety percent" of the earth's population to be people of color and living in "the colonies proper: America, Africa, and Asia," knew well that if indeed socialism purported to be concerned principally with "the mass" of "the governed" having a crucial and critical voice in their government, then people of color should and must have prominent positions in national and international social and political affairs. It could be no other way, according to Du Bois (1995a: 80), or else people of color would, and perhaps should, be pushed to "the last red alternative of revolt, revenge and war": "The footsteps of the long oppressed and staggering masses are not always straight and sure, but their mistakes can never cause the misery and distress which the factory system caused in Europe, colonial imperialism caused in Asia and Africa, and which slavery, lynching, disenfranchisement, and Jim Crow legislation have caused in the United States" (2000: 414). In order to fully realize socialism, Du Bois (1995a: 614) stated that there must be "Freedom," and by "Freedom" he meant *"full economic, political and social equality"* of all people *"in thought, expression and action, with no discrimination based on race or color"* (Du Bois's emphasis). "Freedom" is fundamental to socialism, and without the "full economic, political and social equality" of all respective constituents (citizens) within a particular public sphere, socialism remains an unrealized project of historical, cultural, socio-political and economic change.

Africans, and African Americans in particular, "were not" and have never been "socialists," contends Du Bois (1985a: 304), "nor did they know what communism was or was doing. But they knew that Negro education must be better; that Negroes must have better opportunity to work and receive a wage which would let them enjoy a decent standard of life." For this reason, socialism, being a "democratic program," could not "contemplate the complete subordination of one race to another" (218). It was to be a "program" or "project" of radical social and historical transformation that sought ultimately to establish "world democracy" so that there might be "world peace" (209, 184). Du Bois queries, "Without democracy, what hope is there of Peace?" (237).

The "essence of democracy," for Du Bois, "demands freedom for personal tastes and preferences so long as no social injury results" (215). This is important to point out because democracy was not merely a political project, but a cultural one as well (231). It was Du Bois's unfaltering belief that

> ...the vaster possibility and the real promise of democracy is adding to human capacities and culture from hitherto untapped sources of cultural variety and power. Democracy is tapping the great possibilities of mankind from unused and unsuspected reservoirs of human greatness. Instead of envying and seeking desperately outer and foreign sources of civilization ... in these magnificent mountains a genius and variety of human culture, which once released from poverty, ignorance and disease, will help guide the world. Once the human soul is thus freed, then and only then is peace possible. There will be no need to fight for food, for healthy homes, for free speech; for these will not depend on force, but on increasingly on knowledge, reason and art [242–243].

As long as "the human soul" remained in bondage, so long would the world exist on the brink of "war after war" (184). Under capitalism and colonialism the vast majority of human beings have "for the most part no voice in government" (230). Under these systems it is only "the bloodsucking whites" who "rule and receive large income while others," mostly the "dark" or "native" proletariat, "work and live in poverty" (Du Bois 2000: 417, 1995a: 616, 1985a: 216). Moreover, capitalism and colonialism, comprehended as two sides of the same coin and two of the greatest impediments to "world democracy," had to be eradicated on the grounds that since their inception they have consistently caused the great mass of human beings, who are (it should be borne in mind) "colored," to exist in states and stages of "slavery, cultural disintegration, disease, death, and war" (Du Bois 1985a: 196). And democracy, which for Du Bois was fundamentally predicated upon "free discussion," required at minimum the "equal treatment [of] the colored races of the world" (303, 218).

As stated above, a prerequisite of and for democracy according to Du Bois (1995a: 617) is ever "freedom," and "the real freedom toward which the soul of man has always striven" is, of course, "the right to be different, to be individual and pursue personal aims and ideals." In fact, long before Jacques Derrida, Chantal Mouffe, Cornel West, Nancy Fraser, and a whole host of others engaging in postmodernist discourse and debate on the politics of difference, Du Bois asserted that "the richness of a culture ... lies in differentiation" (617). He contended that "Difference" did not necessarily equal "Dangerous," and that once the bare necessities of "food, shelter, and ... security" were met, then "human friendship and intermingling ... based on broad and catholic reasoning" could lead to "happier ... individual and ... richer ... social" lives (617). He went on to say,

> Once the problem of subsistence is met and order is secured, there comes the great moment of civilization: the development of individual personality; the right of variation; the richness of a culture that lies in differentiation. In the activities of such a world, men are not compelled to be white in order to be free: they can be black, yellow or red; they can mingle or stay separate. The free mind, the untrammeled taste can revel. In only a section and a small section of the total life is discrimination inadmissible and that is where my freedom stops yours and your taste hurts me. Gradually such a free world will learn that not in exclusiveness and isolation lies inspiration and joy, but that the very variety is the reservoir of invaluable experience and emotion. This crowning of equalitarian democracy in artistic freedom of difference is the real next step of culture.
>
> The hope of civilization lies not in exclusion, but in inclusion of all human elements; we find the richness of humanity not in the Social Register, but in the City Directory; not in great aristocracies, chosen people and superior races, but in the throngs of disinherited and underfed men. Not the lifting of the lowly, but the unchaining of the unawakened mighty, will reveal the possibilities of genius, gift and miracle, in mountainous treasure-trove, which hitherto civilization has scarcely touched; and yet boasted blatantly and even answer to every meticulous taste and rare personality [617].

Du Bois's radical democratic theory eschews the elitism of his "Talented Tenth" thesis, what Moses (1978: 138) calls "the conservatism of his intellectual origins," and is predicated upon "the inclusion of all human elements," "the richness of humanity..." "not the great aristocracies, chosen people and superior races," but on "the throngs of disinherited and underfed men." Du Bois, as radical democratic theorist, looks not to the elite, as he once did, but to "disinherited" and "underfed" human beings to bring about the radical transformation of society. In his view, a capitalist society, a so-called "developed society," is to a certain extent a colonized society because it is a society where life and language are directed, defined and deformed to suit the wants and desires of the ruling race, gender, and or class(es) (see Habermas 1984: 374–375). Always and everywhere colonization, like Pandora's box once opened, seeps into every sphere of the life- and language- worlds of both the colonized and the colonizer. It is precisely as Du Bois (1985a: 183, 181, 206) said it would be, a world of "race war," "racial friction" and "disastrous contradiction." Only in "a free world" where "the problem of subsistence is met and order secured" can human beings arrive at "the great moment of civilization." This "moment," representing perhaps *the* highpoint in human history in Du Bois's thought, would foster "the development of individual personality," and these "new" individuals, free from the constant pursuit of their basic needs and capitalist greed — similar to Fanon's "new men" who speak a "new language" to express their "new humanity" (1968: 36) — would pride themselves on "the right of variation." In such a world, human beings "are not compelled to be white in order to be free: they can be black, yellow or red; they can mingle or stay separate." The "free world" Du Bois envisions is a world that puts the premium on the promises, possibilities and potentialities of humble, hard working, ordinary people.

Du Bois's concept of democracy, always and ever engaging "power relations," understood, as Michel Foucault (1997: 292) did, that "in human relationships, whether they involve verbal communication ... or amorous, institutional, or economic relationships, power is always present." It exists on "different levels" and in "different forms," but is a relationship where "one person tries to control the conduct of the other" (292). "[P]ower relations are mobile," meaning "they can be modified" because "they are not fixed once and for all" (292). Power, being "always present," mutates, shifts and changes as human beings and their reality changes, and this makes human beings' relationships to power "mobile, reversible, and unstable" (292).

In fact, Foucault relates that the very notion of a "power relation" is "possible only insofar as the subjects are free" (292). He says, "[I]n power relations there is necessarily the possibility of resistance because if there were no possibility of resistance (of violent resistance, flight, deception, strategies capable of reversing the situation), there would be no power relations at all" (292). In any "power relation" there exists the possibility of "liberation," and "liberation and the struggle for liberation are indispensable for the practice of freedom" (284). Conquered, colonized, colored peoples must be willing to "struggle for liberation," and if they are not, they will never know, or have the possibility of, "the practice of freedom," which for Du Bois rested on radical democracy and or democratic socialism. Du Bois (1995a: 616) cautiously offers a caveat: "No group of privileged slave-owners is easily and willingly going to recognize their former slaves as men." This means, then, that "former slaves" have as one of their life-tasks the reclamation and rehabilitation of their denied humanity, and whether they do so, as Foucault suggests, through "violent resistance, flight, deception, [or any other] strategies capable of reversing the situation," is totally up to them and their specific time and circumstance.

As "the majority of men do not usually act in accord with reason, but follow social pressures, inherited customs and long-established, often subconscious, patterns of action," Du Bois (1995a: 618) believed that "race prejudice ... will linger long and may even increase." He charged peoples of color, and "the black race" in particular, with a special duty, *not* to — as Fanon (1968: 315) said — imitate European civilization and culture in "obscene caricature." On the contrary, Du Bois (1995a: 618) believed that "[i]t is the duty of the black race to maintain its cultural advance, not for itself alone, but for the emancipation of mankind, the realization of democracy and the progress of civilization." Civilization is to progress, and democracy is to be realized, only insofar as "the masses" of human beings gain "the social control" of "the methods of producing goods and of distributing wealth and services. And, the freedom which this abolition of poverty will involve, will be freedom of thought and not freedom for private profit-making" (Du Bois 1985a: 197–198).

Du Bois's Male-Feminism and Pro-feminist Politics

Du Bois's third and final major contribution to the Africana critical theory project is his progressive male or pro-feminist politics. I use the term "male feminist" as Michael Awkward (2000: 89–93) does, and "pro-feminist" as Joy James (1997: 37) does, to denote a male advocate of "women's equality." And, I understand "feminism," as bell hooks (1984: 26, 31) does, to be "the struggle" and "a movement to end sexist oppression." Similar to Frederick Douglass (1992), Du Bois demanded that women's human and civil rights be acknowledged and honored. But, beyond Douglass, he advocated that women have "equal pay for equal work," stating: "We cannot abolish the new economic freedom of women. We cannot imprison women again in a home or require them all on pain of death to be nurses and housekeepers" (1995a: 289, 309).[6]

Many Du Bois scholars have pointed out that Du Bois prophesied that "the problem of the twentieth century" would be "the problem of the color line."[7] However, what many of these scholars have failed to mention is the fact that Du Bois made this statement in 1900, and that he augmented and revised this thesis several times within the remaining sixty-three years of his life. In fact, by the time he published *Darkwater* in 1920, Du Bois (1995a: 308, 311) stressed not only the "sex conditions," "sex equality," and "sex freedom" of women, but he also asserted that "women are passing through, not only a moral, but an economic revolution." Finally, forty-three years before his death, Du Bois—seemingly unbeknownst to the great majority of past and present Du Bois scholars—stated, "The uplift of women is, next to the problem of the color line and the peace movement, our greatest modern cause" (309).[8]

Du Bois developed a "critical sociology," according to Cheryl Townsend Gilkes (1996: 117, 112), that "emphasized that gender, race, and class intersected in the lives of black women to foster an important critical perspective or standpoint." "Standpoint" is a term currently employed in black feminist discourse to denote, as Patricia Hill Collins (1996: 223) points out, the fact that:

> First, Black women's political and economic status provides them with a distinctive set of experiences that offers a different view of material reality than that available to other groups. The unpaid and paid work that Black women perform, the types of communities in which they live, and the kinds of relationships they have with others suggest that African American women, as a group, experience a different world than those who are not Black and female. Second, these experiences stimulate a distinctive Black feminist consciousness concerning that material reality. In brief, a subordinate group not only experiences a different reality than a group that rules, but a subordinate group may interpret that reality differently than a dominant group.

Du Bois believed that women, and African American women in particular, were (within white *and* male supremacist societies) a "subordinate group" who by dint of hard labor and harsh living conditions had developed a distinct feminist, racial, and class consciousness.[9] With "[a]ll the virtues of her sex ... utterly ignored," "the primal black All-Mother of men," "the African mother" endured, on Du Bois's account, "[t]he crushing weight of slavery" only to be re-subjugated in a world that claimed to "worship both virgins and mothers," but "in the end despises motherhood and despoils virgins" (1995a: 304, 300, 301, 300). African American women, in the period after *de jure* "American slavery," where flung into a world were they were dominated and discriminated against simultaneously on account of their race and gender, and exploited in accordance with the (in)human hierarchy of the (white *and* male supremacist) American social order.[10] The chronic experience and effects of the interlocking and intersecting nature of race, gender, class, and as late, sexuality, have led many black feminists (and or "womanists," to use a term Alice Walker popularized) to posit that Africana women experience a reality that is distinctly different from the lived-experiences of those persons who are not black and female. Theses of "double," "triple," and "multiple" jeopardy abound, but curiously, rarely if ever has the thought and text of Du Bois figured prominently in this discourse.[11]

Collins (1990: 27) contends that "[b]eing a biological female does not mean that one's ideas are automatically feminist." On the contrary, it is the "[s]elf-conscious struggle" against and rejection of patriarchal or male supremacist perceptions and practices that qualifies one as either "feminist" or "pro-feminist" (27). Further, and beyond these claims, bell hooks (1981: 189), in a particularly personal moment in *Ain't I A Woman*, stated that as an advocate of feminism she has been "working to destroy the psychology of dominance that permeates Western culture and shapes female/male sex roles," and that she has "advocated [the] reconstruction of U.S. society based on human rather than material values." Pushing this line of thinking further, hooks reveals:

> To me feminism is not simply a struggle to end male chauvinism or a movement to ensure that women will have equal rights with men; it is a commitment to eradicating the ideology of domination that permeates Western culture on various levels—sex, race, and class, to name a few —and a commitment to reorganizing U.S. society so that the self-development of people can take precedence over imperialism, economic expansion, and material desires [194–195].

Feminists then, by hooks's account, are interested essentially in the eradication of "domination" in Western culture and the reorganization of U.S. society in the best interest of all U.S. citizens, as opposed to its rich, white, male constituency. Certainly it could be conjectured that Du Bois spent the great bulk of his life and intellectual energy wrestling with "domination," and was consistently committed to the destruction of "the ideology of domination" that has been and remains a part of "Western culture." He did not shy away from the forms of "domination" that women, and particularly African American women, experienced as a result of white *and* male supremacy. Surely his essays, "The Black Mother" (1912), "Hail Columbia!" (1913), "Woman Suffrage" (1915), "The Damnation of Women" (1920), and "Sex and Racism" (1957), among others, affirm his somber and sincere claim in the last paragraph of "The Damnation of Women": "I honor the women of my race" (1995a: 311).[12]

Divulging the fact that "women of African descent have struggled with the multiple realities of gender, racial, and economic or caste oppression," the African American feminist philosopher, Joy James (2000: 1), similar to Gilkes (1996: 114, 116–117), contends that African American women have "created ... space for a more viable democracy." Democracy, one of the most prevalent and pervasive themes in Du Bois's discourse, as discussed above, has not and will never exist so long as any human group, no matter how small or so-called "minority," is excluded from the civic decision making-processes of their national and the international communities. Du Bois (1969a: 154) included women when he spoke of "peasants," "laborers," and "socially damned" persons who must continually be considered if America, or any nation for that matter, is to achieve anything remotely close to democracy. For instances, in *Darkwater*, in the chapter entitled "Of the Ruling of Men," Du Bois (1969a: 153–154) asserted

> Today we are gradually coming to realize that government by temporary coalition of small and diverse groups may easily become the most efficient method of expressing the will of man and of setting the human soul free....
> No nation, race, or sex, has a monopoly of ability or ideas ... no human group is so small as to deserve to be ignored as a part, and as an integral and respected part, of the mass of men ... above all, no group of twelve million black folk, even though they are at the physical mercy of a hundred million white majority, can be deprived of a voice in government and of the right to self-development without a blow at the very foundations of all democracy and all human uplift ... no modern nation can shut the gates of opportunity in the face of its women, its peasants, its laborers, or its socially damned.

Du Bois directed his intellectual attention to the plight of African American women, and they were in so far as he was concerned, "an integral and respected part" of his beloved "black folk." In fact, the woman of African descent, "the primal black All-Mother of men," could not and would not be held in check neither by white nor male supremacy, because she was leading both a "moral" and "economic" revolution (Du Bois 1995a: 300, 308). Gilkes (1996: 113) contends that "for Du Bois, black women represent a unique force for progressive change in the United States," because of the degree(s) to which they experience and endure various forms of racial and gender oppression and economic exploitation. Du Bois devoted considerable time and energy to extirpating these diverse forms of oppression, and therefore offers critical theory and contemporary critical theorists a multi-perspectival model on which to build an anti-racist, anti-sexist, and anti-imperialist discourse.

Gilkes (1996: 112) reminds us that African American women were an integral part of all three of the "great revolutions" Du Bois prophesied in *Darkwater* which must take place if America (and or the world) is to truly achieve democracy. Here we see most clearly how Du Bois went about confronting and contesting the most daunting existential issues of his epoch: racism, sexism, capitalism, and colonialism. Of the "great revolutions," first, there was the revolt of the masses of colored peoples against colonialism and the color line. This, of course, translated itself in Du Bois's discourse on pan–Africanism and his anti-colonial and anti-racist writings in *The Crisis*, *Phylon*, and *The National Guardian*, amongst other publications and public intellectualism. African American women were cast in a "messianic" or "prophetic" role in the revolution against racial domination and discrimination, because Du Bois believed their sufferings "provided them with a legitimate voice of challenge" (120). Who knew then, or who would know now, more so than many other "Americans," the deficiencies of American democracy than those persons experiencing white and male supremacy and economic and sexual exploitation? Prefiguring Collins's notion of "subjugated knowledge," Du Bois attempted to accent and highlight the "hidden and "suppressed" knowledge produced by African American women as they confronted, combated, and often contradicted both white and male supremacy (Collins 1990: 10).

The second "great revolution" that African American women were to participate in, according to Du Bois, was the revolution of womanhood. He contended that it was the "new revolutionary ideals" of women, and especially African American women, "which must in time have vast influence on the thought and action of this land" (Du Bois 1995a: 311). However, Du Bois's pro-feminism neither begins nor ends with *Darkwater*. On the contrary, Gilkes (1996: 118) has asserted that as far back as his 1883 to 1885 articles for the *New York Globe*, Du Bois displayed "a sensitivity to the contributions of black women." He advocated women's equality and engaged "women's issues" in the *Fisk Herald* in 1885, responding to an article on feminism by observing, "The column on woman's work is interesting, and a first rate woman's rights argument" (Du Bois 1973b: 5). After becoming the editor of the *Fisk Herald* in 1887, Du Bois published a semi-autobiographical novella, *Tom Brown*, which featured a female school teacher protagonist (6). By 1892 he was publishing his "Harvard Daily Themes" in the *Courant*, which was edited by the noted African American women's rights advocate, Josephine St. Pierre Ruffin. Ruffin would found the Women's Era Club (WEC) in 1893 and edit its newspaper the *Women's Era*, and organize a national convention of African American women's clubs that would lead to the formation of the National Federation of Afro-American Women and the National Association of Colored Women (8).

The editorial relationship between Ruffin and Du Bois "was highly significant," maintains Gilkes (1996: 118), because it was Ruffin who introduced Du Bois to Ida B. Wells-Barnett, another founder of the Woman's Era Club, and "a prime mover in the black women's club movement." In dialoguing with Ruffin and Wells-Barnett, among other "clubbers," Du Bois observed firsthand African American social organization, political activism, and, most importantly with regard to the present discussion, feminism. As a result, he developed an unusual (for a nineteenth century male) sensitivity to African American women's sufferings and their contributions to American history, culture, and society in general, and African American history, culture, and community in particular.

In fact, Ruffin's influence, specifically on Du Bois's thought, should not be downplayed because, as Gilkes contends, "[i]t was Ruffin who provided the classic definition of a woman's movement from an African American perspective: she defined the black women's movement as a movement for the benefit of women and men, and she invited men to join women's work and struggles" (118). Ruffin helped Du Bois understand the importance of men simply getting involved in the black women's club movement, but also of black men developing more critical stances toward patriarchy and elitism. Of all the things Du Bois learned from and admired about the black women of the club movement, and some of their progressive white counterparts, it was, according to Gilkes, "their ability to work together across class and color lines in spite of their disagreements" (130). So enduring was Ruffin's influence on Du Bois that half a century later in his *Autobiography* he recalled

> Mrs. Ruffin of Charles Street, Boston ... was a widow of the first colored judge appointed in Massachusetts, an aristocratic lady.... She began a national organization of colored women and published the *Courant*, a type of small colored weekly paper which was spreading over the nation. In this I published many of my Harvard daily themes [1968a: 137].

Du Bois's commitment to women's rights, though full of contradictions, was consistent throughout his career. What many Du Bois scholars have overlooked is the simple fact that for Du Bois, women — African American women in particular — were integral to democracy because "Du Bois's vision" was one that "pointed to" and attempted to produce "a society that could confront, respect, and embrace the gifts of all" (Gilkes 1996: 133).

The third "great revolution" that African American women were to play a pivotal part in was the revolution against economic exploitation. As discussed in the preceding section, Du Bois (1995a: 606) believed that "[t]he emancipation of man is the emancipation of labor and the emancipation of labor is the freeing of that basic majority of workers who are yellow, brown, and black." In "slavery," in "concubinage," as cooks, nurses and washerwomen, Du Bois (1970b: 142) recognized the significance of African American women's work, stating, "economic independence is ... the central fact in the struggle of women for equality." In fact, "the usual sentimental arguments against women at work were not brought forward in the case of Negro womanhood," which helps to highlight how African American women's lived-experiences challenged not only patriarchal notions of "a woman's place," but more specifically African American male and other women's misconceptions about "a woman's place" (142). By acknowledging the significance of African American women's lived-experiences, and the knowledge constructed to cope with those experiences, Du Bois's thought foreshadows the work of both Patricia Hill Collins (1990, 1998) and bell hooks (1981, 1984). By revealing the relevance and significance of African American women's work, and how that work challenges both white and male supremacy, Du Bois's thought, as Gilkes (1996: 126, n. 138) asserts, anticipates the work of both Angela Davis (1981) and Bonnie Thornton Dill (1979).

In brief, Du Bois's discourse, on deep and diverse levels, prefigures and provides a paradigm for Africana critical theory and Africana feminist theory because it simultaneously sought "black liberation *and* gender equality" (Guy-Sheftall 1995: 2), and the "economic emancipation" and the "democratization of modern society" (Du Bois 1985a: 181, 1995a: 615). Du Bois's pro- or male feminism, inextricable from his critical theory of the colonial world, his critique of the deficiencies of Western democracy and the limitations of Eurocentric liberation theory, and his radical re-operationalization of democratic socialism, took into consideration the "subjugated" and or "suppressed" knowledge of a particular group or class, African American women, and attempted to apply it towards the goal of human emancipation (Collins 1995: 232–237). Nowhere is this more evident in Du Bois's discourse, specifically with regard to African American women, than in "The Damnation of Women."

In "The Damnation of Women," Du Bois states that there are three "great causes" in the modern world to which every human being should devote their concern and careful consideration: "the problem of the color line," "the uplift of women," and "the peace movement" (1995a: 309). African American women, Du Bois sardonically remarked, "existed not for themselves, but for men"; "[t]hey were not beings, they were relations and these relations were enfilmed with mystery and secrecy" (229). Where the majority of his African American male contemporaries conceded that "a woman's place is in the home," Du Bois did not associate femininity with fragility or domesticity (11–12).

In "The Damnation of Women," as he invoked the names of the Haitian revolutionists Toussaint L'Ouverture and Jean Jacques Dessalines, Du Bois (1995a: 306–307) also called upon Harriet Tubman, Sojourner Truth, and Mary Ann Shadd; quoted, anonymously, unfortunately, his contemporary Anna Julia Cooper and made reference to Ida B. Wells.[13] In an audacious turn of phrase, Du Bois placed the resistance activities of African American women on par with those of African American men, going so far as to recall Sojourner Truth's classic query to Frederick Douglass, as to "the death of God," if African Americans lose hope and faith in their imminent victory over slavery and white supremacy. Furthermore, African American women, those "long-suffering victims," those "burdened sisters," according to Du Bois, were "sweetly feminine," "unswervingly loyal," "desperately earnest," and "instinctively pure in body and soul," but were also leading "not only a moral, but an economic revolution" (308). Attempting to emphasize the strength and resilience of African American women, Du Bois, with much regality, retorted

> No other women on earth could have emerged from the hell of force and temptation which once engulfed and still surrounds black women in America with half the modesty and womanliness that they retain. I have always felt like bowing myself before them in all abasement, searching to bring some tribute to these long-suffering victims, these burdened sisters of mine, whom the world, the wise, white world, loves to affront and ridicule and wantonly to insult. I have known the women of many lands and nations—I have known and seen and lived beside them, but none have I known more sweetly feminine, more unswervingly loyal, more desperately earnest, and more instinctively pure in body and in soul than the daughters of my black mothers [311–312].

Du Bois's pro-feminist politics have often either been overlooked, or not adequately engaged when, on very rare occasions, they have been discussed. He conceived of African American women as "daughters of sorrow" (1995a: 300), who, like his beloved "sorrow songs" in *The Souls of Black Folk*, were born of "fire and blood, prayer and sacrifice" (1986: 545). These women, these "daughters of sorrow," these singers of the songs of "an unhappy people, of the children of disappointment" are often, as the songs they sing, "neglected" "half despised and above all ... persistently mistaken and misunderstood" (537). For Du Bois, the sorrow songs were "the most beautiful expression of human experience born this side the seas," and African American women, like this majestic music, "remain ... the singular spiritual heritage of the nation and the greatest gift of the Negro people" (537). Concerning the sorrow songs, Du Bois contended

> Little of beauty has America given the world save the rude grandeur God himself stamped on her bosom; the human spirit in this new world has expressed itself in vigor and ingenuity rather than in beauty. And so by fateful chance the Negro folk-song—the rhythmic cry of the slave—stands today not simply as the sole American music, but as the most beautiful expression of human experience born this side the seas. It has been neglected, it has been, and is, half despised, and above all it has been persistently mistaken and misunderstood; but notwithstanding, it still remains as the singular spiritual heritage of the nation and the greatest gift of the Negro people [536–537].

The sorrow songs "stirred men with a mighty power," and it is this power that African American women have contributed not only to African American culture, but to American culture in general (537). By associating African American women with "sorrow" when he refers to them as "daughters of sorrow," Du Bois tropes on his already established interpretation of "sorrow" in the final chapter of *The Souls of Black Folk*—"The Sorrow Songs." The sorrow songs "articulate the message of the slave to the world," they are "the voice of exile" (538–539), and, according to Du Bois (1995a: 298), "the soul longest in slavery and still in the most disgusting and indefensible slavery is the soul of womanhood."

Du Bois (1995a: 304) sternly stated that he would, on that "final judgement day," forgive the white world for many things, but unregrettably remarked that he would never forgive it for its "wanton and continued and persistent insulting of ... black womanhood":

> I shall forgive the white South much in its final judgment day: I shall forgive its slavery, for slavery is a world-old habit; I shall forgive its fighting for a well-lost cause, and for remembering that struggle with tender tears; I shall forgive its so-called "pride of race," the passion of its hot blood, and even its dear, old, laughable strutting and posing; but one thing I shall never forgive, neither in this world nor the world to come: its wanton and continued and persistent insulting of the black womanhood which it sought and seeks to prostitute to its lust.

In Du Boisian discourse, African American women, like the sorrow songs, are sacred and not to be prostituted. The "daughters of sorrow," like "the sorrow songs," have given African Americans, during enslavement and in "freedom," "faith in life, sometimes faith in death, sometimes assurance of boundless justice in some fair world beyond" (1986: 544). Further, for Du Bois (1995a: 310), African American women had "girded themselves for work, instead of adorning their bodies only for play. Their sturdier minds [had] concluded that if a woman be clean, healthy, and educated," then she was "as pleasing as God wills and far more useful than most of her sisters." As Gilkes (1996: 130) observes, "Du Bois's praise of black women was part of his criticism of his brothers." But, even more so, his "praise of black women" also represented a critique of white women. On the one hand, Du Bois's "praise of black women" and his admiration of their ability to "work together across class and color lines in spite of their disagreements," was an indictment against African American male leadership; and, in no small way, himself, considering his noisy and notorious ideological feuds with both Booker T. Washington and Marcus Garvey. On the other hand, Du Bois's "praise of black women," and especially the fact that they had "girded themselves for work" and developed "sturdier minds" which made them "far more useful than most of [their] sisters," was a charge directed against white women and their exclusive political parties and practices.

Du Bois's pro-feminist politics, in many instances, went against the grain of the Victorian values and views of his age. His perspectives on African American women as participants, as opposed to spectators, in African American and American history "anticipated and influenced concepts and ideas we currently use to examine the intersection of gender, race, and class" (132). The "genius" of Du Bois's discourse is evidenced in "his insistence that black women and men were the nexus of international order or 'the world system,' and his articulation of their moral challenge to that order" (134). Du Bois's male-feminism is a contribution not simply to the Africana critical theory project, but also to progressive academics and political activists universally.

As Joy James pointed out in *Transcending the Talented Tenth*, he possessed pro-feminist politics "remarkably progressive for his time (and ours), Du Bois confronted race, class, and gender oppression while maintaining conceptual and political linkages between the struggles to end racism, sexism, and war.... In his analysis integrating the various components of African American liberation and world peace, gender and later economic analyses were indispensable" (1997a: 36–37).

Conclusion: Du Bois and the Ongoing Development of a Critical Theory of Contemporary Society

Despite the problems in his work, I believe that Du Bois was one of the most important thinkers in the modern era, and certainly among the most significant in Africana intellectual history. In my view, his pan–Africanism and anti-colonialism, critique of both capitalism and Marxism, and his male-feminism and pro-feminist politics provide critical theorists, across the disciplines and of many different socio-political persuasions, with a provocative point of departure for rethinking and reconstructing a much needed multicultural, anti-racist and anti-sexist, anti-colonial and anti-capitalist critical theory of contemporary society. In this study I have been interested primarily in that ways in which Du Bois challenges critical theory to take race, gender, and the different dimensions of class in the life-words of people of color seriously. His work helps to point to the fact that what could be termed "traditional critical theory" may very well have extended and expanded the classical Marxist tradition with regard to its neglect of mass culture, media, and social psychology, but it—like the classical Marxist tradition it revises—downplayed and never really developed any sustained or sophisticated theory where race, gender, and colonialism were concerned.

Whatever the deficiencies of his thought and the problems with his approach to critical issues confronting African and other oppressed people, Du Bois forces his readers to think deeply, to criticize thoroughly and move beyond the imperial impulses of the established order. Many critics have made solid criticisms of some aspect of Du Bois's thought, whether pan–Africanist, Marxist, or feminist, and many more have exposed problems with other critics' (mis)interpretations of his theories. But, when analyzed objectively, Du Bois's life-work and intellectual legacy is impressive and inspiring, as is his loyalty to the most radical thought-systems and practice-traditions in Africana and egalitarian intellectual history.

Where some theorists dogmatically hold views simply because they are fashionable or politically popular, Du Bois's philosophy draws from a diverse array of often eclectic and enigmatic sources and, therefore, offers no closed system or absolute truths. His thought, as can be seen from the foregoing analysis, was constantly open and routinely responsive to changing historical and cultural conditions, both nationally and internationally. There are several, sometimes stunning, transformations in his thought that are in most instances attempts to answer conundrums created by changing historical and cultural conditions. In conclusion, then, I want to suggest that it is the openness and consistently non-dogmatic radicalism of Du Bois's project, the richness and wide range and reach of his ideas, and the absence of any finished system or body of clearly defined truths that can be accepted or rejected at ease, which constitute both the contemporary philosophical fascination with and continuing critical importance of W.E.B. Du Bois's life-work and intellectual legacy.

Notes

1. I advance this paper, then, as a continuation of the Africana critical theory project which was initiated in my doctoral dissertation, "Africana Critical Theory: From W.E.B. Du Bois and C.L.R. James's Discourse on Domination and Liberation to Frantz Fanon and Amilcar Cabral's Dialectics of Decolonization," see Rabaka (2001). It need be noted at the outset, and in agreement with David Held (1980: 14), that "[c]ritical theory, it should be emphasized, does *not* form a unity; it does not mean the same thing to all its adherents" (emphasis in original). For instance, Steven Best and Douglas Kellner (1991: 33) employ the term "critical theory" in a general sense in their critique of postmodern theory, stating, "We are using 'critical theory' here in the general sense of critical social and cultural theory and not in the specific sense that refers to the critical theory of society developed by the Frankfurt School." Further, Raymond Morrow (1994: 6) has forwarded that the term "critical theory" "has its origins in the work of a group of German [-Jewish] scholars (collectively referred to as the Frankfurt School) in the 1920s who used the term initially (*Kritische Theorie* in German) to designate a specific approach to interpreting Marxist theory. But the term has taken on new meanings in the interim and can be neither exclusively identified with the Marxist tradition from which it has become increasingly distinct nor reserved exclusively to the Frankfurt School, given extensive new variations outside the original German context." Finally, Best (1995: xvii) uses the term "critical theory" "in the most general sense, designating simply a critical social theory, that is, a social theory critical of present forms of domination, injustice, coercion, and inequality." He, therefore, does not "limit the term to refer to only the Frankfurt School" (xvii). This, then, means that the term "critical theory" and the methods, presuppositions and positions it has come to denote in the humanities and social sciences (a) is not the exclusive domain of Marxists, neo–Marxists, post–Marxists and or Eurocentricists; and (b) can be operationalized to identify and encompass *radical socio-political theory and praxis and other emancipatory efforts and endeavors* developed by continental and diasporan Africans.

2. This reconstruction of Du Bois's philosophy of race is derived in part from a close reading of: "The Conservation of Races" (1897), "The Study of Negro Problems" (1898), "The Present Outlook for the Dark Races of Mankind" (1900), *The Souls of Black Folk* (1903), "Race Friction Between Black and White" (1908), "The Evolution of the Race Problem" (1909), "Race Prejudice" (1910), "The Souls of White Folk" (1910), "The Negro Problem" (1911), "The First Universal Races Congress" (1911), "Does Race Antagonism Serve Any Good Purpose?" (1914), "Of the Culture of White Folk" (1917), "In Black" (1920), "On Being Black" (1920), "Race Intelligence" (1920), *Darkwater* (1920), "The Superior Race" (1923), "On

Being Crazy" (1923), "The Technique of Race Prejudice" (1923), "Color Caste in the United States" (1933), "On Being Ashamed of Oneself: An Essay on Race Pride" (1933), *Dusk of Dawn* (1940), "Prospect of a World Without Race Conflict" (1944), and "The Problem of the Twentieth Century Is the Problem of the Color Line" (1950). See Du Bois (1970c, 1970d, 1970e, 1971b, 1971c, 1971d, 1986a, 1995a, 1996a). I have also consulted several secondary sources, among them, Appiah (1985, 1992), Bay (1998), Bobo (2000), Bruce (1995), Chaffee (1956), Gooding-Williams (1987, 1994, 1996), Holt (1990, 1998), Lott (1997, 2001), Marshall (1994), Martin & Yeakey (1982), Meade (1987), Moses (1993a), Mostern (1996), Outlaw (1995, 1996b, 2000), Rampersad (1996b), Rawls (2000), Reed (1992), Schrager (1996), Sundquist (1993, 1996), Taylor (1981), Taylor (2000), and Wilson (2002).

3. My argument delineating Du Bois's pan–Africanism and anti-colonialism is based primarily on the pieces cited in the text, but also make subtle reference to my readings of "To the Nations of the World" (1900), "The Color Line Belts the World" (1906), "The African Roots of the War" (1915), "Africa and the Slave Trade" (1915), "Africa, Colonialism, and Zionism" (1919), "The Future of Africa" (1919), "Manifesto of the Second Pan-African Congress" (1921), "A Second Journey to Pan-Africa" (1921), "Africa for the Africans" (1922), "Little Portraits of Africa" (1924), "The Pan-African Congress: The Story of a Growing Movement" (1927), *Dusk of Dawn* (1940), "The Future of Africa in America" (1942), "The Future of America in Africa" (1942), "The Realities in Africa: European Profit or Negro Development?" (1943), "The Negro and Imperialism" (1944), "The Pan-African Movement" (1945), *Color and Democracy: Colonies and Peace* (1945), "An Appeal to the World" (1946), "On Britain and Africa" (1947), *The World and Africa* (1947), "Africa Awake!" (1958), *Pan-Africa, 1919–1958* (1958), and "Whites in Africa After Negro Autonomy" (1962). See Du Bois (1954, 1958, 1965, 1970c, 1970d, 1986a, 1995a, 1996a). Among the secondary sources I consulted on Du Bois's pan-Africanism and anti-colonialism, the most noteworthy are Contee (1969a, 1969b, 1971, 1972), Efrat (1967), Gbadegesin (1996), Gershoni (1995), Horne (1986), Ijere (1974), Lewis (1993, 2000), Marable (1986, 1996), Martin & Yeakey (1982), Moore (1970), Reed (1975, 1986, 1997), Stuckey (1987, 1994), Sundquist (1993), and Von Eschen (1997).

4. Du Bois's multidisciplinary method is delineated in greater detail in his "The Atlanta Conferences" address, and the Atlanta University Conference volumes he edited. See Du Bois (1969b, 1978: esp., 53–65).

5. My interpretation and reconstruction of Du Bois's concept of socialism, as well as my general argument here, derives in part from careful and critical investigation of his essays "Socialist of the Path" (1907), "The Negro and Socialism" (1907), "A Field for Socialists" (1913), "Socialism and the Negro Problem" (1913), "The Social Equality of Blacks and Whites" (1920), "Socialism and the Negro" (1921), "The Negro and Radical Thought" (1921), "Class Struggle" (1921), "The Negro and Communism" (1931), "Communists and the Color Line" (1931), "Socialism in England" (1932), "Karl Marx and the Negro" (1933), "Marxism and the Negro Problem" (1933), "The Negro and Social Reconstruction" (1936), "Social Planning for the Negro: Past and Present" (1936), "The Negro and Imperialism" (1944), "Socialism" (1948), "Negroes and the Crisis of Capitalism in the United States" (1953), "Colonialism and the Russian Revolution" (1956), "Ethiopia: State Socialism Under an Emperor" (1955), "Negroes and Socialism" (1957), "A Future

for Pan-Africa: Freedom, Peace, Socialism" (1957), "The Negro and Socialism" (1958), and "Socialism and the American Negro" (1960). See Du Bois (1965, 1970c, 1970d, 1971, 1985a, 1986a, 1995a, 1996a). I have also consulted several secondary sources, among them Aptheker (1961), Cain (1993), DeMarco (1983), Drake (1985), Horne (1986), Lewis (1993, 2001), Marable (1986), Moses (1978), Reed (1997), Robinson (2000), Wright (1985), and Yuan (1998, 2000). It is important to point out, as Wilson Jeremiah Moses (1978: 138) correctly contends, "Du Bois was an anti-capitalist long before he was socialist," and that most serious Du Bois scholars contend that Du Bois initiated his critical engagement of Marxism and Marxist-Leninist derived socialism in 1907 with his *Horizon* essay, "Socialist of the Path." He officially joined the Socialist Party in 1911 on account of his commitments to both racial and economic justice, and because he believed at the time that the Socialists were "the only party which openly recognize[d] Negro manhood." Du Bois, extremely disappointed, resigned from the Socialist Party in 1912 because many of his socialist comrades "openly excluded Negroes and Asiatics" from their "socialist"—which Du Bois desperately desired to interpret as "radically democratic"—theory and praxis. Though he was deeply disturbed by the socialists (and communists) timidity toward concrete criticisms of, as opposed to radical rhetoric against, racial domination and discrimination, he nonetheless "remained a socialist," according Manning Marable (1986: 90), even after his break with the Socialist Party. Moses (1978: 138) maintains that though "Du Bois is remembered as one of the great socialists of the twentieth century ... it is easy to forget the conservatism of his intellectual origins." It must be borne in mind that he "became a socialist by gradual stages," and "[e]ven when he urged Communism, the aging Du Bois did so on black nationalistic rather than on Marxist grounds" (138, 140). In a 1957 interview, Du Bois (1971b: 701–703) stated, "I should call myself a Socialist, although that isn't a very definite term," alluding to the fact that he understood that there were several varieties, several different definitions of "socialism." His brand of socialism, similar to the socialism of George Padmore, C.L.R. James and Kwame Nkrumah, emerged from his pioneering work as a pan–Africanist and his evolving understanding of the ways in which *both* colonialism and capitalism exacerbated anti–African racism, economically exploited Africans, and simultaneously caused unnatural and unnecessary suffering and social misery. Ultimately then, when I write of "socialism" here, I am recollecting a socialism "wholly of Du Bois's own creation," one with "origins independent of the impulses of Western liberal and radical thought" (Moses 1978: 139; Robinson 2000: 186).

6. My commentary on Du Bois's male feminism and pro-feminist politics is primarily drawn from "A Woman" (1893), "The Work of Negro Women in Society" (1902), "The Woman" (1911), "The Black Mother" (1912), "Suffering Suffragettes" (1912), "Suffrage Workers" (1912), "Votes for Women" (1912), "Hail Columbia!" (1913), "The Burden of Black Women" (1914), "Woman Suffrage" (1915), "Votes for Women" (1917), "The Damnation of Women" (1920), "So the Girl Marries" (1928), "The Vision of Phillis the Blessed: An Allegory of Negro American Literature in the Eighteenth and Nineteenth Centuries" (1941), "Sex and Racism" (1957), and "Greetings to Women" (1959). See Du Bois (1980b, 1982a, 1982b, 1983, 1985a, 1986a, 1986c, 1995a, 1996a). I have also consulted several secondary sources, among them Aptheker (1975), Deegan (1988), Diggs (1974), Gilkes (1996), Griffin (2000), James (1996, 1997), Lemons (2001), Lucal

(1996), McKay (1985, 1990), Moses (1975, 1990), Pauley (2000), Reed (1992), Roof (1996), and Yellin (1973). For treatments of male-feminism, and black male-feminism in particular, see Awkward (2000), Byrd & Guy-Sheftall (2001), Carbado (1999), Digby (1998), Douglass (1992), and Jardine & Smith (1987).

7. For example, see the essays in the Du Bois studies anthologies, Anderson & Zuberi (2000), Andrews (1985), Bell, Grosholz, & Stewart (1996), and Clarke (1970).

8. Nellie McKay, Gary Lemons, and Hazel Carby each bemoan the fact that there is a strong tendency in Du Bois studies to read him primarily as a "race man" and downplay his feminist discourse. In her essay, "The Souls of Black Women Folk in the Writings of W.E.B. Du Bois," McKay claims that Du Bois was one of very few black men who wrote "feminist autobiography": "More than any other black man in our history, his three autobiographies [*Darkwater*, *Dusk of Dawn*, and *The Autobiography of W.E.B. Du Bois*] demonstrate that black women have been central to the development of his intellectual thought" (1990: 229, 231). McKay, who is a literary theorist and critic, argues that one of the reasons that so many Du Bois scholars read him as a "race man" is because they often overlook his "more creative, less sociological works, where most of his thoughts on women and his own fundamental spirituality are expressed" (230). "Few people, even those who have spent years reading and studying Du Bois," quips McKay, "know that he wrote five novels and published a volume of poetry" (231). In "When and Where [We] Enter": In Search of a Feminist Forefather — Reclaiming the Womanist Legacy of W.E.B. Du Bois," Lemons laments Du Bois's "womanist activism remains to be fully claimed by contemporary Black men, as he continues to be viewed primarily as a 'race man'" (2001: 72). What perplexes Lemons is that fact that the critics who elide and erase Du Bois pro-feminist politics do not simply do Du Bois a disservice, but rob contemporary men, and black men in particular, of a black male-*feminist* role model. According to Lemons, "not only" was Du Bois's "conception of antiracist resistance feminist-inspired, his worldview was profoundly influenced by Black women" (73). Finally, in the first chapter of her book *Race Men*, "The Souls of Black Men," Hazel Carby offers contemporary academics and political activists a deconstruction of Du Bois as 'race man' that acknowledges that he "advocated equality for women and consistently supported feminist causes" (1998: 12). Carby, who asserts that it is not her intention to claim that Du Bois was "a sexist male individual," is not, however, as concerned with Du Bois's pro-feminist thought — though she gives it a thorough critical treatment — as with many black male intellectuals erasure and omission of that thought in their discourse on Du Bois and obsessive concerns with "the reproduction of Race Men" (12, 25). She states: "If, as intellectuals and as activists, we are committed, like Du Bois, to struggles for liberation and democratic egalitarianism, then surely it is not contradictory also to struggle to be critically aware of the ways in which ideologies of gender have undermined our egalitarian visions in the past and continue to do so in the present" (12). Carby's caveat, like the cautions of McKay and Lucal, essentially asks that we be cognizant of not only our own sexist thought and practice, but also the sexist thought and practice of our intellectual ancestors. My work here, then, registers as an effort to simultaneously incorporate male-feminism into the ongoing development of a critical theory of contemporary society, and an attempt to move beyond one-dimensional interpretations of Du Bois which downplay the multi-dimensionality of his

thought-system. It may be important to note here that because of the richness and wide range and reach of Du Bois's thought, within Du Bois studies there are various research areas and agendas— e.g., history, philosophy, social theory, politics, economics, aesthetics, religion, education, etc.— and, depending on one's intellectual orientation and academic training and discipline, his thought and texts may serve a multiplicity of purposes and may be approached from a wide array of discursive directions. Needless to say, my interpretation(s) of Du Bois have been deeply influenced by my training in and trek through Africana studies, and specifically Africana philosophy, social theory, and politics.

9. For Africana feminist discussions of the intersection and interconnections of race, gender, and class, see Awkward (2000), Busby (1992), Collins (1990, 1998), Davis (1981, 1989, 1998a, 1998b), Guy-Sheftall (1995), hooks (1981, 1984, 1989, 1990, 1991), and James (1996a, 1996b, 1997a, 1997b, 1999). Africana feminist *her*storians have also engaged the overlapping nature of race, gender, and class in the lives of African American women. A few of the better studies are Giddings (1984), Hine (1990), Hine, King, & Reed (1995), Hine & Thompson (1998), and White (1999).

10. For a discussion, consult Angela Davis's essay, "Reflections on the Black Woman's Role in the Community of Slaves," which remains one of the best introductions to African American women's existential universe during enslavement (in Guy-Sheftall 1995: 200–218). Davis (1981), Paula Giddings (1984), and bell hooks (1981) each offer ground-breaking and more comprehensive treatments of African American women's experience during and after enslavement.

11. On "womanism," see Walker (1983). For a discussion of sexuality or sexual orientation's import to the interlocking nature of race, gender, and class, see Davis (1981, 1989), Collins (1990, 1998), Guy-Sheftall (1995), hooks (1990, 1991, 1994), Hull, Bell-Scott, & Smith (1982), James (1996a, 1999), James & Sharpley-Whiting (2000), Lorde (1984), and Smith (1983). With regard to the "jeopardy" theses, see Frances Beale's "Double Jeopardy: To Be Black and Female," and Deborah King's "Multiple Jeopardy, Multiple Consciousness: The Context of Black Feminist Ideology." Both essays can be found in Guy-Sheftall (1995).

12. Each of the aforementioned essays can be found in Du Bois (1995a).

13. Joy James (1997a: 35–61) offers a blistering critique of Du Bois's practice(s) of "non-specificity" and "erasure," especially where Anna Julia Cooper and Ida B. Wells are concerned.

References

Adorno, Theodor W. (1991). *The Culture Industry: Selected Essays on Mass Culture.* Jay M. Bernstien, ed. London: Routledge.

_____. (2000). *The Adorno Reader.* Brain O'Connor, ed. Malden, MA: Blackwell.

Agger, Ben. (1992). *The Discourse of Domination: From the Frankfurt School to Postmodernism.* Evanston, IL: Northwestern University Press.

_____. (1998). *Critical Social Theory.* Boulder, CO: Westview.

Anderson, Elijah, and Tukufu Zuberi, eds. (2000). *The Study of African American Problems: W.E.B. Du Bois's Agenda, Then and Now.* Thousand Oaks, CA: Sage.

Andrews, William L., ed. (1985). *Critical Essays on W.E.B. Du Bois.* Boston: G.K. Hall.

Appiah, Kwame Anthony. (1985). The Uncompleted Argument: Du Bois and the Illusion of Race." *Critical Inquiry* 12, 1 (Autumn): 21–37.
_____. (1992). *In My Father's House: Africa in the Philosophy of Culture*. New York: Oxford University Press.
Aptheker, Bettina. (1975). "W.E.B. Du Bois and the Struggle for Women's Rights: 1910–1920." *San Jose Studies* 1, 2 (May): 7–16.
Aptheker, Herbert. (1948). "W.E.B. Du Bois: The First Eighty Years." *Phylon* 9: 58–69.
_____. (1961). "Dr. Du Bois and Communism." *Political Affairs* 40 (December): 13–20.
_____. (1966). "W.E.B. Du Bois: The Final Years." *Journal of Human Relations* 14 (First Quarter): 149–155.
_____. (1981). "W.E.B. Du Bois and Africa." *Political Affairs* 60 (March).
_____. (1983). *W.E.B. Du Bois and the Struggle Against Racism*. New York: United Nations Center Against Apartheid.
_____. (1989). *The Literary Legacy of W.E.B. Du Bois*. White Plains, NY: Kraus International.
_____. (1990). "W.E.B. Du Bois: Struggle Not Despair." *Clinical Sociology Review* 8, 58–68.
Arato, Andrew, and Eike Gebhardt, eds. (1997). *The Essential Frankfurt School Reader*. New York: Continuum.
Aronson, Ronald. (1995). *After Marxism*. New York: Guilford.
Awkward, Michael. (2000). "A Black Man's Place in Black Feminist Criticism." In James & Sharpley-Whiting (2000: 88–108).
Bell, Bernard W., Emily R. Grosholz, and James B. Stewart, eds. (1996). *W.E.B. Du Bois: On Race and Culture*. New York: Routledge.
Bernstein, Jay M., ed. (1995). *The Frankfurt School: Critical Assessments*. London: Routledge.
Best, Steven. (1995). *The Politics of Historical Vision: Marx, Foucault, Habermas*. New York: Guilford.
Best, Steven and Douglass Kellner. (1991). *Postmodern Theory: Critical Interrogations*. New York: Guilford.
_____. (1997). *The Postmodern Turn*. New York: Guilford.
_____. (2001). *The Postmodern Adventure*. New York:
Bobo, Jacqueline, ed. (2001). *Black Feminist Cultural Criticism*. Malden, MA: Blackwell.
Bobo, Lawrence D. (2000). "Reclaiming a Du Boisian Perspective on Racial Attitudes." *Annals of the American Academy of Political and Social Science* 568 (March): 186–202.
Bohman, James. (1996). "Critical Theory and Democracy." In Rasmussen (1996: 190–215).
Bottomore, Tom. (1984). *The Frankfurt School*. New York: Routledge.
Bouges, Anthony, ed. (1983). *Marxism and Black Liberation*. Cleveland: Hera Press.
Bronner, Stephen Eric. (1994). *Of Critical Theory and Its Theorists*. Malden, MA: Blackwell.
Bronner, Stephen E., and Douglass Kellner, eds. (1989). *Critical Theory and Society: A Reader*. New York: Routledge.
Bruce, Dickson D., Jr. (1992). "W.E.B. Du Bois and the Idea of Double Consciousness." *American Literature* 64 (June): 299–309.

———. (1995). "W.E.B. Du Bois and the Dilemma of Race." *American Literary History* 7, 2: 334–343.

Byrd, Rudolph P., and Beverly Guy-Sheftall, eds. (2001). *Traps: African American Men On Gender and Sexuality.* Indianapolis: Indiana University Press.

Cabral, Amilcar. (1972). *Revolution in Guinea: Selected Texts.* New York: Monthly Review Press.

———. (1973). *Return to the Source: Selected Speeches of Amilcar Cabral.* New York: Monthly Review Press.

———. (1979). Unity and Struggle: Speeches and Writings of Amilcar Cabral. New York: Monthly Review Press.

Carbado, Devon W., ed. (1999). *Black Men on Race, Gender, and Sexuality: A Critical Reader.* New York: New York University Press.

Cain, William E. (1990a). "W.E.B. Du Bois's *Autobiography* and the Politics of Literature." *Black American Literature Forum* 24: 299–313.

———. (1990b). "Violence, Revolution, and the Cost of Freedom: John Brown and W.E.B. Du Bois." *Boundary* 2, 17 (Spring): 305–330.

———. (1993). "From Liberalism to Communism: The Political Thought of W.E.B. Du Bois." In Amy Kaplan and Donald E. Pease, eds. *Culture of United States Imperialism.* Durham, N.C.: Duke University Press.

Calhoun, Craig. (1995). *Critical Social Theory: Culture, History, and the Challenge of Difference.* Malden, MA: Blackwell.

———, ed. (1992). *Habermas and the Public Sphere.* Cambridge: MIT Press.

Carby, Hazel V. (1998). *Race Men.* Cambridge: Harvard University Press.

Chaffee, Mary Law. (1956). "William E. B. Du Bois's Concept of the Racial Problem in the United States." *Journal of Negro History* 41 (July): 241–258.

Clarke, John Henrik, Esther Jackson, Ernest Kaiser, and J.H. O'Dell, eds. (1970). *Black Titan: W.E.B. Du Bois.* Boston: Beacon.

Collins, Patricia Hill. (1989). "The Social Construction of Black Feminist Thought." Signs: Journal of Women Culture and Society 14, 4: 745–773.

———. (1990). *Black Feminist Thought: Knowledge, Consciousness, and the Politics of Empowerment.* New York: Routledge.

———. (1998). *Fighting Words: Black Women and the Search for Social Justice.* Minneapolis: Minnesota.

Connerton, Paul. (1980). *The Tragedy of Enlightenment: An Essay on the Frankfurt School.* Cambridge: Cambridge University Press.

Contee, Clarence G. (1969a). "W.E.B. Du Bois and African Nationalism, 1914–1945." Ph.D. dissertation, American University, Washington, D.C.

———. (1969b). "The Emergence of Du Bois as an African Nationalist." *Journal of Negro History* 54 (January): 48–63.

———. (1970). "W.E.B. Du Bois and *Encyclopedia Africana.*" *Crisis* 77 (November): 375–379.

———. (1971). "A Crucial Friendship Begins: Du Bois and Nkrumah, 1935–1945." *Crisis* 78 (August): 181–185.

———. (1972). "Du Bois, the NAACP, and the Pan-African Congress of 1919." *Journal of Negro History* 57 (January): 13–28.

Davis, Angela Y. (1981). *Women, Race and Class.* New York: Vintage.

———. (1989). *Women, Culture, and Politics.* New York: Vintage.

———. (1998b). *The Angela Y. Davis Reader.* Joy James, ed. Malden, MA: Blackwell.

Deegan, Mary Jo. (1988). "W.E.B. Du Bois and the Women of Hull House, 1895–1899." *American Sociologist* 19, 4 (Winter): 301–311.
DeMarco, Joseph P. (1974). "The Rationale and Foundation of Du Bois's Theory of Economic Cooperation." *Phylon* 35 (March): 5–15.
_____. (1983). *The Social Thought of W.E.B. Du Bois*. Lanham, MD: University Press of America.
Digby, Tom, ed. (1998). *Men Doing Feminism*. New York: Routledge.
Diggs, Irene. (1974). "Du Bois and Women: A Short Story of Black Women, 1910–1934." *Current Bibliography on African Affairs* 7 (Summer): 260–307.
Douglass, Frederick. (1950–1975). *The Life and Writings of Fredrick Douglass*, vols. 1–5. Philip S. Foner, ed. New York: International.
_____. (1992). *Frederick Douglass on Women's Rights*. Philip S. Foner, ed. New York: Da Capo Press.
Drake, William Avon. (1985). "From Reform to Communism: The Intellectual Development of W.E.B. Du Bois." Ph.D. dissertation, Cornell University, Ithaca, NY.
Dubiel, Helmut. (1985). *Theory and Politics: Studies in the Development of Critical Theory*. Trans. Benjamin Gregg. Cambridge: MIT Press.
Du Bois, W.E.B. (1930a). *Africa, Its Geography People and Products*. Girard, KS: Haldeman-Julius.
_____. (1930b). *Africa, Its Place in Modern History*. Girard, KS: Haldemen-Julius.
_____. (1938). *A Pageant in Seven Decades, 1868–1938*. Atlanta: Atlanta University Press.
_____. (1939). *Black Folk Then and Now: An Essay in the History and Sociology of the Negro Race*. New York: Henry Holt.
_____. (1945). *Color and Democracy: Colonies and Peace*. New York: Hartcourt Brace.
_____. (1952). *In Battle for Peace: The Story of My 83rd Birthday*. New York: Masses & Mainstream.
_____. (1958). *Pan-Africa, 1919–1958*. Accra, Ghana: Bureau of African Affairs.
_____. (1962). *John Brown*. New York: International Publishers.
_____. (1965). *The World and Africa: An inquiry into the part which Africa has played in world history*. New York: International Publishers.
_____. (1968a). *The Autobiography of W.E.B. Du Bois: A Soliloquy on Viewing My Life from the Last Decade of Its First Century*. New York: International Publishers.
_____. (1968b). *Dusk of Dawn: An Essay Toward an Autobiography of a Race Concept*. New York: Schocken.
_____. (1969a). *Darkwater: Voices from Within the Veil*. New York: Schocken.
_____. (1969b). *The Souls of Black Folk*. New York: New American Library.
_____. (1969c). *An ABC of Color: Selections from over a Half Century of the Writings of W.E.B. Du Bois*. New York: International Publishers.
_____, ed. (1969d). *Atlanta University Publications, 1896–1916*. Numbers 1–20, 2 volumes. New York: Arno Press.
_____. (1970a). *The Negro*. New York: Oxford University Press.
_____. (1970b). *The Gift of Black Folk: The Negro in the Making of America*. New York: Simon & Schuster.
_____. (1970c). *W.E.B. Du Bois: A Reader*. Meyer Weinberg, ed. New York: Harper and Row.

———. (1970d). *W.E.B. Du Bois Speaks: Speeches and Addresses, 1899–1963*, 2 volumes. Philip S. Foner, ed. New York: Pathfinder Press.

———. (1970e). *The Selected Writings of W.E.B. Du Bois*. Walter Wilson, ed. New York: Mentor Books.

———. (1971a). "Pan-Africa and the New Radical Philosophy." In Du Bois (1971c: 205–209).

———. (1971b). *The Seventh Son: The Thought and Writings of W.E.B. Du Bois, Volume 1*. Ed. with introduction by Julius Lester. New York: Vintage Books.

———. (1971c). *The Seventh Son: The Thought and Writings of W.E.B. Du Bois, Volume 2*. Ed. with intro by Julius Lester. New York: Vintage Books.

———. (1971d). *W.E.B. Du Bois: A Reader*. Andrew Paschal, ed. New York: Collier Books.

———. (1972a). *The Emerging Thought of W.E.B. Du Bois*. Henry Lee Moon, ed. New York: Simon & Schuster.

———. (1972b). *W.E.B. Du Bois: The Crisis Writings*. Daniel Walden, ed. Greenwich, CT: Fawcett.

———. (1973). *The Education of Black People: Ten Critiques, 1906–1960*. Herbert Aptheker, ed. New York: Monthly Review Press.

———. (1977). *Book Reviews by W.E.B. Du Bois*. Herbert Aptheker, ed. Millwood, NY: Kraus-Thomson.

———. (1978). *W.E.B. Du Bois on Sociology and the Black Community*. Dan S. Green and Edwin D. Driver, eds. Chicago: University of Chicago Press.

———. (1980a). *Contributions of W.E.B. Du Bois in Government Publications and Proceedings*. Herbert Aptheker, ed. Millwood, NY: Kraus-Thomson.

———. (1980b). *Selection from Phylon*. Herbert Aptheker, ed. Millwood, NY: Kraus-Thomson.

———. (1980c). *Prayers for Dark People*. Herbert Aptheker, ed. Amherst: University of Massachusetts Press.

———. (1980d). *Selections from the Brownies Book*. Herbert Aptheker, ed. Millwood, NY: Kraus-Thomson.

———. (1982a). *Writings in Non-Periodical Literature Edited by Others*. Herbert Aptheker, ed. Millwood, NY: Kraus-Thomson.

———. (1982b). *Writings in Periodicals Edited by Others*. Herbert Aptheker, ed. Millwood, NY: Kraus-Thomson.

———. (1983). *Selections from The Crisis*. Herbert Aptheker, ed. Millwood, NY: Kraus-Thomson.

———. (1985a). *Against Racism: Unpublished Essays, Papers, Addresses, 1887–1961*. Herbert Aptheker, ed. Amherst: University of Massachusetts Press.

———. (1985b). *Creative Writings by W.E.B. Du Bois: A Pageant, Poems, Short Stories and Playlets*. Herbert Aptheker, ed. Millwood, NY: Kraus-Thomson.

———. (1985c). *Selections from Horizon*. Herbert Aptheker, ed. White Plains, NY: Kraus-Thomson.

———. (1986). *Du Bois: Writings*. Nathan Irvin Huggins, ed. New York: The Library of America Press.

———. (1986b). *Pamphlets and Leaflets*. Herbert Aptheker, ed. New York: Kraus-Thomson.

———. (1986c). *Newspaper Columns by W.E.B. Du Bois*. 2 volumes. Herbert Aptheker, ed. White Plains, NY: Kraus-Thomson.

_____. (1989). *The Souls of Black Folk*. Henry Louis Gates, Jr., ed. New York: Bantam-Doubleday.

_____. (1992). *The World of W.E.B. Du Bois*. Meyer Weinberg, ed. Westport, CT: Greenwood.

_____. (1995a). *W.E.B. Du Bois Reader*. David Levering Lewis, ed. New York: Henry Holt.

_____. (1995b). *Black Reconstruction in America, 1860–1880*. Introduction by David Levering Lewis. New York: Touchstone.

_____. (1996a). *The Oxford W.E.B. Du Bois Reader*. Eric Sundquist, ed. New York: Oxford University Press.

_____. (1996b). *The Philadelphia Negro: A Social Study*. With an introduction Elijah Anderson. Philadelphia: University of Pennsylvania Press.

_____. (1996c). "The Talented Tenth Memorial Address." In Gates & West (1996: 159–179).

_____. (1997a). *The Souls of Black Folk*. Robert Gooding-Williams and David W. Blight, eds. Boston: Bedford Books.

_____. (1997b). *The Correspondence of W.E.B. Du Bois: Volume I — Selections, 1877–1934*. Herbert Aptheker, ed. Amherst: University of Massachusetts Press.

_____. (1997c). *The Correspondence of W.E.B. Du Bois: Volume II — Selections, 1934–1944*. Herbert Aptheker, ed. Amherst: University of Massachusetts Press.

_____. (1997d). *The Correspondence of W.E.B. Du Bois: Volume III — Selections, 1944–1963*. Herbert Aptheker, ed. Amherst: University of Massachusetts Press.

_____. (1998a). "The Socialism of the German Socialists." *Central European History* 31, 3: 189–225 [Special Issue on "W.E.B. Du Bois and the Kaiserreich Articles."]

_____. (1998b). "The Present Condition of German Politics— 1893." *Central European History* 31, 3: 171–189 [Special Issue on "W.E.B. Du Bois and the Kaiserreich Articles."]

_____. (1999). *Darkwater: Voices from within the Veil*. Introduction by Manning Marable. Mineola, NY: Dover.

_____. (2000a). "The Salvation of the American Negro Lies in Socialism." In *Let Nobody Turn Us Around: Voices of Resistance, Reform, and Renewal, An African American Anthology*. Manning Marable and Leith Mullings, eds., Lanham, MD: Rowman & Littlefield.

_____. (2000b). *Du Bois on Religion*. Phil Zuckerman, ed. Lanham, MD: Altamira.

_____. (2001). *The Negro*. Mineola, NY: Dover.

_____. (2002). *Du Bois on Education*. Eugene F. Provenzo, Jr., ed. Walnut Creek, CA: Altamira.

Du Bois, W.E.B. and Booker T. Washington. (1970). *The Negro in the South*. New York: University Books.

Efrat, Edgar S. (1967). "Incipient Pan-Africanism: W.E.B. Du Bois and the Early Days." *Australian Journal of Politics & History* 13, 3 (December): 382–393.

Fanon, Frantz. (1965). *A Dying Colonialism*. Haakon Chevalier, tr. New York: Grove.

_____. (1967). *Black Skin, White Masks*. Charles Lam Markmann, tr. New York: Grove.

_____. (1968). *The Wretched of the Earth.* Constance Farrington tr. New York: Grove.

_____. (1969). *Toward the African Revolution.* Haakon Chevalier, tr. New York: Grove.

Feenberg, Andrew. (1981). *Lukacs, Marx, and the Sources of Critical Theory.* Totowa, NJ: Rowman and Littlefield.

Fontenot, Chester, ed. (2001). *W.E.B. Du Bois & Race:Essays Celebrating the Centennial Publication of The Souls of Black Folk.* Macon, GA: Mercer University.

Foucault, Michel. (1997). *The Essential Works of Michel Foucault, 1954–1984, volume 1 — Ethics: Subjectivity and Truth.* Paul Rabinow, ed. New York: New Press.

_____. (1998). *The Essential Works of Michel Foucault, 1954–1984, volume 2 — Aesthetics, Method, and Epistemology.* Paul Rabinow, ed. New York: New Press.

_____. (2000). *The Essential Works of Michel Foucault, 1954–1984, volume 3 — Power.* Paul Rabinow, ed. New York: New Press.

Friedman, George. (1981). *The Political Philosophy of the Frankfurt School.* Ithaca: Cornell University Press.

Gates, Henry Louis, Jr., ed. (1990). *Reading Black/Reading Feminist: A Critical Anthology.* New York: Meridian.

Gbadegesin, Olusegun. (1996). "Kinship of the Dispossessed: Du Bois, Nkrumah, and the Foundations of Pan-Africanism." In Bell *et al.* (1996: 219–242).

Gershoni, Yekutiel. (1995). "Contributions of W.E.B. Du Bois to Pan-Africanism." Journal of Third World Studies 12, 2 (Fall): 440–443.

Giddings, Paula. (1984). *When and Where I Enter: The Impact of Black Women on Race and Sex in America.* New York: Quill.

Gilkes, Cheryl Townsend. (1996). "The Margin as the Center of a Theory of History: African American Women, Social Change, and the Sociology of W.E.B. Du Bois." In Bernard Bell *et al.* (1996: 111–141).

Gooding-Willliams, Robert. (1987). "Philosophy of History and Social Critique in *The Souls of Black Folk.*" Social Science Information 26: 99–114.

_____. (1991). "Evading Narrative Myth, Evading Prophetic Pragmatism: A Review of Cornel West's *The American Evasion of Philosophy.*" American Philosophical Association Newsletter of the Black Experience 90, 3: 12–16.

_____. (1991/92). "Evading Narrative Myth, Evading Prophetic Pragmatism: Cornel West's *The American Evasion of Philosophy.*" *The Massachusetts Review* 32 (December): 517–542.

_____. (1994). "Du Bois's Counter-Sublime." *Massachusetts Review* 35 (Spring–Summer): 203–224.

_____. (1996). "Outlaw, Appiah, and Du Bois's 'The Conservation of Races.'" In Bernard Bell *et al.* (1996: 39–56).

Gordon, Lewis R. (1995). *Fanon and the Crisis of the European Sciences: An Essay on Philosophy and the Human Sciences.* New York: Routledge.

_____, ed. (1997). *Existence in Black: An Anthology of Black Existential Philosophy.* New York: Routledge.

_____. (2000a). "What Does It Mean to Be a Problem?: W.E.B. Du Bois on the Study of Black Folk." In Gordon, *Existentia Africana: Understanding Africana Existential Thought.* New York: Routledge.

_____. (2000b). "Du Bois's Humanistic Philosophy of Human Sciences." *Annals of the American Academy of Political and Social Science* 568 (March): 265–280.

Gordon, Lewis R., T. Denean Sharley-Whiting, and Renee T. White, eds. (1996). *Fanon: A Critical Reader*. Cambridge: Blackwell.
Gottlieb, Roger S. (1992). *Marxism 1844–1990: Origins, Betrayal, Rebirth*. New York: Routledge.
Griffin, Farah Jasmine. (2000). "Black Feminists and W.E.B. Du Bois: Respectability, Protection, and Beyond." *Annals of the American Academy of Political and Social Science* 568 (March): 28–40.
Guess, Raymond. (1981). *The Idea of Critical Theory: Habermas and the Frankfurt School*. Cambridge: Cambridge University Press.
Guy-Sheftall, Beverly. (1990). *Daughters of Sorrow: Attitudes Toward Black Women, 1880–1920*. Brooklyn, NY: Carlson.
_____, ed. (1995). *Words of Fire: An Anthology of African American Feminist Thought*. New York: The Free Press.
Habermas, Jürgen. (1979). *Communication and the Evolution of Society*. Thomas McCarthy, tr. Boston: Beacon.
_____. (1984). *Theory of Communicative Action*, volume 1. Thomas McCarthy, tr. Boston: Beacon.
_____. (1986a). *Theory and Practice*. Cambridge: Polity Press.
_____. (1986b). *Knowledge and Human Interests*. Cambridge: Polity Press.
_____. (1986c). *Toward a Rational Society*. Cambridge: Polity Press.
_____. (1987). *Theory of Communicative Action*, volume 2. Thomas McCarthy, tr. Boston: Beacon.
_____. (1988). *On the Logic of the Social Sciences*. S. Nicholsen and J. Stark, trs. Cambridge: MIT Press.
_____. (1989a). *The Structural Transformation of the Public Sphere*. T. Burger and F. Lawrence, trs. Cambridge: MIT Press.
_____. (1989b.) *On Society and Politics: A Reader*. Steven Seidman, ed. Boston: Beacon.
Harris, Leonard, ed. (1983). *Philosophy Born of Struggle: An Anthology of Afro-American Philosophy from 1917*. Dubuque, IA: Kendall/Hunt.
Held, David. (1980). *Introduction to Critical Theory: Horkheimer to Habermas*. Berkeley: University of California Press.
Hine, Darlene Clark, ed. (1990). *Black Women in the United States*. Brooklyn: Carlson.
Hine, Darlene Clark, Wilma King, and Linda Reed, eds. (1995). *We Specialize in the Wholly Impossible: A Reader in Black Women's History*. Brooklyn: Carlson.
Hine, Darlene Clark, and Kathleen Thompson. (1998). *A Shining Thread of Hope: The History of Black Women in America*. New York: Broadway Books.
Holt, Thomas C. (1990). "The Political Uses of Alienation: W.E.B. Du Bois on Politics, Race, and Culture, 1903–1940." *American Quarterly* 42, 2 (June): 301–323.
_____. (1998). "W.E.B. Du Bois's Archaeology of Race: Re-Reading "The Conservation of Races." In Katz & Sugrue (1998: 61–76).
hooks, bell. (1981). *Ain't I A Woman: Black Women and Feminism*. Boston: South End.
_____. (1984). *Feminist Theory: From Margin to Center*. Boston: South End.
_____. (1989). *Talking Back: Thinking Feminist, Thinking Black*. Boston: South End.

———. (1990). *Yearning: Race, Gender, and Cultural Politics.* Boston: South End.
———. (1991). *Black Looks: Race and Representation.* Boston: South End.
———. (1994a). *Teaching to Transgress: Education as the Practice of Freedom.* Boston: South End.
———. (1994b). *Outlaw Culture: Resisting Representation.* New York: Routledge.
———. (1995). *Killing Rage: Ending Racism.* New York: Henry Holt.
Horkheimer, Max. (1972). *Critical Theory.* New York: Continuum.
———. (1978). *Dawn and Decline: Notes, 1926–1931 and 1950–1969.* New York: Continuum.
Horne, Gerald. (1986). *Black and Red: W.E.B. Du Bois and the Afro-American Response To the Cold War, 1944–1963.* Albany: SUNY Press.
Hull, Gloria T., Patricia Bell Scott, and Barbara Smith, eds. (1982). *All the Women Are White, All the Blacks Are Men, But Some of Us Are Brave: Black Women's Studies.* New York: The Feminist Press at CUNY.
Ijere, Martin O. (1974). "W.E.B. Du Bois and Marcus Garvey as Pan-Africanists: A Study in Contrasts." *Presence Africaine* 79: 188–206.
Ingram, David. (1990). *Critical Theory and Philosophy.* New York: Paragon House.
Ingram, David, and Julia Simon-Ingram, eds. (1992). *Critical Theory: The Essential Readings.* New York: Paragon House.
James, Joy. (1996a). *Resisting State Violence: Radicalism, Gender, and Race in U.S. Culture.* Minneapolis: University of Minnesota Press.
———. (1996b). "The Profeminist Politics of W.E.B. Du Bois, with Respects to Anna Julia Cooper and Ida B. Wells Barnett." In Bernard Bell (1996: 141–161).
———. (1997a). *Transcending the Talented Tenth: Black Leaders and American Intellectual.* New York: Routledge.
———. (1997b). "Black Feminism: Liberation Limbos and Existence in Gray." In Gordon (1997: 215–225).
———. (1999). *Shadow Boxing: Representations of Black Feminist Politics.* New York: St. Martin's Press.
James, Joy and T. Denean Sharpley-Whiting, ed. (2000). *The Black Feminist Reader.* Malden, MA: Blackwell.
Jardine, Alice, and Paul Smith, eds. (1987). *Men in Feminism.* New York: Methuen.
Jay, Martin. (1984). *Marxism and Totality: The Adventures of a Concept from Lukács to Habermas.* Berkeley: University of California Press.
———. (1996). *The Dialectical Imagination: A History of the Frankfurt School and the Institute of Social Research, 1923–1950.* Berkeley: University of California Press.
Katz, B. Michael, and Thomas J. Sugrue, eds. (1998). *W.E.B. Du Bois, Race, and the City: The Philadelphia Negro and Its Legacy.* Philadelphia: University of Pennsylvania Press.
Kellner, Douglas. (1989). *Critical Theory, Marxism, and Modernity.* Baltimore: Johns Hopkins University Press.
———. (1990a). "The Postmodern Turn in Social Theory: Positions, Problems, and Prospects." In The Frontiers of Social Theory: The New Syntheses. George Ritzer, ed. (pp. 255–286). New York: Columbia University Press.
———. (1990b). "Critical Theory and Ideology Critique." In Critical Theory and Aesthetics. Ronald Roblin, ed. (pp. 85–123). Lewiston, NY: Edwin Mellen Press.
———. (1990c). "Critical Theory and the Crisis of Social Theory." *Sociological Perspectives* 33, 1: 11–33.

_____. (1993). "Critical Theory and Social Theory: Current Debates and Challenges." *Theory, Culture, and Society* 10, 2: 43–61.
_____. (1995). "The Obsolescence of Marxism?" In Magnus & Cullenberg (1995: 3–30).
Kelly, Michael, ed. (1990). *Hermeneutics and Critical Theory in Ethic and Politics.* Cambridge: MIT Press.
Lemons, Gary L. (2001). "'When and Where [We] Enter': In Search of a Feminist Forefather — Reclaiming the Womanist Legacy of W.E.B. Du Bois." In Byrd & Guy-Sheftall (2001: 71–89).
Lewis, David Levering. (1993). *W.E.B. Du Bois: Biography of a Race, 1868–1919.* New York: Henry Holt.
_____. (2000). *W.E.B. Du Bois: The Fight for Equality and the American Century, 1919–1963.* New York: Henry Holt.
Lorde, Audre. (1984). *Sister Outsider: Essays and Speeches by Audre Lorde.* Freedom, CA: The Crossing Press Feminist Series.
_____. (1988). *A Burst of Light: Essays by Audre Lorde.* Ithaca, NY: Firebrand.
Lott, Tommy L. (1997). "Du Bois on the Invention of Race." In Pittman (1997a: 166–187).
_____. (1999). *The Invention of Race: Black Culture and the Politics of Representation.* Malden, MA: Blackwell.
_____. (2000). "Du Bois and Locke on the Scientific Study of the Negro." *Boundary 2* 27, 3: 135–152.
_____. (2001). "Du Bois's Anthropological Notion of Race." In Robert Bernasconi, ed. *Race.* Malden, MA: Blackwell.
Lucal, Betsy. (1996). "Race, Class, and Gender in the Work of W.E.B. Du Bois: An Exploratory Study." *Research in Race & Ethnic Relations* 9: 191–210.
Marable, Manning. (1983/84). "Peace and Black Liberation: The Contributions of W.E.B. Du Bois." *Science & Society* 47: 385–405.
_____. (1983). *How Capitalism Underdeveloped Black America.* Boston: South End.
_____. (1985a). *Black American Politics: From the Washington Marches to Jesse Jackson.* London: Verso.
_____. (1985b). "W.E.B. Du Bois and the Struggle Against Racism." *Black Scholar* 16 (May–June): 43–44, 46–47.
_____. (1986). *W.E.B. Du Bois: Black Radical Democrat.* Boston: Twayne.
_____. (1987). *African and Carribean Politics: From Kwame Nkrumah to Maurice Bishop.* London and New York: Verso.
_____. (1991). *Race, Reform, and Rebellion: The Second Reconstruction in Black America, 1945–1990.* Jackson, MS: University Press of Mississippi.
_____. (1992). *The Crisis of Color and Democracy: Essays on Race, Class and Power.* Monroe, MA: Common Courage Press.
_____. (1993). *Blackwater: Historical Studies in Race, Class Consciousness, and Revolution.* Niwot, CO: University Press of Colorado.
_____. (1995). *Beyond Black and White: Transforming African American Politics.* New York and London: Verso.
_____. (1996a). "The Pan-Africanism of W.E.B. Du Bois." In Bell *et al.* (1996: 193–218).
_____. (1996b). *Speaking Truth to Power: Essays on Race, Resistance and Radicalism.* Boulder, CO: Westview.
_____. (1998). "W.E.B. Du Bois and the Politics of Culture." In Marable, *Black Leadership.* New York: Columbia University Press.

Marcus, Judith, and Zoltan Tar, eds. (1984). *The Foundations of the Frankfurt School of Social Research*. New York: Transaction Books.
Marcuse, Herbert. (1958). *Soviet Marxism*. New York: Columbia University Press.
_____. (1960). *Reason and Revolution*. Boston: Beacon.
_____. (1964). *One-Dimensional Man: Studies in the Ideology of Advanced Industrial Society*. Boston: Beacon.
_____. (1966). *Eros and Civilization*. Boston: Beacon.
_____. (1968). *Negations: Essays in Critical Theory*. Boston: Beacon.
_____. (1969). *An Essay on Liberation*. Boston: Beacon.
_____. (1970). *Five Lectures: Psychoanalysis, Politics, and Utopia*. Boston: Beacon.
_____. (1972). *Counter-Revolution and Revolt*. Boston: Beacon. _____. (1973). *Studies in Critical Philosophy*. Boston: Beacon.
_____. (1978). *The Aesthetic Dimension: Toward a Critique of Marxist Aesthetics*. Boston: Beacon.
_____. (1997). *Technology, War and Fascism*. Douglas Kellner, ed. New York: Routledge.
_____. (2001). *Toward a Critical Theory of Society*. Douglass Kellner, ed. New York: Routledge.
Marcuse, Herbert, Barrington Moore, and Robert Paul Wolff. (1965). *A Critique of Pure Tolerance*. Boston: Beacon.
Marshall, Jessica. (1994). " 'Counsels of Despair': W.E.B. Du Bois, Robert E. Park, and the Establishment of American Race Sociology." Ph.D. dissertation, Harvard University.
Martin, Michael, and Lamont Yeakey. (1982). "Pan-African and Asian Solidarity: A Central Theme in W.E.B. Du Bois's Conception of Racial Stratification and Struggle on a World Scale." *Phylon* 43: 202–217.
Marx, Karl. (1983). *The Portable Karl Marx*. Eugene Kamenka, ed. New York: Penguin.
_____. (1994). *The Selected Writings of Karl Marx*. Lawrence H. Simon, ed. Indianapolis and Cambridge: Hackett.
Marx, Karl, and Friedrich Engels. (1972). *On Colonialism*. New York: International.
_____. (1978). *The Marx-Engels Reader, 2nd Edition*. Robert C. Tucker, ed. New York: Norton.
_____. (1989). *Marx & Engels: The Basic Writings on Politics and Philosophy*. Lewis S. Feuer, ed. New York: Anchor.
McKay, Nellie Y. (1985). "W.E.B. Du Bois: The Black Woman in His Writings— Selected Fictional and Autobiographical Portraits." In Andrews (1985: 230–252).
_____. (1990). "The Souls of Black Women Folk in the Writings of W.E.B. Du Bois." In Gates (1990: 227–243).
Meade, Homer Lee, II. (1987). "W.E.B. Du Bois and His Place in the Discussion of Racism." Doctoral dissertation, University of Massachusetts.
Moore, Richard B. (1970). "Du Bois and Pan-Africa." In Clarke *et. al.* (1970: 187–212).
Morrow, Raymond A., with David D. Brown. (1994). *Critical Theory and Methodology*. Thousands Oaks, CA: Sage.
Moses, Wilson Jeremiah. (1975). "The Poetic of Ethiopianism: W.E.B. Du Bois and Literary Black Nationalism." *American Literature* 47 (November): 411–427.

_____. (1978). *The Golden Age of Black Nationalism, 1850–1925*. New York: Oxford University Press.

_____. (1990). "Sexual Anxieties of the Black Bourgeoisie in Victorian America: The Cultural Context of W.E.B. Du Bois's First Novel." In W.J. Moses, *The Wings of Ethiopia: Studies in African American Life and Letters*. Ames, IA: Iowa State University Press.

_____. (1993a). "W.E.B. Du Bois's 'The Conservation of Races' and Its Context: Idealism, Conservatism, and Hero Worship." *Massachusetts Review* 34, (Summer): 275–294.

_____. (1993b). " Du Bois's *Dark Princess* and the Heroic Uncle Tom." In W.J. Moses, *Black Messiahs and Uncle Toms: Social and Literary Manipulations of a Religious Myth*. University Park: Pennsylvania State University Press.

_____. (1996). "Culture, Civilization, and the Decline of the West: The Afrocentricism of W.E.B. Du Bois." In Bernard Bell et al. (1996: 243–260).

_____. (1998). "W.E.B. Du Bois and Antimodernism." In W.J. Moses, *Afrotopia: The Roots of African American Popular History*. New York: Cambridge University Press.

Mostern, Kenneth. (1996). "Three Theories of the Race of W.E.B. Du Bois." *Cultural Critique* 34 (Fall): 27–63.

_____. (2000). "Postcolonialism after W.E.B. Du Bois." *Rethinking Marxism* 12, 2 (Summer): 61–80.

Nelson, Cary, and Lawrence Grossberg, eds. (1988). *Marxism and the Interpretation of Culture*. Chicago: University of Illinois Press.

Outlaw, Jr., Lucius T. (1983a). "Philosophy, Hermeneutics, Social-Political Theory: Critical Thought in the Interest of African American." In Harris (1983: 60–88).

_____. (1983b). "Race and Class in the Theory and Practice of Emancipatory Social Transformation." In Harris (1983: 117–129).

_____. (1983c). "Critical Theory in a Period of Radical Transformation." *Praxis International* 3, 2 (July): 138–46.

_____. (1995). "On W.E.B. Du Bois's 'The Conservation of Races.'" In Bell and Blumenfeld (1995: 79–102).

_____. (1996a). *On Race and Philosophy*. New York: Routledge.

_____. (1996b). "'Conserve' Races?: In Defense of W.E.B. Du Bois." In Bell et al. (1996: 15–38).

_____. (2000). "W.E.B. Du Bois on the Study of Social Problems." *Annals of the American Academy of Political and Social Science* 568 (March): 281–297.

_____. (2001). "On Cornel West on W.E.B. Du Bois." In George Yancy, ed. *Cornel West: A Critical Reader*. Malden, MA: Blackwell.

Pauley, Garth E. (2000). "W.E.B. Du Bois on Woman Suffrage: A Critical Analysis of His Crisis Writings." *Journal of Black Studies* 30, 3 (January): 383–410.

Rabaka, Reiland. (2001). "Africana Critical Theory: From W.E.B. Du Bois and C.L.R. James's Discourse on Domination and Liberation to Frantz Fanon and Amilcar Cabral's Dialectics of Decolonization." Ph.D. dissertation, Temple University.

Rampersad, Arnold. (1989). "Slavery and the Literary Imagination: Du Bois's *The Souls of Black Folk*." In *Slavery and the Literary Imagination: Selected Papers from the English Institute, 1987*, Deborah E. McDowell and Arnold Rampersad, eds. Baltimore: Johns Hopkins University Press.

_____. (1990). *The Art and Imagination of W.E.B. Du Bois*. New York: Schocken.
_____. (1996a). "Du Bois's Passage to India—*Dark Princess*." In Bell et al. (1996: 161–176).
_____. (1996b). "W.E.B. Du Bois, Race, and the Making of American Studies." In Bell et al. (1996: 289–305).
Rasmussen, David M, ed. (1996). *The Handbook of Critical Theory*. Malden, MA: Blackwell.
Rawls, Anne Warfield. (2000). "'Race' as an Interaction Order Phenomenon: W.E.B. Du Bois's 'Double-Consciousness' Thesis Revisited." *Sociological Theory* 18, 2 (July): 241–274.
Reed, Adolph L., Jr. (1975). "The Political Philosophy of Pan-Africanism: A Study of the Writings of Du Bois, Garvey, Nkrumah, and Padmore and Their Legacy." MA thesis, Atlanta University, Atlanta, GA.
_____. (1985). "W.E.B. Du Bois: A Perspective on the Bases of His Political Thought." *Political Theory* 13 (August): 431–456.
_____. (1986). "Pan-Africanism as Black Liberation: Du Bois and Garvey." In W. Ofuatey-Kudjoe, ed. *Pan-Africanism: New Directions in Strategy*. Lanham, MD: University of America Press.
_____. (1992). "Du Bois's 'Double-Consciousness': Race and Gender in Progressive Era American Thought." *Studies in American Political Development* 6 (Spring): 132–137.
_____. (1997). *W.E.B. Du Bois and American Political Thought: Fabianism and The Color Line*. New York: Oxford University Press.
Robinson, Cedric J. (2000). *Black Marxism: The Making of the Black Radical Tradition*. Chapel Hill: University of North Carolina Press.
Roof, Maria. (1996). "W.E.B. Du Bois, Isabel Allende, and the Empowerment of Third World Women." *CLA Journal* 39, 4: 401–417.
Schoolman, Morton. (1980). *The Imaginary Witness: The Critical Theory of Herbert Marcuse*. New York: New York University Press.
Schrager, Cynthia D. (1996). "Both Sides of the Veil: Race, Science, and Mysticism in W.E.B. Du Bois." *American Quarterly* 48, 4: 551.
Serequeberhan, Tsenay, ed. (1991a). *African Philosophy: The Essential Readings*. New York: Paragon House.
_____. (1994). *The Hermeneutics of African Philosophy: Horizon and Discourse*. New York: Routledge.
_____. (1996). "Fanon and the Contemporary Discourse of African Philosophy." In Gordon, et al. (1995b: 244–254).
_____. (2000a). *Our Heritage: The Past in the Present of African American and African Existence*. Lanham, MD: Rowman & Littlefield.
_____. (2000b). "Identity and Race in the Black Experience: Reflections on W.E.B. Du Bois." In Serequeberhan (2000a: 13–24).
Slater, Phillip. (1977). *Origin and Significance of the Frankfurt School*. London: Routledge.
Smith, Barbara, ed. (1983). *Home Girls: A Black Feminist Anthology*. New York: Kitchen Table.
Stirk, Peter M.R. (2000). *Critical Theory, Politics and Society*. London: Pinter Press.
Stuckey, Sterling. (1987). "W.E.B. Du Bois: Black Cultural Reality and the Meaning of Freedom." In Stuckey, *Slave Culture: Nationalist Theory and the Foundations of Black America*. New York: Oxford University Press.

_____. (1994). "Black Americans and African Consciousness: Du Bois, Woodson, and the Spell of Africa." In Stuckey, *Going Through the Storm: The Influence of African American Art in History*. New York: Oxford University Press.
Sundquist, Eric J. (1993). "W.E.B. Du Bois: African America and the Kingdom of Culture." In E.J. Sundquist, *To Wake the Nations: Race in the Making of American Literature*. Cambridge: Harvard University Press.
_____. (1996a). "W.E.B. Du Bois and the Autobiography of Race." In Du Bois (1996: 3–36).
Taylor, Carol M. (1981). "W.E.B. Du Bois's Challenge to Scientific Racism." *Journal of Black Studies* 11 (June): 449–60.
Taylor, Paul C. (2000). "Appiah's Uncompleted Argument: W.E.B. Du Bois and the Reality of Race." *Social Theory and Practice* 26, 1 (Spring): 103–128.
Von Eschen, Penny M. (1997). *Race Against Empire: Black Americans and Anticolonialism, 1937–1957*. Ithaca, NY: Cornell University Press.
Walker, Alice. (1983). *In Search of Our Mothers' Gardens: Womanist Prose by Alice Walker*. New York: Harcourt Brace & Jovanovich.
_____. (1988). *Living By the Word: Essays*. New York: Harcourt Brace & Jovanovich.
Wellmer, Albrecht. (1974). *The Critical Theory of Society*. New York: Seabury.
West, Cornel. (1980). "Ethics, Historicism and the Marxist Tradition," Ph.D. dissertation, Princeton University, Princeton, New Jersey.
_____. (1988). "Marxist Theory and the Specificity of Afro-American Oppression." In Nelson and Grossberg (1988: 17–34).
_____. (1989). *The American Evasion of Philosophy: A Genealogy of Pragmatism*. Madison: Wisconsin University Press.
_____. (1991). *The Ethical Dimensions of Marxist Thought*. New York: Monthly Review.
_____. (1993a). *Keeping Faith: Philosophy and Race in America*. New York: Routledge.
_____. (1993b). *Beyond Eurocentrism and Multiculturalism, Volume One: Prophetic Thought in Postmodern Times*. Monroe, ME: Common Courage.
_____. (1993c). *Beyond Eurocentrism and Multiculturalism, Volume Two: Prophetic Reflections: Notes on Race and Power in America*. Monroe, ME: Common Courage.
_____. (1998). *The Future of American Progressivism: An Initiative for Political and Economic Reform*. Boston: Beacon.
_____, ed. (1999). *The Cornel West Reader*. New York: Civitas.
White, Deborah Gray. (1999). *Too Heavy A Load: Black Women in Defense of Themselves, 1894–1994*. New York: Norton.
Wiggerhaus, Rolf. (1995). *The Frankfurt School: Its History, Theories, and Political Significance*. Micheal Robertson, tr. Cambridge: MIT Press.
Wilson, Bobby M. (2002). "Critically Understanding Race-Connected Practices: A Reading of W.E.B. Du Bois and Richard Wright." *The Professional Geographer* 54, 1: 31–41.
Wright, William. (1978). "Du Bois's Theory of Political Democracy." *Crisis* 85 (March): 85–89.
Wright, William D. (1985). "The Socialist Analysis of W.E.B. Du Bois." Ph.D. dissertation, State University of New York, Buffalo.
Yuan, Ji. (1998). "W.E.B. Du Bois and His Socialist Thought." Ph.D. dissertation, Temple University, Philadelphia.

_____. (2000). *W.E.B. Du Bois and His Socialist Thought.* Lawrenceville: Africa World Press.
Yellin, Jean Fagan. (1973). "Du Bois's Crisis and Woman's Suffrage." *Massachusetts Review* 14, 2 (Spring): 365–375.

A Theoretical Analysis of Persuasive Tactics Used by Frederick Douglass in "The Meaning of July Fourth for the Negro"

Jason J. Thompson and
Reynaldo Anderson

On July 5, 1852, one of the most renowned figures in African American history, Frederick Douglass, delivered his speech "The Meaning of July Fourth for the Negro" with the hope of persuading America to change its ways. It sparked much interest on the part of both blacks and whites and, arguably, went further than anything else in giving Mr. Douglass the reputation he has today.

In this paper we shall explicate how the social conditions of America at the time the speech was delivered made it very difficult and dangerous for Frederick Douglass to speak to those who gave him the public stage. We will also discuss how Frederick Douglass' address illustrates particular theoretical notions of African American rhetoric later advanced by authors Geneva Smitherman, Molefi Asante, and Henry Louis Gates, Jr. The popular strategies and techniques of African American rhetoric theorized by the aforementioned authors were used by Mr. Douglass in his address and indubitably enhanced the effect his speech had on the audience.

We shall begin by examining the social condition of America during the time the speech was delivered. In the nineteenth century, the climate of America was one filled with virulent racism expressed in such evils as lynchings, peonage, disfranchisement, rapes, beatings, and burnings. White people made it their mission to keep black people down. One of the most salient ways this occurred was through slavery. Black people were forced to perform exhausting tasks with no pay from the white slave owners. Black people were treated like animals, being bought and sold like property. In addition, educational opportunities for black people were denied so as to ensure they could never move ahead. The social climate of America was so turbulent during that time that black people were totally pessimistic about the possibility of change. White people were in power and as long as that remained, there was little likelihood that the unfair social conditions would be transformed.

Frederick Douglass was born during the inauspicious social climate of nineteenth century America. In fact, he was born into and grew up in slavery. He saw and experienced first-hand the aforementioned brutal treatment of black people. However, this did not deter him from being persistent about learning how to read and write. And even more so, the overwhelming circumstances did not stop him from delivering his famous speech.

As we know, Frederick Douglass was a black man. At that point in time, it was very unusual for any black person to give public addresses. It was even more unusual that one would give a speech in front of a predominately white audience. Nevertheless, the fact that he was black did not keep Douglass from taking the public stage. "As a protest speaker, the African American is met with the limitations placed upon all protest speakers, but because he or she is black, a further constraint, based upon socio-historical factors, exists" (Asante, 1998, p.123).

As a black man in a white-dominated society, Douglass had to be precise with his rhetorical strategy. "The rhetorical materials— in fact, the available materials— he or she chooses as a rhetor are limited, and thus the real challenge the African American speaker faces is having to make do or create with the strategies and alternatives prescribed by the social conditions" (Asante, 1998, p.123). Frederick Douglass created strategies and techniques that were powerful and persuasive, yet delicately seasoned, to the mass of people listening while being completely cognizant of the social conditions.

As previously noted, the majority of the people in the audience that Frederick Douglass was speaking to were white. Therefore, he had to be very careful with his use of language in the speech. "The protest speaker must make sure all 'entrances' and 'exits' are covered as he speaks to white audiences; there can be no reckless abandon in language or behavior that will allow misinterpretations or misunderstandings. The protest speaker holds his or her cards close to the flesh when faced with white audiences"

(Asante, 1998, p.126). One way Mr. Douglass does this is by remaining respectful, grateful, and dignified with his words and mannerisms, especially at the beginning part of his speech. He says,

> That I am here today is, to me, a matter of astonishment as well as of gratitude. You will not, therefore, be surprised, if in what I have to say I evince no elaborate preparation, nor grace my speech with any high-sounding exordium. I have been able to throw my thoughts hastily and imperfectly together; and trusting to your patient and generous indulgence, I will proceed to lay them before you [Foner, 1972, p.107].

In this passage, Mr. Douglass cleverly expresses his gratitude to the white people who gave him the public stage. He knew that this was necessary because they offered him the invitation to speak and that an expression of gratitude just might make his speech more effective and possibly alleviate the uneasiness of the moment. This would perhaps make the white audience members more in-tune to the message he was delivering.

Another aspect of Mr. Douglass' speech illustrates the care he took with his language. He attempts to show white people that he does not disapprove of the way their forefathers went about claiming independence. His being careful here is demonstrated in his agreement with some of the deeds of the past. He says,

> Fellow citizens, I am not wanting in respect for the fathers of the republic. They were great men, too—great enough to give frame to a great age. I cannot contemplate their great deeds with less than admiration. They were statesmen, patriots, and heroes, and for the good they did, and the principles they contended for, I will unite with you to honor their memory" [Foner, 1972, p.111].

Mr. Douglass is sure to pay his respects by speaking only kind words about America's forefathers. If he had spoken harsh words before the American people concerning the great effort of their forefathers, then he would have risked being killed by way of lynching or beating. In a situation like this, he did not want to create any enemies. Mr. Douglass was smart enough to know his bounds, keeping in mind that the dominant group in society gives the opportunities and constraints for rhetoric.

Social Transformation

On that day of June 5, 1852, Frederick Douglass' primary goal was to persuade America that it needed to undergo significant social transformation in order to end the discrimination, segregation, and hatred that existed on the country's soil. This was necessary in order for the country to be consistent with what its forefathers fought for when the colonies were under British rule approximately 100 years before the time of this great speech. This was the theme of Mr. Douglass' speech and a major tool in helping him get his persuasive message across to his audience. For instance, in his speech, Mr. Douglass says

> I say it with a sad sense of disparity between us. I am not included within the pale of this glorious anniversary! Your high independence only reveals the immeasurable distance between us. The blessings in which you this day rejoice, are not enjoyed in common. The rich inheritance of justice, liberty, prosperity, and independence, bequeathed by your fathers, is shared by you, not me. The sunlight that brought life and healing to you, has brought stripes and death to me. This Fourth of July is yours, not mine. You may rejoice, I must mourn. (Foner, 1972, p.114).

By making it clear that he cannot rejoice in the celebration, Douglass makes the white audience aware that there was a problem with the country's moral fiber. The audience members would have to see the injustice that was evident based on the words of Mr. Douglass.

In trying to persuade white people that social transformation is the only moral and just thing to do, Mr. Douglass is careful not to overly exert his tonal patterns. If he were, then the white people probably would have had a hard time understanding or following him. "Black protest speakers, trying to persuade white audiences of the need for social transformation, are simultaneously exhibiting distrust of whites by refusing them access into the inner linguistic secrets. Even in the most intense debate over social change, black protest speakers do not share all of their characteristic tonal patterns with white audiences" (Asante, 1998, p.130). The experiences and rhetorical tactics of black people are better understood by themselves. It's similar to the saying, "It's a black thang — you wouldn't understand!"

Modes of Discourse

The rhetorical condition of African Americans during the time of Mr. Douglass' speech was liberatory. African Americans were fighting for their freedom from the system of oppression. In any system of oppression, there is resistance to that oppression. Obviously, Mr. Douglass was part of this fight for freedom from the oppressors. His persuasive speech was something that spoke truth to the immoral structural and power pattern in society. Mr. Douglass' Nommo, which is "the power of the spoken word" (Smitherman, 1977), tried to create a more balanced society and break down the strongholds of oppression. One of the ways he attempted to do this was through three of the four modes of discourse. These modes are signifying, narrative sequencing, and tonal semantics. We will first examine narrative sequencing.

Narrative sequencing is the mode of discourse that concerns the storytelling tradition in Black American culture. (Smitherman, 1977) The foundation of Mr. Douglass' speech was a story. As we mentioned before, the story was about America's forefathers fighting for independence from British rule. In the speech, Mr. Douglass says

> The simple story of it is that seventy-six years ago the people of this country were British subjects. The style and title of your "sovereign people" (in which you now glory) was not then born. You were under British crown. Your fathers esteemed the English government as the home government, and England as the fatherland. This home government, you know, although a considerable distance from your home, did in exercise of its parental prerogatives, impose upon its colonial children such restraints, burdens and limitations as in its mature judgement, it deemed wise right and proper [Foner,1972, p.108].

The point of this narrative sequence is that it helped Mr. Douglass build his argument. Telling the story of how the British government enforced immoral, unjust laws on the colonies helped Mr. Douglass illustrate how America, at that time, was enforcing immoral, unjust laws on black people. This gives Mr. Douglass the chance to fully prove the hypocrisy of America. And he does not stop there in the story. He continues, saying,

> But your fathers, who had not adapted the fashionable idea of this day, of the infallibility of government and the absolute character of its acts, presumed to differ from the home government in respect to the wisdom and the justice of some of those burdens and restraints. They went so far in their excitement as to pronounce the measures of government unjust, unreasonable and oppressive, an altogether such as ought not to be quietly submitted to [Foner, 1972, p.108].

This last part of Mr. Douglass' narrative sequence helps him further drive home the point that as America's forefathers deemed the measures of the English government as oppressive and unreasonable and measures that should not be honored, so shall black people have the same feelings concerning their inauspicious condition under the American government. The condition is slavery. In order to be consistent with the country's past (declaring independence or freedom), Mr. Douglass maintains that black people should be able to step up and claim the liberty they deserve. According to Mr. Douglass, America is false to its past.

The next mode of discourse that Frederick Douglass uses effectively is known as signification, which "refers to the verbal art of insult in which a speaker humorously puts down, talks about, needles—that is, signifies on—the listener" (Smitherman, 1972, p.118). An example of signification in the speech is when Mr. Douglass says

> To side with the right against the wrong, with the weak against the strong, and with the oppressed against the oppressor—here lies the merit, and the one which, of all others, seems unfashionable in our day. The cause of liberty may be stabbed by the men who glory in the deeds of your fathers. But to proceed [Foner, 1972, p.109]

In this passage, Mr. Douglass is signifying on the white people in the audience to make a point concerning the racism that exists against black people. "Sometimes signifying is done to make a point" (Smitherman, 1972, p.118). For example, the right, the weak, and the oppressed in the previous passage are black people in slavery. The wrong, the strong, and the oppressors are white people. Although Mr. Douglass does not say this directly, he means it indirectly. Sometimes signification takes on the form of indirection. (Smitherman, 1977) We also see in the end of this passage that he says, "But to proceed." Today this would kind of be the equivalent of saying, "But anyway," or "But anyhow." People who signify today normally use these phrases.

According to Harvard University's Henry Louis Gates Jr., signification is the language form of black people. (1988) Signification allows black people to invert the meaning of what they are saying thereby critiquing the oppression they suffer from. (1988) Another example of Mr. Douglass signifying comes soon after the previously mentioned passage. In this next passage, he states:

> Feeling themselves harshly and unjustly treated by the home government, your fathers, like men of honesty and men of spirit, earnestly sought redress. They saw themselves treated with sovereign indifference, coldness and scorn. Yet they persevered. They were not men to look back [Foner, 1972, p.109].

Mr. Douglass, once again, is signifying indirectly. He is speaking directly about America's forefathers being treated unjustly and not accepting that type of treatment. He is saying indirectly, however, that like those Americans who persevered against the sovereign indifference demonstrated by Britain, so too will people like himself, Henry Garnet, and Charles Redmond (all of whom were antislavery agitationists) persevere by using their full arsenal against the thresholds of injustice and immorality that exist against their people. Just like the brave forefathers of the past were not men to look back, so shall Douglass, Garnet, Redmond and other blacks do the same. This was a powerful use of signification by Douglass.

Each time Mr. Douglass signifies he makes an adamant point. In the following passage, he signifies to the white audience making another point that is not directly stated. He says:

> We have to do with the past only as we can make it useful to the present and to the future. Your fathers have lived, died, and have done their work, and have done much it well. You live and die and must do your work [Foner, 1972, p.113].

What Douglass is indirectly saying is that the past has done its work by liberating the colonies from British rule and that nineteenth century America has the responsibility of liberating black people from slavery and any other injustice they suffer from. Now the present must do its work by following the example of the past. The theme is liberation.

The third mode of discourse that Mr. Douglass illustrates is that of tonal semantics. "Tonal semantics refers to the use of voice rhythm and vocal inflection to convey meaning in black communication" (Smitherman, 1977, p.134). Tonal semantics are very difficult to pick up on when reading a speech. It is much easier to hear the speech and therefore hear where the speaker's voice inflections change. Nevertheless, we have taken a chance to see if we can detect some tonal semantics in a reading of Mr. Douglass' speech. In the words of Geneva Smitherman, "We gon do our best!"

It is evident that as Mr. Douglass gets further and further into his speech, his voice inflections change from mild and moderate to fiery and intense. For example, toward the end of the speech, Mr. Douglass says

> You shed tears over fallen Hungary, and make the sad story of her wrongs the theme of your poets, statesmen and orators, till your gallant sons are ready to fly to arms to vindicate her cause against the oppressor; but in regard to the thousand wrongs of the American slave, you would enforce the strictest silence and would hail him as an enemy of the nation who dares to make those wrongs the subject of public discourse [Foner, 1972, p.125]!

It's evident here that Mr. Douglass is speaking with great passion. One way we can tell is because there is an exclamation point at the end of the passage. In this passage, he is making the point that America should be consistent. If America is going to shed tears concerning the wrongs of other countries then it should shed the same tears over the wrongs of slavery. If America is going to go to the rescue of other countries, it should rescue black people as well. Mr. Douglass is driving home the notion that America is being hypocritical.

In a different part of the speech, it is easier to recognize the tonal semantics. According to author Geneva Smitherman, one facet of tonal semantics used by African American speakers is rhyme and poetry. (1977) In the speech, Mr. Douglass illustrates this by saying,

Is this the land your fathers loved, the freedom, which they toiled to win? Is this the earth whereon they moved? Are these the graves they slumber in? (Foner, 1972, p.120).

Mr. Douglass uses this rhyme to emphasize a point he was making about how wrong it was for African Americans to be bought and sold, therefore being treated like animals. Mr. Douglass emphasizes that he does not believe that this type of inhuman treatment is consistent with the freedom that America's forefathers fought and died for. He hopes this rhyme will be yet another technique that will help bring about social change.

Another passage of Mr. Douglass' speech illustrates tonal semantics. In this example, Mr. Douglass is again speaking with great passion with hopes that his powerful words will shake the audience members and incite change for the better. Mr. Douglass says

> The minister of American justice is bound by the law to hear but one side; and that side is the side of the oppressor. Let this damning fact be perpetually told. Let it be thundered around the world that in tyrant-killing, king-hating, people-loving, democratic, Christian America the seats of justice are filled with judges who hold their offices under an open and palpable bribe, and are bound, in deciding the case of a man's liberty, to hear only the accusers [Foner, 1972, p.121]!

Here, we can infer that Douglass raises his voice while delivering this part of the speech. He uses the very strong word "damning" to signify the strength of his message. The exclamation point in the end also indicates that he is speaking very energetically during this part of the speech. Nevertheless, sometimes one has to be forceful and take a chance in order to get change.

Rhetorical Tools

In Frederick Douglas's speech there are a number of instances where he uses the rhetorical tools simile and metaphor. Similes and metaphors allow the rhetor to use analogies that ultimately give life to what he or she is saying. These rhetorical tools make great illustrations and therefore help to drive home the point of what is being said. In the following passage, Mr. Douglass uses a simile. Similes are phrases that compare two things using "like" or "as." Mr. Douglass says

> As a sheet anchor takes a firmer hold when the ship is tossed by the storm, so did the cause of your fathers grow stronger as it breasted the chilling blasts of kingly displeasure [Foner, 1972, p.109].

With this similie, Mr. Douglass is describing the firm hold America's forefathers had in their fight for liberty despite how difficult the tyrants of Great Britain made things. No matter how arduous things became, America's forefathers did not give up — their resolve remained strong. Similarly, Mr. Douglass is saying black people shall remain strong despite the terrible injustices committed against them by America.

In the next passage, Mr. Douglass uses a metaphor to get his point across. Metaphors are phrases that compare two things without the use of "like" or "as." Metaphors use a lot of detail. In this instance, Mr. Douglass says

> Great streams are not easily turned from channels worn deep in the course of ages. They may sometimes rise in quiet and stately majesty, and inundate the land, refreshing and fertilizing the earth with their mysterious properties. They may also rise in wrath and fury, and bear away on their angry waves the accumulated wealth of years of toil and hardship. They, however, gradually flow back to the same old channel and flow on as serenely as ever. But, while the river may not be turned aside, it may dry up and leave nothing behind but the withered branch and the unsightly rock, to howl in the abyss-sweeping wind, the sad tale of departed glory. As with rivers, so with nations [Foner, 1972, p.108].

Here, Mr. Douglass is comparing America to a great stream. Essentially, he is saying that America is not too old to change her ways, that there is still hope that America could undergo a significant transformation for the better. America is not like an old, great stream in that it is used to flowing to the same channel time after time. Because America is young, she can change the plethora of immorality that exists on her soil against black people. Because she is young, she can dissolve the wicked system of slavery. America is puerile, not set in her ways.

Mr. Douglass uses another metaphor, albeit simpler than the previous one, to describe how the white people he is delivering the speech to should embrace the Fourth of July celebration day. Mr. Douglass says,

"Cling to this day-cling to it, and to its principles, with the grasp of a storm-tossed mariner to a spar at midnight." (Foner, 1972, p.110–111).

The use of the "storm-tossed mariner" metaphore provides greater depth to what Mr. Douglass is saying. Obviously, a storm-tossed mariner has to have a very firm grip on his ship when there is a spar. In comparison, so too should the great number of American citizens have a stout grip on the Fourth of July celebration day as they bask in the fruits of their forefathers' labor. American people should hold on to the day as tightly as possible, realizing that their freedom was earned at a high price.

Conclusion

We should be continually reminded that the root of society should always be harmonious and coherent. When society is out of equilibrium, it is the responsibility of the rhetor to restore harmony, compatibility, and communal balance. The human being has the ability to affect society. We can say, without hesitation, that Frederick Douglass put forth an incomparable effort to restore moral equilibrium in a completely immoral American society.

Frederick Douglass transcended the constraints of his time and overcame his circumstances in an effort to transform his and other African American peoples' terrible social condition. He did a marvelous job putting the strategies and tactics of African American rhetoric to practice. The day of harmony, coherence, and compatibility is closer to being thanks to Mr. Frederick Douglass and other African American trailblazers before and after him.

References

Asante, M.K. (1998). *The Afrocentric Idea*. Philadelphia: Temple University Press.
Foner, P. S. (1972). *The Voice of Black America*. New York: Simon and Schuster.
Gates, H.L. (1988). *The Signifying Monkey: A Theory of Afro-American Literary Criticism*. New York: Oxford University Press.
Smitherman, G. (1977). *Talkin and Testifyin*. Boston: Houghton Mifflin Company.

The Philosophy of the Black Power Movement Using Ntu as a Theoretical Construct
Paul Easterling

The Black Power Movement is one of the most significant and important movements of the Civil Rights movement and in the African's overall struggle for liberation in America. Janheinz Jahn, in the book *Muntu*, defines "Ntu" as "the universal force which, as such, never occurs apart from its manifestations: Muntu (human being), Kintu (thing), Hantu (time and place) and Kuntu (modality) ... NTU is what Muntu, Kintu, Hantu and Kuntu all equally are" (Muntu, 101). Ntu is everything we are and everything the world is; it is all that we see around us, everything we do. "Black power can be clearly defined for those who do not attach the fears of white America to their questions about it," is the definition given by Stokely Carmicheal, also known as Kwame Toure, in an essay entitled "What We Want" (1966, Carson, 283). In this essay, I will use this definition, along with others and different ways organizations exercised and used Black Power in the Civil Right movement to analyze the philosophy of the Black Power movement, using the theoretical paradigm outlined above.

Muntu

Toure continues his definition by saying, "We should begin with the basic fact that black Americans have two problems: they are poor and they are black. All other problems arise from this two-sided reality: lack of education, the so-called apathy of black men. Any program to end racism must address itself to that double reality." To address these issues Toure saw as our problems, it must shown that being Black as one of our problems is saying that our humanity, or Muntu, is a problem. Our Blackness cannot be a problem; if that is so, then how do we justify our existence? This is the point Du Bois was addressing when he said, "Blacks are often studied as problems instead of as people who face problems," (Gordon, 23). This notion of us being the problem must be addressed. Otherwise, we are questioning our own Muntu, for which we have been fighting against the oppressor.

In the book *Black Power: The Politics of Liberation in America*, Toure also said, "Black people in the United States must raise hard questions, questions which challenge the very nature of the society itself: its longstanding values, beliefs and institutions" (34). To confront America with a query of its own nature, instead of America questioning our nature and humanity will force America to address us as Muntu. That is one of the main purposes of the Black Power movement and the Civil Rights movement as a whole, to force America and the world to recognize our collective Muntu. Toure goes on to say, "To do this, we must first redefine ourselves. Our basic need is to reclaim our history and our identity.... We shall have to struggle for the right to create our own terms through which to define ourselves and our relationship to the society, and to have these terms recognized" (34–35). Once again, this leads to the most essential part of us. To redefine ourselves, to reclaim our history and identity, is to reclaim our humanity.

Kintu

There were different Kintu (things) and methods that were used during the Black Power movement. Toure used marches, rallies and picket signs, and Bobby Seale stormed the California capitol building with rifles and shotguns and patrolled the police in their own neighborhoods. This could not have been done in Alabama. The use of the Kintu, this time weapons as compared to picket signs, is what made the Black power movement in Oakland what it was. The Kintu that was used in the manner it was, was made possible by the Hantu (place) in which it was done.

Hantu

In his essay "What We Want," Toure claims that "In such areas as Lowndes, where black men have a majority, they will attempt to use it to exercise control. This is what they seek: control. Where Negroes lack a majority, black power means proper representation and sharing of control" (Carson, 283). This addresses the Hantu of a specific area. In Oakland, California, Black people are not the majority; they would have to use some representation in the Governor's cabinet or a place in the state legislature instead of being just a sheriff.

Moreover, the time in which Toure's essay was written and Seale's march on the California capitol took place must be noted. If one was to take the stance that Toure did in the 1920s or 1930s, the reaction of the people would have been very different from the reaction of the 1960s. The fact that the 1960s was a time of social unrest and America's eye had been turned to the South, people could not have reacted in the manner that it would have if they had been thirty to forty years earlier. However, if this movement were to take place in present day America, the reaction would again be much different.

Kuntu

The establishment of the Black Panther Party Platform and program "What We Want, What We Believe" was also a way that Bobby Seale and Huey P. Newton defined Black Power:

1. "We want freedom. We want power to determine the destiny of our Black community....
2. We want full employment for our people....
3. We want an end to the robbery for the capitalist of our Black Community....
4. We want decent housing fit for shelter of human beings....
5. We want education for our people that exposes the true nature of this decadent American society. We want education that teaches us out true history and our role in present-day society....
6. We want all Black men to be exempt form military service....
7. We want an immediate end to *police brutality* and *murder* of Black people....
8. We want freedom for all Black men held in federal, state, county and city prisons and jails....
9. We want all black people when brought to trial to be tried in court by a jury of their peer group of people from their Black communities, as defined by the Constitution of the United States....
10. We want land, bread, housing, education, clothing, justice, and peace. And as our major political objective, a United Nations

supervised plebiscite to be held throughout the Black colony in which only Black colonial subjects will be allowed to participate, for the purpose of determining the will of Black people as to their national destiny" (Carson, 346–7).

This is the platform the Black Panther Party used to define and to establish Black power. This platform was created and presented to the United States in Oakland, California, rather than Lowndes County, Alabama, because of the Kuntu of California.

"Politically, black power means what it has always meant to SNCC: the coming together of black people to elect representatives and to force those representatives to speak to their needs. It does not mean merely putting black faces into office." These words of Toure speak the Kuntu (modality) of one as an individual (Carson 283–4). It is one thing to just have a Black face in office occupying the position, but that is not power. This is evident in such representatives as Clarence Thomas and Ward Coneley; they are men of African descent but they do not represent the African community in America. The person must have the right Kuntu to lead and represent the people properly.

Amalgamation

Another point that Toure brings up is "In Lowndes County, for example, black power will mean that if a Negro is elected sheriff, he can end police brutality. If a black man is elected tax assessor, he can collect and channel funds for the building of better roads, schools serving black people — thus advancing the move from political power into the economic arena" (Carson 283). This concept can be looked at from different ways: First, in the Hantu that is Lowdnes County, Alabama, Black Power would be looked upon differently than it would be in Oakland, California, where the Black Panther Party arose from using Black Power as its platform. Whereas Black Power may be a sheriff in Alabama, it is state representative in California as was discussed earlier. Secondly, the modality, or Kuntu, of the area, is also very significant. If Toure and his constituents were to take the posture that Seale and his took, the outcome would have been very different. The mob law of the South would have reacted more violently, while California, being the West, could not react the same way because of its high-profile visibility.

In the book *Black Power: The Radical Response to White America*, Charles V. Hamiliton explains some of the aims of and issues facing Black power: "Black Power must (1) deal with the obviously growing alienation of Black people and their distrust of the institutions of this society; (2) work to create new values and to build a new sense of community and belonging; and (3) work to establish legitimate new institutions that make participants, not recipients, out of a people traditionally excluded from the fundamentally racist processes of this country" (Wagstaff, 126). First, Black power having to deal with the alienation of Black people is addressing the Muntu that Black people are denied by this country. Because of the distrust of this society deals with the Kuntu of the people. The fact that our people have been denied their Muntu and alienated from society, the Kuntu of distrust is one that Black power as an institution will have to confront.

Muntu and Kuntu are also evident in the second point that Hamiliton raises about to creating new values to build a new sense of community and belonging. For a people to be able to reflect and reassess their current values and to build new ones and to build a sense of community is Muntu recognizing its Kuntu, and rebuilding it as to adapt to the Kuntu of the society in which the people live. Thirdly, establishing new institutions is establishing new Hantu and Kuntu. For example, if a school that teaches Black Power or an Afrocentric academy were built, that is a place where the people could go and be taught; this is where a new Kuntu can be established and taught to the people.

Analysis

The Black Power movement had to deal with the different manifestation of Ntu throughout the struggle, otherwise it would have fallen short in the dealing with the problems that the African community in America had to deal with. The manifestation of Ntu in the Black Power movement was shown in the struggle for our collective Muntu, the use of Kintu in our struggle, the Hantu in which the movement took place and the Kuntu of the movement and the people. Any current social movement or any movement that may arise in the future will also have to address the presence of Ntu or it will fall short in its efforts for liberation. The manifestation of Ntu as Muntu, Kintu, Hantu and Kuntu is what makes Ntu apparent in all that we do and all that we are. From our struggle for liberation to our everyday dealings with life we must recognize the presence and power that is Ntu.

Conclusion

It has been shown that the presence of Ntu is very important when looking at our social movements and even our everyday lives. We must recognize and confront this force in all that we do. Using Ntu as a theoretical construct to understand the Black Power movement is only one way of doing so. The Black Power movement is a very significant movement in our history and it must be studied using different theoretical constructs in order understand it and to do it justice.

References

Carmichael, Stokely and Charles Hamilton. *Black Power: The Politics of Liberation in America.* New York: Random House, 1967.

Carson, Clayborne, David J. Garrow, Gerald Gill, Vincent Harding, Darlene Clark Hine, eds. *The Eyes on the Prize Civil Rights Reader.* New York: Penguin Books, 1991.

Gordon, Lewis R. *Existentia Africana: Understanding Africana Existential Thought.* New York and London: Routledge, 2000.

Jahn, Janheinz. *Muntu: African Culture, and the Western World.* New York: Groove Press Inc., 1961.

Wagstaff, Thomas, ed. *Black Power: The Radical Response to White America.* Beverly Hills: Glencoe Press, 1969.

African American Intellectual History: Philosophy and Ethos
Malachi Crawford

Theory and Methods

This paper broadly surveys African American intellectual history from the life of Frederick Douglass to the appearance of systematic nationalist and Black existential systems of thought within Africana Studies departments (see Table 1). In the past, historians have placed African American intellectual history within a dialect of integrationist or Black nationalist thought, such as Harold Cruse in his book *The Crisis of the Negro Intellectual*. Even on a continuum of extremes, allowing room for moderation between the two ideologies, the prognosis is theoretically conflicting. The data herein centers on the philosophy and ethos of several African American leaders with an attempt at showing influence of ideas.

The theory that drives the research proposes that African American intellectual philosophies depend on having African Americans realize their humanity. All African American intellectual thought asks the question, "How might Blacks come to realize their own humanity?" Similarly, African American philosophies differ on the means that each system of thought takes in resolving the problem. The theory comes from Janheinz Jahn's two concepts of being: Muntu and Kuntu. The theory argues that there are two forms of humanity that African American intellectuals attempt to resolve.

In *Muntu*, a text on African philosophical thought, Janhienz Jahn defines the Bantu word for Muntu as being. Existence within Muntu centers on the interconnectedness of all things within the universe and the special place that humans have in the natural order of the world. The first type of humanity, then, acknowledges basic existence as a human.

The second form of humanity discussed herein comes from Jahn's concept of Kuntu. Designation, or identity, is the primary form of existence within Kuntu. According to Jahns, identity is another form of humanity without which humans are simply things or animals. The force of Kuntu rests in knowing that there are differences in the cosmological and ontological makeup of human beings—for example, there are differences between men and women. Therefore, the second form of humanity arises from an appreciation of the differences between humans. Without the appreciation of such difference, humans could not respect the quality of different characters or the uniqueness of various opinions. In the case of African Americans, two details of humanity—both formulated by Du Bois—take precedence: African identity and African enslavement in America (see Table 2).

The experience of American enslavement is paradoxical in relation to African American humanity. Enslavement in America intentionally called for the dehumanization of Africans and African culture. However, because the system had such a dramatic impact on African livelihood, enslavement necessarily became a fixed component of African American identity. As we shall see, the consequences of underestimating or oversimplifying the influence of enslavement have been tested throughout African American intellectual thought. With this said, the two forms of humanity mentioned above are interconnected—not separate—and should not be categorized as such.

Table 1

Name	Philosophy	Birth Date	Birth Place
Frederick Douglass	Humanistic Nationalist	1817–1895	Tuckahoe, MD
Alexander Crummel	Black Nationalist	1819–1898	New York, NY
W.E.B. Du Bois	Systematic Nationalist	1868–1963	Great Barrington, MA

The location and circumstances that African American intellectuals are born in becomes important in placement and comprehension of their philosophical views toward African American humanity. As Table 1 indicates, of the three African American intellectuals surveyed, only one, Frederick Douglass, grew up in a slave holding state. The other two intellectuals, Crummel and Du Bois, were born to free parents. Consequently, an analysis of Douglass' speeches reveal his determined position towards the existence of humanity within all humans. This paper begins with an analysis of a contemporary of Douglass, Alexander Crummel, and Black Nationalism.

Alexander Crummel: Black Nationalist

One of the pillars of Black Nationalist thought is believing in the need for the moral redemption of African Americans. This comes as a direct consequence of the disabling effect that enslavement has had on the basic humanity of African Americans. Enslavement challenged the essential human practices, interaction, and cultural connectedness of Africans taken to America. Africans were politically, legally, and socially relegated to the position of property — or thing — in the minds of Americans. African existence on a human level became simple organic matter. Thus, African American leaders prioritized human dignity and decency in their efforts to redefine African American humanity. Alexander Crummel, one of the primary influences and founders of Black Nationalism, was zealous in this regard.

Progressive northern whites contributed significantly to the political philosophies of Alexander Crummel. Although his commitment to and study of religion began early in his life, in 1844 Alexander Crummel reached priesthood within the Evangelical church. Because the philosophy of most progressive whites cared little for African American agency and held a hegemonic paradigm of culture, Crummel and many other African American intellectuals of his time, such as Booker T. Washington, retained Eurocentric perspectives on African culture. Nevertheless, the church gave Crummel his first real chance at disseminating his views to large bodies of African Americans. Perhaps as a result of his early life within the Evangelical church and personal scholastic background, Crummel placed European concepts of governmental order — elitism — over African ones—eldership. Consequently, Crummel perceived traditional African culture as backwards.

Along with other traditional Black Nationalists, Crummel saw European culture as the model for implementation in African American society. Crummel employed his training in the Episcopal Church and his elitist ideology to design a system of thought that could combat the dehumanizing effects of enslavement. The combination of the two influences directly affected Crummel's political ideologies while in Liberia. From 1853 to 1873,

Crummel preached the need for Africans to become civilized. Interestingly enough, Alexander Crummel, like subsequent Black Nationalists Edward Blyden and Elijah Muhammad, saw religion as the vehicle through which people disseminate culture. Faith and practice in Christianity were the agents of socialization forced on the indigenous peoples within the state of Liberia. Crummel deliberately disregarded the sovereignty of traditional African culture.

Again, this pattern of thought is traceable to many African American intellectuals influenced by progressive whites during this period of time. Given this engagement, Crummel became an African colonizer with European values. Despite these setbacks, Alexander Crummel advanced crucial political concepts, such as political independence, toward the struggle for African American liberation.

Frederick Douglass: Humanistic Nationalism

Unlike the other two intellectuals surveyed in this study, Frederick Douglass was born into slavery. Moreover, Douglass was a salve in Maryland, the state with the worst reputation for the treatment of slaves in America. Douglass' life represents a series of transitions in perception and analysis of American society. He, more than any other American, articulated the degratory effects of American enslavement. Because of his beginnings, Douglass' view and analysis of American society are valid even today.

According to Douglass, the purpose of American enslavement was to erode and degrade the humanity of African people. Douglass is unequivocal in his position here. In *My Bondage and My Freedom*, Douglass makes the case that if American enslavement centered on economics, African Americans didn't see that side of enslavement. Common farm animals were kept better than slaves. The upkeep of slaves required whatever was necessary to keep them alive. The cruelty that Douglass saw and experienced while in enslavement led him to defend the fundamental principals of humanity.

The philosophical propositions of Frederick Douglass focus on the commonalties, or humanness, that all people share. This philosophical tradition represents the first form of humanity: Muntu. According to Douglass, before difference (opinion) can be recognized, discredited or validated, there must be an initial recognition of the right of a people to express and engage in the intercourse of ideas. As Douglass stated, "I do not presume to be a leader, ... , but if I have advocated the cause of the Negro it is not because I am a Negro, but because I am a man" (Litwack and Meier, 1988).

Thus, humanistic nationalism negates racialized concepts of identity. Conflict based on race or difference is a learned manifestation of human thought. Therefore, humanistic nationalism makes, firstly, an ethical appeal to the will and morals of a people. Moreover, because humanity is the central component of humanistic nationalism, those things necessary to sustain life and basic human needs, such as food, shelter and living conditions, are of paramount importance. If human beliefs can be changed, then so can human practices. Douglass' solution during the Reconstruction Era, like that of Du Bois, was essentially one of political empowerment.

William E.B. Du Bois: Systematic Nationalism

The philosophies and theoretical paradigms of W.E.B. Du Bois are a combination of previous African American intellectual thought and his own ideas on the problems and needs of African Americans. Du Bois had the opportunity of hearing, debating, and being mentored by a host of nineteenth century African Americans. Alexander Crummel committed himself to the belief that an elite group of intellectuals would advance the causes and positions of African Americans. During Crummel's life in Washington, D.C., he had the opportunity to disseminate his beliefs in a powerful group of African Americans. Du Bois participated in the beginning years of the American Negro Academy, an elitist organization that Crummel founded. Unlike Alexander Crummel, Du Bois did not call for emigration from America. Du Bois also had an opportunity to discuss and exchange ideas with Frederick Douglass, Henry Highland Garnet, and John Mercer Langston.

In *The Souls of Black Folk*, Du Bois exposes his theories on how to go about solving the problems of African Americans. Du Bois poses the question "How might African Americans manage the crucial aspect of enslavement with an African heritage?" Because of the negative designation of these dual realities, a conflict in identity occurs. This *twoness* of identity gives African Americans a unique perspective on American society. Consistently, the text offers strategies for improving the circumstance of African Americans.

Du Bois' strategy for the social upliftment of African Americans called for political empowerment. Unlike Booker T. Washington, Du Bois thought that the social and economic advancement of African Americans could only be secured with political rights. Like Douglass, Du Bois based his analysis on the years immediately following the Civil War and the failure of such reconstruction era organizations as the Freedmen's Bureau. Du Bois also believed that the African American community needed persons trained in industrial education, but insisted that industrial education should not be the primary focus of African American education and that an elite group of African American intellectuals would be necessary for the advancement of the race.

The theories that Du Bois posits on the problems of African Americans come from an emphasis on the second form of humanity (Kuntu) shown in Table 2. While Washington's concerns rested with the immediate needs of African Americans as a people — food, shelter, and land — Du Bois was concerned with the pillaging and exploitation that African Americans suffered as a result of how they were perceived in society. Indeed, many of Du Bois' works center on the loyalty that African Americans show in the face of blatant human degradation.

Du Bois' view and expression of African American identity is a fundamental transcendence in African American intellectual history. How do African Americans find a meaningful designation in African culture and the enslavement of Africans in America? Assigning an arbitrary value to either one would be detrimental to the basic humanness (Muntu) of African Americans.

Table 2
M + [K(1) x K(2)] Humanity

Philosophy System of Thought	Muntu Human Existence	Kuntu African Culture	Kuntu African Enslavement
Humanistic-Nationalist*	Primary logic	Reference	Strategic Focus
Black Nationalist*	Primary logic	Strategic Focus	Resource
Systematic-Nationalist*	Reference	Primary logic/ Strategic Foci	Strategic Foci/ Resource
Religious Nationalist	Primary logic	Reference	Resource/ Reference
Black Existentialist	Strategic focus	Reference	Primary logic
Black Marxist	Primary logic/ Strategic Focus	— — —	Reference

An asterisk (*) indicates the philosophies discussed in this study.

Table 3

Name	Correspondence	Contemporaries
Alexander Crummel	Henry Highland Garnett W.E.B. Du Bois; Paul L. Dunbar; John E. Bruce; Francis J. Grimke; Anna J. Cooper; Samuel Crowthery; Thoas S. Sidney; Ira Aldridge; Ssanuel R. Ward	Frederick Douglass; Martin R. Delany; Daniel A. Payne; John Mercer Langston; Henry M. Turner; Booker T. Washington; Nat Turner; St. Claire Drake; W.E.B. Du Bois; John E. Bruce; T. Thomas Fortune; Edward Blyden
Frederick Douglass	Henry Highland Garnett; James McCune Smith; Harriet Tubman; Martin R. Delany; Lewis Woodson; Soujoutner Truth; William Lloyd Garrison; John Brown; Charles L. Redmond; Rev. Charles Lawson; Gerrit Smith; George Latimer	Harriet Tubman; Soujourner Truth; Booker T. Washington; John Merer Langston; Henry Highland Garnet; Martin R. Delany; Nar Turner; John Brown; Denmark Vessey, David Walker; Edward Blyden; John E. Bruce; T. Thomas Fortune
William E.B. Du Bois	Carter G. Woodson; Eugene Kinkle Jones; Booker T. Washington; Alexander Crummel; Frederick Douglass; Langston Hughes; Robert R. Moton; Edward M. Stanton	Booker T. Washington; T. Thomas Fortune; Henry M. Turner; Carter G. Woodson; Marcus Garvey; Langston Hughes; Zora N. Hurston; Daniel A. Payne; Frederick Douglass

Correspondence and Contemporaries

One of the more interesting components of this study involved researching the correspondence and contemporaries of each intellectual in an effort to locate influence of ideas and strategies. Some of Alexander Crummel's philosophies on social advancement, such as industrial education for indigenous Africans within the state of Liberia, may well be traced to his connection with W.E.B. Du Bois. Crummel and Du Bois served together at the American Negro Academy, which Crummel founded the academy a year before his death in 1898. Essentially the ANA — an elitist institution — brought some of the most prolific African American leaders together in efforts to strategically liberate the African American community at the dawn of the twentieth century. Du Bois offered Crummel connections and insights into the economic philosophies of Booker T. Washington. Furthermore, Crummel kept close contacts with the friends he made at the New York African Free School. Some of his classmates were Henry Highland Garnet, Samuel R. Ward, and Ira Aldridge. Although Crummel may not have interacted with Frederick Douglass on a personal level, his relationship with Martin R. Delany helped him further understand the elder statesman.

Frederick Douglass' main vein of correspondence, however, came via newspaper articles or public rebuffs of certain African American political positions. Douglass was bitterly agitated by emigrations proposals of expatriation. Douglass felt that African Americans had too large a stake in the founding of America (both physically and psychologically) to simply walk

Table 4

Name	Publications	Date	Occupations
Alexander Crummel	The Duty of a Rising	1856	Priest, educator, businessman
	The Progress of The Future	1861	
	The Greatness of Christ	1882	
	Africa and America	1882	
Frederick Douglass	Narrative of the Life of Frederick Douglass	1845	Orator, statesman politician
	Editor of North Star	1847-51	
	Frederick	1861-60	
	What to the Slave is the Fourth of July	1852	
	My Bondage and My Freedom	1855	
	Douglass' Monthly	1860–63	
	New National Era	1870–73	
William E. B. Du Bois	The Conservation of Races	1897	Orator, philospher, sociologist, historian, editor
	The Philadelphia Negro: A Social Study	1899	
	The Souls of Black Folk, Essays and Sketches	1903	
	The Development of a People	1904	
	Darkwater, Voices from Within the Veil	1921	
	My Evolving Program for Negro Freedom	1944	
	The Crisis	— — —	

away from the country. Douglass corresponded chiefly with persons of similar social and political views as himself, such as Harriet Tubman, John Brown, and Sojourner Truth. During Douglass' last years of life, he involved himself with the National Negro Convention. At the convention he debated with the likes of Henry Highland Garnet and Du Bois.

When the previous two intellectuals were at the apex of their public careers, W.E.B. Du Bois was just a child. Du Bois entered the public arena in the twilight years of an elite class of African American intellectuals, such as John Mercer Langston, Ida B. Wells, Douglass, Crummel, Henry Highland Garnet, and Martin R. Delany. Du Bois had the opportunity to listen to and grasp the seasoned philosophies of the best and brightest African American intellectuals. Consistently, Du Bois' strategies for African American liberation were an admixture of his own ideas and those African American intellectuals that came before him. Du Bois corresponded with both Frederick Douglass and Henry Highland Garnnet, and Booker T. Washington and Martin R. Delany.

Publications

African American intellectual publications during the middle to late nineteenth century represented both the philosophical, theoretical, strategical, and academic abilities of African Americans. "Progress of Civilization along the West Coast of Africa" is a speech that Alexander Crummel gave various times throughout his stay in Liberia. The piece, written in 1861, represents Crummel's attempt at providing a solution to the crisis brewing in America over the enslavement of Africans.

Frederick Douglass' two most remembered works are "What to the Slave is the Fourth of July," a speech given in Rochester, New York, in 1852, and his autobiography *The Life and Times of Frederick Douglass*. First published in 1845, Douglass reprinted his autobiography under the title *My Bondage and My Freedom* in 1855. One of the major reasons for the revision to his first autobiography was the change in his relationship with William Lloyd Garrison. In his speech "What to the Slave is the Fourth of July," Douglass describes the hypocrisy of Americans celebrating their independence and propounding notions of "liberty, justice and freedom for all," while a whole people in America remained in chattel slavery. One of Douglass' greatest accomplishments was his devotion to the cause and struggle of his people. From 1847 until 1873, Douglass committed himself to publishing and editing newspapers dedicated to the political disenfranchisement of African Americans.

Similar to the publishing tradition of Frederick Douglass, Du Bois wrote a large volume of works that described and analyzed the social position of African Americans. Among Du Bois' most notable works are *The Philadelphia Negro: A Social Study* (1899) and *The Souls of Black Folk* (1903). He was also known for his editing and direction of the *Crisis*, the political magazine of the NAACP. *The Philadelphia Negro* was the first sociological study done in America. Consistently, Du Bois describes the *twoness* of African American identity and the consequences of American racism in *The Souls of Black Folk*. The text also serves as a direct attack on the strategy of industrial education proposed by Booker T. Washington. Along with articles for the New York Age and New York Globe, Du Bois utilized the *Crisis* spread to his strategies on race to African American intellectuals.

Table 5

Name	Organizations	Positions
Alexander Crummel	Union of Colored Ministers; American Negro Academy (later called the National Negro Academy); St. Luke's Church (Washington, D.C.); National Negro Convention; New York African Free School	Principal of Mount Vaughan High School, Cape Palmas, Liberia; Priest of St. Luke's Church
Frederick Douglass	National Colored Labor Union; National Negro Convention American Anti-Slavery Society; East Baltimore Mental Improvement Society; National Council of Women; Women's Suffrage	U.S. Minister to Haiti (1889); Recorder of Deeds (Washington, D.C.); Vice Presidential nominee, Presidential candidate. Editor of North Star
William E.B. Du Bois	American Negro Academy; Niagara Movement; NAACP; Krigwa Players; First Universal Races Congress (1911); Cultural and Scientific Conference for World Peace; the First Conference of Negro Land Grant Colleges; National Negro Convention; Alpha (1909)	Secretary of the First Pan-African Conference; Consultant to the Founding Convention of the United Nations presided at the Fifth Pan-African Conference; Chair of the Dept. of Sociology (Atlanta University) founder of Alpha Phi Phylon.

Organizations

During the course of their lives, Crummel, Douglass, and Du Bois participated in a range of social organizations. Table 5 does not suggest that Crummel and Douglass were members of the same organization (as the two intellectuals disagreed on the method toward African American advancement). Douglass and Crummel were, however, in organizations with Du Bois. Douglass served in the National Negro Convention with Du Bois, while Crummel founded and participated with Du Bois in the American Negro Academy.

Analysis

The three systems of thought presented here all center on the manners in which African American intellectuals attempted to resolve the problems associated with African American humanity. Traditionally, Black Nationalism has attempted to solve the humanistic struggles of African Americans by proudly proclaiming the identity of Africans while rejecting traditional African culture. Black nationalists see African identity as the key to solving the problems associated with African American human existence. Conversely, humanistic nationalists have attempted to disregard race-based differences. The humanistic nationalist is concerned with the general welfare of humans, especially when differences in the distribution of food and land are based on arbitrary human will. Lastly, systematic nationalists always present a strategic background of upliftment with any theory that they posit.

These systems of thought are not stationary, or categorical, as all human thought is an amalgam of influenced ideas. The systematic nationalism of Afrocentrists—and systematic nationalism in general—is the direct conception of evolved Black Nationalism. So too, Afrocentricity and Black existential thought are the dual theories of systematic nationalism — the systems of thought are inseparable. If African Americans forget the influence that enslavement has had on their humanity, they fall prey to the circumstances faced by the members of the Moorish Science Temple. Similarly, when African Americans over depend on the experience of enslavement in America, they necessarily fall into defeatists' discussions of nihilism.

References

Conyers, James L. Jr. *Black American Intellectualism and Culture*. Stanford, CT.: JAI Press Inc., 1999.

_____, and A. Barnett. *African American Sociology.* Chicago: Nelson-Hall Publishers, 1999.

Cruse, Harold. *The Crisis of the Negro Intellectual.* New York: Morrow, 1967.

Douglass, Frederick. *My Bondage and My Freedom.* Toronto: Dover Publications, Inc., 1969.

Du Bois, William E.B. *The Souls of Black Folk, Essays and Sketches.* Chicago: A.C. McClurg, 1903.

Frederickson, George M. *Black Liberation.* New York: Oxford University Press, 1995.

Gordon, Lewis R. *Existence In Black.* New York, NY: Routledge, 1997.

_____. *Existentia Africana.* New York: Routledge, 2000.

Jahn, Janheinz. *Muntu: African Culture and the Western World.* New York: Grove Press, 1990.

Litwack, and A. Meier. *Black Leaders of the Nineteenth Century.* Chicago: University of Illinois Press, 1988.

Moses, Wilson Jeremiah. *Classical Black Nationalism.* New York: New York University Press, 1996.

_____. *The Golden Age of Black Nationalism.* Hamden, CT: Archon Books, 1978.

Part 3: Critical Analysis

Afrocentricity and African Psychology
Kevin Cokely

The growing influence of Afrocentricity in the discipline of African/Black psychology has not been without growing pains. This paper seeks to explore the tension between the construction of knowledge in African-centered psychology and the methods it uses to provide evidence. It is argued that the ability of an African psychology to advance as a discipline will be compromised if it becomes a primarily oppositional and polemical project which only reacts to the oppression of White supremacy. Furthermore, continuing use of a methodology steeped in the Western empiricist tradition will leave Afrocentric scholarship vulnerable to Eurocentric critique, and ultimately, discredited. A closer examination of the scholarship of influential African-centered psychologists reveals a deviation from a central tenet of Asante's Afrocentricity, the tenet of pluralism without hierarchy. This brings us to the moral question of "To what extent should Afrocentric scholarship reflect a responsibility to articulate moral values which promote human transformation?" A close examination of certain beliefs from "race men" in both African and European psychological scholarship reveals some uncomfortable similarities. The chapter concludes by offering some thoughts about how the future success or failure of African psychology with be largely determined by how it deals with the construct of race.

Afrocentricity in African Psychology: The Tension Between Gnosis and Method

The continued growth of African psychology as a legitimate discipline will depend on its ability to meet three challenges: 1) to create theories and methods which are more than just "darker" reflections of and or reactions to European thought; 2) to provide internal critiques of these theories and methods which are free of ideological partisanship; and 3) to fully expose its ideas to external critiques with the belief that they will withstand refutation. The discipline of African psychology should be a self-sustaining project which continually contributes new insights into the behavior, character, and spirit of African descended people. To make a difference in the lives of African people, African psychology must represent a balance between scholarship and activism. It should also seek to understand the psychological nature of those forces which dehumanize and oppress people of African descent.

The early history of Black psychology can be traced back to a disillusionment with the overwhelmingly White American Psychological Association and its failure to address the societal ills that were negatively impacting the collective psychology of Africans in America. This disillusionment occurred during a time when African Americans were becoming more racially and culturally conscious and reconnected to Africa. Historical beginning not withstanding, I believe that Black psychology's legacy must be more than a reactionary movement to the racism and White supremacy present in psychology. The advancement of African psychology will be compromised if it becomes a primarily oppositional and polemical project which only "counterpunches" the oppression of White supremacy. In other words, this more traditional approach is a necessary but insufficient component for the continued growth of the discipline.

One indication of Black psychology's growing influence is the intellectual scrutiny it has undergone. Several scholars have attempted to categorize Black/African psychology based on various intellectual and political criteria. Karenga's classification[1] is arguably the most prevalent one while Kambon's classification[2], created to complement Karenga's, is the most ideologically driven. Karenga divides Black psychology into three schools of thought: Traditional, Reform, and Radical. Kambon describes the ideologies which roughly correspond to the schools of thought as Racial integrationists/cultural assimilationists, Black-American nationalists, and Pan-African cultural nationalism. Karenga characterizes the Traditional approach as being reactive and defensive, with no interest in developing a Black psychology. Kambon describes these individuals as racial integrationists and cultural assimilationists, because their ideology is based in Eurocentric training and miseducation in psychology. Karenga characterizes the Reform approach as one that attacks racism and recognizes the existence of a Black psychology which emphasizes racial oppression and the continuing legacy of American slavery. Kambon calls these individuals

Black-American nationalists, because race is their primary analytical framework while culture remains relatively insignificant. Karenga characterizes the Radical approach as adopting an Afrocentric conceptual framework which emphasizes African culture and philosophy. Kambon calls these individuals Pan-African cultural nationalists, because they advocate that race and culture are the foundation of African self-identity. The focus of this essay is on the last categories because they currently represent the most publicized and arguably influential intellectual perspectives within African psychology. They are also heavily influenced by the philosophy that Asante[3] refers to as Afrocentricity.

Asante has described Afrocentricity as a philosophy which places African people at the center of any analysis.[4] This means that instead of Africans being continually treated as mere objects of primarily European curiosity, or derisively as "the other," they become the authors of their own destiny and interpreters of their own experience by becoming subjects of study. Quite simply, objects are persons or things which occupy space and have no function or purpose other than to be studied and discussed. According to the New World Dictionary of the American Language (1980), "object" has been colloquially used to refer to a person that arouses pity or ridicule. On the other hand, subjects are under the control and authority of another. From the Afrocentric perspective, being the subject of analysis requires Africans to be in control of every phase of intellectual study, ranging from the conceptual and theoretical all the way to the methodological and interpretive. In short, Afrocentric analysis requires the analyzer to be properly located culturally.

In incorporating an Afrocentric perspective into any disciplinary framework, a fundamental question must be answered: Does Afrocentricity represent a racial or cultural theory?[5] Asante has addressed this issue in several of his writings. In terms of advancing Afrocentricity into a rigorous intellectual movement, he says the following:

> A rigorous discipline is necessary to advance the intellectual movement toward a meaningful concept of place. In saying this I am challenging the Afrocentrist to maintain inquiry rooted in a strict interpretation of place in order to betray all naive racial theories and establish Afrocentricity as a legitimate response to human conditions.[6]

Asante's statement suggests that he is aware of the temptation for some Afrocentric scholars to engage in racialized scholarship. In doing so, he believes that this will compromise the intellectual integrity of the movement. In *Afrocentricity and Culture*, he makes the following comments,...

> Patterned behaviors by African ethnic groups are cultural, not rigid or fixed, but related to history and experience. Culture can vary over time, but in the case of the African culture, it will always be articulated in a similar way.[7]

Here, Asante is using a cultural analysis, as evidenced by his use of the words "history and experience," in contrast to a racial analysis implied by his words "not rigid or fixed."

Asante recognizes that Afrocentricity as a liberatory educational paradigm becomes particularly vulnerable to criticism when it can be reduced to racialized rhetoric. Some of the more sensational media depictions of Afrocentricity are a result of this racialized rhetoric. An obvious example is the rhetoric of Leonard Jeffries, who has publicly stated that Whites are biologically inferior because of their lack of melanin and because their genes were malformed by the Ice Age. Statements such as this made by "Afrocentric scholars" make the Afrocentric enterprise fodder for scholarly and general public ridicule.

Aside from the discipline of history, there is perhaps no greater intellectual presence of Afrocentricity than in psychology. Given the often repeated characterization of Afrocentricity as an attempt to raise Black self-esteem, it is not surprising that Afrocentricity would find its way into the discipline of psychology. For comparative purposes it is important to note that European psychology's roots can be traced back to the British empiricists' branch of European philosophy (i.e. John Locke's essay "Concerning Human Understanding," 1690; David Hume's *A Treatise of Human Nature*, 1740) where psychology remained content as primarily philosophical reflections on the human condition until its obsession to prove itself a real science caused it to split from philosophy. Afrocentric psychology's roots, while influenced by Afrocentric philosophy, clearly has influences predating Asante's articulation of Afrocentricity (i.e. Cheikh Anta Diop's "Two Cradle Theory," Franz Fanon's anti-colonialist critique, Aime Cesaire's Negritude movement). Regardless of whether it is European or African psychology, the relationship between philosophy and psychology must be examined in order to understand psychology proper.

As one of the main disciplinary proponents of Afrocentricity, Afrocentric psychology has a responsibility to produce knowledge that "advance(s) claims which no person is able to refute."[8] When claims are advanced as facts that are speculative, specious, and or morally suspect, they work against advancing the interests of Afrocentric psychology in particular and the philosophy of Afrocentricity in general. Afrocentric psychology and philosophy converge on the construct of world views. A review of the Afrocentric psychology literature in particular shows a heavy emphasis on the world views paradigm. Because the world views paradigm is considered to be foundational for understanding Afrocentric psychology, it must be subjected to a rigorous internal critique so that it can withstand external refutation. For that reason, the world views paradigm is analyzed, with particular attention being paid to epistemology. Finally, an ethical analysis of the content of certain Afrocentric psychologists' rhetoric and theory-building is compared to that of a prominent European race psychologist J. Philippe Rushton.

Worldview

The world views paradigm basically states that one can trace in the origin of human beings a fundamental division of thoughts, beliefs, values, and actions between groups of people. Of primary concern here is whether the acquisition of a world view is conceived of rigidly or flexibly. A secondary and related concern is whether these groups of people are perceived as racial, cultural, or as suggested by Kambon,[9] both. Both concerns involve the area of philosophical inquiry pertaining to categories. Categories, in philosophical terms, represent "ultimate or fundamental divisions or kinds."[10] Mudimbe makes the following observation about categories:

> Western interpreters as well as African analysts have been using categories and conceptual systems which depend on a Western epistemological order. Even in the most explicitly "Afrocentric" descriptions, models of analysis explicitly or implicitly, knowingly or unknowingly, refer to the same order [p. x].[11]

Thus for Mudimbe, the only difference between Eurocentric and most current Afrocentric models of categorization lies in their ideology, because both are still governed by a Western epistemology. In short, Eurocentric and Afrocentric categorizations may differ in the way they describe the nature of differences between the two, but both still rely on dualistic notions of world view. This point is well taken and will be elaborated on shortly.

The world views paradigm is a product of attempts to explain human origins. For illustrative purposes, I will reference Kobi Kambon.[12] In his textbook, *African/Black Psychology in the American Context: An African-Centered Approach*, he describes two competing models of human origins. He calls the first one the Divine Causation/Creation Model, which asserts that all humanity and all other life forms were created by a Spiritual

Creator Force. Kambon says that this model was prevalent among African intellectuals and was later adopted by some European intellectuals. He calls the second one the Evolution Model, which asserts that humans evolved over time from lower order, sub-human forms (i.e. apes) to the present *homo sapien sapiens*. Kambon says that this model denies the intervention of a spiritual force, and he explains that it is clear how this model of evolution grew out of a European world view. Kambon goes on to say that regardless of which model is used, it was generally thought "the different races derived from a common hominid ... ancestry who migrated over the globe and somehow underwent biogenetic mutation in the process in order to adapt to the distinct physical environments in which they found themselves."[13] Kambon calls this the "Common Origins Model." However, he also entertains the possibility of a more controversial model, the "Independent Origins Model," which states that the different races evolved in geographical isolation from each other. Although Kambon does not attempt to resolve this debate, (though the general tone of his academic writings strongly suggests that he believes the "Independent Origins Model"), he does make the following statement:

> It is clear that fundamental differences in historical reality, and obviously some biogenetic differences as well, do indeed exist between racial collectives of human beings, and these differences seem to have some degree of relationship to their functioning and behavior. Thus, whether Africans and Europeans have common origins or not, they do manifest distinct biogenetic and psychological makeups which are best explained by the concept of "cultural reality" or world view differences.[14]

This rigid categorization of world views is a staple in Afrocentric psychological discourse, and becomes an important point to critique. One potential criticism that can be leveled is that the language and tone used to describe the Afrocentric and Eurocentric world views contradicts Asante's Temple School of Afrocentricity's insistence on pluralism without hierarchy. Examine the following description of world views from Kambon:[15]

It does not take a genius to quickly figure out that the African world view is the more desirable of the two. Assuming that this world view schematic is accurate (and this author believes that it is), the question becomes how to use and interpret it. There are essentially two approaches taken in Afrocentric psychology. The first, and most prevalent in Afrocentric psychology, I refer to as the "Mutually Exclusive Approach." This approach takes the position that racial-cultural groups are biogenetically predisposed to their respective world views. This fatalistic approach asserts that racial groups throughout the world, regardless of their cultural traits,

	African	European
Cosmology	Interdependence, collectivism Human-Nature Oneness, Unity	Separateness/Alienation Independence, Human-Nature Conflict/Control Over Nature
Ontology	Spiritual Basis of Nature	Material Basis of Nature
Axiology	Emphasis on Person-to-Person, Human-to-Human Relations	Emphasis on Person-to-Object, Human-to-Object Relations
Epistemology	Emphasis on Affective-Cognitive Synthesis	Emphasis on Cognitive Over Affective Processes
Values and Customs	Complementarity-Understanding	Intervention-Oppression and Aggression
Psycho-Behavioral Modality	Humanism-Religious	European/White Supremacy (Racism/Anti-African)

political power, economic status, or religious beliefs, all manifest the same race-based world view. On this point Kambon makes the following statement:

> They (world views) are deeply rooted in the genetic history of race family groups, and are therefore indigenous to race families.[16]

Kambon cites several Afrocentric scholars including himself, Marimba Ani, Cheikh Anta Diop, Wade Nobles, and Bobby Wright to substantiate his point. Kambon asserts that to deviate from normal, natural relationships by identifying with a group that is not your own indigenous cultural group is an abnormal and unnatural circumstance. This assertion becomes unwieldy when one tries to determine what constitutes an indigenous cultural group, particularly for those individuals who identify with multiple cultural groups or who have a multi-cultured lineage. If an individual has a Black father and White mother, what is her indigenous cultural group? Does this individual not have a world view? Or is her world view half African and half European? How would a biogenetic determinist view (i.e. Mutually Exclusive Approach) go about determining the extent to which she is Afrocentric or Eurocentric in her world view? An equally problematic implication of the Mutually Exclusive Approach is that it would label a European who sees the African world view as more desirable as abnormal, unnatural, and culturally disordered. This view seems to contradict the humanistic thrust of the Afrocentric world view. Finally, in a twist of irony, many Afrocentric psychologists who adhere to the Mutually Exclusive Approach unwittingly use the same dichotomous logic that they are so critical of with Europeans. Kambon includes the following quote from Marimba Ani (1997):

> The mode or determining structure in the western (European) World view is that of power, control and destruction. *Realities are split into pairs of opposing parts* [author's emphasis] ... one ... becomes valued while (the other) is understood as lacking value. *One is "good" and the other is "bad."* [author's emphasis]. Other opposing pairs in the European world view are "knowledge/opinion," "objective/subjective," "science/religion," "mind/body," "male/female," "man/boy," "*white/black,*"[author's emphasis] ... and so forth, and the mode of thought is literal-concrete.[17]

The entire world views paradigm is replete with dualistic logic, yet for some reason it is not brought under the same critical scrutiny as the ill-fated European world view. On trying to understand traditional African systems of knowledge, Mudimbe makes the following observation:

> My own claim is that thus far the ways in which they have been evaluated and the means used to explain them relate to theories and methods whose constraints, rules, and systems of operation suppose a non–African epistemological locus.... To what extent can their perspectives modify the fact of a silent dependence on a Western episteme?[18]

Here we see that Mudimbe's critique can easily be applied to the world views paradigm, more so in its presentation than its accuracy (although its accuracy has yet to be proven with Afrocentric methods). By this I am suggesting that while the act of categorizing world views dualistically may provide a useful heuristic for understanding general cultural differences, the presentation of world views as organically opposite and conflictual poses many problems. This is not to say that differences don't exist between world views. I am simply suggesting that the differences may be exaggerated, particularly if race, rather than ethnicity/culture, is the theoretical frame of reference.

Although in print Afrocentric psychologists are careful not to explicitly attach any absolute values to either of the world views, it is quite apparent that all discussions of world view differences are inherently value-laden, with the obvious conclusion usually being that the Afrocentric world view is not only relatively superior for African Americans compared to the Eurocentric world view, but is also absolutely superior for humanity to the

Eurocentric world view. This latter view will be examined next, as it represents the second of the two approaches. In the final analysis, it seems that the acquisition of any world view must be much more environmental than Afrocentric psychologists have generally discussed in their academic writings.

The second and somewhat less popular approach in Afrocentric psychology I call the "Mutually Inclusive Approach." This approach is similar to the Mutually Exclusive Approach in that it identifies basically the same characteristics which make up the Afrocentric and Eurocentric world views. However, the primary proponent of this approach, Linda James Myers, has labeled the world views as optimal and suboptimal, respectively.[19] According to Myers, the optimal world view derives from the beliefs, values, and practices of ancient Africans. This optimal world view is anti-racism and anti-sexism. In fact, any "ism" that is hegemonic and oppressive in nature is antithetical to the optimal world view. The suboptimal world view is an unhealthy world view that is arrested in its development. It represents, among other things, all of the "isms" of the world. Myers believes that in many instances before one can adopt the optimal world view, one must participate in the suboptimal world view. In this sense, it is a necessary stage toward human actualization. Although she does not state it, Myers apparently avoids explicitly naming the world views "Afrocentric" and "Eurocentric" to allow for the possibility that individuals may consciously operate under a non-indigenous world view orientation. Here we see that Myers and Kambon are ideologically at odds with each other, because Myers does not pathologize the European who adopts the optimal Afrocentric world view. Instead, Myers would characterize any individual, regardless of ethnicity, who adopts a suboptimal world view as operating in a less than desirable psychological state.

Although Myers comes closer to Asante's "pluralism without hierarchy" than Kambon, both fail to achieve this goal. Perhaps it is wrong to assume that Afrocentric psychology seeks pluralism without hierarchy. If this is the case, then Afrocentric psychology deviates from a central tenet of Asante's Afrocentricity. Whatever the case may be, Afrocentric theorists in psychology need to address this very important issue.

Epistemology

Central to the Afrocentric psychology project are deconstructive challenges regarding the nature, types and origin of knowledge. Questions such as "What can we know?" and "How do we come to know it?" are extremely important to the Afrocentric psychologist. For example, Kambon has characterized the African way of knowing reality as emphasizing an affective-cognitive synthesis, while the European way of knowing reality emphasizes cognitive over affective processes. This epistemic statement serves as part of the foundation of Afrocentric theory-building. The challenge for Afrocentric psychologists, as noted by Banks,[20] is to develop Afrocentric methods that verify their ideas. Of importance here is the distinction between knowing and believing. Knowing implies verifiability, while believing does not. Instead, believing is dispositional and attitudinal — that is, it involves a predispositional cognitive schema which does not require the rigor of provability. It would be naive to suggest that knowing does not usually involve believing, because even the knower has certain beliefs about the issue in question. For example, I know that the death penalty differentially impacts African Americans because of statistics, but I also believe that it differentially impacts African Americans because the justice system is inherently corrupt and racist.

One can also believe something and yet not know it. I believe that O.J. Simpson was guilty of murder and yet I do not know this to be true. Furthermore, one can believe in something and yet know that the opposite is true. Jury nullification is a classic example of this, where the jurors (example predominantly African American) believe that the African American defendant should not be found guilty, even though they know that he is guilty of the crime for which he has been charged. Afrocentric psychologists must be careful that their ideological programmes result in the construction of knowledge rather than beliefs. While it is expected that their knowledge involves beliefs, it becomes an intellectually weaker proposition when beliefs are espoused without benefit of knowledge. Beliefs without knowledge are akin to the old riddle "If a tree falls in the woods and no one is there to witness it, does it make a sound?" It most certainly does, but how do we know without someone there to verify it? Hountondji wryly notes, "A fake science is not always, or necessarily, a false science."[21] He goes on to say that "It may contain useful information or reveal objective facts."[22] Similarly, many Afrocentric beliefs espoused by Afrocentric theoreticians may very well be true, but without methods that both test and protect the theories and ideological programme, the beliefs will never materialize into knowledge.

The assertion that world views are biogenetically transmitted bears the burden of providing sufficient evidence. Beyond rote citation of Diop's Two Cradle Theory and Bradley's Iceman Inheritance, the latter of which makes rather dubious and largely unsupported claims, what evidence do Afrocentric psychologist provide? To his credit, Kambon is the only

Afrocentric psychologist who has systematically conducted an empirical research program which attempts to provide evidence of world view differences. Given that Kambon has already stated his belief that world views are biogenetically transmitted, any differences that he finds would be unsurprisingly racialized. While Kambon is obviously not the only Afrocentric psychologist who has written about world view differences,[23,24] he is the only one who has attempted to conduct an empirical program of research which would lend the appearance of rigorous science. His results, because they are empirically based, take on an air of credibility, which lends more authority to his theorizing. It is for this reason that he must be thoroughly critiqued, in order that we can address any potential shortcomings of his research program.

Kambon's research, like that of many other psychologists, relies primarily on self-report and questionnaire data. As is widely known, and as acknowledged by Kambon himself, the validity of questionnaire data can be limited because of social desirability, the desire of the subjects to misrepresent their true attitudes and beliefs in order to meet some perception of approval. While Kambon downplays this phenomenon, he does not provide any evidence of how he controls for it. This is particularly important because of the strongly-worded nature of the questionnaires that he uses. Consider, for example, the following items from Kambon's African Self-Consciousness Scale: "Blacks should form loving relationships and marry only other Blacks"; "It is good for Black husbands and wives to help each other develop racial consciousness and cultural awareness in themselves and their children"; and "African culture is better for humanity than European culture." Higher scores on these items are indicative of higher African self-consciousness. The last item in particular is evidence that Asante's "pluralism without hierarchy" is not part of Kambon's Afrocentricity.

In Kambon's textbook referred to earlier, he provides research evidence for the existence of world view differences between Africans and Europeans. His research evidence consists of largely non-empirical and historical-cultural studies as well as one illustrative empirical study conducted by him.[25] The results of the study were difficult to understand (example they report that African females and males scored "significantly more Afrocentric" on five of the seven world view dimensions while European females and males scored "significantly more Eurocentric" on six of the seven world view dimensions). The only way that these results could occur would be to compare both groups, in which case the numbers would have to be equal (i.e. if one group is significantly higher on five dimensions than another group, then the other group would have to be significantly lower on five dimensions as well). Kambon then concludes that this study "indicates that world view differences do appear to be basic in the beliefs, attitudes and perceptions of contemporary Africans and Europeans in America...."[26] World view differences may exist, but this study, based on a sample of 181 college students, is not generalizeable beyond the very narrowly defined college population. (It should be noted that Kambon is certainly not the only research psychologist who overgeneralizes from limited data and inadequate methodology. I suspect that in my writings I have done so too. That seems to be the nature of much published correlational psychological research).

A more serious critique of Kambon's research was rendered by Stephen Howe.[27] Howe reviews a 1990 study by Bell, Bouie and Baldwin examining Afrocentric cultural consciousness in African American male-female relationships. Using direct quotes, Howe immediately lists the characteristics of the European American and African American world views, making sure he mentions that all of the citations come from "the little band of Afrocentric academics, primarily Asante and the article's co-author Joseph Baldwin."[28] Howe then mentions that there was no coherent account of the sample of 88 men and 89 women who were selected. This sample took the African Self-Consciousness Scale and tested the participants' attitudes on heterosexual relations. Sample statements that they responded to included "In mate selection and or evaluation, Black men and Black women should consider Black cultural beliefs and values (or cultural consciousness) as a main or primary criterion." Howe's point is that even though the statistical analysis indicated that Afrocentric cultural consciousness is positively related to attitudes that prioritize an Afrocentric value orientation in Black heterosexual relationships, the study is tautological in nature. In other words, no truth can be inferred nor knowledge derived from this study because its internal logic is essentially repetitive.

Paradoxically, it should be noted that for all the criticism of the European world view and Western approaches to science, Kambon and other African-centered psychologists essentially use the same methods of inquiry to examine African phenomena. These methods are steeped in the Western empiricist tradition, where research is conducted using the scientific method. This poses perhaps the greatest challenge for advances in Afrocentric psychology. As Banks so astutely noted about Afrocentric psychology, "it must be vigorous in the establishment of methodologies which insure the proliferation of theory through defense against refutation from outside the system."[29] What Banks is referring to is a sort of preemptive strike against critiques like Stephen Howe in the form of what I call "methodological inoculation." The methodological inoculation would consist of methods designed to be consistent with the internal logic of the ideological programme of research. Stephen Howe's critique, while thorough and somewhat ideological itself, would not have been nearly as effective if Afrocentric psychologists and other social scientists created a truly Afrocentric methodology that is distinctly different than Eurocentric methodology. As long as Afrocentric psychologists claim that there are distinct African and European world views, yet continue to use methods that clearly has roots in a Eurocentric world view, they will continue to be critiqued by Eurocentric scholarship, and ultimately discredited. Asante poses the question "How can the oppressed use the same theories as the oppressor?"[30] I am proposing that for Afrocentric psychology, a similar question needs to be asked — that is, "How can the oppressed use the same methods as the oppressor?" As Banks has noted, "the role of methodology is to protect theory from falsification."[31] Eurocentric methods which stem from logical positivist inquiry can never really advance the interests of the Afrocentric ideological programme.

The Ethical Question

When the proverbial smoke clears, the Afrocentric psychology project must be clear about its purpose. Its purpose should not contradict the larger Afrocentric intellectual movement, which, Asante reminds us, is transcendent in its discourse and committed to a more humanistic vision of the world.[32] Thus, there is a profoundly ethical component to Asante's Afrocentricity. When contradictions to this vision exist vis-à-vis morally dubious declarations of superiority and inferiority, or goodness and evilness, Afrocentric scholars are presented with an ethical question: To what extent should Afrocentric scholarship reflect a responsibility to articulate moral values which promote human transformation? Furthermore, should a type of moral particularism be practiced which rejects universal principles of morality and effectively insulates itself from intrinsic and extrinsic critique?[33]

Consosant with Asante's discourse on Afrocentricity, I believe that Afrocentric scholarship should articulate moral values which promote human transformation. However, I do not agree that the belief in moral particularism advances the Afrocentric project. Moral particularism could be practiced in such a way that racism and notions of White supremacy are viewed as morally evil when practiced by Europeans, but similar beliefs among Africans are not critiqued with the same moral compass. Let me say that while I do not believe that Africans or so-called Black people can be racists, I do believe that they can harbor racialized ideas which are essentially reactions to the oppression of White racism and supremacy. A closer examination of certain beliefs from "race men" in both African and European psychological scholarship reveals some uncomfortable similarities.

J. Philippe Rushton

J. Phillipe Rushton is a European professor of psychology at the University of Western Ontario. His research has focused on testing for racial differences in behavior. His thesis is essentially that racial differences in behavior do exist which can only be adequately explained from an evolutionary perspective.[34] On ethnocentrism, Rushton has this to say:

> Despite enormous variance within populations, it can be expected that two individuals within an ethnic group will, on average, be more similar to each other genetically than two individuals from different ethnic groups. According to genetic similarity theory, people can be expected to favor their own group over others.[35]

Here Rushton is arguing for a biological basis for ethnocentrism. This belief alone is enough to categorically dismiss Rushton as unscientific and racist, because most population geneticists have shown that there is more genetic variability within groups than exists between groups.[36] Although in the passage cited above, Rushton refers to ethnic groups, when in fact he is really talking about so-called racial groups. He makes a very elementary mistake by apparently using ethnicity and race interchangeably. One does not have to look very far to produce examples which challenge his assertion. For example, Latinos consist of Puerto Ricans, Mexicans, Cubans, Panamanians, Dominicans, and many other Spanish speaking groups. Puerto Ricans, who are usually of African-descent, would be expected to be genetically more similar to Cubans of European descent rather than African Americans. While I am not suggesting that this could not be the case, I am saying that Rushton has not provided evidence that would disprove this example.

In Rushton's chapter entitled "Genes Plus Environment," he reviews an adoption study by Scarr and Weinberg where 7-year old black, interracial, and white children were adopted by white families.[37] The purpose of the study was to determine the extent to which genetic vs. environmental factors were responsible for the poor cognitive performance of black children. While Scarr and Weinberg attribute the poorer performance to the dominant role of the social environment, Rushton offers another explanation:

> A more straightforward interpretation of the results consistent with the other data presented in this book, is that blacks have lower mental ability than whites because of their African ancestry.[38]

The other data presented in Rushton's book includes ranking of racial groups (i.e. Blacks, Whites, and Orientals) on criteria such as brain size, aggressiveness, rule-following, strength of sex drive, and size of genitalia. Rushton's ranking shows that Blacks have the smallest brain size, are least likely to follow rules, are the most aggressive, have the strongest sex drive, and have the largest genitalia. Rushton also presents data showing that Black babies have a shorter gestation period than white babies, and physically mature at a greater rate. This supposedly explains Blacks precocity in sports throughout life. Rushton does not even entertain more complex social-psychological explanations for Black dominance in many sports. On challenges to the usefulness of the race construct, Rushton says the following:

> The view that race is only a social construct is contradicted by biological evidence. Along with blood protein and DNA data..., forensic scientists are able to classify skulls by race.... Constructs in science are only useful if they have explanatory power. The three macro racial categories show much predictive and construct validity. As has been shown, racial categories better organize disparate data than is possible using only ethnicity, religion, or sociopolitical grouping.[39]

Rushton concludes by acknowledging that Africa is the cradle of humankind. However, racial differentiation (either by Multiregional or Single Origin theories)[40] has resulted in Black people being more prone to commit crime, more sexually active and therefore more likely to contract AIDS, and having a diminished cognitive capacity compared to Whites and Asians. While this brief review is not intended to be a critique of Rushton per se, it is presented to give the reader a sense of the general tone and, I believe, the paucity of moral consciousness in Rushton and his research.

Bobby Wright

Bobby Wright was an African psychologist and director of the Garfield Park Comprehensive Community Mental Health Center in Chicago. Although he died in 1982, his influence as a teacher, college educator, and researcher on some of the leading Afrocentric psychologists and other social scientists still resonates very powerfully today. He served as a mentor to Kobi Kambon, who dedicated his most recent textbook to him. Bobby's commitment to and love for African people is without question. However, because his ideas and overall spirit are so integrally part of Afrocentric psychology, it is necessary that we examine them more closely. In his book, *The Psychopathic Racial Personality and Other Essays*, Wright presents a very simple yet incendiary thesis:

> In their relationship with the Black race, Europeans (Whites) are psychopaths and their behavior reflects an underlying biologically transmitted proclivity with roots deep in their evolutionary history. The psychopath is an individual who is constantly in conflict with other persons or groups. He is unable to experience guilt, and is completely selfish and callous and has a total disregard for the rights of others. This premise is supported by overwhelming scientific evidence.[41]

The scientific evidence that Wright cites includes the writings of Frances Cress Welsing, whose theory of color confrontation and racism contains some highly speculative scientific musings.

Wright, like Rushton, relies heavily on the evolutionary history of racial groups to make some very strong statements about the personality of racial groups—in this case, Whites. Although both are proponents of biological determinism, each arrives at a different conclusion as to the nature of the groups based upon their own ideology. What is most striking and different about Wright in comparison to Rushton is his aggressively polemical style. Indeed, this style is characteristic of many Afrocentric psychologists and other scholars, and is consistent with Asante's description of Afrocentric rhetoric as being "combative and antagonistic."[42] However, the tone often times betrays any commitment to a more humanistic vision of the world, and therefore seems to be incompatible with the ethical nature of Asante's Afrocentricity. Wright goes on to say the following:

> The psychopath is usually sexually inadequate with a very limited capacity to form close interpersonal relationships. The European's sexual inadequacy psychologically explains why there is a constant projection toward Blacks as being super sexual beings and as having not sexual inhibitions.[43]

A preoccupation with racial sexual functioning is a common theme for both Wright and Rushton. Again, both draw entirely different conclusions based upon their ideology. Wright pathologizes Europeans as sexually inadequate, and uses the sexual atrocities many Europeans committed against Africans during their enslavement as scientific evidence.

Kobi Kambon

Following in the tradition of these "race men," Kambon indicates that several questions about Europeans have been asked in the Pan-African Nationalists community (of which many of the Afrocentric psychologists would identity with). These questions included.... What is the nature of the Europan/Caucasian/Eurasian?"; "Are Caucasians members of the same species as Africans or the Black race?"; and "Are they human beings or some other life form?"[44] While Kambon admits that these sort of questions are more emotion-driven than a substantive academic exercise, he does not rule out the possibility that there may be some evidence that demonstrates that the nature of Europeans is dramatically different than Africans and other members of the human race. In the most racialized and perhaps most provocative statement in his book, Kambon shares these thoughts:

> No strong evidence has been generated to date which denies the Caucasian's claim to humanity; however, there does appear to be a preponderance of evidence suggesting that the Caucasian is clearly atypical relative to other human groups and could possibly represent an aberration of the so-called human strain for beings (Ani, 1994). The trunk and skeletal traits, as well as hair type, body hair, facial characteristics and lack of pigmentation generally, clearly distinguish them from Africans. One can also clearly observe the psychology of aggressiveness, xenophobia, territoriality, lack of social harmony and social development, selfishness, deficient morality, and basal sexuality, which all contrast with that of the African human form. Thus, there is an array of evidence which some might argue appears to be strongly in favor of the conclusion of an unusual biophysiology, as well as a defective-deficient psycho-genetic condition in the Caucasian strain of the human community. These are unquestionably very important issues which must be investigated further by the African-centered sciences. [45]

Kambon's connection of phenotype to psychological traits and behaviors occurs less frequently in Afrocentric psychology than it does in race psychology. Nevertheless, in this case, his words almost mirror that of Rushton, who believes that the biogenetic make-up of Africans predisposes them to criminality, having an unstable family unit, and being oversexed to the point of being irresponsible and perpetuating the AIDS epidemic. A moral particularist stance would defend Wright and Kambon by rationalizing that they are both just reacting to the hundreds of years of oppression that Africans have experienced in their interactions with Europeans. However, as I have argued elsewhere, while their positions are understandable, they are still inexcusable, because they lack the very principled and ethical reasoning that they have noted lacks in much of White people's attitudes and behavior toward Black people.[46] And ultimately, they do not advance the discipline of African psychology.

Conclusion

In this chapter I have attempted to examine the growing tension between gnosis and method in Afrocentric psychology. By gnosis, of course, I am referring loosely to knowledge and knowledge construction. The construction of knowledge lies primarily in the ability to develop appropriate methods which will unearth irrefutable evidence. Afrocentric psychology has, for the most part, failed to do this. In many cases, it has relied on the same methods (example comparative studies of Africans and Europeans) that it has been so critical of in the past. Thus, any theories derived from the Afrocentric research programme remain vulnerable to harsh critique.

I also addressed the moral question of whether Afrocentric scholarship should promote human transformation. If Afrocentric psychology is going to move to the next level of critical scholarship, then it cannot, in rhetoric or substance, mimic the discourse of European race psychologists. In matters of the conscience, Africans have historically always been on the side of truth, justice, and righteousness, the cardinal principles of MAAT. That is why we have the moral authority to critique European culture and condemn racism and White supremacy. How the discipline of African psychology deals with the construct of race will be predictive of its future success or failure. If race is treated as a social and psychological construct that is related to but distinct from ethnicity, then the ability of African psychology to offer correctives on ill-advised, poorly conceptualized research on African descended people is greatly enhanced. However, if race is treated as a biological fact, is continually confounded with ethnicity and culture, and continues to generate an inordinate amount of intellectual energy, then the ability of African psychology to "liberate the African mind" will be a dream deferred, an opportunity wasted, and a historical mandate unfulfilled.

Notes

1. Maulana Karenga, *Introduction to Black Studies* (Inglewood: Kawaida 1996).

2. Kobi Kambon, *African/Black Psychology in the American Context: An African-Centered Approach* (Tallahassee: Nubian Nation 1998).

3. Molefi Kete Asante, *Afrocentricity* (Trenton: Africa World Press 1988); "Afrocentricity and culture." In M. K. Asante & K. W. Asante (Eds.) *African Culture: The Rhythms of Unity* (Trenton: African World Press 1990a).

4. Molefi Kete Asante, *Kemet, Afrocentricity and Knowledge* (Trenton: African World Press 1990b).

5. Sandra Van Dyk, "Toward an Afrocentric perspective: The significance of Afrocentricity." In D. Ziegler (ed.), *Molefi Kete Asante and Afrocentricity: In Praise and Criticism* (Nashville: James C. Winston 1995). Dyk poses this question of whether Afrocentricity is a racial or cultural theory at the beginning of her essay, yet never answers the question.

An interesting note about this edited book is that the title is somewhat deceptive. In point of fact, there was mostly praise and very little criticism of Asante's ideas.

6. Molefi Kete Asante, "Afrocentricity and culture." In M. K. Asante & K. W. Asante (eds.) *African Culture: The Rhythms of Unity*, p. 5.

7. *Ibid.*

8. Curtis Banks, "Theory and Method in the Growth of African American Psychology." In R. Jones (ed.), *Advances in African American Psychology*. (Hampton: Cobb & Henry Publishers 1999), pp. 3–8.

9. Kobi Kambon, *African/Black Psychology in the American Context: An African-Centered Approach* (Tallahassee: Nubian Nation 1998).

10. A. R. Lacy, *A Dictionary of Philosophy*, pp. 38 (New York: Routledge 1996).

Lacy states that the notion of categories first appeared in the work of Aristotle. He then discusses the contribution that Immanuel Kant made in understanding categories, noting that the only way we can make sense of the world is to impose some structure that originates from the mind. Interestingly, this idea is prevalent in cognitive and social psychology, the latter of which applies the ideas of categories to the act of stereotyping.

11. V.Y. Mudimbe, *The Invention of Africa: Gnosis, Philosophy, and the Order of Knowledge*, p. x (Bloomington and Indianapolis: Indiana University Press 1988).

12. Kobi Kambon, *African/Black Psychology in the American Context: An African-Centered Approach* (Tallahassee: Nubian Nation 1998).

13. *Ibid.*

14. *Ibid.*, p. 117.

15. *Ibid.* It should be noted that the world views schematic Kambon provides is informed by the contributions of the Afrocentric psychologist Wade Nobles. In fact, the psycho-behavioral modality description comes straight from Nobles.

16. *Ibid.*, p. 123.

17. Marimba Ani, *Let the Circle Be Unbroken: African Spirituality in the Diaspora*, pp. 5–6 (New York: Nkonimfo 1997). Ani goes on to make a powerful critique about the limitations of Western science. In her critique, she makes the following statement: "Spirit is, of course, not a rationalistic concept. It cannot be quantified, measured, explained by or reduced to neat, rational, conceptual categories as Western thought demands."

18. V.Y. MUDIMBE, *The Invention of Africa: Gnosis, Philosophy, and the Order of Knowledge*, p. x (Bloomington and Indianapolis: Indiana University Press 1988).

19. Linda James Myers, *Understanding an Afrocentric World View: Introduction*

to an Optimal Psychology (Dubuque, IA: Kendall/Hunt 1988). It is very interesting to note that although Myers' work is considered must reading in Afrocentric psychology reading circles, Kambon only mentions her twice in his 564-page book, and this was in the context of her service as past president of the Association of Black Psychologists. The fact that none of her work in world views was referenced confirms the ideological nature of his scholarship, and suggests that he philosophically disagrees with her, although they are both African-centered.

20. Curtis Banks, "Theory and Method in the Growth of African American Psychology." In R. Jones (ed.), *Advances in African American Psychology* (Hampton, VA: Cobb & Henry Publishers 1999), pp. 3–8.

21. Paulin Hountondji, "Scientific Dependence in Africa Today." *Research in African Literatures, 21* (1990b). 3: pp. 5–15.

22. ____, *African Philosophy: Myth or Reality*, p. xix, (Bloomington and Indianapolis: Indiana University Press 1996).

23. Na'im Akbar, "Afrocentric social science for human liberation." *The Journal of Black Studies,* 14(2), (1984a).

24. Wade Nobles, "African Philosophy: Foundations for Black Psychology." In R. L. Jones (ed.), *Black Psychology*, 2nd ed. (New York: Harper & Row Publishers 1980a).

25. Joseph Baldwin and Reginald Hopkins. "African-American and European-American cultural differences as assessed by the world views paradigm: An empirical analysis." *The Western Journal of Black Studies,* 14(1), (1990), pp. 38–52.

26. *Ibid.*, p. 137

27. Stephen Howe, *Afrocentrism: Mythical Pasts and Imagined Homes* (London and New York: Verso Press 1998). Howe teeters back and forth between a dispassionate, objective critique and a predictable Eurocentric diatribe. In the introduction he states, "I do not seek to imply that all, or even most, Afrocentric writers are deliberate intellectual frauds—though I think some certainly are." He astutely notes that many anti–Afrocentric polemicists (example Dinesh D'Souza) appear to not have read much of the Afrocentrists' works. He correctly points out the excesses in some of the truth-value claims made by Afrocentrists (example Leonard Jefferies' belief in the innate superiority of black 'Sun People' and biological inferiority of White people because of the Ice Age). However, his cynicism and true lack of objectivity is apparent in statements such as "The main Afrocentrists have university posts, but their work has little to do with 'meticulous research." He disregards the serious intellectual contributions of Afrocentric scholars such as Wade Nobles, who operates outside the "mainstream/Eurostream" academy, and minimizes the serious intellectual contributions of Jacob Carruthers and Asa Hilliard, the latter whom he categorizes as being a part of "Wild Afrocentricity." This polemical act is intellectually irresponsible, because he does not critically review the academic writings of Dr. Hilliard.

28. *Ibid.*, p. 245

29. Curtis Banks, "Theory and Method in the Growth of African American Psychology." In R. Jones (ed.), *Advances in African American Psychology* (Hampton, VA: Cobb and Henry Publishers, 1999), p. 8.

30. Molefi Kete Asante, *The Afrocentric Idea* (Philadelphia: Temple University Press 1998).

31. Curtis Banks, Theory and Method in the Growth of African American Psychology. In R. Jones (ed.), *Advances in African American Psychology* (Hampton, VA: Cobb and Henry Publishers, 1999), p. 5.

32. Molefi Kete Asante, *The Afrocentric Idea* (Philadelphia: Temple University Press 1998).

33. A. R. Lacy, *A Dictionary of Philosophy*, pp. 98 (New York: Routledge, 1996).

Lacy defines moral particularism as situational ethics, where each moral situation is considered independently and in isolation from other moral situations, so that no universal moral principles can be generalized.

34. J. Philippe Rushton, *Race, Evolution, and Behavior: A Life History Perspective* (New Brunswick: Transaction Publishers 1997).

35. *Ibid.*

36. Margaret Wetherell and Jonathan Potter, *Mapping the Language of Racism: Discourse and the Legitimation of Exploitation* (New York: Columbia University Press 1992).

Wetherell and Potter, as many other social scientists before and after them, discuss the falsity of the concept of race. They cite population geneticists as arguing that there is more within group genetic variation than between groups. They characterize arguments regarding race as ideological when they misinterpret the natural with the social, and mistake phenotypical characteristics as the underlying cause of social relations. They argue that central to racist discourse is the notion that there are natural divisions between people, and that these groups of people can be assigned certain traits. Racist discourse also contains theories about the origins of group differences. At this point some may argue that some Afrocentric scholars discourse meets the aforementioned criteria to be considered racist. I have a fundamental problem with this assertion for the simple reason that I do not believe that African people (or any other people of color) should own a term that is so rooted in the history of White supremacy and European aggression against African people. While I believe that all racialized discourse is ultimately morally problematic, African people do not have the political power to systematically deprive Europeans of their so-called inalienable rights. This, in my mind, is the defining feature of racism.

37. S. Scarr and R. Weinberg, "IQ test performance of black children adopted by white families." *American Psychologist, 31* (1976).

38. J. Philippe Rushton, *Race, Evolution, and Behavior: A Life History Perspective* (New Brunswick: Transaction Publishers 1997), p. 190.

39. *Ibid.*, pp. 235–236.

40. The Multiregional and Single Origin theories are equivalent to Kambon's Independent Origins and Common Origins theories, respectively. In print, both Rushton and Kambon subscribe to the Single/Common Origins theories, though one could challenge the extent to which both are communicating their true beliefs.

41. Bobby Wright, *The Psychopathic Racial Personality and Other Essays* (Chicago: Third World Press 1984), p. 2.

42. Molefi Kete Asante, *The Afrocentric Idea* (Philadelphia: Temple University Press, 1998), p. 186.

43. Bobby Wright, *The Psychopathic Racial Personality and Other Essays* (Chicago: Third World Press 1984), p.

44. Kobi Kambon, *African/Black Psychology in the American Context: An African-Centered Approach* (Tallahassee: Nubian Nation 1998), p. 170.

45. *Ibid.*

46. Kevin Cokley, "To Be or Not to Be Black: Problematics of a Racial

Identity," in *Of the Quest for Community and Identity: An Africana Philosophical Anthology* (in press). (Rowman & Littlefield). I argue that preoccupations with race and a Black racial identity lead to essentialist notions of Blackness which ultimately hurt the goal of Black unity. I propose that identity should be reframed in ethnic, rather than racial, terms.

The Black Male Narrative: An Afrocentric Assessment
James L. Conyers, Jr.

Introduction

The African American male narrative is a parable that has unfurled in a number of ways. Paramount has been the topologies placing categories—regarding patterns of espies and perspectives. Transient has been the consistent manner to locate a sense of agency, to reclaim the meaning and purpose of gender and social responsibility of Black men in America. Repeatedly confronted with racism–racialism, labeling, and physical endangerment—on a day to day basis, Black men endeavor to maintain sanity through a presage of spiritual austerity. Phrased this way, in the process of addressing dysfunctionalism on a per diem basis, the barometer to measure abstinence of substance abuse is to be taken each day at a time. In general and in hypothesis, the African American male narrative has commonalities which reach across social class lines. A good example which explores this phenomena are the documentaries by Charles Dutton (*The Corner*), and Bernie Casey (*The Dinner*), and the gathering of the Million Man March[1] in October of 1995. In the early 1900s, Booker T. Washington's narrative *Up from Slavery* and W.E.B. Du Bois' *Souls of Black Folk* provided an example of the intellectual historical genre of knowledge, with a focus on the Black male narrative.

It appears to some extent an oxymoron to address the idea of a Black male narrative. Consequently, because of the historical pattern of involuntary migration and colonialism, Black men, like Black women, have been referred to as chattel property and non-human beings. Therefore, to review the concept of a Black Male narrative is to review the voice, axiom, and prism of spirit from a subordinated posture of dexterity. Likewise, not to place hierarchy or endorse segregation from the concept of Africana Womanism, the scientific objective is to examine patterns and commonalities of the suffrage of Africana people; in this case, emphasis is placed on the Black Male narrative. The primary variables which link these commonalities are racism, prejudice, and discrimination. Even more important, the term "Black Male Narrative" can be described as the ideas, folklore, common sense, mother wit, spirituality, secular processes, intuition, lens, prism and perseverance to explain and appraise the overall condition of Africana life across gender lines. Using concepts from phenomenology, this can be referred to as "truth of correctness." Truth of correctness" can be defined as a "Statement being made or a proposition being held. We then go on to verify whether the claim is true. We carry out whatever kind of experiencing is needed as a confirmation or a disconfirmation of the statement."[2]

Moreover, the focus of this essay examines the concept of the African American male narrative in the organizational formation of a bibliographical essay. Secondary sources have been reviewed and analyzed to address heritage, reflection, and tradition. Hence, the sources probed are the following: a lengthy critical analysis of Carter G. Woodson's *Mis-Education of the Negro*; an annotated summary of Barbara Adams' oral history biography entitled *John Henrik Clarke: The Early Years*; S. Jay Walker's article, "Nat Turner and John Brown–Du Bois Uses of History;" Charles P. Henry's *Culture and African American Politics*; and a brief biographical sketch of Malcolm X. Table 1.0 provides the name, title, and copyright year of the selected secondary sources reviewed in this bibliographical essay.

TABLE 1.0[3]
Selected Secondary Sources

Name	Title	Copyright Year
Carter G. Woodson	*Mis-Education of the Negro*	1933
S. Jay Walker	"Nat Turner and John Brown: Du Bois Uses of History."	1975
Charles P. Henry	*Culture and African American Politics*	1990
Barbara Adams	*John Henrik Clarke: The Early Years*	1995
James L. Conyers, Jr.	"Malcolm X: A Brief Biographical Sketch"	1999

Overall, this essay has drawn upon eclectic sources, which address the concept of the Black male narrative — postulating a framework to study conscientious subservience from an alternative perspective and lens. Subsequently, it draws attention to an Afrocentric perspective. In summary, the conclusion of this essay will focus on soliciting queries to examine what is referred to as the African American narrative. I begin this essay with an adage from the *Akan* which reads: "When you don't know when you have been spit on, it does not matter too much what else you think you know.[4] From this proverb, the central message is that *principal*, or *general principal*, is the operative point in which decisions and relations transact. Once this informal mode of communication is violated, further dialog and engagement could be articulated as a nexus which ascends to testimonials of emptiness (i.e., "Whatteverrr" said in a long-winded way).

Carter G. Woodson: The Mis-Education of the Negro

Carter G. Woodson is regarded as one of the pioneers in the development of African American history and Black Studies. His contributions to these bodies of knowledge within and outside the academy are certainly important. Blassingame and Berry describe the importance of Woodson's contributions to the field of African American history:

> Carter G. Woodson's organization of the Association for the Study of Negro Life and History in 1915 was one of the most important forces in creating an interest in African history in the United States. In his life time many African nationalists corresponded with Woodson.[5]

Woodson's research on African America nearly sixty years ago, is, without much difficulty, applicable to the spiritual, physical, and mental condition of black people in contemporary times. Furthermore, his examination of the African American community centers around issues and schema of adversity and social and economic empowerment, which appears to be the seat of the problem that confronts Blacks.

Accordingly, probing the residual affects of colonialism and the concept of assimilation provides a contextual analysis for investigating self-loathing, xenocentricism, and nihilism. In fact, from this mantra of discovery, the idea of the cultural continua ... is a way for Africans in the diaspora to appreciate why people need to have culture grounded in their own reflection of reality as a ontological praxis. Woodson's cogency to inquire into truth, knowledge and reality are the criteria used to examine the nature of western education not being effective in regard to African Americans. Furthermore, as Joseph T. Durham cites ... there were a reported 216 African American preparatory boarding schools in 1916.[6] He writes about this in length, saying

> These schools, along with other African American academies, are an important reminder of where the education of blacks has been. Frequently underfunded by their denominations, they still survived often by the sheer dogged determination of the local pastor who started the school and by the noble efforts of the Alpha men who served a principal. These schools, especially the boarding schools sought to take students from barren home environment and instilled virtues of industry, sobriety, self control and godliness in their charges. The alumni produced are a testimony to the excellence these schools fostered. The boarding schools offered a select environment that could be replicated today. Many of today's youth, encapsulated in the pathology of the urban ghetto, could be rescued if they were placed in a different milieu. The boarding schools of yesteryear provided, around the clock, an atmosphere, which fostered excellence and responsibility. Modern educators might well consider the duplication of the wholesome atmosphere that was fostered by the academies of another era.[7]

What's more, Woodson's book is a testament that challenges scholars to transform and recenter the conventional wisdom of higher education. He points out that through this transition of philosophy, Blacks would begin to seek the auxiliary analysis and views to posture cultural autonomy. Equally important, this is relevant in revising and reinterpreting history, with emphasis on African Americans, Americans, and world history.

Again, this survey of Woodson's work spotlights the meaning and function of psychoanalysis in Black Americana phenomena from an interdisciplinary perspective. Detractors might say that identifying the relativity of Woodson's scholarship in contemporary times is ahistorical. On the other hand, his rationale can be employed today, as a way to discuss the conflicts and dilemmas of African Americans in all facets of various professions—so much so that Pan Africanists, Cultural Nationalists, and Afrocentric scholars have directed their attention to this book in making critical and suggestive arguments for an African centered pedagogy.

In addition, Woodson focuses on the restraints of institutional and individual racism within educational, political, social, and economic institutions. Quite interestingly, Jawanza Kunjufu acknowledges that the conspirators who certify and aid in institutional racism are parents, educators, and white liberals who deny the existence of racism and through their muteness allow institutional racism to survive.[8] In many ways we relate *The Mis-Education of the Negro* to the present day plight of African Americans not so much because of the lack of progress gained by African

Americans, but possibly because of the structural organization format of the enforcement of racialism.

From an etymological analysis, the title of the book infers that Woodson had reservations about the education of African Americans in Black and White institutions of higher education. He referred to this problem as "missing the mark" as a result of the focus on classical education rather than vocational educational. Na'im Akbar explains the distinction between these two functions:

> Education is a process by which you are more actively capable of manifesting what you are. When you increasingly manifest what somebody else wants you to be — which may or may not be critical to your survival as a life form — you are actually trained. So we are in a world where we have all been severely miseducated. We are in a world where we have all been well trained but not very well educated.[9]

Precursor of Afrocentric School of Thought

In contemporary times, Pan Africanists, Cultural Nationalists, and Afrocentric scholars acknowledge Woodson's book as a classical study of critical theory. Critical Theory refers to an interchange rather than counter point of view from the Eurocentric hegemonic perspective. In a systematic way, he examined the function of the Eurocentric hegemonic perspective of subordination in two ways: (1) the all-weather racist thought and action and (2) the institutionalization of racism articulated through public policy. Woodson makes note of this, indicating how African Americans assimilate into western culture and values. In an historical perspective, Blacks are trained to study African phenomena from the perimeter of world history. Adding to this commentary, Yosef ben-Jochannan explicates the atomization of western disciplines:

> We have plainly seen that Western Scholars have failed to understand that departmentalization, or in fact fragmentation, of educational discipline is European; not African. For this reason, and many others of course, they cannot see or admit Philosophy in the religion, mathematics, science, law, engineering, etc. of Africa that produced the "Diagram of the Law of Opposites" I now place before you for your examination of the philosophical complexities it contains.[10]

An Akan proverb reads, "Real tragedy is never resolved. It goes hopelessly forever!"[11] To maintain an historical view, whenever studying a body of information, it is important to review the diachronic background of that data to surmise contextual clarity. In the case of Woodson's *Mis-Education of the Negro*, he studies the social ecology of race relations in the United States during the 1920s and 1930s, remaining postured in an era of Jim Crow laws. Phrased another way, races were separated on the basis of physical differences. Woodson's major thesis in this book addresses two queries: (1) Have institutions of higher education failed African Americans to develop schools, businesses, and social institutions? (2) Why are African Americans not allowed to define what is important in the academic curriculum and social environment at predominantly black colleges?

Despite the fact that this book was written in a period of social, political, and economic abandonment for African Americans, the residual's and crevices are relevant. Educational transcendence was the method which enabled Woodson to establish a posture of reflexivity concerning the condition of Black life and culture and the consequences of assimilation. On the other hand, Black neo-conservative scholars and professionals are confronted with going through a transitional crisis of marginality in lieu of institutional racism that effects them individually and collectively. Likewise, there were (are) Blacks who have exhibited a xenocentric perspective (i.e. Black snitches). Thus, they are not able to assist "as a group" or act in the capacity of "leadership" to aid and assist the masses of African Americans. Jacob Carruthers cites from Woodson to elaborate on this topic by saying: "The so-called modern education with all its defects, however, does others so much more good than it does the Negro, because it has been worked out in conformity to the needs of those who have enslaved and oppressed weaker peoples."[12] Paradoxically, many would consider Woodson's critique of American education as radical. His reservations about the miseducation of African Americans challenges a Eurocentric hegemonic perspective's acquisition of authority and power to subordinate African Americans. Intrigued by Woodson's query, he distinguishes a scientific approach of research to study the creation and consequences of subordination.[13] Concurring, with Woodson's antithesis, he acknowledged limitations to critically appraise the setting and to write about the acculturation of Black Education due to his experience in higher education.

> Woodson points out the drawbacks which confront African Americans being trained in educational institutions. First, he makes reference to the ethos of Africans being miseducated to despise themselves. Consequently, this method and theory of learning if effective could have an trickle down effect to mentally stabilize a selected group of formalized educated Blacks. Second, once African American scholars or professionals have obtained degrees of higher education, they are confronted with the glass ceiling of

institutional racism. These two points recursively, are fundamental grounds why African Americans in essence need to re-define their prism of reality, predicated on their historical and cultural experiences—while in following logically their conjuncted energy to surmount purposive impediments. Moreover, Woodson has presented primal information and focuses on the organized strategy, for the status quo to historically abort African Americans to dislocate themselves from continental Africana phenomena. Evidently, Woodson has laid before us query for Africana people to accept the challenge of becoming their own educators.

Commentary

In conclusion, this book is a requisite for scholars to develop an understanding, appreciation, and critical study of the Black male educational narrative. At present, social scientists are probing unexplored grounds to advance scholarship of discovery. Withal, there is the use of the word. Negro, in both the present and latter uses, which Woodson uses to imply a fundamental query concerning the plight of African Americans. From a common sense perspective, can this query ever be answered? This investigation of ideology, with reference to the topology of race men and the black elite, is integral for engagement. As a side note, the objectives for this probe of topologies are: (1) describing the role these constituencies perform in the shaping of African America; and (2) examining how Black social movements and leadership are studied and described from a Eurocentric hegemonic frontier perspective. Furthermore, these values and norms are not congruent to the black experience and lumps Africana ethnic groups into the American melting pot of assimilation.

Woodson acknowledged these problems and wrote extensively about these issues and the schemas of race, gender, and class. In summary, the past is relative to the present, with relevance to patterns and postures of the interactions of different racial and ethnic groups. Thus, the critical issue and question at hand is African Americans being physically and culturally disconnected with the continent of Africa. In this sense, Woodson's position is considering Africana people from their own shared authority of phenomena.

John Henrik Clarke: The Early Years

Barbara Adams has produced an oral history biography examining the life, folklore, ideas, and philosophies of the late Dr. John Henrik Clarke. The organizational structure of this study is two-fold: oral histories conducted with the subject, who is now deceased, and selected lectures by Clarke including, "The History of African Americans in Harlem," and "Kwanzaa Celebration on the Nature and Harmony of Africans." Clarke could have rightfully been considered one of the senior historians in the United States prior to his death in the summer of 1998. However, Clarke was more than a historian; he was a headmaster of world civilization, philosophy, literature, linguistics, politics, sociology, psychology, business, and so on. Phrased another way, Clarke was the living testimony of a "scholar activist."[14]

Adams raised questions concerning why there had there not been a biography written on Clarke, and who would Clarke give permission to organize and write this epic of the early years of his life. Equally important, my analysis of his commentary centers on two points: the necessity for black biographies to be written by African Americans from an Afrocentric perspective; and the essential function of recognizing and paying homage to our elders, who have consistently been in the struggle for liberation and to advance the cause for the masses of African Americans.

Nat Turner and John Brown: Du Bois' Uses of History

The use of history by Du Bois, as discussed by Jay Walker in this article, is interesting on a number of points. I make this contention based on the fact this article focuses primarily on the heroics and shortcomings of John Brown as written in a biography by W.E.B. Du Bois. Jay Walker, the author of this article, reveals that Du Bois had presented two manuscripts for publication: one about Nat Turner, and the other about John Brown for the American Crisis Biography series. The biography on John Brown was accepted for publication. Although Du Bois' rhetoric may seem somewhat radical, he prepares the biographical study of Brown within the tradition of a trained historian. This is exhibited by Du Bois' references to African American folk culture.[15]

As Du Bois writes about Brown, he points out the subject's sensitivity to and advocacy for the abolishment of enslavement. Du Bois' use of primary data and sources provides him the flexibility of interpretative analysis of Brown's narrative. Moreover, the biography of John Brown written by Du Bois is an epic and advancement to discovery scholarship on and about the subject.

Relevantly, Du Bois addresses the problems of interpretative analysis and historians' quest to be objective. Jay Walker makes the following statement: "That is why we, once again , must seize our own history, why we must write better biographies on Nat Turner and make better studies on plantation economy and do better research on the genetic properties of intelligence. Otherwise all propaganda will continue to exist on one side, while we stand stripped and silent."[16] Unfortunately, this is a web of transformation in which Du Bois consistently found himself entangled. Finally, I propose that the task for Africanologists is to advance the position of African people throughout the diaspora. In doing this there will be a need to focus writings and publications on Africans in contemporary periods, African elders, African ancestors and European institutions that have taken an anti–African position in their efforts to exploit African people.

Culture and African American Politics

Charles Henry examines the cultural, social and political development of African Americans, especially the diversity of social and political thought among Blacks. Postured from a critical frame of reference, he addresses issues concerning the problem of interpreting leadership topologies. For example, Henry discloses that a "bottom to the top approach" would exhibit an equilibrated methodology regarding African Americans participation in electoral politics. This representation exists in folklore, music, history, oral tradition, and sacred and secularism dimensions of Black culture and kinship. Henry supplies as a context speaking to the importance of communication as a primary medium in African American political science. Also, his use of folklore renders a holistic exegesis to outline and assess historical and cultural experiences of Blacks.17

The inquisition that shapes and guides this study began in depicting and measuring the social and political condition of the African American community. Power dynamics which constitute change support the concept of pluralism as an alternative epistemology for socio-political thought. Henry correlates politics and culture as the ontology of Black socio-political orientation. He supports this assertion by deducing — on the basis of race, gender, and class— that worldview and explication of social and or political philosophy differentiates substantially. Perhaps this is why he addresses the question — European Americans often ask, "What else does the Negro want?"

Henry provides a review of literature which focuses on socialization, leadership, organization, and public policy. The philosophy of this study veers to probe the thematic schema of culture and the Afro-American

Jeremiad. Culture is a form of expression that regulates history, motif, and ethos. Henry points out how through allegorical collaboration — of which culture, language, and ciphers are attributes— African Americans develop a composite political existence. Also, he argues that personal magnetism is the centerpiece of African American social and political leadership — this is supported by Henry using quotes at the beginning of chapters from prolific Black orators and writers such as Zora Neal Hurston and Martin Luther King, Jr. Explicitly, the common theme in using these quotations is call and response, correct entrance and exit, and the use of metaphors to distinguish adversity. Admittedly, these issues have been the central theme in the conceptualization time and space in the Afro-American Jeremiad. Henry credits the black church's adoption of a holistic perspective concerning issues and schemas of race, gender, and class, categorically on a sacred and secular basis.

Malcolm X

Malcolm X was born Malcolm Little on May 19, 1925, in Omaha, Nebraska. His parents, J. Earle and M. Louise Little, were both active members of the Universal Improvement Association, and wrote for the UNIA paper, the *Negro World*. At an early age, while living in Omaha, the Littles house was burned down by local arsonists. From Omaha, Nebraska, the family then moved to Milwaukee, Wisconsin, and in 1929 to Lansing, Michigan. In Lansing, Malcolm's father was killed, his body cut in half. Some accounts have stated that local white hate organizations killed Earle Little. Others have speculated that he committed suicide. His mother went into a depression and the children eventually became wards of the state. Malcolm X moved about, living with friends and family, and in children's homes around the state. He progressed through his elementary years of education, but, was discouraged to proceed with interest in studying law as a profession.

Unfortunately, his behavior became a problem and he was sent to a detention home in Mason, Michigan. After that Malcolm was sent into foster care and his siblings were sent to foster care families or sent to live with relatives. Malcolm began having negative encounters with teachers and felt that he was kept from professional advancement because of his race. The student of honors began to fall off as neglected youth and his formal education ended in the eighth grade.

Malcolm worked on the trains as a bus boy for a short period of time while living with his half-sister Ella in Boston. Often during Malcolm's trips on the train, he would stop in New York City. After leaving his employment on the railroad cars, he moved to New York, where he took a number of jobs including drug-trafficking, distribution of prostitutes, gambling, and fencing stolen goods. In the mid 1940s, Malcolm was a part of a burglary gang, and in 1946 he was convicted of burglary and sentenced to ten years in the Charleston State Penitentiary. While incarcerated, Malcolm's siblings and an older inmate introduced him to the teachings of the Honorable Elijah Muhammad. Reluctant at first, he eventually began to continue his studies and in 1950 identified his affiliation and religious conversion to Islam. In 1952, he was released from prison. Soon after his release from prison, he lived with his brother Philbert in Detroit, where Philbert was the minister of Muslim Temple Number One. Malcolm sold furniture during the day and worked for the Nation of Islam in the evenings and in his spare time. In 1953, the Honorable Elijah Muhammad named Malcolm Assistant Minister to Muslim Temple Number One in Detroit, Michigan. In 1954, was sent out to recruit and establish temples in Boston and Philadelphia. In June of that year, he was appointed by Muhammad to become the minister of Temple Number Seven in Harlem, New York. It was in this capacity—the chief leadership figure of the Nation of Islam in New York—that he received notoriety. In 1958, Malcolm married Betty Saunders. By 1963, Malcolm had broken with the Nation of Islam. Later on in 1963, he established two organizations: Muslim Mosque Incorporated and the Organization of Afro-American Unity, which was molded after the OAU. In March of 1964, Malcolm made his hajji to Mecca. Before his assassination in 1965, Malcolm X's ideological phase was moving in the direction of global Pan Africanism.[18]

Conclusion

In summary, the objective of this study was to examine the concept of the Black Male Narrative. Circumvented through the use of an eclectic assembly of secondary sources, the purpose was to study and trace patterns of personhood, identity, and existence. To some, the focus on Africana males is located within a conflict perspective whereas the axiological base examines Africana phenomena as dysfunctional social agents. Lewis Gordon addresses this issue of existence by writing, "The human condition occasions many questions, but two recurring ones are: "What are we?' and 'What shall we do?' These are also questions of identity and moral action. They are questions, further, of ontological and, as we observed, teleological significance, for the former addresses being and the latter addresses what to become–in a word, purpose."[19]

As far as addressing the idea of the cultural milieu, people of Africana decent are desperate to find meaning, value, norm, and mores in their daily lives, to operate in a hostile racist-racialist society through the lens of an Eurocentric perspective. Barbara Sizemore discussed this issue, "Black people are defining themselves. Having discarded the meaningless name, Negro, they are crying, 'I'm black and I'm proud.' The demands of Black Literature and Black History are attempts at restructuring the temporal–spatial arrangements of history to accommodate the presence and past of other pseudospecies, to remove the constraints on the dissemination and distribution of knowledge, and to permit the installation of the worth of blackness as a value in the black community."[20]

Identity and existence are addressed and reaffirmed from a collective pose, rather than one trying to encounter his individualism to draw relationship of memory and self rather than to the cultural parameters of their ethnic group identity. We hope to gain some insight from this discussion and begin to augment engagement centered on a philosophy of liberation for people of Africana decent.

Notes

1. See Haki Madhubuti and Maulana Karenga, Eds, *Million Man March/Day of Absence: A Commemorative Anthology*, Chicago: Third World Press and Los Angeles: University of Sankore Press, 1996; This is a valuable reference work providing speeches, commentaries, and photographs recorded from the Million Man March.
2. Robert Sokolowski, *Introduction to Phenomenology*, New York: Cambridge University Press, 2000, p. 158.
3. Table 1.0 formulated by James L. Conyers, Jr., to provide an illustration of the selected secondary sources examined in this study.
4. Janet Cheatham Bell, Ed., *Famous Black Quotations*, Chicago, Illinois: Sabayt Publications, 1986, p. 2.
5. John Blassingame and Mary Frances Berry, *Long Memory*, New York: Oxford University Press, 1982, p. 408.
6. Josep T. Durham, "Alpha Men and African American Academies," *Sphinx Magazine*, Summer 1999, http:www.apa1906.org, p. 2.
7. Durham, Op. Cit., p. 7.
8. Jawanza Kunjufu, *Countering the Conspiracy to Destroy Black Boys*, Volume 1, Chicago: Afro-American Publishing Company, 1984, p. 1.
9. Na'im Akbar, *From Miseducation to Education*, Jersey City, New Jersey: New Mind Productions, 1982, p. 3.
10. Yosef ben-Jochannan, *In Pursuit of George James Stolen Legacy: A Study*

of African Origins in Western Civilization, Ithaca, New York: Cornell University, Africana Studies and Research Center, 1980, p. 14.

11. Janet Cheatham Bell, *Famous Black Quotations*, Chicago: Sabayt Publications, 1986, p. 19.

12. Jacob Carruthers, *Science and Oppression*, Chicago: Northeastern Illinois University Kemetic Institute, 1972, p. 1.

13. Richard T. Schaefer, Racial and Ethnic Groups, see the remainder of the citation.

14. See Barbara Adams, *John Henrik Clarke: The Early Years*, Chesapeake Bay, Virginia: United Brothers and Sisters Publications, 1995. This is an oral history biography with the late John Henrik Clarke. The author provides some insight into the views and narrative of the subject.

15. See essay written by S. Jay Walker titled, "Nat Turner and John Brown: Du Bois' Uses of History," in *Black World*, Volume XXVI No. 4, February 1975, pp. 4–11.

16. *Ibid.*, pp. 11.

17. See Charles P. Henry, *Culture and African American Politics*, Bloomington, Indiana: Indiana University Press, 1990. An excellent source which surveys intellectual thought and ideology in Africana political thought. The author examines this phenomena across the boundaries of periodization and secular institutions within the African American community.

18. See the following sources: James H. Cone, *Martin and Malcolm and America: A Dream or a Nightmare*, Maryknoll, New York: Orbis Books, 1991; Malcolm X, *Malcolm X Justice Seeker*, New York: Steppingstones Press, 1993; Bradford T. Stull, *Amid the Fall, Dreaming of Eden: Du Bois, King, Malcolm X, and emancipatory composition*, Carbondale, Illinois: Southern Illinois University Press, 1999; William W. Sales, From *Civil Rights to Black Liberation: Malcolm X and the Organization of Afro-American Unity*, Boston, MA: South End Press, 1994; Bruce Perry, *Malcolm: The Life of a Man Who Changed Black America*, Barrytown, NY: Station Hill Press, 1991; David Gallen, *Malcolm X: As They Knew Him*, New York: Carroll and Graf, 1992; David Gallen, editor, *The Malcolm X Reader*, New York: Carroll and Graf, 1994; and Victor E. Wolfenstein, *The Victims of Democracy*, Berkeley, California: University of California Berkeley.

19. Lewis Gordon, *Existentia Africana*, New York: Routledge, 2000, p. 7.

20. Barbara A. Sizemore, "Social Science and Education for a Black Identity," in James A. Banks and Jean D. Grambs, Eds, *Black Self Concept: Implication for Education and Social Science*, New York: McGraw and Hill, 1972, p. 16

What Is Afrocentric? Applying Afrocentric Analysis to a Non-Fiction Text

Sandra Van Dyk

The theory of Afrocentricity and its accompanying methodology developed by Molefi Kete Asante in *Afrocentricity: The Theory of Social Change* (1980) and subsequent books (1990, 1992), offers Africanist scholars a method of analysis that can be useful in exploring fiction and non-fiction texts in the field of African American Studies. African American texts, including both fiction and non-fiction, have traditionally been defined as texts written by African American authors, but in the culturally hybrid world we occupy, this designation may well be oversimplified. Diversity of nationality, culture and ethnicity abounds within as well as outside of the African diaspora. The answer to the question, "Who is African?" can be complex. As Afrocentric theory has developed in the midst of this complexity, questions have arisen concerning its effectiveness in understanding and analyzing literature. It is this writer's opinion that Africological method, properly applied, can assist contemporary scholars in finding their footing in this difficult terrain, enabling them to culturally situate texts related to African people and subjects.

Debates have raged in the field of literary studies in the last three decades about who should be privileged to analyze the literature of African people and by what method(s) (Neal, 1969; Gayle, 1971; Gates, 1990; Joyce, 1994). Some have argued, combining racial and cultural arguments, that only African American scholars are equipped to analyze and critique texts written by African Americans (Neal, 1969). Others have argued that any scholar can analyze any text irrespective of race of author or critic (Gates,

1990). The Afrocentrist takes a somewhat different position, stating that texts dealing with material related to people of African descent, irrespective of author's race, can most effectively be understood and adjudged as having or not having an African cultural location by the scholar who applies the methods of Africalogy developed by Molefi Kete Asante.

Asante's theory of Afrocentricity represented a turning point in the field of African American Studies, from reactions to white supremacist definitions of African people to the development of a movement of cultural and intellectual self-definition potentially more powerful and more sophisticated than the Black identity movement of the 1970s. Asante laid down an Africalogical method which is useful as a framework for analyzing and critiquing texts related to African people and subject matter and, more importantly, as a framework for culture creation in its own right. Applying Africological methodology can enable the scholar to define Afrocentric literature as well as to determine how it is related to and different from other literatures both within and outside of the African diaspora and how that literature has changed over time. It will assist the scholar in differentiating between non–Afrocentric, pre–Afrocentric and Afrocentric texts.

An interesting body of literature to examine in this regard is African American protest literature of the 1960s and 1970s. This literature contains many of the themes of liberation, self-reliance, cultural pride and community self-development Asante later incorporated into the theory of Afrocentricity (Malcolm X, 1967; Sanchez, 1973; Karenga, 1978). The writing of well-known historian Lerone Bennett, Jr., who did much of his writing in this time period, is an example of protest literature. His work expresses a sharp Black consciousness and a commitment to Black community development similar to concepts later found in Asante's work. However, Bennett's book, *The Challenge of Blackness* (1972), exemplifies a telling difference between much of the writing before 1980 — particularly Black protest writing — and writing produced after 1980. The task of analyzing the literature from these two periods is useful to identify the differences, if any, between that written during the 1960s and 1970s and literature written after 1980. It also enables the scholar to fully appreciate the contributions made by pre–Afrocentric literature to the later development of the theory and method of Afrocentricity and to more clearly understand the departures of Afrocentric thinking from earlier philosophical traditions.

Afrocentric Method

According to the methodology of Afrocentric analysis (or "Africalogy," as Asante refers to it), one begins one's analysis by first choosing a subject field for the focus of the investigation from one of Afrocentricity's three major categories: social/behavioral, cultural/aesthetic, or policy issues. One must then adopt one of Asante's three paradigmatic approaches: "functional (dealing with needs, policy and action); categoral (dealing with issues of schemes, gender, class themes and files); or etymological (dealing with language, particularly in terms of word and concept origin)" (1990a, p. 13).

Once the researcher has organized the basic structure of his or her project, Asante suggests that the Afrocentric practitioner begin with determining the cultural location of the researcher. The person doing the research positions himself in relation to the phenomena under study. Asante emphasizes the primacy of cultural location to the process and method of Afrocentric analysis. The researcher's process of analysis must begin with introspection and must be conducted throughout with introspection as an integral part of the research process. This is particularly important when engaging in research across cultures or races. The Caucasian researcher, for instance, must understand the implications of white identity and white skin privilege for the research situation and for both his structuring and interpretation of research projects (McIntosh, 1988). The Caribbean researcher must understand the dynamics of racism in America to understand the attitudes and responses of African Americans to the dominant American culture. In the case of researching across cultures, Asante suggests a dual collection paradigm in which two researchers, one from the cultural context being studied, collect and assess similar data, comparing results and evaluating for cultural nuances (1990b). Once the researcher determines whether or not the use of the dual collection paradigm is appropriate, the analysis of the text can begin.

Example of Analysis of a Non-Fiction Text

A perusal of Bennett's book, *The Challenge of Blackness* (1972), using the contexts of the cultural/aesthetic subject field and the etymological paradigm, reveals that Bennett occupies an ideological position typical of the 1960s and 1970s. While Bennett clearly writes with a strong Black consciousness, he writes from a position deeply influenced by and in response to European oppression and cultural dominance. Aspects of his writing which this writer believes are characteristic of literature of this time period include: 1). writing which expresses a Black racial consciousness but without a reference to cultural identity; 2). writing in response to oppression; 3). writing that affirms the dominant American cultural values; 4). writing with frequent, and almost exclusive, reference to Western scholars as standards of knowledge and behavior.

Clearly akin to the Afrocentric perspective Asante articulates and, many would suggest, contributing to it, Bennett recognizes (nearly in Asante's later language) that "Blacks must be educated from the center of themselves (1972, p. 41) ... redefin[ing] the concept of knowledge within the perspective of our own needs and interests" (p. 36). He sees the need for the remaking of history (p. 39) and urges the development of Black Studies as a means to that end (p. 35ff). He recognizes the task of the Black artist [or writer] to "emancipate him[her]self from the white cultural structure" (p. 192). Bennett characterizes African American history as "turning American history inside out" (p. 199)—a current result of the contemporary Afrocentric perspective as the strong resistance to it attests. He expresses the need to "develop a new frame of reference which transcends the limits of white concepts ... a total intellectual offensive" (p. 35). Bennett's concepts certainly challenge white supremacy and champion Black intellectual development. His ideas are an important, though usually unrecognized, precursor to the formal theory of Afrocentricity.

Bennett also speaks of the model of the scholar-activist and the role of the community in helping to define the perspectives of Black intellectuals. Like Asante, Bennett seeks to "institutionalize the Black experience to ensure a Black presence in the land" (p. 37). He deals with nomenclature, aware that those European experiences that are universalized, such as the Renaissance, are more accurately spoken of when particularized. Interestingly, Bennett suggests "the white Renaissance" (instead of the European Renaissance), again couching his ideas in terms of color.

In his work, Bennett cogently discusses the problems and issues confronting the African American artist and intellectual, but in *The Challenge of Blackness* is not able to go far enough in his analysis. He writes from within the European oppressive structure, detached from the African past. He expresses a *Black* race consciousness without a clear recognition of African cultural identity as the source of African American understanding. He writes, " Blackness is a way, perhaps the only way to the primordial, unplumbed center of our being.... Blackness is an antidote to the Puritan curse" (p. 2). Bennett identified "Blackness" as the source of what is needed and recognized, even suggesting that the idea of "Blackness" is reactive, formed in response to white oppression.

What Bennett and others of his time period were not able to see, however, is that the concept and nomenclature "Black," though asserted to signify race pride, in actuality kept African Americans captive to the white supremacist system of "othering" and, in many ways, defined by white reflections of their identity, as Morrison suggests in *Playing in the Dark* (1992). This leaves African Americans estranged from the African cultural moorings that would enable them to locate themselves outside of the American hegemonically racist context. To relate "Black" people to the classical African context connects them to a different — and powerful — cultural root. This implies that the issue with European society is primarily one of culture, not color, thus illuminating the fact that systems of racism are part of a cultural construct and are embedded in the thought processes, behaviors and social structures of white societies in lethal and complex combination with the European class structure. Approaching these issues Afrocentrically relegates Eurocentricity to its proper place as one of a number of cultural perspectives, different from African and other cultural perspectives thereby reducing the impact of European hegemonic claims and opening space in the global dialogue for new possibilities. Even more importantly, it provides people of African descent a place from which to speak with authority about their own experience.

Though it is excellent in many respects, much of Bennett's 1972 book is characterized in terms of the "Black rebellion" against white racism "inventing itself by countermoves in the white darkness" (p. 29). This is no doubt due to its historical context of the struggle for civil rights in that time period, but it also signifies some of the limitations of pre–Afrocentric thinkers and activists who were still thinking and acting inside the circle of white oppression. Bennett, as did other African American social and political writers of the time, challenged the "perpetuating rituals" of the European and insisted on expressing a voice that had been stifled by the dominant culture. But, at the same time, his writing did not escape the confines of oppression. He often seemed to be battering at the gates of American society by asserting moral claims against Euro-American values, writing that "Blackness is the regal repository of the values Europeans claimed and never lived" yet, in this writer's opinion, failed in adequately recognizing 300 years of European refusal to live up to those values and in assessing the lack of real possibilities for fundamental change (1972, p. 2). Bennett identified African American interests with European social and or political goals: "Black people embody the most advanced social and economic interests of this society. Action on their behalf is action on behalf of the real interests of America" (1972, p. 81).

Although Bennett recognized the definitive identity of African American people and saw the need for radical social transformation, his work was not freed from white oppression. It was not until Asante's development of the theory and methodology of Afrocentricity that people of African descent had a systematic intellectual approach to breaking out of that circle and were able to see an identity beyond the negative identity provided by American society, which is driven by color identification and white constructions of "The Other" largely based on color. Standing in a different place — an African place — is a profound shift in thinking that makes the ideas of liberation and victory both possible and real for African people.

Another way one sees the effects of oppression on the writing of Bennett and others is their continual use of and reference to European scholars in their work. Sartre, Hegel and Marx are more frequent travelers with pre–Afrocentric writers than continental African, African American or other diasporan scholars. Obviously, the American scholar is and should be conversant with scholars from all world cultures, but must at the same time demonstrate both the need and the possibility for analysis from African reference points. That is not to say that the Afrocentric scholar should neglect knowledge of European thought and culture or refrain from cross-cultural comparisons of literatures, but only to say that when engaged in Afrocentric analysis and expression, the scholar should be appropriately grounded in African referents. Literature exists which speaks from African reference points with a perspective of liberation in the work of Abarry (1993), Asante (1980, 1987, 1990a, 1990b), Baldwin [Joseph] (1986, 1990), Kershaw (1989, 1993), Keto (1989), Myers (1987), Nobles (1985), Richards (1981), Welsh-Asante (1985, 1993) and others. This literature is not concerned with victimization nor is it speaking in reaction to white oppression; it is focused on building the cultural connections between contemporary Africans in the diaspora and their African past, and develops literature with a strong cultural location from which to articulate a critique of the present and a vision for the future.

Rather than utilizing terms such as "minority," "majority" and "people of color," Afrocentric analysis introduces language such as "location," "relocation," "centeredness," and "inclusion" as indicators of new ways of thinking which enables the scholar to classify phenomena in relation to an African rather than a European norm. Afrocentrists are reclaiming values such as living in harmony, fostering cultural development, thinking holistically, establishing communities based on human concern and including the spiritual dimensions of life in the definition of reality. They are shifting their analysis to an overarching theory of culture rather than to a fragmented theory of class or race.

In acknowledging the failures of the struggles for civil rights and Black power, Bennett rightly argued that attacking European oppression on the level of its legal structure, as groups within the Civil Rights Movement did, was ultimately ineffective in eradicating racism and white privilege.

Further, he argued that the Black rebellion lacked "a revolutionary conception and an overall revolutionary structure" (1972, p. 29). He also suggested that to define the struggle as one of class could end up polarizing those within the African American community (p. 113). The Black middle class, under those circumstances, is put in the position of having to betray itself (p. 57ff). Bennett saw the problem faced by Africans in American as a "white problem," (p. 127). He correctly defined important issues and accurately identified the direction of the cause but saw it only in part. The primary issue is not one of color, but culture. In his idealism, Bennett urged America to live up to its own promise when, in reality, the idea of America since its inception has been to provide a cultural home for the Euro-American, most particularly for the Euro-American male.

Conclusions

In summary, using the Africalogical method of analyzing *The Challenge of Blackness*, six areas of difference from Afrocentric literature can be identified. The first difference is one of focus. Looking from an African center, Bennett is largely concerned with issues of race and color, making frequent use of terms such as "colored," "Black," and "Negro" to describe Africans in America. Though some may consider these words to be dependent on historical period, groups or individuals referring to themselves as "Africans" have always existed throughout the history of Africans in America. Since terms depicting color do not connect people of African descent either geographically or culturally to a particular physical or, for that matter, symbolic location, they find themselves stranded, both actually and metaphysically, in foreign and hostile territory. White construction and or acceptance of these terms is a further indictment of white America's degradation of African culture and ongoing efforts to separate African people from their roots and from their very identities.

Second, a difference in themes directs the literatures. Bennett's book focuses predominantly on themes of victimization, rebellion and struggle. Afrocentric literature, making the African person the subject rather than the object of study, moves the reader beyond the roles of victim, rebel and struggler to the role of positive activist and culture creator. It emphasizes reestablishment of relationships among peoples of the African diaspora and the development of myths, language and symbols to express these new understandings and relationships.

Third, the nature of discourse is different. Afrocentric analysis of Bennett's text reveals submission to the rhetoric of oppression through acceptance and use of such terms as "minority," "people of color," and "Third World" current in that time period. Afrocentric literature seeks to change the nature and language of discourse itself, removing what Asante terms oppressive rhetorical conditions (1987). It introduces culturally relevant ideas such as location, relocation, bilocation, and so on. and the recognition and expression of the ideas of people of African descent as equal to those of other cultural, national or political groups. Power is often expressed in language before it is expressed in politics. When new language and ways of expression gain currency, power relationships can ultimately change; hence the ongoing turmoil over political correctness of language and discourse in contemporary society.

Fourth, Afrocentric and pre–Afrocentric literatures express different values. Bennett was concerned with the place of African Americans in the dominant American system and with affirming the positive values of a culture which, for Africans, had been an oppressive and rejecting culture. Afrocentric literature is concerned with identifying, developing, expressing and demonstrating Afrocentric values such as social harmony and the essential spirituality of humankind, which have been part of African people's cultures wherever they have lived, whether as enslaved or free peoples. This literature also urges actualizing those values in a global context, which moves beyond the American context and emanates from a different intellectual, social and political framework. Indeed, it can remove African peoples from their intellectual imprisonment by oppressive white supremacist and Eurocentric ideas and perceptions of the world.

A fifth concern with Bennett's work, as representative of other pre–Afrocentric texts, is the use of different reference points. The work examined made frequent use of Eurocentric terms and references to thinkers such as Hegel, Sartre, and Marx as sources of analytical perspectives. Clearly, the informed Afrocentric scholar must insist that the European scholar deal with writers and thinkers from African contexts by deliberately employing the rich sources available in the course of his work. When Europeans encounter the work of Afrocentrists, they must become familiar with a new body of knowledge drawing from different cultural perspectives and experiences that may challenge their assumptions, ideas and practices. Afrocentrists create space for their own positions to be stated in academic discourse when they embed their work in analytical perspectives arising from African cultural locations.

Finally, the two literatures differ in their expression of the key issues leading to social, political and economic change. In *The Challenge of Blackness* (1972), Bennett is still searching for places to effect change, whether in social, political or economic situations. The Afrocentric scholar believes that the present revolution is being fought at the level of culture, of which these same social, political and economic situations are a part. Afrocentric analysis leads one to the position that to attack the legal structure — a primary emphasis of the Civil Rights Movement — is only to touch a part of the problem, perhaps the most tractable part. Asante suggests in *The Afrocentric Idea* (1987) that once one succeeds in changing the language a society uses and also in changing its canon, the body of work that educated people believe should be common knowledge and the most debatable symbol, one will begin to create space for varied cultural perspectives representative of the global spectrum of literatures. At that point, the most profound revolution — the restructuring of what is taught, known, believed, and, hence, done — will have begun.

References

Abarry, A. S. (1993). "Mpai oratory." In K. Welsh-Asante (ed.) *The African Aesthetic: Keeper of the Tradition*. (pp 80–101), Westport, CT: Greenwood Press.
Asante, M. K. (1980). *Afrocentricity: The Theory of Social Change*. Buffalo, NY: Amulefi Publishing.
_____. (1987). *The Afrocentric Idea*. Philadelphia, PA: Temple University Press.
_____. (1990). *Kemet, Afrocentricity and Knowledge*. Trenton, NJ: Africa World Press.
_____. (1992). Afrocentric metatheory and disciplinary implications. *The Afrocentric Scholar*. 1, 98–117.
Baldwin, J. A. (1986). "African (black) psychology." *Journal of Black Studies*. 67, 235–249.
_____, and R. Hopkins. "African-American and European-American cultural differences as assessed by the worldviews paradigm: An empirical analysis." *The Western Journal of Black Studies*. 13, 45–51.
Bennett, L. (1972). *The Challenge of Blackness*. Chicago: Johnson Publishing.
Gates, H. L. Jr. (1990). Introduction. "Tell me sir ... what is black literature?" *PMLA* 105, 11–22.
Gayle, A. Jr., (1971). *The Black Aesthetic*. New York: Doubleday.
Joyce, J. (1994). *Warriors, Conjurers and Priests: Defining African Centered Literary Criticism*. Chicago: Third World Press.
Karenga, M. (1978). *Essays on Struggle: Position and Analysis*. San Diego, CA: Kawaida.
Kershaw, T. (1989). "The emerging paradigm in Black Studies." *Western Journal of Black Studies*. 14, 3–52.
_____. (1993). "Afrocentricity and the Afrocentric method." *Western Journal of Black Studies* 16, 160–168.
Keto, C. T. (1989). *The Africa-Centered Perspective of History*. Blackwood, NJ: K.A. Publishing.
McIntosh, P. (1988). "White privilege and male privilege: A personal account of coming to see correspondences through work in Women's Studies." *Working*

Paper No. 189. Wellesley, MA: Wellesley College Center for Research on Women.

Morrison, T. (1992). *Playing in the Dark.* Cambridge, MA: Harvard University Press.

Myers, L. J. (1987). "The deep structure of culture." *Journal of Black Studies.* 18, 72–85.

Neal, L. (1969). "The black arts movement." *The Drama Review.* 12. 4–12.

Nobles, W. (1985). *Africanity and the Black Family.* Oakland, CA: The Institute for the Advanced Study of Black Family Life and Culture.

Richards, D. M. (1981). *Let the Circle Be Unbroken.* Published by Dona Richards.

Sanchez, S. (1984). "A blues book for blue black magical women." In M. Evans (ed.) *Black Women Writers: 1950–1980.* (pp. 415–450). NY: Anchor Books.

Welsh-Asante, K. (ed.) (1993). *The African Aesthetic: Keeper of the Tradition.* Westport, CT: Greenwood Press.

_____. and M.K. Asante (eds.). *African Culture and the Rhythms of Unity.* Westport, CT: Greenwood Press.

X, Malcolm. *Malcolm X and Afro-American History.* NY: Pathfinder Books.

Part 4: Pan Africanist Thought

The Return: Slave Castles and the African Diaspora
Tanya Y. Price

Dozens of large structures, customarily called "castles," and over 40 European-built "forts" that once protected them, are situated along the modern-day Ghanaian coastline (Broadi-siaw, 1998) as testimony to the exchanges of goods and people that took place between Europeans and local Africans from the late fifteenth century onwards (Huggins 1995:30).

The Cape Coast "castle" is one of the largest castles in Ghana. The massive, whitewashed structure is situated on a rock outcropping along the shore at Cape Coast, Ghana. The Swedes originally built the Cape Coast Castle in 1652, with the local Fanti rulers reluctantly providing permission for its construction. Its original purpose was to protect Swedish trade interests against the Portuguese, Spanish, Dutch, or any other European powers trading in the area. Over time this trade became increasingly exploitative from the African point of view, as Europeans accumulated the wealth precipitating the development of capitalism as an economic system. Europeans also enjoyed a monopoly in the technology needed for gun and cannon manufacture (Rodney 1972:75–91)—guns that African nations needed to defend themselves against slave-raiding by their local enemies. The medium of exchange shifted from ivory, to gold, to enslaved human beings. The resultant destruction reached all the way into Northern Ghana (Der 1998:31–32), and hundreds of miles into West Africa's interior, where "[m]en, women and children were wrenched from the anchor of tradition and family...." (Huggins 1995:30). Some of the enslaved were war captives, others sentenced to slavery by crime or indebtedness. Still others were randomly kidnapped. As the notorious European trade in Africans reached its height the eighteenth through nineteenth centuries, the dungeons underneath the slave "castles" of Ghana held up to 1,000 Africans at any one time as full ship-loads of captives were collected for the harrowing two-month voyage to the Americas (Boadi-siaw, 1998). According to Holloway (1990:8), some 13,070 of 106,506 or 12.3 percent of all enslaved persons imported into Charleston, South Carolina (a principle U.S. slave port) between 1733 and 1807 were from the Gold Coast, or present-day Ghana. Ghana was, therefore, a significant supplier of enslaved Africans to the United States.

The first known African captives arrived in the English colonies of North America in 1619. Although the transatlantic slave trade was officially ended by constitutional amendment in 1808, an ongoing domestic U.S. slave trade and illegal overseas trading continued through the Civil War. The last enslaved Africans were not freed until 1865. It was not until the 1970s or so that African Americans and others from the Diaspora began making the "reverse middle passage" to the West African coast in significant numbers. By this time, the slave "dungeons," as Sister Imahkus Ninzinga Robinson, her husband, Nana Okofo, and the local expatriate African American community refer to them, had become foci for the spiritual return of African Americans and others from the African Diaspora.

The Robinsons, originally from Brooklyn, New York, and their associate, Bongo Shorty, originally from Jamaica, started their company "One Africa Productions" in 1990. The three associates describe themselves as a "grassroots family organization of African Descendants who have relocated to our ancestral land and can provide a unique and stimulating introduction into Ghana for brothers and sisters who are returning home." One Africa produces a play that emphasizes the experiences of people from the Diaspora within the "castles," hence, their insistence on naming the structures "slave dungeons" rather than "castles." According to One Africa, the dungeons are "our Plymouth Rock," the symbolic sites where the African people disembarked from the continent for the last time and the place where African Americans and other Diaspora Africans were born as identifiable groups of people. The history of the slave castles and the dungeons below them are testimony to the shifting nature of the European cultural, economic and political domination that enabled the structures to be built on Ghanaian soil in the first place, and serve as a backdrop for the controversies that continue to rage around the castle.

In the *American Anthropologist*, Bruner refers to slave "castles" as:

> site(s) to be struggled over, a transition point between the passage of goods and peoples from the interior of Africa to Europe and the New World, " and "...dominant localities that define boundaries, that tell us who has the right to be inside the castle, within the center of power, in

control, and who is outside, on the periphery. Castles are a dynamic presence, places that produce movement between home and abroad sites for the construction of narratives of time and narratives of space [Bruner 1996:302].

Ghanaians, African Americans and African descendants arriving from other areas of the Diaspora experienced the highly charged symbolic sites of the castles and dungeons of Ghana in different ways, corresponding to their varying histories and frames of reference. While many Ghanaians experience the slave castles and forts as only a painful aspect, of their ongoing history, African Americans tend to focus on the slave castles and dungeons as symbols of their severed African identity. According to Huggins, "Slavery did what death could not do.... [It] rudely severed the natural family inks between past and present generations, which is the essence of African tradition," thus removing African Americans from "the consciousness of continuing generations" (1995:34). The castles, forts and other structures associated with the slave trade were, at all times, impregnated with deeply-held cultural meanings and memories for those returning from the Diaspora. For African Americans, returning to the slave dungeons is a symbolic reconnection with their African heritage, a reunion with the ancestors left on the other side of the Atlantic. These shifting cultural meanings and historical interpretations produced conflict over the historical representation of the castles, conflicting ideals over how the castles were to be utilized, and controversy over who should be allowed to enter the castles. In this paper, I will attempt to decipher some of these meanings as they manifested themselves during my own visit to the Cape Coast Castle, as I accompanied Dr. Nancy Dawson of Southern Illinois University on a trip to the region under the auspices of the African Cultural Continuities Study-Abroad Program. We traveled with a group of 13 students from the Black American Studies Program, between July and August of 1998. I observed my own reactions and those of others, with all the passion of a participant and the fascination of an observer.[1]

What Is the Black (African) Diaspora?

Although the notion of an "African Diaspora" has gained wide acceptance in recent years across the humanities and social sciences, the exact nature of the phenomenon of Diaspora is open to interpretation. Evidence suggests earlier explorations and visitations by Africans to other continents (see Van Sertima: 1976) and provides conclusive support for an

Arabian trade in enslaved Africans that pre-dated the European trade by some 1,000 years, and eventually fed into the European trade (Rodney 1972: 97,143; Anderson 1995:31). The European slave trade, however, is conceived of as the catastrophic event that spread people of African descent to Europe and the Americas. During this process, Africans predominantly from the western and central regions of the continent were forcibly removed from their cultural environments. After an overwhelmingly painful process of capture, forced marching to the coast, entombment for a period of time in overcrowded, disease-ridden slave dungeons, and finally crossing the dreaded middle passage on slave ships, Africans were taken to Europe, the Americas and the Caribbean Islands to face hundreds of years of enslavement. Upon residence in the Americas under slavery conditions, Africans gradually adopted to the new physical and cultural environments they inhabited. In 1941, anthropologist Melville Herskovits described a process whereby "Negroes, coming from different tribes and speaking different languages, have by a hitherto unrecognized least common dominator in tradition and speech found it possible to preserve elements of their heritage" (1941:19). Herskovits recognized that African culture was far from weak under contact, as Frazier (1948) and others had presupposed. Instead, inherent within the culture was an internal strength and resiliency that resisted assimilation (1941:19). Through a process of adaptation, Africans retained some of their African traditions, transformed others to fit new environments and conditions, and blended others with the cultures of those existing around them. "This African retention manifested itself in a continuum from pure African carryovers to behavior indistinguishable from that which characterizes the dominant culture of European derivation" (1941:xxv). Through this process, Africans retained some distinctive cultural traits of their own, while existing in a world where people with predominantly European ancestry were economically and politically, if not numerically, dominant. Herskovits traced African culture of a more or less "pure" form to a relatively restricted area of the Diaspora, (namely, the Caribbean and South America), while other, more subtle survivals "which, because they represent the deepest seated aspects of African tradition, have persisted even where overt forms of African behavior and African custom have completely disappeared," were found in other areas (1941:53). The subordinate cultural and economic position of most African cultural survivors in relationship to their European oppressors assured that they were perceived as a people apart in the various societies in which they eventually settled. Never completely absorbed into their cultural environments, nor no longer fully African in culture, some African people of the Diaspora found themselves ensnared in an identity crisis which Du Bois labeled a "double consciousness"—that is, the desire to be both Black and American (or by extension, English, Caribbean, and so on) while remaining unable to fully achieve either identity (1996:102). In order to escape from this double bind, some people from the African Diaspora, particularly the middle class, educated strata of those who could afford the trip, have been returning to the African continent in an attempt to reconnect with their cultural roots. As former centers of the slave trade in Africa, present-day Ghana, Nigeria, Sierra Leone, Senegal and Gambia are logical places for retreat, reflections, and historical re-examination. The thread of African cultural memory that survived slavery in varying degrees among different groups, along with shared historical identity and disadvantaged economic, social and political positions vis-à-vis dominant group members in places where African descendants have settled mark out the African Diaspora as a cultural area in the anthropological sense.

In recent years, Paul Gilroy's concept of the "Black Atlantic" has become widely accepted. Gilroy, an Afro-British professor of literature, argues against what he calls the "tragic popularity of ideas about the integrity and purity of cultures" (1993:7). Instead, Gilroy suggests that scholars study the "Black Atlantic," a complex transnational and transcultural formation combining disparate elements of Africa, the Americas, the Caribbean and Britain. Gilroy uses the image of ships to capture the notion of the middle passage and back-to-Africa movements, as well as circulating ideals, activities and cultural artifacts. In essence, the Black Atlantic is seen as "a living, micro-cultural, micro-political system in motion" (1993:4). Although Gilroy's concept is intriguing, I, along with other anthropologists, disagree with anti-essentialists and some post-modern theorists who privilege identity as "constructed, hybrid, fragmented and conjuntual" over any notion of identity as essence, fixed, or rooted in a specific cultural tradition. Anti-essentialists fail to acknowledge that by their very nature, cultural identities are not only "multiple and constantly shifting," ... are historically anchored to specific locations (Lavie and Swenburg, {quoting Alarcon} 1996:3–4). Not only does Gilroy deny the "roots" of African Americans and Afro-Britons cultural identities and the importance of African cultural retentions that Herskovits describes, he fails to adequately confront the tactics of creative resistance against the "Eurocenter" (the United States and Western Europe) that such "essentialized" identities make possible. Contemporary African-American culture is, in part, the "result of a long history of confrontations between unequal cultures and forces, in which the stronger culture struggles to control, remake, or eliminate the subordinate partner" (1996:9). Instead, African Americans have used identity politics as a tool to subvert the economic and political dominance of the state in creative ways. Through the strategic use of alternate identities, Diaspora Africans have managed to "creolize (decenter) and destabilize" the dominant Europeanized culture. The state, in turn, resists attempts for people of African descent to define themselves (hence, the furor over African American Studies and Afrocentricity in the United States). "Essentialism," therefore, is a process of using cultural identities for the purpose of healing and recovery. European, Native American and Asian culture are also part of the mix that make both American and African American culture, however, this fact does not de-emphasize the importance of Africa in African American cultural construction. The return to Africa, then, is a means of converting pain into progress, of healing, and recovering the task of overcoming subordination in exchange for political empowerment.

The First Encounter and the Play

The Cape Coast slave castle, along with the Elmina Castle and their attendant forts, dominate a large portion of the shoreline of Cape Coast and Elmina, and are visible over much of the area. Before entering inside the Cape Coast castle, our group first experienced it from the outside. We gazed at its thick, off-white stone walls bathed in brilliant sunlight, and observed the inexpressible beauty and power of the ocean beneath it. We also observed the Fanti fishermen below, as they beached their boats and spread their nets on the ground for repair before the next day's fishing. The Fanti seemed to live in harmonious coexistence with the castles. Some of us could not resist descending to one of the many large boulders beneath the castle and watching the crashing waves from its perch. Others bought tourist items from young traders and Ghanaian school children that approached us yielding addresses and pleas to "write back." I took some video footage of the scene, where I remarked on my difficulty in believing that a site of such beauty could also be the location of such tragedy. From this vantage point it was evident that the castles didn't hold the same significance for most Ghanaians as they did for African Americans, save their commercial exploitative value as centers for African American tourism and resources for the economic development that such tourism would bring (Bruner 1996:290). For the school children and traders, we were "Black Americans," or *obruni* (white man or foreigner), world travelers with the wealth and resources which they could never achieve in their present condition as residents of an exploited, "underdeveloped" nation. (One Fanti child actually addressed me as, "White man.") Before asking for money or addresses, the local children recited a well-rehearsed speech about the similarity between themselves and African Americans: "It is only because of the European that our African brothers and sisters are apart." The speech seemed less than sincere. It was my suspicion that the children reacted to us more as rich tourists than as brothers and sisters. The speech appeared as nothing more than a public performance to give Diaspora Africans, who wanted nothing more than to be seen as brothers and sisters returning home, a reason to give, and give generously. By American standards our group was quite poor, having won scholarships, sacrificed, begged and borrowed for the privilege of traveling to Ghana. In relation to Ghana's economically subordinate position in the world economic system, however, it is difficult to blame the children for trying to capitalize on our comparative wealth. The group ate lunch at an attractive wooden restaurant on stilts located within 50 feet of the castle. I ate there with mixed feelings—regret that a restaurant would be constructed on a site that was, for me sacred ground, and guilt and shame that I would even consider eating there. Ironically, the restaurant burned down before we left the country, leaving nothing but one stilt, still buried in the sand. I silently hoped that it would never be rebuilt.

The Tour and the Play

One pays a fee to enter the castle—a larger fee for foreign tourists, a lesser fee for Ghanaian nationals. There was a small museum in the castle, however, I declined to enter it, wanting to form my own impressions and ideas about what I was about to see. The experience of the Cape Coast castle began with a conventional tour, conducted, I assumed, by an employee of the Ghanaian government. Molefi Asante, a prominent Temple University professor and originator of the Afrocentric approach to African American culture, happened to be touring the castle with his group at the same time as Nancy Dawson's group. A man with an African accent walked along with Asante's group. I didn't know the man's identity, but, he was learned, probably a professor. He contradicted the government docent loudly and consistently, his running commentary forming a counterpoint to what one assumes was the official Ghanaian interpretation of events that the docent offered. At one point, the tour group entered a large room that had been fit with wooden floors and florescent lights. The docent was explaining the historical uses of the room, when someone asked if this was the way the room appeared during the slave trade. Before the guide could offer a sufficient explanation, the man with the accent launched into a diatribe about how it was a shame that the entire room had been modernized. Shortly after this, the docent mentioned the "triangular slave trade," and the man launched into a diatribe about how the term "triangular trade" was a misnomer for the systematic, complex commercial exchanges that constituted the trans–Atlantic trade in human beings. I reacted to the man's constant interruptions with both annoyance and interest — annoyance with his rudeness and insensitivity, interest in the underlying meaning of this series of exchanges. These exchanges illustrated in vivid form the struggle over meaning from the viewpoint of Ghanaians and Africans from the Diaspora. I understood that the cultural diversity of the Diaspora would lead to slight differences in historical interpretation among each group, but this exchange illustrated how profoundly different these views of history were. I concluded that the man of African origin was probably a U.S. immigrant intent on proving that, as a resident of the Diaspora who originated from the African continent, he understood the complexity and brutality of slavery, unlike the "unenlightened" African guide from the continent.

We then entered a walkway that passed over a courtyard, where a wooden structure under construction was visible below and to our left. As the guide explained that a souvenir stand was being constructed, students and professors alike shook their heads in disgust that place was being commercialized. The last leg of the "conventional tour" took us into the men's and women's dungeons, where the captives were actually held, as we were told, hundreds to a room, sometimes for two or three years, until a ship-full of Africans could be gathered for transport to the Americas. At the entrance of the dungeons, a Ghanaian priest stood ready to perform rites of reconciliation and atonement for the role that Ghanaians played in the tragedy of the slave trade. Group members paid the priest a few Cedis, after which he recited a prayer and poured imported Gin upon the altar. Upon entering the cell, I was struck by the darkness. The only light source was a tiny slit cut into a wall many feet above our heads. The few flash photos I attempted to take were too dark to see. A few narrow gutters, perhaps one-half inch deep, were cut into the solid stone floor to help channel accumulated urine, blood, feces and vomit away from the cell. On the way back to the large courtyard at the center of the castle, I crawled into a small, stifling hot cell with low ceilings, where I was told, Africans who revolted starved to death or died of thirst, whichever came first. Scratch marks were still visible where suffering people dug their fingers into the stone walls in agony. At the conclusion of the tour, I marveled at the strength and resiliency of any human who survived these torturous conditions with the mental fortitude to continue their lives. Following the "conventional tour," we prepared to view the play.

Sister Imahkus Ninzinga Robinson, Nana Okofo, and Bongo Shorty stood in the central courtyard of the Cape Coast castle, ready to begin the production "Thru the Door of No Return — The Return." Their organization, One Africa Productions, produced the play especially for the consumption of African Americans and others from the African Diaspora; therefore, no one of European descent is allowed to attend the play when a group from the Diaspora pays to view it. Earlier, Imahkus informed us that she preferred the Cape Coast castle over the Elmina castle as a site for the production; while Elmina was older, Cape Coast was "less spoiled," closer to its original state, and therefore a more meaningful site to commune with the ancestors. The group sat in anticipation on folding chairs as Imahkus made her opening remarks and recited a prayer. A candle was distributed for everyone in attendance. Finally, the action began, as several African women and men, dressed in the traditional manner, took center stage. The play depicted Africans minding their own business, on the way to the market or the fields, when Europeans entice them with cheap trinkets. Interestingly, the actors playing Europeans were wearing plastic Mick Jagger and Bean masks, their brown arms showing from beneath the folds of their costumes. Obviously, the symbolism of the stock European characters was more important than the accuracy of the costuming. The vain local chief is enticed by the trinkets, after which the Europeans introduce intoxicating beverages. The Europeans get the African men drunk, at which time they chain the ankles of the men, the women and children while the men sleep off the stupor. They awaken to the cracks of whips and gunfire, as they are led off into dungeons, the men screaming in anguish, the women crying and singing mournfully. At this point, the women in the audience follow the chained women into the women's dungeon and the men follow their counterparts into the men's dungeon.

The women carried their candles into the dark dungeon, where we stood in a circle, prayed, and evoked the names of our ancestors who never had the opportunity to return to Africa. The point was emphasized that we were returning in their place. At the conclusion of the ceremony, several of the women cried and all offered generous hugs and words of love for the Ghanaian women, who cried along with us. Crying along with the African women was therapeutic. Through the ceremony, we experienced an emotional connection between ourselves and the actresses in the play, who may have been our distant kin, for all we knew. We were discovering our connection, and they were empathizing with us and the struggles our kin had encountered as slaves in a strange land. Whatever lingering resentment that existed among the African Americans toward Africans who may have facilitated the sale of their ancestors to Europeans, at that moment evaporated. Finally, upon leaving the dungeons, we went out through the "door of no return." This door is said to be the last "piece" of his homeland any captive experienced before being transported to the "New World." Once through the door, we stood along the ocean-side, singing the "Redemption Song," and other freedom songs from the Diaspora, with Bongo Shorty accompanying on drums. After two or three songs, we re-entered, back through the door of no return, in a triumphant atmosphere of dancing, drums and singing.

Identity and the Ceremony

The meaning of the play and ceremony was clear: it had constructed a "three-part narrative of initial horror, diaspora resistance, and joyous return" (1996:301) through which we filtered our own pasts. Standing in the dungeon, we experienced a temporary liminal state (Turner 1982) during which an important emotional change occurred. We symbolically connected our ancestors on the African continent with those in the Americas. We had crossed the waters of Atlantic to achieve a great reunion. While our African ancestors left through the door, never to return, we had, with great difficulty, returned on our own will as their representatives, thus completing the circle. At the same time, we had reconciled with our living relatives on the mother continent, the healing strength of redemption making us a stronger people. Once the union of our living and dead ancestors was created, we could return to our lives in the Diaspora as changed people, with a new, more positive outlook on life.

This ceremony, along with countless other redemptive ceremonies and a noted revival of interest in African culture in Africa and abroad, are part of a larger process of identity formation. Africans at home and in the Diaspora are in the process of building bridges based on shared similarities of history, place, and experience. Most of us have agreed to "strategically suspended our unshared historical specificities" (Lavie and Swedenburg: 10) in exchange for the advantage of creating a politically unified front against cultural, political and economic oppression by the Eurocenter. The play at Cape Coast castle and other forms of creative cultural production will continue to aid in the forging of such political and social identity for years to come.

In 1995, a posthumously published book by Howard University historian Nathan Irvin Huggins vividly captured the connection of the slave trade with the African American experience when he stated:

Everything that has happened to us since — brutal passage, plantation slavery, centuries of oppression, violence and discrimination — is all linked to such places. To see the urban ghetto in its fullest perspective, one must walk in the Cape Coast dungeon. To really understand Attica prison, one must know the meaning of Elmina, and others, too.

Many black Americans like myself want to find their way back through that horror, into and through these dungeons, to the source of their being. Not because we wish to deny our history as it has developed from these castles, but because we come to find in the experience itself, from the beginning in those dungeons, the essence of our special humanity that the slave experience and all the rest could not destroy (1995:34–35).

Notes

1. Nearly ten years earlier, during a stay in southern Nigeria, I had peered westward across the Atlantic from Lagos harbor, imagining how I may have been the first in my family to behold the Atlantic view from the African side. Experiencing the physical remnants of the slave trade, however, adds an extra dimension to a deeply emotional experience.

2. Attention should be called to the fact that although African descendants are often criticized for claiming their African heritage when they are, in fact, products of cultural syncretization, White Americans have rarely been criticized for claiming "whiteness" or "European" as an essential identity when in reality, *all* cultures are constructions " resulting from the intermingling of disparate cultures." The myth of White cultural homogeneity has been sustained by European and American dominance of the global political economy (Lavie and Swedenburg 1996:10).

3. Many of the group expressed the sentiment that the dungeons were sacred ground that people of European descent should not be allowed to enter — at least not with a group of Africans from the Diaspora. One African American woman was said to have become so enraged when a White man refused to stop taking pictures in the dungeons, she drowned him in the ocean. The same sentiment is expressed in Howard film professor Halie Gerima's 1993 film *Sankofa*.

References

Anderson, S.E. 1958. *The Black Holocaust for Beginners*. New York: Writers and Readers Publishing.

Broadi-siaw, Samuel. 1998. Unpublished lecture delivered at University of Cape Coast, Ghana, July.

Bruner, Edward M. 1996. "Tourism in Ghana: The Representation of Slavery and the Return of the Black Diaspora." *American Anthropologist*, 98(2): 290–304.

Der, Benedict G. 1998. *The Slave Trade in Northern Ghana*. Accra:Woeli Publishing Services.

Du Bois, W.E.B. 1996. *The Souls of Black Folk*. In *The Oxford W.E.B. Du Bois Reader*. New York: Oxford University Press (originally published 1903).
Frazier, E. Franklin 1948. *The Negro Family in the United States*. New York, Dryden Press.
Gilroy, Paul 1993. *Black Atlantic: Modernity and Double-Consciousness*. London: Verso.
Herskovits, Melville 1941. *The Myth of the Negro Past*. Boston: Beacon Press.
Holloway, Joseph E. 1991. "The Origins of African-American Culture." In *Africanisms in American Culture*, Joseph E. Holloway, ed. Pp. 1–18.
Huggins, Nathan Irvin 1995. *Revelations*. New York: Oxford University Press.
Lavie, Smadar and Ted Swedenburg. 1996. Introduction. In *Displacement, Diaspora, and Geographies of Identity*. Smadar Lavie and Ted Swedenburg, eds. Durham: Duke University Press, pp. 1–25.
Rodney, Walter 1972. *How Europe Underdeveloped Africa*. Washington, D.C.: Howard University Press.
Turner, Victor 1982. *The Ritual Process: Structure and Anti-Structure*. Ithaca, N.Y.: Cornell University Press (originally published 1969).
Van Sertima, Ivan 1976. *They Came Before Columbus*. New York: Random House.

The Shebanization of Knowledge
Miriam Ma'at-Ka-Re Monges

> *Hearken. O ye who are my people, and give ye ear to my words. For I desire wisdom and my heart seeketh to find understanding.... Now to what under the heavens shall wisdom be compared...? It is a source of joy for the heart, and a bright and shining light for the eyes.... It maketh the ears to hear and hearts to understand, it is teacher of those who are learned, and it is a consoler of those who are discreet and prudent.... As for a kingdom, it cannot stand without wisdom and riches cannot be preserved without wisdom.... Wisdom is the best of all treasures.*
> Kebra Nagast Chapter 24

With these words, Makeda, the Queen of Sheba, set out on a quest for wisdom. I envision her quest as a model for the roots of an epistemological paradigm, which I have entitled the "Shebanization of Knowledge." I will stand on the shoulders of an Afrocentricity paradigm, and use "circles of discussion" that highlight the centrality of African ideals and values as a valid frame of reference for examining data and expanding upon the story of Queen Makeda and King Solomon (Asante 6). I see her quest for wisdom as a tool which will assist in deconstructing linear philosophical interpretations of knowledge where King Solomon is perceived as holding all wisdom and Makeda, the Queen of Sheba, is perceived as the recipient of all wisdom.

> Through wisdom I have dived down into the great sea, and have seized in the place of her depths a pearl whereby I am rich [Busby 16].

I first encountered the words attributed to Makeda, Queen of Sheba, while reading Margaret Busby's *Daughters of Africa* (16). As I was reading the compelling passage, I was dazed, but spiritually fulfilled. It was comparable to the first time that I discovered that Africa was not a jungle, but a land of great kingdoms to which Europeans came for a first class university education. Or when I discovered that the Africans in America were not passive, enslaved people who waited for the Emancipation Proclamation to free them, but that many were freedom fighters. Previously, in the story of Solomon and Sheba, I had been taught that Makeda, *Queen of Sheba*, was basically an appendage to King Solomon. Certainly, according to tradition, he possessed great wisdom; she, however, had the wisdom to pursue more knowledge.

> I went down like the great iron anchor for the night on the high seas, and I received a lamp, which lighteth me, and I came up by the ropes of the boat of understanding [Busby 16].

Who was Makeda, Queen of Sheba, and the archetype for this knowledge paradigm? Clearly, she has captured the public imagination for millennia. In addition to being included in religious texts, there are many popular books, such as Jacki Lyden's *Daughter of the Queen of Sheba: A Memoir* which was on the New York Times best seller list for many months, devoted to her. We also have European classical composer Handel's opera, *The Arrival of Queen of Sheba*, and numerous pieces of artwork. What we do know for certain is muddled in a web of religion, national history, archeology, and public fascination.

From where did she come? The exact geographical origin of Makeda, Queen of Sheba, has been the subject of many debates. James B. Pritchard's *Solomon and Sheba* explored her Southern Arabian roots. The sacred text of Ethiopian Orthodox Church, the *Kebra Nagast*, or the *Book of the Glory of the Kings* (of Ethiopia) placed her solidly in Ethiopia. Zachariah Cherian Mampilly wrote a compelling story in *The Queen of Sheba's Nigerian Roots*. The Jewish historian Josephus referred to her as the queen of Ethiopia and Egypt (179–181).

The evidence that she was from Southern Arabia is compelling, because it was and still is the primary place where frankincense and myrrh trees grow. Nevertheless, the historical division between Southern Arabia and Ethiopia is not tidy. I can state with certainty that her spiritual home is Ethiopia. It is where her spirit is most honored, and where the traditions that she is believed to have initiated are still venerated. I will not argue her place of origin.

Makeda, Queen of Sheba, was financially rich and politically powerful. The religious texts assert that she ruled a country that was a principal source of the precious commodities frankincense and myrrh1. In ancient times, frankincense and myrrh were used for sacred rituals and for medicinal purposes. They were also used to fight poisons, pain, female problems, and malaria, among other things (Beek 45–47).

It is also not the purpose of this paper to speculate on the accuracy of the historical data about Makeda, Queen of Sheba, and her relationship with King Solomon. There are several versions. The *King James Bible* focuses their relationship on a meeting of the minds and exchanging of gifts. The *Kebra Nagast*, or *The Book of the Glory of the Kings* (of Ethiopia), chronicles that it went much further and resulted in the birth of a child, Menelik. The Kebra Nagast also explains how they came to possess the Ark of the Convenant (Chapters 32, 33). This paper will limit itself to conjecturing on the spiritual expression of their relationship and how it can be used as a model for knowledge.

It is not critical to my analysis to determine which account is true. It is, however, essential to my analysis that the narratives of the Bible and the *Kebra Nagast* do represent the truth for many people, such as the Ethiopians, Orthodox Christians, and the Rastafarians. (Just as it is not essential to a spiritual analysis of what is commonly called Jesus "Sermon on the Mount," whether it took place on a mountain as is stated in Matthew 5:1, or on a level plain as is stated in Luke 6:17 [*African Heritage Bible* 1383] The Beatitudes, which is the basis of the Sermon, represent the truth to many people and can be analyzed for sacred meaning.)

> I went to sleep in the depths of the sea, and not being overwhelmed with the water I dreamed a dream. And it seemed to me that there was a star in my womb, and I marveled thereat, and I laid hold upon it and made it strong in the splendour of the sun... [Busby 16].

According to the *Kebra Nagast*, Queen Makeda sent Tamrin, her trusted advisor and head of her camel caravans, to make arrangements with King Solomon of Israel to secure trade routes (Chapters 22, 23). When Tamrin returned he told her that the routes were secured. He also told her of Solomon's wealth and power.

After much thought, Makeda decided to make the long and arduous trip to Israel "to prove him with hard questions" (*Kebra Nagast* Chapter 24; *African Heritage Study Bible* 1 Kings 10:1; 2 Chronicles 9:1). King Solomon was famous for offering his wisdom through proverbs and parables. The "hard questions" with which Makeda wanted to "prove him" referred to uncovering the meaning of his parables and proverbs. The *African Heritage Study Bible* informs us that "a proverb is a short, memorable saying that expresses a truth or gives us a warning, such as the Book of Proverbs written by Solomon." (454) Traditionally, among people of African descent, proverbs have been a method through which wisdom are passed on. For example, the *Akan* and the *Ashanti* are well known for expressing their religious beliefs through proverbs (*African Heritage Bible* 454). Therefore, Queen Makeda was following well-established African cultural tradition. It is my belief that she wanted to gain more insight and sharpen her leadership skills.

She relied on the wisdom of a higher, more holistic, intuitive inner self. Her spiritual transformation became the dominant force in the changing of the ancient Ethiopian culture. Moreover, she not only came closer to African spiritual holism — she also found love.

King Solomon

King Solomon was the king of Israel. He was building a temple to house the Ark of the Covenant, and had sent out a request for almug wood (*African Heritage Bible* 2 Chronicles 2:8–9). These were red sandalwood trees, which had a beautiful garnet color.

He was well known because he had brought peace, prosperity, and abundant wealth to Israel.

Tamrin

Tamrin was a trusted advisor and the head of the Queen of Sheba's camel caravan (*Kebra Nagast* Chapter 23). She sent him to make arrangements with King Solomon and other leaders to secure trade routes and barter frankincense, myrrh, and almug trees. When he returned he told her that indeed the routes were secured. He also told her stories of King Solomon's wealth and power and that King Solomon was a learned man who spoke with authority, but still gave kind and compassionate answers to his subjects. Tamrin told her story after story about King Solomon's wisdom (*Kebra Nagast* Chapter 24).

Shebanization of Knowledge and the Search for Wisdom

> I went in through the doors of the treasury of wisdom and I drew for myself the waters of understanding (Busby 16).

Makeda, Queen of Sheba, asked Tamrin countless questions about Solomon. She decided that she wanted to meet him herself. She made the long and arduous camel trip because she was in search of a deeper level of wisdom. This search is as old as humankind, and is certainly as old as ancient Egypt. "Know thyself.... Quest for wisdom and truth occupied the lives of elders but it was also a quest actively pursued by initiates [of priesthood] who knew it as the pathway to establish proper order. Life was meaningless without this order." (Asante 81).

Webster's dictionary informs us that wisdom is "[t]he quality of knowing what is true and right coupled with just judgment as to action; discernment, insight.... The power of judging rightly and following the soundest course of action, good judgment discretion." (2181). Makeda, Queen of Sheba, traveled to King Solomon based on specific data that she had received and her intuition, which told her that she had more to learn.

Giving

The Biblical narrative says she also functioned on the spiritual principle of reciprocity and giving. According to the Biblical scripture, Queen Makeda gave King Solomon 120 talents of gold. A talent equals 131 pounds Thus she gave him 15,720 pounds of gold. This was in addition to giving him almug trees in exchange for wisdom (*African Heritage Bible*). Whether this is mathematically accurate is not pertinent. What is pertinent is the obvious value of the wisdom sought. The intangible was a very precious commodity.

Menelik

According to the *Kebra Nagast*, Menelik was a son who was born of the relationship between Makeda and King Solomon (Chapters 32, 33). As he grew older, he continually asked questions about his father. Queen Makeda told him all about Solomon, and eventually he visited his father. It was a spiritually rewarding and loving visit for both of them. When Menelik left to return home, King Solomon assigned several priests to return to Sheba with him. These priests conspired to take the Ark of the Covenant, in which the Ten Commandments were believed to be housed.

Without Menelik's knowledge, they took the Ark and escaped before King Solomon realized it was missing. They brought it to Ethiopia and set it up in holy and highly guarded quarters. The Ethiopian people developed rituals and sacred texts around it. This is considered the establishment of the Ethiopian Orthodox Church. Menelik was made king. There is no more information about Makeda, Queen of Sheba, after Menelik became king. It is, however, believed that their descendants ruled Ethiopia (up to Haile Selassie, Ras Tafari).

The Ark of the Covenant

> I went into the blaze of the flame of the sun, and it lighted me with the splendour thereof, and I made of it a shield for myself, and I saved myself by confidence therein, and not myself only but all those who travel in the footprints of wisdom [Busby 16].

The Ark of the Covenant is central to the Ethiopian version of the story of Queen Makeda and King Solomon. Arks are very ancient spiritual commodities that have been part of African culture since ancient Egypt. For example, during the 25th Dynasty Kushite Kemetic Pharaoh Piankhi worshipped at the Ark of Ra before he went into battle (Budge xxi; Monges 119).

To the people of Ethiopia, the Ark of the Covenant not only housed the Ten Commandments, which were written by God, it represented the energy of God. In their sacred text, the *Kebra Nagast*, it is written that it was given to them because, unlike the Israelites, they were true to God's words. They were righteous enough to be entrusted with God's power. When they received the Ark of the Covenant, which they also refer to as Zion:

> Zion shone like the sun, and the majesty thereof they were dismayed. And they arrayed Zion in her apparel, and they bore the gifts to her, and they set her upon a wagon, and they spread out purple beneath her, and they draped her with draperies of purple, and they sang songs before her and behind her. [Kebra Nagast Chapter 55].

To the Ethiopians, like the ancient Jewish people, the energy that emitted from the Ark was strong enough to destroy idols and humans and to redirect the road of the people of Ethiopia. The search for wisdom began by Makeda, Queen of Sheba, lead to much more than her getting answers to a few hard questions. It led to the Ethiopians' possession of the Ark of the Covenant.

Yin and Yang, Energy and African Wholism

The words of artist and activist Paul Robeson can lead us into another way of viewing the relationship of Queen Makeda and King Solomon. Paul

Robeson believed it was useful for African Americans to study Eastern philosophy. He asserted that "Negro students who wrestle vainly with Plato would find a spiritual father in Confucius or Lao-tze...." (Stuckey 26). The reward would be that African Americans would come closer to African holistic thinking. Historian Sterling Stuckey summarizes that "Robeson had systematized his thinking on the need for creative equilibrium between the spiritual and the material, between a life of *intuition and feeling* and one of *logical analysis*. In a word, he called for a synthesis of the cultures of East and West" (Stuckey 33). Using the guidance of Robeson, I have applied the principles of yin and yang to the relationship of Queen Makeda and King Solomon. I envision that their relationship was like a mandala of yin and yang energy. Eastern Taiji master, Chungliang Al Huang, explains yin and yang in this manner:

> The yin/yang symbol is the interlocking, melting together of the flow of movement within a circle. The similar — and at the same time obviously contrasting — energies are moving together. Within the black area there is a white dot and within the white fish shape, there is a black dot. The whole idea of a circle divided this way is to show that with a unity there is duality and polarity and contrast. The only way to find real balance without losing the centering feeling of the circle is to think of the contrasting energies moving together and in union, in harmony, interlocking.... It's a kind of consummation between two forces, male and female, mind, and body, good and bad [Huang 12].

The ultimate goal is to reach a balanced state. Huang further enlightens us about the limitations of Western culture: "where the tendency is to identify with one force and to reject the contrasting element. If you identify with only one side of the duality, then you become unbalanced" (12).

Yin as the earthy, feminine, dark, passive, and absorbing force epitomizes the characteristics of the energy of Makeda, Queen of Sheba. Her goal was to absorb the wisdom of King Solomon. She was warm, receptive, expansive, and open to receiving knowledge. Yang as the masculine complementary principle of heaven, light, active, and penetrating force represented King Solomon's energy. His role was to provide light and to penetrate the mind of Makeda, Queen of Sheba. King Solomon's masculine yang energy was focused and potent.

In the Eurocentric worldview, these forces are antithetical, but in the Eastern and African worldviews they are complementary. They are distinct characteristics of a fundamentally harmonious universe. In spite of the Eurocentric historical emphasis on the masculine yang energy of King Solomon, both were equally important.

The complementary characteristics need each other and each carries the seed of the other. Yin and yang flow and dance together like the moon and the stars.

Shebanization of Knowledge and Energy

> [Wisdom] maketh the ears to hear and hearts to understand, it is teacher of those who are learned, and it is a consoler of those who are discreet and prudent.... [*Kebra Nagast* Chapter 24]

One of the domino effects of the Queen of Sheba's visit to prove King Solomon "with hard questions" (1 King 10:1; 2 Chronicles 9:1) was that their energy was fused together and consequently more energy was formed. This new energy was evident in the creation of new religions—the Ethiopian Orthodox Church and Rastafarianism, and, in the infusion of new energy into established religions—Christianity, Islam, and Judaism.

The science of quantum physics can help us explore the depths of their relationship further. In the world of quantum physics, "[t]he dance of subatomic particles never ends and it is never the same" (Zudav 212). The Shebanization of Knowledge is like a dance of subatomic particles. The more we excavate information about the ancient past of African people, the more there is to know. The more we destroy old misconceptions, the more energy we have to create new paradigms. Author Gary Zudav, who wrote about quantum physics and spirituality, further informs us on the invisible:

> Subatomic particles forever partake of this unceasing dance of annihilation and creation. In fact, the subatomic particles are the unceasing dance of annihilation and creation. This twentieth century discovery with all its psychedelic implications, is not a new concept. In fact, it is very similar to the way that much of the world's population, including the Hindus and the Buddhists, view their reality [Zudav 217].

Zudav, perhaps due to a lack of knowledge, does not specifically include traditional Africans in this picture of the world's population. There are, however, numerous examples of Africans viewing reality from similar lenses of annihilation and creation.

The Ethiopians rejoiced when they received the Ark of the Covenant. They also experienced the annihilation of their old belief system as they witnessed the creation of the new system.

> And their idols, which they had made with their hands and which were in the forms of men, and dogs, and cats, fell down, and high towers ... fell down also and were broken in pieces. For Zion shone like the sun, and at the majesty thereof they were dismayed [Kebra Nagast Chap. 55].

The Dogon are a thought-provoking African ethnic group. They are from the territory at the border between Mali and Upper Volta. With no more aid than the naked eye, they amassed a very ancient knowledge system which included knowledge of the existence of the two companions of the star Sirius. This phenomenon has been generally explained away by attributing Dogon astronomical knowledge to outside, recent sources (Pale Fox 14). However, French anthropologist Germaine Dieterlen supplied evidence that the Dogon have known about and formed rituals around the two companions of Sirius since at least the thirteenth century (Pale Fox 14).

More pertinent to this analysis is that the Dogon also provide us with a distinct example of the dance of the creation and annihilation of spiritual energy. This passage also provides us with evidence that their perception of energy was similar to that of Albert Einstein; that is to say, it has a wave-particle duality. Let us further examine their view of reality.

According to their belief system:

> The present world is conceived as having come out of a first seed formed by God.... It contains the essence of creation, including the four basic "elements" (air, earth, water, and fire) and the "word" creator, that is to say, life manifesting itself within, in the form of eight segments, animated by a motion that is both vibratory and spiraling." [Griaule and Dieterlen 63].

The Dogon philosophy further explores the energy dance:

> [T]he plant dies and is reborn the following year from the seed it has formed. In like manner, man-even already in the fetal state where he is fish-like — will be animated by spiritual principles of the same essence. This explains the identical structure of the fish egg and the grain. Man is *consubstantial* with the grain, the symbol of which he bears in his clavicles (emphasis supplied) [Griaule and Dieterlen 63].

The issue of man or humans being consubstantial with the grains equates energy and matter. Afrocentric psychologist Wade Nobles adds further insight to the concept that matter is energy and energy is the spirit of the Divine. In *Kemet and the African World View,* he affirms

> To the Ancients, all the elements of the universe were "consubstantial" that is to say that nature of all things was of the same spirit or Ka. The

> Divine willed first itself to be and then manifested itself as complimentary male-female gods who in having the attributes (the Ka) of the Divine manifested themselves as man and women. Hence, all things are endowed with the spirit of God (i.e., the Ka of God) [Nobles 107].

Nobles further explains that the ancient Egyptians used mythology as a scientific textbook. They explained creation in accounts of physical and spiritual generation — one of masturbation and one of spitting (Nobles 107). The underlying law being revealed here is (1) that Being, as represented by the creation story, is simultaneously "spiritual" and "physical" and (2) that the reality (creation) is the consequence of both the idea (conception) and the act (masturbation). Human reality results, therefore, from both thinking and doing (Nobles 107).

Shebanization of Knowledge

The Afrocentric epistemology validates knowledge though a combination of historical understanding and intuition. Afrocentric scholar Norman Harris states that what is known, what can be proven, is demonstrated through the harmonization of the individual consciousness with the best traditions in the African past. Again, by way of contrast, the Eurocentric epistemology validates knowledge though a combination of objectivity and "scientific method," wherein it is assumed that similar results obtained through similar conditions is an indication of reality (Harris 156).

Moreover, there is an assumption of the superiority of the scientific method. Harris enlightens us on the error of this assumption by referring to Carl Jung's comments that

> scientific materialism has merely introduced a new hypostasis that is an intellectual sin. It has given another name to the supreme principle of reality and has assumed that this created a new thing and destroyed an old thing. Whether you call the principle of existence "God," matter, energy, or anything else you like, you have created nothing; you have simply changed a symbol [Harris 156].

I agree with Harris that what they have succeeded in doing is to create disharmony.

Shebanization of Knowledge and Womanism

> I saved myself by confidence therein, and not myself only but all those who travel in the footprints of wisdom (Busby)

I have used the accounts of Queen Makeda and King Solomon to begin to explore a different knowledge paradigm. The new physics, quantum mechanics, tells us clearly that it is not possible to observe reality without changing it (Zudav 30). I seek to help change the perspective on Makeda, Queen of Sheba. This will add more energy to the complex mandala that surrounds the relationship of Queen Makeda and King Solomon. The Shebanization principle of knowledge states that intuitive and feminine energy is as essential as the rational and masculine energy. I will not end, but I will stop this exploration with words of wisdom from Katie Canon:

> As an interpretive principle, the Black Womanist tradition provides the incentive to chip away at oppressive structures, bit by bit. It identifies those texts that help Black womanists to celebrate and rename the innumerable incidents of unpredictability in empowering ways [Canon 56].
> "For you shall go out in joy, and be led back in peace" [Isaiah 55:12].

Notes

1. This is commonly stated in the Bible, *Kebra Nagast*, and *Koran*.
2. They do not focus on Queen Makeda but her son as the ancestor of H.R.H. Haile Selassie.
3. I use the term "Sheba" in as much as it is commonly used as the country of origin of Makeda.
4. Kushite Kings ruled the 25th Dynasty of Kemet

References

Asante, Molefi. *Kemet, Afrocentricity, and Knowledge*. Trenton: Africa Word Press, 1990.

Beek, Gus W. "The Land of Sheba." *Solomon and Sheba*. Ed. James Pritchard. New York: Praeger, 1974. 40–63.

Bennett, Lerone. *Before The Mayflower: A History of Black America*. New York: Penguin Books, 1993.

Budge, E.A. Wallis. *The Queen of Sheba and Her Only Son Menyelek aka The Kebra Nagast* London: Oxford University Press, 1932.

Canon, Katie. *Katie's Canon: Womanism and the Soul of the Black Community*. New York: Continuum Publishing Co., 1995.

Griaule, Marcel and Germaine Dieterlen. *The Pale Fox*. Trans. Stephan C. Infantino, Ph.D. New York: Continuum Publishing Co., 1986.

Harris, Norman. "Afrocentrism: Concept and Method: A Philosophical Basis for an Afrocentric Orientation," *The Western Journal of Black Studies*, Vol. 16, No. 3 (1992): 154–159.

Huang, Chungliang A. *Embrace Tiger, Return to Mountain: The Essence of Taiji.* Berkeley: Celestial Arts, 1997.
Josephus. *The Complete Works of Josephus.* Trans. Wm. Whiston. Scotland and Philadelphia: Nimmo and Porter and Cates, 1981. 179–181.
Lyden, Jacki. *Daughter of the Queen of Sheba: A Memoir* New York: Penguin, 1998.
Mampilly, Zachariah C. *The Queen of Sheba's Nigerian Roots* Africana.com. 19 January 2000 <http:www.africana.com/index_20000119.htm>
Monges, Miriam Kush. *The Jewel of Nubia: Reconnecting the Root System of African Civilization.* New Jersey: African World Press, 1997.
Nobles, Wade. "Ancient Egyptian thought and the Renaissance of African (Black) Psychology." *Kemet and the African Worldview: Research, Rescue and Restoration* eds. Karenga and Carruthers. Los Angeles: University of Sankore Press, 1986. 100–118.
"On the Wisdom of Solomon." *Daughter's of Africa: An International Anthology of Words and Writings by Women of African Descent from the Ancient Egyptian to the Present.* Ed. Margaret Busby. New York: Ballantine Books, 1992. 15–16.
Pritchard, James Ed. *Solomon and Sheba* New York: Praeger, 1974.
Stuckey, Sterling. "The Cultural Philosophy of Paul Robeson." *African American Sociology: A Social Study of the Pan-African Diaspora*, ed. Conyers and Barnett. Chicago: Nelson-Hall Publishers, 1998, p. 23–36.
The Original African Heritage Study Bible. Gen. ed. the Reverend Cain Hope Felder, Ph.D. Washington, D.C., Winston: 1993.
"Wisdom." *Webster's New Universal Unabridged Dictionary.* 2nd ed. New York: Random House, 1996.
Zudav, Gary. *The Dancing Wu Li Masters: An Overview of the New Physics.* New York: Bantam Books. 1980

Why Write "Black"? Reclaiming African Culture Resource Knowledges in Diasporic Contexts

George J. Sefa Dei

In this paper, I discuss knowledge production as a decolonizing exercise. I affirm the importance of local cultural resource knowledges as relevant to challenging hegemonic knowledge forms. It is argued that to question Eurocentric knowledge as the only valid way of knowing, the learner must be equipped with the appropriate intellectual and political tools. Specifically, I interrogate Afrocentric knowledge as reclaiming the notions of "community" and "multiple selves and identities" in order to provide the African learner with a critical lens to undo any form of intellectual enslavement or the subversion of the human mind. In conclusion I point to the implications of my discussion for transformative educational practice in Euro-Canadian/American contexts.

Introduction

One would think that producing knowledge for decolonization purposes is easy. After all, this is, I would submit, what the academy (schools, colleges and universities) ought to do. Unfortunately, even in the academy the anti-racist, -feminist, -colonial pedagogue must work within the confines and structures of the very systems one opposes. Language remains, nonetheless, an important tool for decolonizing minds. Critical language is helpful in destabilizing taken-for-granted assumptions about society. Critical language is valuable for decolonizing imperial knowledge.

I set out to write this paper from notes previously made for an address to a local gathering of social activists, educators, parents and students. It was a gathering of peoples who espouse the idea of reclaiming their Africaness in Diasporic contexts. As I penned my thoughts, I was confronted with a question: Who is going to be the audience for my "academic paper"? Unable to resolve the questions, challenges, ambiguities, tensions and contradictions summoned by such a question, I satisfied myself that I would let each of my readers decide how they found themselves implicated in the discussion. But this was not the end. I also found myself asking, What is the goal and purpose in using critical writing to challenge the ideological and material assumptions behind conventional educational practice? I thought about what a student in my graduate course, "The Principles of Anti-Racism," said a few days before: "The discourse of race must include White Euro-Americans. It cannot simply be minorities who are writing, teaching and speaking race." When I tried to point out that many White scholars have been doing so for a very long time, I appeared to have hit a brick wall. This was not apparent to the student since if one looks at the academy, one finds only minorities teaching subjects about race and difference. Then another student shot back, "But who should be singing our song for us?" This intervention only confused and muddled the discussion further.

This paper takes the position that all knowledge is raced, classed, gendered and sexualized, and is produced in particular contexts to satisfy specific interests (see also Banks, 1993). In broaching the subject matter of knowledge production, I speak from an African identity. I use the multiple identities of being "African" to recapture the cultural resource knowledges of local peoples and thereby advance the decolonization project in the academy. An African identity is based on who one is and what makes the self whole. It is not based on exclusion (see Roediger, 1993, on "White identity"). The study of African identity is the study of the historical, cultural and political construction of that identity (see Giroux, 1997, and Harris, 1993, on "Whiteness"). The prevailing discourse of African cultural deficiency and intellectual inferiority needs to be continually ruptured. Minoritized bodies in our academies need to challenge the sense of entitlement members of the dominant group have, the sense that society is simply "theirs."

Textual representation of colonial and imperial discourses emanating from minoritized communities attests to the existence of competing and alternative claims to knowledge about space, society and the construction of the nation. Today, we are having to deal with the paradox of liberalism where all is difference but, at the same time, difference is irrelevant.

This paper theorizes insurgent responses to racialized and gendered discourses of valid knowledge, and addresses how local peoples negotiate their identities and politics across several historical domains to contest and (re)create knowledge. Colonialist discourse and discursive practices continue to construct and shape global politics of knowledge production about difference. There are historical implications (legal, social, political and economic) of the colonial and imperial state in establishing racial, class, gender and sexual ideological stereotypes of minoritized groups in society. Racially minoritized communities, in particular, are caught between the dominant White construction of the nation and the Diasporic challenge to such monolithic and homogenous conceptions. Radical or transformative scholarship situates and locates individual and collective identities and subjectivities in understanding current political practice. Agency and resistance can be understood within the trope of difference. Differences among cultures and local communities inform political resistance and the rupturing of established histories and texts. In the context of narrated histories, there are powerful lessons of resistance that can and do inform current progressive politics for social and educational change across geographical space and discursive boundaries. In order to affirm difference, it is evoked in pluralistic contexts.

Knowledge, Difference and the Institutionalization of Dominance

While conventional academic paradigms constrain us from being subversive and from challenging dominant knowledge, the space of marginality does allow for resistance and subversion. It also allows for a learning of resistance and empowerment. Thought regulates and structures action, that is, the nature and directionality of action. The institutionalization of thought is the project of education (Itwaru, 1999). In order to rupture the "institutionalization of thought," we must see education as more than teaching someone to think. We must question what passes as thought and recognizes that thought itself is socially produced, maintained and sustained.

Itwaru (1999) enthuses that it is through the institutionalization of thought that knowledge maintains domination. To be creative is not to imitate stable knowledge. To be creative is to challenge conventional thought. A decolonized mind guards against imitative intellectualism. It sees creativity as emerging in the challenge to existing hegemonic ideas. For example, Afrocentric discourse (Asante, 1987, 1988, 1991) as oppositional knowledge seeks to break the prison house of Eurocentric perception. Afrocentric knowledge ruptures the fetishization and complacency of Western thought. It challenges the Hegelian dialectic that constructs the "other" as a threat to be neutralized, destroyed and negated. As many have observed, it is this same dialectic which evidences a need for the existence of the 'other' in order to affirm the 'self' (Hall, 1979; 1991). Given its self-referential nature, Eurocentric discourse judges others, but not the self. It is an academic project that judges the other through the lens of the self. In calling this "Euro-egocentrism," Itwaru (1999) gestures to the problem of self-concealment and self-congratulation that leaves unproblematized the view that one's reality is the only reality worth talking about (see also Hunter, 1983). Within Eurocentric thought, reality is defined as singular and fixed. This definition of reality is imposed on others. A non–Eurocentric worldview that sees multiple realities, realities which are not fixed or frozen in time and space, is oppositional to conventional reason.

Itwaru (1999) clearly argues that an imperial order sees the colonized as the inferior other. The "other" is devoid of person and personhood, and is disconnected from indigenous identity, ancestry and history. Insecure of its own existence, the imperial order must continually move to destroy and devalue critical thought and action. In other words, the imposed order anticipates resistance and takes action to destroy it. Hegemonic education has been instrumental in maintaining the imperial order. Hegemonic education marginalizes certain voices and co-opts existing structures and relations of power to establish domination. Hegemonic education thrives on the existence of relations of dependency. In the academy, for example, relations of dependency allow some African and minority scholars to be less Afrocentric than even non–African and dominant scholars. More importantly, the project to sustain hegemonic education is concomitant with the denigration of alternative knowledge systems to Eurocentric worldviews. Critical oppositional knowledge is devalued by denying it an authentic voice, the indigenous self-identity that, in actuality, creates and produces such critical knowledge. Consequently, the authority of the indigenous self is questioned. And, the claim to "indigenous" as referring to those whose authority resides in origin, place, history and ancestry is refuted. Through the use of critical discourse as resistance, the "indigenous" can and must be reclaimed and redefined within a conceptual frame that ascribes it authority.

In pluralistic contexts, difference is presented for material consumption. Sameness is glorified, while difference is left uncelebrated. Yet, the irony is that this sameness is revoked when the other is constructed as different in order to affirm the self. To talk about difference is to affirm our multiple selves and different identities. Today, there is a never-ending struggle to represent oneself. Identity cannot be taken for granted — it is struggled for and acclaimed. In examining how the self and the subject are understood for personal politics, we must be critical of discursive approaches that end up over-subjectivizing, individualizing and privileging certain subject voices and narrative. Embedded in this approach is a celebration of identity and difference that may limit our understanding and pursuit of a collective politics for change.

Afrocentric Knowledge: The Interrogation of Its Relevance

To challenge Eurocentric knowledge as the only valid way of knowing the learner must have with the appropriate intellectual tools. Afrocentric politics insists that even if the seeds of Eurocentric knowledge have been sowed, the critical learner cannot allow it to germinate. The learner must employ critical education to undo any form of intellectual enslavement and or the subversion of the human mind. Asante (1987, 1988, 1991) and others conceptualize Afrocentric knowledge as a paradigm shift in the sense of its being an alternative, non-hegemonic way of knowing and reading the world informed by African peoples' histories and experiences. Afrocentricity is about the investigation of phenomenon from a perspective grounded in African-centered values, epistemological constructs and philosophies. The Afrocentric discursive approach is to center one's analyses and perceptions from the view of the African subject (Asante, 1991). The process of dehistoricizing the rich contributions of African peoples, rather than understanding Africa on its own terms, has contributed to inferiorizing Africa. Africa continues to be misread by dominant academic discourses. Dehistoricization is a part of the colonialist and imperialist project on Africa. As African peoples, we need to speak about our achievements and successes in history. Afrocentric knowledge reminds us of the impossibility of forgetting the African past, history and culture. Of course, we cannot allow such accomplishments to sidestep a critique of failures and disasters. Afrocentric learning seeks to challenge this approach.

An important site for resisting imperial knowledge is the use of local cultural knowledges as discursive frames of reference. Today, many local peoples are having to confront the powerful political force of Euro-American hegemony in the promotion of global knowledge. Local and indigenous communities are having to use their own creativity and resourcefulness to deal with the challenges of an exploitative transnational economy. By "indigenous," I mean long-term occupancy of a place (Fals Borda, 1980; Fals Borda and Rahman, 1991) and the knowledge that comes with such occupation. Indigenous knowledge encapsulates the commonsense ideas and cultural knowledges of local peoples concerning the everyday realities of living. This knowledge refers to the mental constructs and thought processes, as well as the norms, values, ideas and beliefs of local peoples which help to guide social living (Dei, 1999a). Through the application of such knowledge, local peoples are engaged in the process of decolonizing minds and social action. Thus, the process and politics of decolonization are informed by the need to affirm and reclaim local indigenousness.

Afrocentric discourse is a dialectical reading of the world that borrows from other knowledges, including knowledges which are framed in the Eurocentric tradition. Like other knowledge systems, Afrocentricity shares some ideas about nature-society-culture interrelationships. Scheurich and Young (1997) highlight the ontological, epistermological and axiological positions that may characterize different knowledge systems. The ontological position speaks to the primary assumptions people have and or make about the nature of reality. In African systems of thought, the ontological viewpoint stresses that to understand reality is to have a complete or holistic view of society. This view stresses the need for a harmonious coexistence among nature, culture and society. There is the idea of mutual interdependence among all peoples such that the existence of the individual and or subject is only meaningful in relation to the community one is a part of. On the other hand, the epistemological position argues that there are different ways of knowing reality. Thus, in African systems of thought, knowledge is seen as cumulative and as emerging from experiences of the social world. Practice and experience are seen as the contextual basis of knowledge. Knowledge is for survival, and the two go hand-in-hand. While membership in community gives rights, there are important matching responsibilities. The axiological position maintains that there are "disputational contours of right and wrong or morality and values ... [that are] ... presumptions about the real, the true and the good" (Scheurich and Young, 1997: 6). In African systems of thought, therefore, cultural, spiritual and ideational beliefs, values and practices are evaluated within the history and contexts of communities as societies striving to set their own moral tone. While these ideas may be shared by other indigenous peoples, it is the privileging of certain core social values for reward (e.g., responsibilities over rights; community over individual; peaceful co-existence with nature over control or domination of nature) that sets different knowledge systems apart.

In this context, exercising intellectual agency means engaging in a process of recuperation, revitalization and reclamation of African indigenous knowledge as a necessary exercise in empowerment. We cannot underestimate the power of ideas or the role of social forces in generating relevant knowledge for collective resuscitation, spiritual rebirth and cultural renewal. Thus, a discursive project affirming the past cannot be interpreted unproblematically as a call to retrogress to a previous state of primitivity. It should be read as a political agenda to interrogate the African past, culture, tradition and history in order to learn from the sources of empowerment and disempowerment as African peoples search for ways towards the future.

Local peoples everywhere are speaking out about knowledge as a crucial part of the decolonization process. Knowledge is useful in helping to disabuse minds of the lies and falsehoods that have been told about their lives. Knowledge can be used to find authentic and viable solutions to a people's problems. For Africans, this means challenging the insulting idea that others know and understand them better than they know and understand themselves (see Prah, 1997).

Long ago, Franz Fanon (1963) pointed out that decolonization can only be understood as a historical process that ultimately culminates in changing the social order. To decolonize human minds is to call into question the whole colonial situation and its aftermath, and the continued devaluation of the knowledges of subordinate groups. Knowledge is transformative in local cultural contexts if it subverts and helps people break with the ways by and through which dominant ideologies have defined and shaped the local human condition. Transformative knowledge must provide an endogenous understanding, informed by experience and practice, of the local social reality.

All knowledges can be contested in terms of boundaries and spaces, yet it cannot be denied that all local peoples have intellectual agency. Such agency is useful in confronting and dealing with the historic inferiorization of local experience and the devaluation of the rich histories and cultures of marginalized groups. In searching for social understanding and solutions, minoritized groups are utilizing knowledges that integrate the body, mind and soul. They are posing new questions that denote an acknowledgement of their own power and agency. For example, rather than ask, How come? or Why is it that? we cannot have an inclusive curriculum for our children in schools? We begin to pose the new question, How are we going to have inclusive curriculum for the children? This question means taking control of our own affairs. It means devising the means to stem the path of "miseducation." A sense of power is located within all knowledges. As Foucault (1977) long ago observed, "power and knowledge directly imply one another ... there is no power relation without the correlative constitution of a field of knowledge, nor any knowledge that does not presuppose and constitute at the same time power relations" (p.175) (see also Foucault, 1980, 1983). A discursive analysis of power helps to explain how identities are produced, refracted and reiterated through everyday political practice. Power is necessary to survive, critique and create the new dream and the shared vision. Power is relevant to challenging the materiality of social existence and domination.

In the Canadian context, specific incidents and experiences poignantly demonstrate how powerful societal structures, representations and images construct social meanings about African peoples. Knowledge and power can exclude, malign and establish advantage, as well as help in resisting marginality. The bombings of the United States embassies in Kenya and Tanzania last year, and the story of these bombings as told by the Western media are a case in point. While we share the human loss and the devastation, we must also question how such stories are presented to us for consumption. In my reading, it was obvious that some lives were considered more precious than others. The question is, Why? Similarly, early in 1998, a police officer was murdered in Toronto. It took some time before the suspects were apprehended, and, for many Black and African peoples in Toronto, it was an agonizing wait. We live in a society where images of Black people committing crimes are erroneously conveyed in the coverage of social events by a particular Toronto newspaper. The anxiety African peoples felt over the murder can be captured in the community's "holding of [its] collective breadth." We all sighed with relief when the suspects were later identified as non–Black. The question is, Why do we find it necessary to shoulder collective guilt for an individual action?

These incidents confirm that an interrogation of the past experience of African peoples in North America is a necessary component of the process of decolonization. Every history must teach something, otherwise it is not a history worth talking about. The history of African peoples in North America is one of survival and resistance in the face of huge odds. We can read about such resistance in the social actions and practices of local groups (and their allies) in contesting hegemonic social formations and knowledges, as well as unraveling and dislodging the strategies of domination (Haynes and Prakash, 1991: 3).

The African presence in Canada dates back to 1604. Like every other group, African peoples have contributed immensely to building the Canadian nation. Our forbearers collectively organized to address educational, employment, legal and immigration issues. There have always been traditional problem-solvers within African communities—community leaders, church leaders, parents' groups and associations and so on. These leaders have led the way in providing education for youth in homes, churches and community sites. Many African peoples have drawn on the inspiration and foresight of our foremothers and forefathers. In fact, there is a saying that if any African stands tall today, it is because he stands on the backs of his ancestors. This is why it is said that no African worth his salt can claim to have paid his dues. If one insists that he has, the question asked is, How much was paid and to whom?

I provide this short historical narrative in order to contextualize certain questions for us as African peoples. For example, what have we learned from our past and its rich histories? How do we build on such histories and ensure our collective survival? What new leadership and communitarian strategies are required? How do we utilize our African identities and spiritual sense of collective self to develop and offer solutions to the many problems that currently afflict our communities? How are we claiming collective responsibility for our own well-being? To address these questions, we must rethink and reaffirm our understanding of community.

Affirming "Community"

It is fashionable today in critical scholarship to offer a lucid critique of the essentialist discourses that cultivate and promote community, emphasizing its homogenizing tendencies. Yet what is left uncritiqued is the fact that dominant groups also engage in essentializing although it is masked by the perception of race neutrality and dominate groups hold on power. Critical academic engagement requires that we start talking about how difference both fractures and enhances the community's political agenda. It is important for academic and political work to avoid presenting communities as static, homogenous entities, particularly when this becomes a starting point for critique. In fact, an anti-colonial reading of the notion of community recognizes its multiple evocations. This approach critiques the dominant view of what community means. A mode of resistance can be evoked in community with a politicized understanding of what it is to offer social critique. Community can be a forum for critical discussion and change. No community has ever been static. In fact, the critique of static traditionalism which is so often leveled against proponents of a communitarian ethic is frequently misguided. Static traditionalism, it can be said, exists only in the minds of its critics. Communities grow, and their issues and interests shift depending on history and context.

A discussion of community raises some pertinent questions. For example, how do we understand the grounds on which some people choose to come together? What are the contexts in which 'community' is evoked? What political choices are being made? Do we distinguish the notion of community from how it is lived and practiced? Is the metaphor relevant (albeit problematic) in devising political strategies? Do we simply dismiss knowledges and understandings that legitimize community? In other words, striving to comprehend why people form communities in the first place and also to acknowledge that communities themselves can be critical and self-reflective are useful exercises. For minoritized populations living in dominant contexts, the Diaspora is a hostile place. This hostility influences the particular options and strategies that are open to and prevail among those who are minoritized. Understanding the nature of the hostility they encounter is crucial in order not to deny the intellectual agency and power of local subjects and the pragmatic political choices they make. While not everyone sees himself as belonging to a community, this fact cannot serve as the basis for denying the existence of community. Those who exercise their intellectual agency to define a community for their actions must have their knowledges affirmed and legitimatized. We must learn about the particular insurgent responses to racial, ethnic, class, gender, cultural and language hostility that necessitate the evoking of community, just as we must unravel the practices that seek to protect privilege, power, property and a sense of entitlement for the dominant.

Colonial knowledge still serves to undermine the ability of local peoples to liberate their lands, resources and energies from alien control. Maintaining local cultural resource knowledges is one way to resist imperial and colonial subordination of the aspirations and dreams of marginalized communities. Within communities, institutionalized structures and processes of government, the economy, religion and education are shaped by cultural values and belief systems. Culture is not conceptually separate from societal and institutional construction and development. All cultures are imbued with elements of tradition and modernity. Indigenous cultures and local peoples have historically had sophisticated, literate forms and technologies and well-advanced spiritual values. The knowledges of marginalized groups represent different points on a continuum, and they evidence the sharing of ideas from multiple sources.

Caution has usually been expressed about constructing a romanticized past during the process of indigenous cultural reclamation and affirmation. Yet this exhortation is part of the insidious attempt by dominant and Eurocentric scholars to control and, at the same time, invalidate the ability of indigenous peoples t redefine their cultural selves. From the anti-colonial perspective, all cultural groups have the authority to define their cultural identities. Certainly, the success of any mission to reclaim cultural knowledge poses a threat to Eurocentric control.

I am asserting that there is nothing meaningless about the term "community." As Price (1998) notes, "'community' can refer to different conceptions of social identity." The term can operate or function as an enabler or a mobilizing force in the fight for social justice and the redistribution of power and material advantage. Rather than abandon the term, we must retheorize community. We must look for new and alternate ways to speak of community that acknowledge and give some sense of history and of the loyalty, commitment and interdependence among peoples. Thus, community must be dealt with critically as denoting "deep movements of allegiance, commitment and identification" (Price, 1998: 4). Nonetheless, there are, even in communities, complex processes through which racial, class, gender and sexual ideologies are produced and sustained. Such ideologies are linked to material conditions to produce particular discursive effects. In social movement politics, community can be a vehicle for perpetuating ideologies of race, class, gender and sexuality.

Given the great complexity of our world today, academic and discursive practices must be sophisticated enough to account for the tensions, contradictions and structural ambiguities that pervade claims for particular identities. To claim community is to engage in a powerful linguistic, cultural and discursive practice. As Price (1998: 3–4) further states, we can speak of community in some multiple, non-exclusive combinations of: 1) "spatial community" in which boundaries are defined for the pursuit of socially meaningful interactions; 2) "affective/relational community" in which community draws on some bonds of affinity — it becomes a mutually-shared experience of the values, attitudes, beliefs, concerns and aspirations of a collective; and 3) "moral community" as defined in meaningful participation and belonging in a citizenry to achieve common goals defined as the collective good. Within these various concept of community, tensions, struggles, ambiguities and contradictions are captured and articulated, and yet the integrity of the collective membership is maintained. As members of community(ies), individuals have multiple, rather than single, affinities and allegiances resulting in profound complexities that challenge easy categorizations and designations. Yet, each community also maintains and reinforces certain processes of inclusion and exclusion in order to ensure that identities and histories are not obliterated.

As community is not an undifferentiated category, so also is the local community faced with competing interests, oppressions and marginalities. Fortunately, it is within communities that local knowledges are nurtured and made relevant for daily human survival. To survive is to co-exist with other peoples. Learning to exist collectively demands a conscious attempt to redress multiple forms of oppression as they play out within and among communities. An important question to ask is How do colonial and imperial relations, social alienation and cultural ideology interface in understanding contemporary human experience? As has already been pointed out, there are multidimensional experiences of identity and resistance to oppression and subordination. The powerful correlations among racial, class, gender and sexual exploitation and oppression demand the adoption of a collective approach to understanding human subjectivities and social resistance. Subjective experiences of human struggles against oppressions are not simply diverse, but also intertwined. While we move away from the homogenizing tendencies of race, class and gender discourses, we must simultaneously acknowledge the larger global, structural and historical forces that account for commonalities in human experiences. To this end, we must reject the liberal notion of "individuality" and interrogate the problematic postmodernist take on the autonomous, differentiated subject.

My use of the concept "multiplex oppression" borrows from Collins' (1990, 1993) idea of the "matrix of domination" and Brewer's (1993) articulation of the "simultaneity of oppressions." In working with the concept, I draw on the distinction between "intersecting" and "interlocking" oppressions (see Dei, 1999b) and utilize the latter to denote a specific political engagement and personal complicity in the struggle over inseparable oppressions. To understand intersecting and interlocking oppressions, we must search for an alternative, complex, comprehensive discursive framework that accounts for differing material circumstances and experiences among subjects. Racism (as one form of oppression) is irreducible to class relations or oppression. Yet, race cannot be understood as independent or completely autonomous from other social relations and identities (e.g., ethnicity, gender, sexuality). Today, there are complex readings of race, class and gender identities that move beyond simplistic Black and White, low, middle, upper class, and male and female distinctions. The complexities of race, class, gender and sexual identities are further conflated by religion, culture and language as other important markers of identity.

The politics of identity is important in how we understand multiple and interlocking identities. The danger of situational politics (race politics in Canada; gender politics in Africa) demands that we locate and work towards intersections. The discourse of relative or particular saliency of different social identities must recognize four crucial ideas: 1) all oppressions have certain things in common (e.g., the use of power to establish material and symbolic advantage; working within structures; 2) oppressions interlock and a discussion of one form of oppression must necessarily entail others; 3) oppressions are neither the same nor equal in their consequences—they differ in their intensities depending on situations and contexts; and 4) as anti-racists, we can, when we choose, maintain the salience of race and racism and yet not sacrifice an integrative analysis for a reductive, additive model of oppressions.

The shifting and complex nature of social existence demands a sophisticated rendering of human experiences. Identities are fluid and overlapping, and knowledge must be able to deal with nuances, ambiguities and contradictions in human experiences. Academic knowledge must move beyond binaries and the establishment of hierarchies. Similarly, sophisticated analysis can help eschew pragmatism over dogma and extremism. An important challenge to understanding community politics is dealing with the problem of mathematizing oppressions. Mathematizing oppressions through an addictive model is a positive discourse which limits our understanding of oppressions to strictly objective analyses. It is seductive to argue that there is less racism today than yesterday, but this assertion provides a false sense of security. An addictive approach means one can examine one form of oppression and then, from this examination, apparently understand human experience.

The consequences of oppressions are varied. There are material, economic, political, spiritual, social, emotional and psychological dimensions of oppressions that cannot be subjected to purely quantitative and materialist analysis. Furthermore, understanding history and context is crucial to knowing human experiences and the nature of social identities. Social relations/identities are raced, classed, gendered and sexualized. Race, class, gender and sexuality are not simply identities, but sites of difference and sites of power. This necessitates our moving beyond bland pluralism (see Stasiulis, 1990; Brewer, 1993; Collins, 1993). As a site of difference, the subject cannot be understood within an essentialist, homogenized discourse (Mohanty, 1990). Looking for both the similarities and the differences that co-exist among racialized groups will ensure that we avoid totalizing and essentializing discourses. There are also pedagogical implications to recognizing difference. Acknowledging difference allows for subjectivity to engage in social resistance.

How then do we move beyond the problematic and competitive hierarchy of oppressions? There are multiple subject locations and simultaneous oppressions and privileges that impact human lives. The human subject can oppositionally reconstruct and claim identity, and then use that identity as a perspective and motivation for political and academic work in differing contexts. The subject can be simultaneously privileged and oppressed. Experiences are differentiated and complicated by race, class, gender and sexual identities. The systems of power embedded in social identities and differences cannot be understood in isolation form one another. An integrative approach to understanding oppressions/identities legitimizes the multiplicity of relations of power based on race, ethnicity, class, gender and sexuality.

Integrative anti-racist practice (Dei, 1996) articulates the salience of race as an important entry point. That is, anti-racism advocates for social change in which race is acknowledged as a central axis of power and racist inequities are ameliorated. The politics of anti-racism demand that race comes first, that its salience is primary, even when other dimensions of oppressions co-exist with racial ones. To deal with the "matrix of domination" (Collins, 1990, 1993), the "simultaneity of oppressions" (Brewer, 1993) and "multiplex oppressions," integrative anti-racist practice must further recognize/articulate the following: 1) tensions and limitations (for example, are we doing justice to all oppressions when we bring them together?); 2) the nature of social movement politics (what are we fighting for and is there a shared or common understanding?); 3). the location of power (who wields power in the movement for change?); 4) the way in which the discourse of change is being produced (how are the issues of voice, representation, appropriation and resistance dealt with?); and, finally, 5) the role of human agency and collective action.

Lessons for Educational Practice

In the remainder of this paper, I will spell out the implications of the foregoing discussion for educational change in the context of Canadian schooling. There is a wide body of research information on the subject of Black/African youth and schooling (Dei, et al., 1997; Brathwaite and James, 1996; Black Educators Working Group (BEWG), 1993; Canadian Alliance of Black Educators (CABE), 1992; Board of Education, Toronto, 1988). Without a doubt, there are many success stories in our school systems. But there are also some troubling failures that call for immediate redress. For example, a large proportion of students are disengaged in schools because of the complex dynamics of the culture, environment and organizational life of mainstream schools, and the intersections of these realities with societal and family forces (e.g., racism, unemployment, family abuse and violence, etc.) (see Dei, et al., 1997; Brathwaite and James, 1996; Codjoe, 1997). Physical presence masks the problem of student disengagement in soul and mind, as well as the high cost of academic success to personal and cultural identity.

Compounding these problems is a disturbing resistance, largely in defense of the status quo, to anti-racism educational change. For all the talk about change, equity is not at the forefront of change agenda. The discourse of educational responsibility has become an escape route for not interrogating institutional structures and systems. Failure to make the important conceptual distinction between blaming victims and asking people to take responsibility has meant that Black and racial minority families are continually pathologized for the educational problems of their youth. Current processes of deracialization render race and skin color insignificant (e.g., color-blind approach to schooling). But, as McLaren (1997) correctly argues, "not to see color ... really amounts in ideological terms to be blind to the disproportionate advantage enjoyed by white people in nearly all sectors of society" (11). Similarly, the dangerous and seductive argument about the lack of self-esteem accounting for minority youth's schooling problems avoids an interrogation of the structures and processes of educational delivery that may be creating the self-esteem or identity problem in the first place. Generally, the "cult of individualism" (see Scheurich, 1993) has succeeded in personalizing the problem of educational failure. There is no need to take a critical look at the structures for teaching, learning and administration of education. The cult of individualism also makes it easier for the school system to take credit for successes and deny responsibility for failures.

Students do not go to school as disembodied youth. Racial, class, gender and sexual identities have implications for knowledge production. Educational theory cannot be separated from teaching practice. Besides the philosophical argument for multiple knowledges in schools, there is also pragmatic recognition of the limits of theory. Any and all theorizing of oppressions must be grounded in actual political practice. Theorizing on race, difference and anti-racism does not, in and of itself, certify as anti-oppression work. Similarly, educational theorists cannot hope to engage in effective anti-racism efforts if classroom practices are not duly informed by the philosophical reasons for promoting equity and justice.

Today, the theoretical and practical case for excellence in schools is decoupled from the struggle for equity. And yet, to teach equity is to promote academic excellence. Excellence and equity are inextricably linked. For educators, the challenge is not simply to ensure that excellence is accessible, but to ensure that excellence is also equitable. Equity considerations must be situated in the broader definition of education. This means placing equity issues at the forefront of educational change. There can be no education today that is not anti-racist, anti-classist, anti-sexist and anti-homophobic. To bring equity to the forefront of current discussions about educational change, we must move beyond mere rhetoric into concrete action.

A broader definition of equity must take the notion of difference seriously. For example, addressing issues of educational access and equitable outcomes requires theoretical and practical consideration of the interlocking of race, class, gender and sexuality with other forms of difference. Acknowledging difference is vital to ensuring opportunity of access and opportunity for outcomes. Each identity is contingent on the others. The social effects of race cannot be understood outside of an acknowledgment of the interlockings of difference. Race and difference provide the contexts for power and domination in society. Difference can be a marker of exclusion and inclusion. As a form of identity, difference accords power and privilege for some, while meting out punishment and penalty for others.

The fight for social justice can be pursued in a manner that recognizes the severity of issues for particular disadvantaged groups in our communities. This is both the product and the lesson of history. A failure to deal with the lessons and the legacy of history will only ensure that we continue to reproduce existing systemic inequities. Working with a broader understanding of equity within school systems, the severity of issues for specific disadvantaged groups can be acknowledged. An unmasking of the seduction of the liberal discourse on social justice requires an understanding of the intensities of oppressions depending on their situational and contextual variations. There are relative saliencies of different identities depending on contexts.

Social change entails power sharing among groups. Dealing with representation is central to structural transformation in schools both in terms of physical bodies and knowledge production. The questions of who is teaching the youth and how and why, can be addressed. Physical bodies in positions of influence represent power and knowledge. The presence of physical bodies constitutes structural hegemonic rupturing. Bodies can rupture hegemonies in terms of discourse as well as institutional practice. Bodies have implications for how we produce knowledge about ourselves and others. Identity is linked to knowledge production. Raced, classed, sexualized and gendered knowledge allows us to see and not see privilege and oppression. In many ways, the particular identities we choose to claim allow us to put on blinders when it comes to owning up to our complicities in oppression. In disowning our complicities, we can be duplicitous. The sites from which we oppress or dominate are those sites upon which we least want to cast our gaze. What identities offer to us by way of privilege cannot mask the vital roles we might play in using collective and individual agencies for social resistance. There is a fear of rupturing a stable sense of place and space. In anti-oppression work, it is important for progressive politics of change to criticize domination.

The emotional and spiritual well-being of the individual and the collective is the bedrock of educational transformation. Transformation is only possible if it proceeds from a development of the inner self and human spiritual values. In rethinking schooling and education, the complex linkages between the natural, spiritual, social, cultural, political and economic dimensions of life and society offer important social knowledge for teaching and learning. This will be a new form of schooling that presents education and learning as emotionally-felt experiences (see also wa Thiong'o, 1986). Education, conceived broadly to mean the varied options, strategies and ways through which people come to know their world and act within it, draws on the interlocking of indigenous knowledges, spiritualities, cultures and identities. The spiritual development of the learner is an important dimension in effective education. Unfortunately, in the practice of educational change, not many specific educational strategies anchor the 'spiritual' in the physical and material aspects of schooling. Educators need to approach schooling in its broader context to encompass emotional and spiritual empowerment of the learner. We must explore learning as an emotionally and spiritually informed educational exercise. Educational change must confront a major challenge facing contemporary education — the reconciliation of the secular and the sacred. Rather than shying away from the spiritual dimensions of education, educational practices and teachings may help reconcile mainstream secularity with individual and community understandings of spirituality. To be successful in enhancing learning outcomes for a diverse student body, educators must tap indigenous, traditional and culturally-based knowledges as important sources of knowledge.

Specific educational initiatives could ask learners to situate learning in their understanding of self and personhood and in the interactions of nature, society and culture. Educators can redefine success broadly to include both the academic and the social. The social implies an ability to understand the self, personhood and one's connection to the group, as well as what this means for communal responsibility and civic duty. Working with a concept of community which recognizes diversity and difference helps do away with rugged individualism.

There is a broad range of interests in our diverse communities. As educators, we must use the strengths embedded in our differences to our advantage rather than engage in practices that only serve to accentuate current obsessions with individual and capabilities rights. To establish, strengthen and support local communities, we must all recognize our responsibilities to a larger collective. Education is the "socialization of human-centered knowledge." It is about teaching the importance of matching individual rights with social responsibilities. Consequently, all educational stakeholders (students, teachers, parents and community workers, etc.) must define their responsibilities as offering support, advice, encouragement and help, and they must engage in concrete action to effect change. We all have to work collectively to set the agenda, priorities and goals for the future of our communities.

It is important for all educational stakeholders to see the issues that affect the delivery of education in a broader perspective and to work with allies by making linkages and connections.

Most indigenous cultural knowledge systems speak to the importance of mutual interdependence.

This linkage extends beyond the local community. All progressive workers must strike meaningful and purposeful working relationships and link the issues in a spirit of genuine partnership — partnership in which questions of power are not evaded, but confronted, discussed and dealt with in a manner that is beneficial to all parties. The play of power cannot be pursued as a zero-sum game. We cannot hope to remove one form of oppression while leaving other forms intact. Whether we be academics, learners, students, teachers, parents or community workers, there are enormous challenges ahead of us. In exchanging and sharing ideas and experiences, as well as engaging in political practice for change, we must maintain the faith that the future contours of our communities lie across geographical spaces and contexts. We must all redefine our individual and collective responsibilities. Today the call for accountability and transparency means moving beyond the bland and seductive politics of inclusion. It is not simply the appearance of inclusion that matters, but also the desire to hold people (in positions of authority and power) accountable for their actions. For far too long policies for anti-racism, equity and social justice have merely existed "on the books" with no political will to implement them meaningfully into schools.

References

Asante, Molefi K. 1987. *The Afrocentric Idea*. Philadelphia: Temple University Press.
_____. 1988. *Afrocentricity*. Trenton, N.J.: Africa World Press.
_____. 1991. "The Afrocentric Idea in Education." *Journal of Negro Education* 60(2): 170–80.

Banks, James. 1993. "The Canon Debate, Knowledge Construction and Multicultural Education." *Educational Researcher* 22(5): 4–14.
Black Educators Working Group (BEWG). 1993. *Submission to the Ontario Royal Commission on Learning*. Toronto.
Board of Education, Toronto. 1988. *Education of Black Students in Toronto: Final Report of the Consultative Committee*. Toronto: Board of Education.
Brathwaite and C. James. 1996, eds. *Educating African Canadians*. Toronto: James Lorimer and Co.
Brewer, Rose M. 1993. "Theorizing Race, Class and Gender: The New Scholarship of Black Feminist Intellectuals and Black Women's Labour." In Stanlie James and Abena Busia. (Eds.) *Theorizing Black Feminisms*. New York: Routledge, 13–30.
Canadian Alliance of Black Educators (CABE). 1992. *Sharing the Challenge I, II, III: A Focus on Black High School Students*. Toronto.
Codjoe, H. 1997. *Black Students and School Success*. Unpublished Ph.D. Dissertation, Department of Educational Policy Studies, University of Alberta, Edmonton, Alberta.
Collins, Patricia Hill. 1990. *Black Feminist Thought*. London: Harper Collins.
_____. 1993. "Toward a New Vision: Race, Class and Gender as Categories of Analysis and Connection." *Race, Sex and Class* 1(1): 25–45.
Dei, George J.S. 1996. *Anti-Racism Education: Theory and Practice*. Halifax: Fernwood Publishing.
_____. 1999a. "African Development and Indigenousness." In G. J. S. Dei, B. Hall and D. Goldin-Rosenberg, eds. *Indigenous Knowledges in Global Contexts: Multiple Readings of Our World*. Toronto: University of Toronto Press. [Forthcoming]
_____. 1999b. "The Denial of Difference: Reframing Anti-Racist Praxis." *Race, Ethnicity and Education*. [Forthcoming]
_____. J. Mazzuca, E. McIsaac and J. Zine. 1997. *Reconstructing "Dropout": A Critical Ethnography of the Dynamics of Black Students' Disengagement From School*. Toronto: University of Toronto Press.
Fals Borda, O. 1980. *Science and the Common People*. Yugoslavia.
_____ and M. A. Rahman, eds. 1991. *Action and Knowledge Breaking the Monopoly with Participatory Action Research*. New York: The Apex Press.
Fanon, Franz. 1963. *The Wretched of the Earth*. New York: Grove Weidenfeld.
Foucault, M. 1977. "The Body of the Condemned." (From *Discipline and Punish: The Birth of Prison*.) In Paul Rabinow (ed.). *The Foucault Reader*. New York: Pantheon Books, 170-8.
_____. 1980. *Power/Knowledge: Selected Interviews, 1972–77*. C. Gordon, ed. Brighton: Harvester Press.
_____. 1983. "The Subject and Power." In H. Dreyfus and P. Rabinow, eds. *Michel Foucault: Beyond Structuralism and Hermeneutics*. Chicago: University of Chicago Press, 208–26.
Giroux, H. 1997. "Rewriting the Discourse of Racial Identity: Towards a Pedagogy and Politics of Whiteness." *Harvard Educational Review* 67(2): 285–310.
Hall, Stuart. 1979. "Ethnicity: Identity and Experience." *Radical America* (Summer 1979): 9–20.
_____. 1991. "Old and New Identities: Old and New Ethnicities." In A. King, ed. *Culture, Globalization and the World System*. New York: State University Press, pp. 41–68.

Harris, C. 1993. "Whiteness as Property." *Harvard Law Review* 106 (8): 1709–91.
Haynes, D. and G. Prakash. 1991. "Introduction: The Entanglement of Power and Resistance." In D. Haynes and G. Prakash, eds. *Contesting Power: Resistance and Everyday Social Relations in South Asia.* Delhi: Oxford University Press, 1–22.
Hicks, E. 1991. *Border Writing.* Minneapolis: University of Minnesota Press.
Hunter, Deborah A. 1983. "The Rhetorical Challenge of Afro-Centricity." *Western Journal of Black Studies* 7(4): 239–43.
Itwaru, A. 1999. "Creativity, Resistance, Transformation: An Instance in the Life of an Othered Other." Public Lecture, Department of Sociology and Equity Studies in Education, OISE, University of Toronto.
McLaren, P. 1997. "Unthinking Whiteness, Rethinking Democracy; Or Farewell to the Blonde Beast: Towards a Revolutionary Multiculturalism." *Educational Foundations* 11(2): 5–39.
Mohanty, C. 1990. "On Race and Voice: Challenges for Liberal Education in the 90s." *Cultural Critique* 14: 179–208.
Prah, K. 1997. "Accusing the Victims—In My Father's House: A Review of Kwame Anthony Appiah's *In My Father's House.*" CODESRIA Bulletin (1): 14–22.
Price, E. 1998. "First Thoughts Toward a Thesis Proposal." Unpublished Paper, Department of Sociology and Equity Studies in Education, OISE, University of Toronto.
Roediger, D. 1993. *The Wages of Whiteness.* London & New York: Verso.
Scheurich, J. 1993. "Towards a White Discourse on White Racism." *Educational Researcher* 22(8): 5–16.
_____ and M. Young. 1997. "Coloring Epistemologies: Are Our Research Epistemologies Racially Biased?" *Educational Researcher* 26(4): 4–16.
Stasiulis, D. 1990. "Theorizing Connections: Gender, Race, Ethnicity and Class." In P. Li, ed. *Race and Ethnic Relations in Canada.* Toronto: Oxford University Press, 269–305.
Trueba, T. 1994. "Reflections on Alternative Visions of Schooling." *Anthropology and Education Quarterly* 25(3): 376–93.
Wa Thiong'o, N. 1986. *Decolonizing the Mind: The Politics of Language in African Literature.* London: James Currey.

"There Was No Better Place to Go"? Quintard Taylor, Afrikancentricity,[1] and the Historiography of the Afrikan Experience in the American West

Ahati N. N. Toure

Biographical Sketch

When Quintard Taylor, Jr.—fresh from completing his Ph.D. in the history of African peoples at the University of Minnesota-Minneapolis—secured a position in 1977 as a professor of history at California Polytechnic State University in San Luis Obispo, he decided to pack up his belongings and travel by car. Stopping at a remote gas station along old US 6, just west of Amarillo, Texas, his passenger asked for the key to the rest room. The station owner replied that the rest room was out of order, a satisfactory answer until a short time later a European customer approached him for the same rest room key and was granted it. Taylor, affronted by this blatant display of racism, challenged the man with the question, "Haven't you heard of the Civil Rights Act?" The Texan's reply was blunt but eloquent. He shoved the muzzle of a shotgun into Taylor's stomach and retorted, "Haven't you heard about my shotgun?"[2]

That unpleasant and potentially fatal experience sums up the nature of the promise and disappointment that characterized the quest for freedom and opportunity, as Taylor tells the story, that the American West represented for thousands of Afrikans who traveled to the region from the American South across two centuries. In a sense Taylor's journey to the West, like those Afrikans who preceded him, is one similarly fraught with the expectations of hope and possibility that motivated them.

A southerner by birth, Taylor was raised in Brownsville, Haywood County, in western Tennessee, not far from the border with Arkansas. Along with neighboring Fayette County to the south, which borders Mississippi, Haywood County was one of the two predominantly Afrikan counties in the state. Taylor's grandfather, John Henry Taylor, had migrated after the Civil War to apartheid-ruled western Tennessee from New Orleans, escaping from a past of enslavement in search of freedom and opportunity. John's son and Taylor's father, Quintard, Sr., grew up to become the foreman on a cotton plantation owned by two brothers who lived in Memphis and New York City. Taylor has arisen from quite humble beginnings, recalling that in the 1960s he chopped cotton for $2.50 a day, although that sum might increase to as high as $7 for a long day of harvesting.[3]

Growing up in the segregated South, he was certainly aware of the limitations imposed upon the aspirations of Afrikans under the white supremacist dictatorship that prevailed there. His father had only gotten as far as the second grade, while his mother had spent a year at the predominantly Afrikan Lane Teacher's College in Jackson, Tennessee. Taylor himself attended the segregated high school named after the famous Tuskegee Institute agricultural scientist George Washington Carver. From there he went on to Raleigh, North Carolina, and St. Augustine's College, founded in 1867 to teach newly emancipated Afrikans.[4] He completed an undergraduate degree in American history in 1969. Afterward, he accepted admission to the University of Minnesota-Minneapolis, where he obtained M.A. and Ph.D. degrees in American urban history and in the history of African peoples in 1971 and 1977.

Between earning his masters and doctoral degrees, Taylor began teaching, lecturing as an assistant professor in the Black Studies program at Washington State University-Pullman from 1971 to 1975. After completing his doctorate, he accepted a position in history at California Polytechnic State University, working there for 13 years between 1977 and 1990. During that time he spent a year, from 1987 to 1988, as a Visiting Fulbright Professor of History at the University of Lagos's Department of History at Akoka, Lagos, in Nigeria, West Afrika. By 1990, Taylor had moved on to positions at the University of Oregon in Eugene: professor in the Department of History from 1990–1999; and department chair from 1997–1999;

adjunct professor in the Folklore and Ethnic Studies Program from 1990–1994; acting director of the Ethnic Studies Program from 1992–1993; and an endowed chair as a Knight Distinguished Professor of Liberal Arts and Sciences from 1998–1999. In 1999 he moved to take a position as an endowed chair at the University of Washington in Seattle as the Scott and Dorothy Bullitt Professor of American History.[5]

During some 30 years of scholarship and teaching, Taylor has certainly become one of the foremost authorities on the Afrikan experience in the United States' western region. A man who has demonstrated a keen scholarly interest in the Afrikan struggle for citizenship rights,[6] he has to date authored or edited five books, 19 book reviews and at least 58 articles, introductions, and essays in journals, magazines, books, and encyclopedias on various subjects, most of them focused on the Afrikan experience in the American West.

His research and writing have been awarded with distinction. His survey history of Afrikans in the west, *In Search of the Racial Frontier: African Americans in the American West, 1528–1990* (1998), garnered a Pulitzer Prize nomination in history, while his *The Forging of a Black Community: A History of Seattle's Central District, 1870 through the Civil Rights Era* (1994) became the fifth book selected since 1968 for the Emil and Kathleen Sick Series in Western History and Biography.[7] His essay "From Esteban to Rodney King: Five Centuries of African American History in the West," which appeared in *Montana: The Magazine of Western History* (Winter 1996), won the Vivian A. Paladin Award for the best article to appear in *Montana* in 1996–1997. Early in his career he also received the Carter G. Woodson Award for the Best *JNH* Article of 1978–1979 for "The Emergence of Black Communities in the Pacific Northwest, 1865–1910," published in the *Journal of Negro History* (Fall 1979).[8]

Major Themes

Taylor's work on the Afrikan presence in the American West — with a particular interest in the Pacific Northwest — evinces a number of themes regarding its nature, impact, and significance in the region. His chief concern is the integration of that history into the writing of the West's history, including the New Western History, which has a historiographical focus that includes examinations of issues of caste (race), gender, and European ethnicity. He has also championed its incorporation into the writing of national Afrikan history in the United States. In this regard, four principal themes appear to predominate in his work.

Establishing the significance of the Afrikan presence in the West is, of course, a principal theme. Although the most neglected Majority World[9] group in terms of western historical inquiry, Afrikans, like Latinos, First Nations peoples (so-called Native Americans or American Indians), and Asians, were and remain a significant presence in the history of the western region[10] for several reasons, argues Taylor. Among the foremost is simply the fact that the Afrikan presence in the West, beginning in 1528, predates the Anglo-British invasion from the East, and precedes by nearly a century the 1619 arrival, under the English regime, of indentured Afrikans in Jamestown, Virginia. Enslaved Afrikans accompanied and facilitated the Spaniard invasion and conquest of what would later become Mexico and, later still, the southwestern United States. For a time, in the late sixteenth century, enslaved Afrikans brought into New Spain even outnumbered both the European and half caste European/First Nations populations (mestizos) before merging with them through intermarriage and cultural assimilation. Taylor argues the numbers of enslaved Afrikans brought into the Spanish colony — nearly 200,000 between 1521 and 1821— were comparable to the 345,000 brought into what became British North America.[11] Afrikan people could be found in various Spanish-controlled regions that later became provinces of the United States, including California, New Mexico, and Texas.

Moreover, notes Taylor, even under Anglo-American occupation the Afrikan presence was significant. Among the largest regions for Afrikan enslavement were Texas and the First Nations (so-called Indian) Territory of the Cherokee, Creek, Choctaw, Chickasaw, and Seminole (the so-called Five Civilized Tribes), whom the Americans deported from their original lands in the Southeast in 1830s. By 1860, 13 of Texas's 105 counties were predominantly Afrikan, while in the First Nations Territory enslaved Afrikans comprised 17.5 percent of the resettled First Nations population.[12] Hence, the Afrikan presence was significantly large and contributed mightily to the economic production of the region.

Taylor also maintains that Western history cannot be written without an account of the Afrikan presence because their influence was disproportionate to their numbers. Even in states in which enslavement was illegal, the question over its expansion into the West would stir fierce debate and convulse Europeans into bloody confrontations, as in Kansas during the period leading to the American Civil War. Enslavement was, further, a de facto reality in the Pacific Northwest, and Afrikans resisted through lawsuits and flight from their enslavers.[13] While Afrikan numbers were minuscule in nineteenth century Oregon and Washington — some 150 or more in 1860 — they, nonetheless, constituted "a permanent black presence," sufficient in numbers to ensure that they "lived in 14 of the 19 Oregon counties and eight of the 19 counties of Washington Territory."[14]

Further, Taylor contends, the western experience cannot be written without cognizance of the fact that Afrikan influence was also felt in significant ways that positively affected Anglo-American invasion and occupation. Afrikan soldiers stationed in the West from 1866 to 1917 assisted in vanquishing the last of the First Nations peoples' resistance to European colonialism and aggression, put down European labor resistance to monopoly capitalist mining interests, policed the United States border with Mexico, and generally protected the interests and security of European settlers. James Beckwourth discovered Beckwourth's Pass, a major route for travel to California, while others accompanied Euro-Americans in various explorations of the region. Some 133,500 Afrikans rushed in to settle areas of Colorado, Nebraska, Kansas, and Oklahoma to establish homesteads on lands stolen from the First Nations peoples.[15]

Afrikans even rose to positions of prominence among Europeans. The formerly enslaved Barney L. Ford had by 1890 become "one of the most successful businessmen in Colorado," while George Washington Bush of Thurston County, Washington Territory, became by the 1850s "one of the most successful farmers in the territory." Farther to the south, in San Francisco, California, William Alexander Liedesdorff had by 1848 "served as U.S. Vice-Consul to Mexico and treasurer of the San Francisco city council," and built "the first hotel in the city and operated the first steamboat line in San Francisco Bay." Fifty years later, William Gross, who had opened the second hotel in Seattle as well as a restaurant and barbershop, became, with accumulated real estate holdings, "one of the wealthiest individuals in Seattle."[16]

Afrikans also made their presence felt in many ways through the nineteenth and twentieth centuries. They vigorously resisted apartheid policies in housing, employment, and education through lawsuits, direct action protest tactics, and the dissemination of their opinions through the publication of their own newspapers. Afrikan citizenship rights activism in the American West had, in some instances, national implications during and after World War II. The United States Supreme Court's decision in 1954 (Brown v. Board of Topeka, Kansas) to strike down the legality of apartheid in public education had repercussions across the United States. In the area of arts and culture, many of the great jazz artists, as well as writers of the Harlem Renaissance, such as Arna Bontemps, Langston Hughes, Charles Mingus, and Lester Young, hailed from the American West. By the twentieth century, particularly after World War II, the Afrikan presence grew into a significant demographic presence among Majority World groups.

Although generally one among a number of much larger groups of Latinos or Asians in various parts of the region, Afrikans became the largest Majority World group in Seattle from World War II to 1990.[17]

A second theme in Afrikan history in the West, as in the history of Afrikans in the United States generally, involves migration and urbanization. During the nineteenth century, Afrikans sought to escape European terrorism and dictatorship in the United States. Many fled to Mexico or to British-held territory on the West Coast and the Pacific Northwest — only to find themselves back in the European settler state with the advent of American military occupation and a massive influx of Anglo-American settlers. But like the Anglo-Europeans, some Afrikans also went in search of gold in California or flooded the Great Plains states of Nebraska, Kansas, and the Dakotas in an effort to establish all–Afrikan farming communities in which they could rule themselves and prosper independently of European persecution and dictatorship.

In the twentieth century, the most dramatic population increases came during World War II in response to the lure of defense factory jobs. The chronic labor shortages of the region and the aggressive recruitment outside of the region brought thousands of Afrikans to cities all across the West, including Los Angeles, San Francisco, and Oakland, California, Seattle, Washington, and Portland, Oregon.

Urbanization is another important and related theme in both the 1800s and the 1900s. To the Pacific Northwest came "approximately ten thousand Afro-Americans [who] participated in the migration of two million people" to that region after the Civil War. Most Afrikans settled in the larger cities like Portland and Seattle, but others went to smaller towns like Roslyn, Washington, or Butte and Helena, Montana,[18] Indeed, throughout the West as early as 1870, "most African American westerners (outside Texas and Indian territory) resided in cities and towns. African Americans in Colorado, California, Utah, Montana, and Nevada lived in cities from the beginning of their settlement."[19]

In addition to urbanization, Taylor is also very much concerned with the nature of Afrikan life in those cities. His attention is drawn to the ways in which Afrikans organized themselves, established institutions that created a sense of cultural and community ethos, interacted with other nationalities within their localities, and acted to defend their citizenship rights in the face of European hostility and subordination. Indeed, he takes pains to emphasize the dynamic of Afrikan agency, the self-conscious effort of Afrikans in the urban areas of the American West to transcend mere reaction to European oppression and to define and shape an affirmative consciousness of themselves as a group.

The multi-national encounter is, thus, a third important focus in Taylor's work. Because Afrikans were not the only Majority World group subject to European persecution, Taylor is interested in exploring the ways in which the experiences of the various nationalities differed or were similar, and the ways in which they either similarly or differently negotiated their resistance. Taylor is also concerned with looking at the ways in which Afrikans interacted with various Majority World groups, and explores points of contention, competition, conflict, and cooperation. In his essay, "Blacks and Asians in a White City: Japanese Americans and African Americans in Seattle, 1890–1940," he engages in a comparative analysis of Japanese and Afrikan communities, their strategies for social advancement, and the outcomes in terms of education, economic development, and citizenship rights.[20] In other essays that explore Afrikan migration to and settlement in Seattle and Portland, he looks at the interactions of Afrikans, Asians, and First Nations peoples.[21] In *In Search of the Racial Frontier* he extends that examination to Afrikan/Latino relations as well.

A fourth concern of Taylor's work, and one he investigates in some detail, is the oppression Afrikans faced in both the nineteenth and twentieth centuries and the ways in which they organized to resist. Resistance in terms of the struggle for citizenship rights is a constant theme in his exploration of the experiences of Afrikans throughout the West. Segregation in housing and education and restricted employment opportunities were the reality throughout the region in both the nineteenth and the twentieth centuries. Taylor's concern is to explore in detail the history of the Afrikan citizenship rights struggle in the West so as to balance its significance with the more celebrated citizenship rights struggles in both the northeastern and the southeastern United States.[22]

Historiographical Analysis

Interestingly, Taylor's work falls within two schools of research interest. One is what in the European academy is called the New Western History, an exploration of the American experience in the West that borrows heavily from the historiographical, theoretical, and methodological research issues and directions raised by Africana Studies, Chicano Studies, First Nations Studies, and Ethnic Studies, all of which, following the lead of Africana Studies, emerged in the 1970s. The New Western History — a primarily Euro-American-dominated area of scholarship — rejects as sclerotic and irreparably inaccurate the Eurocentric assertion of a mythical, heroic, Euro-American agrarian pioneer who progressively "tamed" a "wild" and "underutilized" land. The late nineteenth century historian Frederick Jackson Turner and his disciples would distill and transmogrify this popular Caucasian supremacist notion into academic discourse and offer it as an explanation for the alleged uniqueness and "democratic" achievement of the national Anglo-American character.[23] In its place, the New Western History addresses itself to a complexity surrounding the historical experience in the region, including the presence of non Anglo-European peoples engaged in conquest (Spaniards, French, and Russians), the various struggles of Majority World peoples (Afrikans, Latinos, First Nations peoples, Asians), and the bewilderingly multi-tribal character of European immigration to the region, particularly in response to the monopoly capitalist labor demands of the nineteenth century. In short, the New Western History embraces an exploration of the roles of class, caste ("race"), European tribalism (ethnicity), culture, gender, conquest, colonialism, migration, immigration, urbanization, capitalist exploitation of workers, capitalist destruction of the natural environment, and ecology in the West of the sixteenth through the twenty-first centuries.[24] Hence, Taylor's work can be accommodated within the scope of the New Western History's historiographical inquiry.

Yet, at best, this fact may largely be coincidental and fortuitous. The substance of Taylor's work owes very little on a conceptual or theoretical ground to the New Western History, flowing, as it does, from a tradition that predates it. Drawing his primary inspiration from "Black Americanist" or "African Americanist" historiography,[25] Taylor extends its scope into the exploration of the experience of Afrikans in the West. His research explores themes such as enslavement, abolition, migration, urbanization, the struggle for citizenship rights, white supremacist persecution, cross-cultural encounters with other Majority World peoples, and Afrikan contributions to American life that are all very much a part of the historiography that explained the Afrikan presence in the European settler state as a whole — largely conceived, as Taylor rightly points out, as the South, North, Midwest, and East, to the neglect of the West.

That historiography, exemplified in classic survey histories like those of the distinguished scholars John Hope Franklin in *From Slavery to Freedom: A History of African Americans* (1947, 1956, 1967, 1980, 1988, 1994), Benjamin Quarles in *The Negro in the Making of America* (1964, 1969, 1987, 1996), Lerone Bennett, Jr., in *Before the Mayflower: A History of Black America* (1962, 1964, 1966, 1969, 1982, 1987, 1993, 2000), or more recent efforts like those of Robin D. G. Kelley's and Earl Lewis's edited work *To Make Our World Anew: A History of African Americans* (2001) and Darlene Clark Hine's, William C. Hine's, and Stanley Harrold's *The African-American*

Odyssey (2000), bridged the seventeenth through twentieth centuries with the contention that the central theme of Afrikan struggle was the quest for greater Americanization and the fullest democratization of American society.[26] Taylor, likewise in his trail-blazing survey of the Afrikan experience in the American West, *In Search of the Racial Frontier*, accomplishes the same, bridging the Afrikan experience in a continuity that extends from the sixteenth century into the final decade of the twentieth century. His motive arises not from the New Western History's concern to extend the history of the West beyond 1890 and the closing of the frontier,[27] but rather from the need to chronicle a much-neglected Afrikan experience in that place of 19 western states "on and beyond the ninety-eighth meridian— North Dakota to Texas westward to Alaska and Hawaii."[28]

Indeed, the New Western History's inquiry beyond the nineteenth into the twentieth (and now, the twenty-first) century was framed in contradistinction to Turner's contention that the region's history had terminated a decade prior to the end of the 1800s. For New Western historians — who have repudiated in large measure the ethnocentric romanticism of the "Old West" of "virtuous and heroic white cowboys" and "savage and feral Indians" that had conceptually arrested American western history — the notion that the history of the West did not end with the demise of Anglo-European-centered notions of frontier exploration and settlement provides an enormously important epistemological and historiographical breakthrough. Yet for Taylor, whose central concern is to uncover the history of a people in a region in which that people's history has been overlooked, the Turner thesis, in truth, has no relevance. This explains why Taylor almost never mentions Turner in his work.[29]

It is, perhaps, Taylor's citizenship rights orientation that prompts him to pose the Afrikan experience more in terms of issues of "discrimination" than exploitation and dictatorship, a position the New Western historians would presumably share, at least to some degree, with a Pan Afrikan nationalist analysis.[30] Nonetheless, migration and urbanization in the post–Civil War era, in addition to "discrimination," reflect important themes that are examined in Afrikan historiography in the United States as a whole. Consequently, that these phenomena take place in the western region is incidental to place, for they form part of the national pattern of the Afrikan experience in the European settler state. The New Western History, by contrast, is primarily a Euro-American reevaluation of the nature of the western historical experience that adds to its reconceptualization a cognizance of the existence of Asians, Latinos, and First Nations peoples, without which that reevaluation would remain unintelligible. It is a revival of a field of regional studies within the traditional American historical tradition that had grown marginalized and moribund. Energized by the social revolt of Majority World peoples in the European settler state — particularly as that revolt asserted itself in the academy — the New Western History involves, simultaneously, an awakening of a sense of conscience. It is an acknowledgment of the reality of the multi-national and multi-centered history of the region.

Yet even this advance in human understanding has proved limited. Taylor, in an essay titled "Through the Prism of Race: The Meaning of African-American History in the West," acknowledges the work of scholars in the field in stimulating this reappraisal of the multi-national (as well as class and gender) dimension of the region's history. But he also looks beyond them to the "innovative scholarship on African-American history and black studies that emerged in the 1970s and 1980s."[31] This praise for New Western historians is, perhaps, ironic in light of the fact that the New Western historian Clyde A. Milner, II, in his introduction to his *A New Significance: Re-Envisioning the History of the American West*, in which Taylor's essay appears, never mentioned Afrikans at all. Apparently, Milner simply overlooked them among the region's "Native Americans, Mexican Americans, Asian and Asian Americans."[32] Milner does, however, mention Taylor's essay, which appears to have been tacked on as an afterthought and as a concluding statement in the book. Indeed, Taylor, in his essay, objects very strenuously to precisely this systematic omission of Afrikans in the New Western History's European-dominated discourse.[33]

It may be that this omission is sufficiently indicative of the point that the story of Afrikans in the West still thrives outside of the boundaries of the New Western History's discourse, although logically it should and does, at least theoretically, fall within it. This conclusion is amply illustrated in Paul Wirt's *Terra Pacifica: People and Place in the Northwest States and Western Canada*. In it, Taylor attempts to fit his work within the concern of the New Western History, although it is to some extent a forced, somewhat unnatural, fit. In fact, in Taylor's essay, "'There Was No Better Place to Go'— The Transformation Thesis Revisited: African-American Migration to the Pacific Northwest, 1940–1950,"[34] he merely dusts off a subject he has explored in essays in 1978 and 1981.[35] Taylor engages a debate within the New Western History regarding the so-called transformation thesis: whether the second World War ended the western region's colonial dependency on eastern capital and established it as an autonomous economic power in its own right. But it appears Taylor does not attempt to resolve, and is not seriously interested in resolving, that debate. He only uses the argument as an occasion to insert the significance of the Afrikan experience in the region within the context of an important theme in the

New Western History. As he says, he wants to assess "the impact of the presence of black Pacific Northwesterners on the rest of the region's inhabitants" and to use "the joint prism of African-American and Pacific Northwest history" to examine the debate.[36]

Ultimately, Taylor's exploration has little direct relevance to the macro-level focus of the transformation thesis except insofar as he demonstrates there was both transformation (that is, a change from) and continuity with previous trends in the Afrikan experience in the region following and as a result of World War II. The specifics of his discussion — the fact that Afrikan gains in employment were complicated by white supremacist oppression, that those gains in employment and economic and social advancement were uneven in the region, that Afrikans were also compelled to challenge segregation in housing, and that all of these challenges entailed sustained citizenship rights activism against entrenched European domination — all of this, as has been noted above, he had previously explored without reference to this debate in the New Western History.

Moreover, the Black Americanist nature of the historiographical focus that underlies the work — which is infused with an implicit American patriotism as well as a certain optimism regarding the prospects of the quest to dissolve the barrier of caste (otherwise called race) and to achieve equal American status with the European population — also sidesteps issues of conquest, power, and capitalist expansion and exploitation, critical themes in the New Western History's reexamination of the western regional experience. Taylor's interpretation, an integrationist one within the context of Afrikan cultural and intellectual thought, is focused on *the struggle to become American* and the obstacles in the pursuit of that quest. A Pan Afrikan nationalist interpretation within Afrikan thought would significantly differ, being primarily focused upon *the struggle against, and to achieve independence from, American colonial status*. In the latter case, themes of conquest, power, imperialism, colonialism, capitalism, global, national, and local Afrikan self-determination, and solidarity with the struggles of other Majority World peoples against European colonialism, become critical issues of historical interpretation and scholarly inquiry.[37]

The differences are perhaps most clearly underscored in Taylor's discussion of the buffalo soldiers in his critically-acclaimed survey history, *In Search of the Racial Frontier*. The buffalo soldiers are those Afrikans of the Ninth and Tenth Cavalries and the Twenty-fourth and Twenty-fifth infantries of the United States Army who between 1866 and 1917 were stationed in the West and used, among other purposes, to crush the last of the First Nations peoples' resistance to European colonialism, to neutralize incipient revolutionary struggle within Mexico, and to crush European worker movements against monopoly capitalism. A Pan Afrikan nationalist historical inquiry with respect to the buffalo soldiers would have agreed with Ho Chi Minh's assessment of the uses of colonized people in imperial expansion when he argued "international capitalism draws all of its vital force from the colonial countries. It finds there ... above all, native soldiers for its counterrevolutionary army." In his view, "Imperialism ... hurls the proletarians of one colony against those of another."[38] Indeed, this issue of American military expansionism and its use of Afrikans to assist in the conquest of other Majority World peoples resisting European imperialism has been a continuing concern throughout Afrikan history in the European settler state, whether it involved the American struggle against Japan, Vietnam, the Philippines, Iraq, the First Nations of the so-called North American continent, or fellow Afrikans in post-independence Congo. In some instances, as in the 1898 Spanish American War, many Afrikan soldiers in the United States Army joined the Filipino resistance against American occupation of the islands.[39] Taylor, however, who spends an entire chapter on the buffalo soldiers, concludes: "Both nineteenth- and twentieth-century African Americans were proud of the buffalo soldiers, who joined the still-small pantheon of African American heroes."[40]

Agents of conquest, themselves victims of conquest — important, even central, themes in a Pan Afrikan nationalist historiography — become, in an integrationist interpretation, heroes and evidence of a significant contribution to the European settler state's cultural life and history. Hence, Taylor's view is ultimately, and significantly, more conservative even than that being articulated in some domains of the New Western History's critique of the western experience, in which conquest is seen as anything but heroic.[41] Indeed, the chief goal of the integrationist is to become a part of the European settler state, not to fundamentally transform it. The central goal is to banish Afrikan exclusion, not to fundamentally restructure, or even to question, the terms of the political and socioeconomic arrangement.

If there is a central theme in Taylor's work that agrees with this conclusion, it is his emphasis on citizenship rights, the struggle against segregation in housing and education, restrictions and limitations in employment, and the quest to secure opportunities for social and economic advancement that plays such a central role in the Afrikan experience in the nineteenth and twentieth century American West. Such a research emphasis flows from what James L. Conyers, Jr., has identified as the phenomenon of "social ecology": the macro- and micro-level political, cultural, economic, epistemological, and axiological dynamics that shape the experience, formation, and expression of personal and group consciousness, and that ultimately influences the direction of scholarly research interest by offering an ideological framework for interpretative analysis.[42] As mentioned earlier, Taylor grew up in caste-ruled western Tennessee, and pursued an undergraduate degree at the historically Afrikan St. Augustine's College in Raleigh, North Carolina, during the most vigorous years of the southern citizenship rights movement. The citizenship rights tradition — the drive to overcome caste barriers to fulfill the quest for complete and unqualified American status— inform his thinking and the nature of the history he sees in the West. From the nineteenth through the twentieth centuries, Afrikans came to the West to escape enslavement, white supremacist terrorism and dictatorship (and even, although unsuccessfully, Americans) in pursuit of freedom, opportunity, wealth, land, entrepreneurship, employment, and advancement. The notion that there was "no better place to go" constitutes Taylor's definition of the geographical and ideological limits of the Afrikan struggle: to become fully enfranchised as Americans or bust. One must stand and fight on the ground of achieving full and complete American status because there is no other, and no better, place to go.[43]

Conclusion

In the end, Taylor's work significantly advances the knowledge of the Afrikan experience in the United States and points to the urgent need to explore its varied dimensions in a region in which the systematic study of Afrikan people has been ignored. Thus, his research within the school of the New Western History helps to effect the penetration of Afrikan realities into European scholarly discourse. With this said, however, it is evident that the body of Taylor's work demonstrates that it is less a part of the New Western History than it is of that vision of Afrikan historiography in the European settler state (that is considerably older than the New Western History) that is classically "Black Americanist" or "African Americanist." Many of the important themes of Taylor's research — issues of migration and urbanization, the struggle against caste and white supremacist subordination, citizenship rights and the quest for integration, and the significance of the Afrikan contribution to American life — accord with those themes of scholarly inquiry that have long been explored and/or celebrated concerning Afrikan people in other regions of the United States. In sum, Taylor's important contribution is that he has expanded the scope of Afrikan history in the European settler state, tying the experience in the American West to that larger, national Afrikan experience so as to make it a part of an organic whole.

As the New Western History has virtually ignored Afrikans, whether the field succeeds or perishes will have little meaningful impact upon Taylor's work. On the other hand, the degree to which the New Western History begins to take the Afrikan presence seriously as part of the scope of its examination of the dimensions of conquest, power, and multi-nationality in the West is the degree to which Taylor's work (and hopefully the work of others less conservative in outlook) can expand the scope of exploration within the field and its reevaluation of what the history of the American West really means.

At the same time, Taylor's conceptual limitations point to the need for Africalogical inquiry and a Pan Afrikan nationalist historiography that deals with themes of culture and power that are central to an understanding of the Afrikan experience in the struggle for national sovereignty, and against European colonial dictatorship and world hegemony. As James L. Conyers, Jr., has stated, the Africalogical enterprise deals with the ideological repertoires of an Afrikan-centered perspective, global Pan Afrikanism, and cultural nationalism as modes of interpreting the Afrikan experience in the United States and worldwide.[44]

Hence, for Afrikan-centered scholars, there are certain assumptions that inform the interpretative framework in which the history of Afrikan people in the European settler state must be understood. One important consideration, as Bayo Oyebade has outlined, is the assumption that it is a dimension of Afrikan history and culture that is without "any dichotomy between the African past and African-American history." The history of Afrikans in the United States is "an integral part of African history," and thus, "[t]o be valid, any study of African-American experience must be rooted in African culture."[45] This is because, as Conyers has aptly noted, "the cultural and historical foundations of African Caribbean and American history are found in Africa."[46] Indeed, as Molefi K. Asante has maintained, "one cannot write fully without a self-conscious attempt to place the historical enterprise in an organic relationship to African history." Further, he has noted, the definition of what constitutes Afrikan history can be seen in this light: "The geographical scope of the African world, and hence, the Africalogical enterprise, includes Africa, the Americas, the Caribbean, various regions of Asia and the Pacific. Wherever people declare themselves as African, despite the distance from the continent or the recency of their out-migration, they are accepted as part of the African world." As a result, one "cannot study Africans in the United States or

Brazil or Jamaica without some appreciation for the historical and cultural significance of Africa as source and origin.... Thus, if one concentrates on studying Africans" in the United States, "it must be done with the idea in the back of the mind that one is studying African people, not 'made-in-America Negroes' without historical depth."[47]

The rather revolutionary implication of this idea is that it is incompatible with any Eurocentric notion that would ground Afrikan political, historical, or cultural identity in a genesis under any form of European domination. As Omowale Malcolm X cogently and perceptively observed, Afrikans in the European settler state are not Americans, but merely Afrikans who were brought to America. Any perceived or asserted discontinuity between Afrikan history and identity flowing from the Afrikan continent and Afrikan history and identity in the European settler state is, from an Africalogical perspective, a colonial history, an epistemological abortion, and, argues Oyebade, a Eurocentric mythology.[48]

There are, of course, other profound political implications that are inherent in this perspective. "Afrikan-centered education recognizes that the whole of human life is a political system and, therefore," notes the late Afrikan psychologist and revolutionary theorist Amos N. Wilson, "it interprets its materials politically. It is through political, economic and military action that we must change our circumstances."[49] Thus, a key to understanding the political implications of this experience is the Pan Afrikan nationalist emphasis upon the reclamation of national power and national sovereignty — what the historian John Henrik Clarke identified as the only true purpose of Afrikan education. Indeed, Clarke proposed, the Afrikan objective in the United States was to regain the capability and reality of "the structure and the management of the state," adding that Afrikans in the European settler state, struggling against European colonial subordination, were without a state, and, therefore, without an authentic nationality.[50] He went on to say, the "*nation is the ultimate goal of all people who walk on this earth*"[51] (original emphasis).

Wilson, echoing Clarke, maintained that the academic enterprise for Afrikan-centered scholars implicitly embraced the revolutionary project of Afrikan national liberation. "We must understand the tremendous value of the study of history for the *re-gaining* of power. If our education is not about gaining real power, we are being miseducated and misled and we will die 'educated' and misled"[52] (original emphasis).

Notes

1. The late Afrikan historian John Henrik Clarke declared: "I never use the word Afrocentricity. I don't believe in it. I don't compromise with the word Afrikan. I think it should have been from the beginning, 'Afrikancentricity' or nothing." See Kwaku Person-Lynn, ed., "On My Journey Now: The Narrative and Works of Dr. John Henrik Clarke, The Knowledge Revolutionary," *The Journal of Pan African Studies, Special Issue* 1, no. 2 (Winter–Fall 2000) and 2, no. 1 (Spring–Summer 2001): 176–177.
2. Dan Krieger, "The Struggle for Freedom Continues," *San Luis Obispo County Telegram-Tribune*, 22 June 1996, available from http://www.sanluisobispo.com/stories/0796/krigr1.htm1; Internet.
3. Ibid.
4. Ibid.
5. Quintard Taylor, Jr., *Curriculum Vitae*; available from http://faculty.washington.edu/qtaylor/vita.htm; Internet.
6. Chris Kenning, "MLK Associate to Visit Campus for Celebration," *Oregon Daily Emerald*, 15 January 1998; available from http://www.darkwing.uoregon.edu/~ode/archive/v99/2/980115/mlk.htm1; Internet.
7. Quintard Taylor, *In Search of the Racial Frontier: African Americans in the American West, 1528–1990* (New York: W. W. Norton, 1998); and Quintard Taylor, *The Forging of a Black Community: A History of Seattle's Central District, 1870 through the Civil Rights Era* (Seattle: University of Washington Press, 1994). See also Taylor, *CV*.
8. Quintard Taylor, "From Esteban to Rodney King: Five Centuries of African American History in the West," *Montana: The Magazine of Western History* 46 (Winter 1996): 2–23, reprinted in *The American West: The Reader*, eds. Walter Nugent and Martin Ridge (Bloomington: Indiana University Press, 1999); and Quintard Taylor, "The Emergence of Black Communities in the Pacific Northwest, 1865–1910," *Journal of Negro History* 64 (Fall 1979): 342–351, reprinted in *From Reconstruction to the Great Migration, 1877–1917*, Vol. 4 of *Black Communities and Urban Development in America, 1720–1990*. 10 vols, ed. Kenneth L. Kusmer (Hamden, CT: Garland Publishing, 1991). See also Taylor, *CV*.
9. In explanation of the use of terms such as Majority World, citizenship rights, caste, First Nations, white supremacist dictatorship, European colonial subordination, European settler state, and similar terminological innovations, I present the very cogent analysis offered by Amos N. Wilson: "When we get ready to create revolution we must *re*define the world and *re*define words; there's no way around it.... There is a connection between naming and dominion, between naming and bringing into reality. When we permit another people to name and define, we permit another people to gain dominion and control over us." (original emphasis) See Amos N. Wilson, *The Falsification of Afrikan Consciousness: Eurocentric History, Psychiatry and the Politics of White Supremacy* (Brooklyn, NY: Afrikan World InfoSystems, 1993), 22.
10. He defines the U.S. western region as comprising the 19 states on and west of the 98th meridian, from North Dakota to Texas and westward, including Hawaii and Alaska.
11. Taylor, *Racial Frontier*, 30.

12. Ibid., 55–56, 67.
13. Quintard Taylor, "Slaves and Free Men: Blacks in the Oregon Country, 1840–1860," *Oregon Historical Quarterly* 83 (Summer 1982): 165–167.
14. Taylor, 169.
15. Quintard Taylor, "Blacks in the American West: An Overview," *Western Journal of Black Studies* 1 (March 1977): 6.
16. Ibid., 5.
17. Quintard Taylor, "Blacks and Asians in a White City: Japanese Americans and African Americans in Seattle, 1890–1940," *Western Historical Quarterly* 22 (November 1991): 428. For a comprehensive treatment of the significance of the Afrikan presence in the U.S. western region from the sixteenth through the twentieth centuries, see also "From Esteban to Rodney King: Five Centuries of African American History in the West," in *The American West: The Reader*, eds. Walter Nugent and Martin Ridge (Bloomington: Indiana University Press, 1999), 275–294; "African American Men in the American West, 1528–1990," *The Annals of the American Academy of Political and Social Science* 569 (May 2000): 102–119, and "Bibliographic Essay on the African American West," *Montana: The Magazine of Western History* 46, No. 4 (Winter 1996): 18–21; also available from the National Parks Service at http://www.cr.nps.gov/history/aaw.htm; Internet.
18. Taylor, "The Emergence," 342.
19. Taylor, *Racial Frontier*, 192–193.
20. Taylor, "Blacks and Asians," 401–429. The fuller and more extensive study can be found in *The Forging of a Black Community: A History of Seattle's Central District, 1870 through the Civil Rights Era*, in which Taylor explores all of the major themes already outlined: issues of employment, economics, politics, citizenship rights, Afrikan and Asian interactions, Afrikan community ethos, and the internal contest between citizenship rights and Black Power strategies in the face of European oppression through both the nineteenth and twentieth centuries.
21. Quintard Taylor, "The Great Migration: The Afro-American Communities of Seattle and Portland During the 1940s," *Arizona and the West* 23 (Summer 1981): 109–126; Quintard Taylor, "'There Was No Better Place to Go': The Transformation Thesis Revisited, African American Migration to the Pacific Northwest, 1940–1950," in *Terra Pacific: People and Place in Northwest America and Western Canada*, ed. Paul Wirt (Pullman: Washington State University Press, 1998), 205–219; and Quintard Taylor, "Black Urban Development — Another View: Seattle's Central District, 1910–1940," *Pacific Historical Review* 58 (November 1989): 429–448. See also (with Donald Grinde) "Red v. Black: Conflict and Accommodation in the Post-Civil War Indian Territory, 1865–1907," *American Indian Quarterly* 8 (Summer 1984), reprinted in *Peoples of Color in the American West*, eds. Sucheng Chan, Douglas Henry Daniels, Mario T. Garcia, and Terry P. Wilson (Lexington: D.C. Heath and Company, 1994).
22. In addition to that referenced above, see also Quintard Taylor, "The Civil Rights Movement in the Urban West: Black Protest in Seattle, 1960–1970," *Journal of Negro History* 80 (Winter 1995): 1–14.
23. See Frederick Jackson Turner, "The Significance of the Frontier in American History," in *Frontier and Section: Selected Essays of Frederick Jackson Turner*, ed. Ray Allen Billington (Englewood Cliffs, NJ: Prentice-Hall, 1961), 37–62. See also Turnerian disciple Walter Prescott Webb, *The Great Plains* (Boston: Ginn, 1931).

24. An enormously abbreviated list of New Western History scholars would include Carl Abbot at Portland State University, Armando Alonzo at Texas A&M University, David Danbom at North Dakota State University, William Deverell at the California Institute of Technology, and John Findlay at the University of Washington, who focus on various aspects of the twentieth century West; Susan Armitage at Washington State University, Anne Butler at Utah State University, Sarah Deutsch at Clark University, Kathleen Underwood at Grand Valley University of Michigan, who explore various dimensions of western women's history; Gordon Bakken at California State University–Fullerton, Stephen Haycox at the University of Alaska–Anchorage, Nancy Taniguchi at California State University–Stanislaus, and John R. Wunder at the University of Nebraska–Lincoln, who examine various perspectives on western legal history; Francisco Balderrama at California State University–Los Angeles, Albert Camarillo at Stanford University, Arnoldo De Leon at Angelo State University, Mario Garcia at the University of California–Santa Barbara, Ricardo Griswold Del Castillo at San Diego State University, and David Weber at Southern Methodist University, who explore various aspects of Tejano, Chicano, Mexican, and Mexican American history and US–Mexico relations; Peter Boag at Idaho State University, Dan Flores at the University of Montana, Mark Harvey at North Dakota State University, and William Cronon at University of Wisconsin–Madison, who investigate western environmental history; Sucheng Chan at the University of California–Santa Barbara, Ronald Takaki at the University of California-Los Angeles, Liping Zhu at Eastern Washington University, who, among other things, explore various dimensions of Asian history in the region; Gary Anderson at the University of Oklahoma, Philip Deloria and Vine Deloria, Jr. at the University of Colorado-Boulder, R. David Edmunds at the University of Texas–Dallas, Donald Fixico at the University of Kansas, Frederick Hoxie at the University of Illinois, Peter Iverson at Arizona State University, and Elliott West at the University of Arkansas–Fayettville, who explore various themes in First Nations history; and David Emmons at the University of Montana, Neil Foley at the University of Texas–Austin, and Chris Friday at Western Washington University, who explore various issues of race (caste) and/or labor in the region.

25. A Black Americanist or African Americanist historiography is principally concerned with the process by which Afrikans struggle to succeed in the quest of integrating or assimilating as equals and as Europeans within the mainstream of European culture in the United States. On the cultural level, this process ideally entails either complete absorption into the European genetic and or cultural mainstream, or a form of hybrid Euro-Afrikan ethnic identity (Americans of Afrikan descent), comparable to the ethno–European American identities of Irish-Americans, Italian-Americans, or Jewish-Americans. On the political level, this process inheres in the struggle for American citizenship rights as the central and only legitimate teleology of the Afrikan experience. Such a historiography champions that the struggle for unproscribed Europeanization — even if with the preservation of some elements of a distinctive Afrikan cultural identity — is the only credible interpretation of the nature and purpose of Afrikan struggle in the United States.

Concomitant with that is the notion that Afrikan history in the United States is primarily an *American*, not Afrikan, phenomenon. See Robert Ernst, "Negro Concepts of Americanism," *Journal of Negro History* 39, no. 3 (July 1954): 206–219 for an essay which arguments accord with this "Black Americanist" view.

26. John Hope Franklin and Alfred A. Moss, Jr., *From Slavery to Freedom: A History of African Americans*, 7th ed. (New York: Alfred A. Knopf, 1994); Benjamin Quarles, *The Negro in the Making of America* (New York: Simon and Schuster, 1996); Lerone Bennett, Jr., *Before the Mayflower: A History of Black America* (Baltimore: Penguin Books, 1993; Chicago: Johnson Publishing, 2000); Robin D. G. Kelley and Earl Lewis, eds., *To Make Our World Anew: A History of African Americans* (New York: Oxford University Press, 2000); and Darlene Clark Hine, William C. Hine, and Stanley Harrold, *The African-American Odyssey*, combined vol. (Upper Saddle River, NJ: Prentice-Hall, 2000).

27. Turner argued that the year 1890 signaled the end of the American frontier, and therefore, the ending of the history of the American West. New Western historians, by contrast, argue that the history of the region continued and continues into the twentieth and the twenty-first centuries. Turner's notion was grounded in a romanticism of Caucasian supremacist mythology surrounding Anglo-European conquest, settlement, and exploration. He argued this romanticized version of the Anglo-European expansion into the region constituted the central core of the region's history.

28. Taylor, *Racial Frontier*, 18.

29. He is mentioned twice in the introduction to *Racial Frontier*, on pages 19 and 21, but is altogether left out of the journal articles reviewed.

30. A Pan Afrikan nationalist historiography is concerned with the struggle for the end of white supremacist colonial rule by cultural, political, economic, military, and territorial independence from the European people of the United States. Unlike its counter notion, it recognizes the existence and motive of an integrationist or assimilationist dynamic in the course of the history of Afrikan struggle in the United States, but it does not credit it as the singular, principal, or legitimate struggle of Afrikan people. Further, whereas a Black or African Americanist historiography is principally concerned with explicating the Afrikan experience in the United States as an *American* experience, a Pan Afrikan nationalist historiography views the Afrikan experience in the United States as an *Afrikan* experience, centered in and flowing from the history of the Afrikan continent itself.

Pan Afrikan nationalism is distinct from Afrikan nationalism in that the former may be defined as the movement toward national independence from Europe (including the United States, a European settler state) that embraces the notion of a unified Afrikan world family or Afrikan world community and that affirms solidarity with the struggles of other peoples in the world against colonialism, cultural subordination, and human oppression and exploitation. Adhering to Omowale Malcolm X's definition, Afrikan nationalism, strictly speaking, simply means the struggle of Afrikans in the United States to realize national independence, state sovereignty, and authentic nationality apart from the American/European economic, political, and cultural complex.

31. Quintard Taylor, "Through the Prism of Race: The Meaning of African-American History in the West," in *A New Significance: Re-Envisioning the History of the American West*, ed. Clyde A. Milner, II (New York: Oxford University Press, 1996), 289.

32. Clyde A. Milner II, "Introduction: Envisioning a Second Century of Western History," in *A New Significance*, xi–xiii.

33. Taylor, "Through the Prism," 289. Taylor, critiquing both New Western History and Afrikan scholarship, charges "the experiences of African Americans

west of the ninety-eighth meridian have yet to be addressed in any systematic, comprehensive manner." In "From Esteban to Rodney King," 275, he also noted: "Much of New Western History scholarship easily reconciles Asian American, Chicano, or most nineteenth- and twentieth-century Native American history, which are axiomatically 'western' in orientation. Yet anomaly continues to define black western history. There is the uneasy sense that it is imposed on regional historiography to appease contemporary sensibilities rather than because it is central to the historical narrative. Scholarship on African American westerners continues to be viewed as an interesting footnote to a story focused largely on the rural South, the urban East, and the Midwest."

34. Taylor, "No Better Place," 205–219.

35. Quintard Taylor, "Migration of Blacks and Resulting Discriminatory Practices in Washington State Between 1940 and 1950," *Western Journal of Black Studies* 2 (March 1978): 65–71; and Taylor, "The Great Migration," 109–126.

36. Taylor, "No Better Place," 205.

37. As an example, see John Henrik Clarke's *Africans at the Crossroads: Notes for an African World Revolution* (Trenton, NJ: Africa World Press, 1991), *Who Betrayed the African World Revolution? And Other Speeches* (Chicago: Third World Press, 1994), *Christopher Columbus and the African Holocaust: Slavery and the Rise of European Capitalism* (Trenton, NJ: Africa World Press, 1992), and Clarke, ed., *New Dimensions in African History: The London Lectures of Dr. Yosef ben-Jochannan and Dr. John Henrik Clarke* (Trenton, NJ: Africa World Press, 1991).

38. Bernard B. Fall, ed., *Ho Chi Minh on Revolution, Selected Writings, 1920–66* (New York: Frederick A. Praeger, 1967), 40, 42.

39. For an interesting treatment of the complexity of Afrikan responses to the Filipino liberation struggle against American imperialism, see Willard B. Gatewood, Jr., *Black Americans and the White Man's Burden, 1898–1903* (Urbana: University of Illinois Press, 1975).

40. Taylor, *Racial Frontier*, 190–191.

41. Perhaps in the forefront of this critique was Patricia Nelson Limerick in her ground-breaking (within the context of the New Western History) book titled *The Legacy of Conquest: The Unbroken Past of the American West* (New York: W. W. Norton, 1987).

42. According to Conyers, a reference to social ecology involves "examining the social environmental characteristics and identifying these environmental factors" that shape a person's "ideas, philosophies, memory, and ethos." See James L. Conyers, Jr., "Charles H. Wesley, African American Historiography and Black Studies: An Historical Overview," in *African American Sociology: A Social Study of the Pan-African Diaspora*, eds. James L. Conyers, Jr. and Alva P. Barnett (Chicago: Nelson-Hall, 1999), 264.

43. Taylor does point out, however, that in the eighteenth and nineteenth centuries many Afrikans attempted to escape altogether from the United States to western regions under the control of the Spanish, British, and Mexicans. Ultimately, however, most failed, as these areas were eventually overrun by Americans and absorbed into the European settler state. But Taylor's assessment that Afrikans had no other alternative than the United States is not altogether historically accurate. Afrikans who had settled in various parts of the West, or even who sought to leave the South, also considered West Afrika as an alternative to the American West. As an example, Afrikans in Oklahoma had pursued the option of

repatriation to Gold Coast (now Ghana) under the movement of Chief Alfred Sam and the Rev. Orishatukeh Faduma. See Robert A. Hill, "Before Garvey: Chief Alfred Sam and the African Movement, 1912–1916," in *Pan-African Biography*, ed. Robert A. Hill (Los Angeles: African Studies Center, University of California, Los Angeles, and Crossroads Press, African Studies Association, 1987), 57–77. There are also some quite interesting discussions on both efforts and interest in West Afrikan settlement as an alternative to settlement in the western United States in Nell Irvin Painter, *Exodusters: Black Migration to Kansas After Reconstruction* (New York: W. W. Norton, 1986), 82–95, 137–145. See also Cyril E. Griffith, *The African Dream: Martin R. Delany and the Emergence of Pan-African Thought* (University Park: The Pennsylvania State University Press, 1975). That the West Afrikan resettlement effort ended in frustration had more to do with the fact that Afrikans lacked sufficient economic resources and infrastructure that would have allowed them to get to *"that* better place."

44. James L. Conyers, Jr., "Nathan Huggins's Report to the Ford Foundation on African American Studies: A Reflective Analysis a Decade Later," in *Black American Intellectualism and Culture: A Social Study of African American Social and Political Thought*, ed. James L. Conyers, Jr. (Stamford, CT: JAI Press, 1999), 267.

45. Bayo Oyebade, "African Studies and the Afrocentric Paradigm: A Critique," *Journal of Black Studies* 21, no. 2 (December 1990): 235–236.

46. James L. Conyers, Jr., "Africana Cosmology, Ethos, and Rap: A Social Study of Black Popular Culture," in *African American Jazz and Rap: Social and Philosophical Examinations of Black Expressive Behavior*, ed. James L. Conyers, Jr. (Jefferson, NC: McFarland, 2001), 187.

47. Molefi K. Asante, "Afrocentricity and the Quest for Method," in *Africana Studies: A Disciplinary Quest for Both Theory and Method*, ed. James L. Conyers, Jr. (Jefferson, NC: McFarland, 1997), 78–79.

48. Oyebade, "African Studies," 236.

49. Wilson, *Falsification*, 17–18.

50. John Henrik Clarke, "The Restructuring of the African Village Away From Home," in *John Henrik Clarke: Master Teacher*, ed. Barbara Eleanor Adams (Brooklyn, NY: A&B Publishers, 2000), 160.

51. Ibid., 155.

52. Wilson, *Falsification*, 13. Clarke related: "I have called for Afrikan people throughout the world to liberate themselves, to move toward self-reliance. I've asked for Pan Afrikan nationalism.... I've tried to seek an operational definition of Pan Afrikanism that is effective throughout the Afrikan world under different conditions.... What I'm working toward, and calling attention to the possibility of, is something that will take us from under the tutelage, the power and the domination of other people without giving us the right to dominate other people. I'm calling for an 'Afrikan world community.'" He defined the objective of the global Afrikan struggle in these terms: "We have to stop flinching from the fact that once we love ourselves, people will call us separatists and call us racists. We have to restore to Afrikan people the independence, the dignity and the connection that was destroyed by slavery and colonialism." See Person-Lynn, "On My Journey Now," 151, 163.

A Quintard Taylor Bibliography

Books

Shirley A. Moore and Quintard Taylor, eds., *Above the Rockies of Prejudice: African American Women in the American West, 1598–2000* (Norman: University of Oklahoma Press, 2001)

Lawrence B. de Graaf, Kevin Mulroy, and Quintard Taylor, eds., *Seeking El Dorado: African Americans in California, 1769–1997* (Los Angeles: Autry Museum of Western Heritage; Seattle: University of Washington Press, 2000)

In Search of the Racial Frontier: African Americans in the American West, 1528–1990. New York: W. W. Norton, 1998.

The Forging of a Black Community: Seattle's Central District, from 1870 through the Civil Rights Era. Seattle: University of Washington Press, 1994.

The Making of the Modern World: A History of the Twentieth Century. Dubuque, IA: Kendall/Hunt Publishing, 1990.

Journal Articles

"The Civil Rights Movement in the Urban West: Black Protest in Seattle, 1960–1970." *Journal of Negro History* 80 (Winter 1995): 1–14.

"Blacks and Asians in a White City: Japanese Americans and African Americans in Seattle, 1890–1940." *Western Historical Quarterly* 22 (November 1991): 401–429.

"The Question of Culture: Black Life and the Transformation of Black Urban America." *Essays in History: The Journal of the Historical Society of the University of Lagos, Nigeria* 6 (December 1989).

"Black Urban Development – Another View: Seattle's Central District, 1910–1940." *Pacific Historical Review* 58 (November 1989): 429–448.

"Slaves and Free Men: Blacks in the Oregon Country, 1840–1860." *Oregon Historical Quarterly* 83 (Summer 1982): 165–169.

(with Donald Grinde). "Native American and Black Interaction in the American Southeast During the Colonial Period." *Hampton Institute Journal of Ethnic Studies* 9 (May 1981).

"The Great Migration: The Afro-American Communities of Seattle and Portland During the 1940s." *Arizona and the West* 23 (Summer 1981): 109–126.

(with Alonzo Smith). "Racial Discrimination in the Workplace: A Study of Two West Coast Cities During the 1940s." *Journal of Ethnic Studies* (Spring 1980).

(with Dennis A. Warner, Karen P. Swope and Michael Balasa). "South by Northwest: An Educational Television Series Designed to Teach Regional Black History." *Integrated Education* 18 (January–August 1980).

"The Emergence of Black Communities in the Pacific Northwest: 1865–1910." *Journal of Negro History* 64 (Fall 1979): 342–351.

"Frente Negra Brasileira: The Afro-Brazilian Civil Rights Movement, 1924–1937." *Umoja: A Scholarly Journal of Black Studies* 2 (Spring 1978).

"Migration of Blacks and Resulting Discriminatory Practices in Washington State between 1940–1950." *Western Journal of Black Studies* 2 (March 1978): 65–71.

"Blacks in the American West: An Overview." *Western Journal of Black Studies* 1 (March 1977): 4–10.

"The Chicago Political Machine and Black-Ethnic Conflict and Accommodation." *Polish-American Studies* 29 (Spring 1972).

Articles in Books, Book Chapters/Introductions

"Introduction. The Twenty-Fifth Infantry Regiment: Buffalo Soldiers and the Quest for American Freedom." In *History of the Twenty-Fifth Regiment, United States Infantry, 1869–1926* by John H. Nankivell. Lincoln: University of Nebraska Press, 2001.

"Contested Regional Stories: Race and Region in The African American Pacific Northwest: The Saga of Susie Revels Cayton and Beatrice Morrow Cannady." In *The Pacific Northwest: A Region in Transition*, edited by William Robbins. Corvallis: Oregon State University Press, 2000.

"From Esteban to Rodney King: Five Centuries of African American History in the West." *Montana: The Magazine of Western History* 46 (Winter 1996): 2–23. Reprinted in *The American West: The Reader*, edited by Walter Nugent and Martin Ridge. Bloomington: Indiana University Press, 1999.

"Introduction. The African American Experience in Nebraska." In *Visions of Freedom on the Great Plains: An Illustrated History of African Americans in Nebraska*, edited by Bertha W. Calloway and Alonzo Smith. Virginia Beach, VA: Donning Company Publishers, 1998.

"Introduction." In *The Colored Cadet at West Point: Autobiography of Lieutenant Henry Ossian Flipper*, by Henry O. Flipper. Lincoln: University of Nebraska Press, 1998.

"'There Was No Better Place to Go': The Transformation Thesis Revisited, African American Migration to the Pacific Northwest, 1940–1950." In *Terra Pacific: People and Place in Northwest America and Western Canada*, edited by Paul Wirt. Pullman: Washington State University Press, 1998.

"Mary Ellen Pleasant." In *By Grit and Grace: Women Who Shaped the Pioneer West*, edited by Glenda Riley and Richard Etulain. Golden, CO: Fulcrum Publishing, 1997.

"Blacks and Asians in a White City: Japanese Americans and African Americans in Seattle, 1890–1940." *Western Historical Quarterly* 22 (November 1991). Reprinted in *Major Problems in the History of the American West: Documents and Essays*, 2nd ed., edited by Clyde A. Milner, II. New York: Houghton Mifflin, 1997.

"Through the Prism of Race: The Meaning of African-American History in the West." In *A New Significance: Re-Envisioning the History of the American West*, edited by Clyde A. Milner II. New York: Oxford University Press, 1996.

"Contentious Legacy: The Nigerian Youth Movement and the Rise of Ethnic Politics, 1934–1951." In *Ethnicity, Religion and Nation-Building*. Vol. III of *Nigerian Studies in Religious Tolerance*, edited by C.S. Momah and Hakeem Harunah. Lagos, Nigeria: University of Lagos Press/Center for the Propagation of Religious and Ethnic Tolerance, 1995.

"Slaves and Free Men: Blacks in the Oregon Country, 1840–1860." *Oregon Historical Quarterly* 83 (Summer 1982). Reprinted in *Peoples of Color in the American West*, edited by Sucheng Chan, Douglas Henry Daniels, Mario T. Garcia, and Terry P. Wilson. Lexington: D.C. Heath and Company, 1994.

(With Donald Grinde). "Red v. Black: Conflict and Accommodation in the Post-Civil War Indian Territory, 1865–1907." *American Indian Quarterly* 8 (Summer 1984). Reprinted in *Peoples of Color in the American West*, edited by Sucheng Chan, Douglas Henry Daniels, Mario T. Garcia, and Terry P. Wilson. Lexington: D.C. Heath and Company, 1994.

"The Emergence of Black Communities in the Pacific Northwest, 1865–1910." *Journal of Negro History* 64 (Fall 1979). Reprinted in *From Reconstruction to the Great Migration, 1877–1917*. Vol. 4 of *Black Communities and Urban Development in America, 1720–1990*. 10 vols, edited by Kenneth L. Kusmer. Hamden, CT: Garland Publishing, 1991.

"Black Urban Development: Another View, Seattle's Central District, 1910–1940, A Case Study." *Pacific Historical Review* 58 (November 1989). Reprinted in *The Great Migration and After, 1917–1930*. Vol. 5 of *Black Communities and Urban Development in America, 1720–1990*. 10 vols, edited by Kenneth L. Kusmer. Hamden, CT: Garland Publishing, 1991.

Other Contributions

"African American Men in the American West, 1528–1990." *The Annals of the American Academy of Political and Social Science* 569 (May 2000).

"Race and Ethnicity in the Southwest: African American and Arizona History." *Arizona Attorney* 34 (February 1998).

"African Americans on the American Frontier." In *The Reader's Encyclopedia of the American West*, edited by Howard R. Lamar. New Haven: Yale University Press, 1998.

"A View of the Buffalo Soldiers Through Indigenous Eyes: A Response." *Raven Chronicles* 7 (Summer/Fall 1997).

"Comrades of Color: Buffalo Soldiers in the West, 1866–1917." *Colorado Heritage* 18 (Spring 1996).

"African Americans in the Enchanted State: Black History in New Mexico, 1539–1990." In *History of Hope: The African American Experience in New Mexico*, edited by Thomas Lark. Albuquerque: The Albuquerque Museum, 1996.

Articles on Sarah Breedlove Walker, Mary Ellen Pleasant and Oakland, California. In *Encyclopedia of the American West*, edited by Charles Phillips and Alan Axelrod. New York: Macmillan Publishing Company, 1996.

"The Black Towns," "African Americans in the West" (and discussions of black communities in Idaho, Montana and Seattle). In *Encyclopedia of African American Culture and History*, edited by Jack Salzman, David Lionel Smith, and Cornel West. New York: Macmillan Publishing Company, 1995.

"Swinging the Door Wide: World War II Wrought a Profound Transformation in Seattle's Black Community." *Columbia: The Magazine of Northwest History* 9 (Summer 1995).

"In Search of Nigeria: My Year as a Fulbright Scholar at the University of Lagos." In *The Fulbright Experience in Benin*, edited by Frank J. Salamone. Williamsburg: William and Mary Press, 1994.

"African Americans in Pacific Northwest History: Retrospect and Prospect." *Columbia: The Magazine of Northwest History* 7 (Fall 1993).

"Disparate Images: Black Life in Contemporary Japan, Review of Regge Life's Documentary Film, 'Struggle and Success: The African-American Experience in Japan.'" *Annual Bulletin of the University of Oregon Center for Asian and Pacific Studies* (August 1993).

"The Evolution of Post-Bellum African American Culture." In *Encyclopedia of Social History*, Vol. II, edited by Mary Kupiec Cayton, Elliot J. Gorn, and Peter W. Williams. New York: Charles Scribner's Sons, 1993.

"Beatrice Cannady, An Early Twentieth Century Oregon Civil Rights Activist: An Historical Vignette." In *Voices of Kuumba: An Anthology of the Northwest African American Writers Workshop*, Vol. 4, edited by Linda Harris, Joseph Franklin, and Lillian Whitlow. Portland: Metropolitan Arts Commission, 1992.

"Reflections on Two Decades in Pursuit of African American History in the Pacific Northwest." In *Voices of Kuumba: An Anthology of the Northwest African American Writers Workshop*, Vol. 3, edited by Joseph Franklin and Linda Harris. Portland: Metropolitan Arts Commission, 1991.

Biographical entries for Jesse Jackson, Otto Kerner, Burke Marshall, and Huey P. Newton. *Historical Dictionary of Civil Rights in the United States*. Westport, CT: Greenwood Press, 1991.

Biographies of Lloyd Bentsen and Richard Gephardt. *Encyclopedia of World Biography*. New York: McGraw Hill, 1991.

"The Troublesome Presence: Black Americans and the United States Constitution." *Proceedings of the International Conference on Federalism in a Changing World*. Ile Ife, Nigeria: Obafemi Awolowo University Press, 1988.

Biographies of John B. Connally, Estes Kefauver, John W. McCormack and Edmund Muskie. *Encyclopedia of World Biography*. New York: McGraw Hill, 1986.

"Slave Family Life on the Fazenda and Plantation: A Comparison of Brazil and the United States, 1750–1850." *Proceedings of the First Annual Conference on Records, Family History and Genealogy*, Vol. 11. Provo, Utah: Brigham Young University Press, 1980.

Book Reviews

Review of *The Chinese in Vancouver, 1945–80* by Wing Chung Ng. *Pacific Historical Review* (forthcoming).

Review of *Race, Place and the Law, 1836–1948* by David Delaney. *American Historical Review* 104 (December 1999).

Review of *Minorities in Phoenix: A Profile of Mexican American, Chinese American and African American Communities, 1860–1992* by Bradford Luckingham. *Pacific Historical Review* 65 (February 1996).

Review of *W.E.B. Du Bois: Biography of a Race* by David Levering Lewis. *Reviews in American History* 22 (December 1994).

Review of *Seattle, 1921–1940: From Boom to Bust* by Richard C. Berner. *Pacific Historical Review* 63 (August 1994): 452.

Review of *Black San Francisco: The Struggle for Racial Equality in the West, 1900–1954* by Albert S. Broussard. *Pacific Historical Review* 63 (May 1994): 266.

Review of *The End of American Exceptionalism: Frontier Anxiety from the Old West to the New Deal* by David M. Wrobel. *Oregon Historical Quarterly* 94 (Summer Fall 1993).

Review of *The Civil War in Louisiana* by John D. Winters. *Gulf Coast Historical Review* 9 (Fall 1993).

Review of *Black Dixie: Afro-Texan History and Culture in Houston* edited by Howard Beeth and Cary D. Wintz. *Western Historical Quarterly* 24 (May 1993): 255.

Review of *Seattle, 1900–1920: From Boomtown, Urban Turbulence, to Restoration* by Richard C. Berner. *Pacific Historical Review* 62 (February 1993): 109.

Review of *George Washington Williams: A Biography* by John Hope Franklin. *African Concord* (Lagos, Nigeria), January 1989.

Review of *Mainstream and Margins: Jews, Blacks and other Americans* by Peter I. Rose. *Religious Studies Review* 10 (July 1984).

Review of *Death in a Promised Land: The Tulsa Race Riot of 1921* by Scott Ellsworth. *Oral History Review* 11 (Summer 1982).

Review of *The American Law of Slavery, 1810–1860: Considerations of Humanity and Interest* by Mark V. Tushnet. *Journal of Economic History* 42 (1982).

Review of *The Black Worker*, Vol. 6, *The Era of Post-War Prosperity and the Great Depression, 1920–1936* edited by Philip Foner and Ronald L. Lewis. *Umoja: A Scholarly Journal of Black Studies* 6 (Spring 1982).

Review of *Sexual Racism: The Emotional Barrier to an Integrated Society* by Charles Herbert Stember. *Umoja: A Scholarly Journal of Black Studies* 3 (Fall 1979).

Review of *The Black Towns* by Norman L. Crockett. *Utah Historical Quarterly* 47 (Fall 1979).

Review of *Red Over Black: Slavery Among the Cherokee Indians* by Rudia Halliburton, Jr. *Umoja: A Scholarly Journal of Black Studies* 2 (Summer 1978).

Review of *Roots: The Saga of an American Family* by Alex Haley. *Minnesota History* 45 (Spring 1977).

Mulattos, Freejacks, Cape Verdeans, Black Seminoles, and Others: Afrocentrism and Mixed-Race Persons

Rhett Jones

> *In Latin America no one wants to be black.*
> — Anani Dzidzienyo

The worldwide dominance of Europe, with its construction of empires and smug celebration of self, had as its counterpart the denigration of African peoples. Wherever they had power, Europeans constructed a system in which Blacks were regarded as morally, intellectually, culturally, and physically inferior to whites. In their enslavement, exploitation, and oppression of people of color, the colonizing powers above all feared an alliance between them. Therefore, they worked not only to divide Native American nations from one another and to separate Africans from the same nation, but to divide Africans from Indians. Throughout the colonial Americas, the settlers worked to divide red people from black ones. This was achieved, in part, by attaching to blackness a stigma, by establishing a racial hierarchy in which persons of African ancestry were at the bottom, a position intended, some settlers argued, by God.

This paper examines how persons of this culturally despised African identity have coped by examining the various strategies some adopted to escape from Africanity. Because their African heritage sometimes manifested itself in obvious physical characteristics, those who wished to escape the stigma of blackness were confronted with a seemingly inescapable dilemma. They literally had to create an identity for themselves that denied their physical appearance and rejected their blackness. This paper examines some of the ways in which this was achieved.

Finding Race: Two Opposing Forces

In the American colonies, settlers deliberately played Indians and blacks against each other, whether the colonizing power was English (Willis, 1970: 43; McLoughlin, 1984: 264–265), French (McConnell, 1968: 8), Portuguese (Degler, 1971: 213), or Spanish (Palmer, 1976: 189). Blacks were used in battle against the Indians and Indians were employed to track down runaway slaves (Jones, 1977). Using one group against the other dated back to the earliest years of settlement. Indians cooperated with the Spaniards and hunted down rebellious blacks on the island of Hispanola in 1522, and helped to put down the black rebellion in Mexico City in 1537 (Rout, 1976: 121). In 1533, as part of a treaty signed with the Spaniards on Hispanola, Indians were required to search for and return all runaway slaves to the Spaniards. The treaty stipulated they were to be paid for this service. In working out a peace treaty with Maroons, Spanish authorities in sixteenth-century Mexico gave them Indian lands, thereby not only achieving peace, but creating hostility between the two groups (Pereira, 1994). In English South Carolina, a government committee suggested a group of commissioners should be appointed to decide on rewards given Indians who killed or captured black runaways (Wood, 1974: 265). In French Louisiana, a number of slaves were rewarded with their freedom for bravery in battle against the Natchez Indians in 1729 (McConnell, 1968: 8; Brawley, 1970: 16). In the 1720s and again in the 1730s, the English imported their Miskito Indian allies from Central America to be used to track down and defeat their troublesome Maroon population (Bridges, 1828: II, 141; Campbell, 1988: 54). In neither case were the Miskito successful in forcing the Maroons into the kind of major decisive battle the English sought, but they did succeed in locating and destroying hidden Maroon croplands and herds—successes which some historians believe led Maroons to sign peace treaties with the English in the 1730s. On the other side of the coin, the massive revolt led by Tupac Amaru in the 1780s to drive the Spaniards out of Peru and restore the Inca was defeated in part because of the support provided the Spanish government by its troops of African descent.

In addition to using blacks and Indians against one another, whites used other ways to separate them. In the Spanish Americas, for example,

Indians were given legal protection that was denied blacks. The Spaniards gradually concluded that Native Americans were a childlike people in need of uplift, and that if proper patience were demonstrated Indians could become a part of civilization. But while they were being taught, they had to be protected from whites, from blacks, and even from the Catholic church. As a consequence, Indians were exempt from the Inquisition, while blacks (and whites) were not. Blacks were regarded as a difficult, dangerous, and unruly people. While baptized Indians did not, for example, fully understand the teachings of the Catholic Church, blacks did and might from the perspective of the Spaniards, consciously enter into pacts with the devil against the Church (Palmer, 1976). Indians and blacks were both aware of these differences between them (Jones, 1991). Morner (1967: 60–61) argues that while Indians were legally ranked above blacks in the Spanish American hierarchy by virtue of the various legal protections they enjoyed, in practical terms they were below blacks. Most persons of African descent, whether slave or free, spoke Spanish and understood the workings of the Spanish colonial system. They shrewdly took advantage of it. Indians, on the other hand, were unfamiliar with the system and so were exploited and abused, often by those who were supposed to be their protectors.

Spanish church and state therefore tried to minimize contact between Native Americans and blacks, not only because they feared the possibility of a black–Indian alliance, but because they were afraid persons of African descent would abuse and take advantage of Native Americans. They especially worked to prevent social, sexual, and marital relations between Indians and blacks, and did everything possible to prevent Indians and blacks from living together. Black men who entered into sexual relations with Indian women could be castrated (Morner, 1967: 40). The situation was not very different in Portuguese-controlled Brazil, which in the latter Eighteenth century permitted marriages between whites and Indians, but discouraged those between Indians and blacks. In 1771, a Native American officer was reduced in rank because he married a black woman (Morner, 1967: 50). In the English settlements, whites tried to eliminate situations where Indians and blacks might meet and thereby establish close personal relations. They attempted to limit the number of Indians coming into colonial settlements and to keep blacks out of Indian country (Willis, 1970: 43).

These laws impacted both peoples of color. Rout suggests that Native Americans may have initially seen no meaningful difference between the Spaniards and their African slaves as the two people arrived together, worked together, shared a common language, and were both regarded as outlandish foreigners. But as the Indians gradually came to understand that the Spaniards regarded Africans as inferior, they were prone to adopt the same attitude (Rout, 1976: 121). In the southeastern part of what is now the United States, Indians were very much influenced by the development of slavery and the racist justifications for it. Even after being removed from their homeland to Oklahoma territory, the Cherokee continued to hold racist attitudes toward blacks, and like the Choctaw, Creek, and Chickasaw, they passed harsh racist laws against blacks that were little different from those passed by neighboring slaveholding whites (McLoughlin, 1984: 278–279). The severe treatment of blacks in the Cherokee nation produced slave rebellions in 1841, 1842, and 1850. In Mexico, blacks found Indians to be easy, convenient, and relatively defenseless targets for the hostility they developed as a result of their treatment by whites (Palmer, 1976: 64). Palmer (1976: 84) concludes that Indians and blacks were never able to unite in common rebellion against the Spaniards in Mexico not only because of the Spanish policy of divide and rule, but because of the "perverse phenomenon of the oppressed directing their violence at each other rather than toward the oppressors."

The same efforts made to separate Native Americans from Africans and Afro-Americans were also made to divide them from whites. While the strategies varied over time and space and were influenced by such factors as economics, demographics, settlement patterns and goals, religion, and nationality in general, the Europeans who populated the Americas sought to maintain a racial hierarchy by drawing firm and fast lines among the races. Such lines may have been deliberately and consciously constructed as Bennett (1970), Morgan (1975), and others have suggested, or they may have been the virtually inevitable consequence of empire building. Jordan (1968) touched a firestorm of scholarly controversy when he suggested that racism was an "unthinking decision," not at all planned by the colonists but a by-product of the social orders they created. While Williams (1944) had earlier argued that slavery led to racism and not the other way around, Jordan maintained the two developed together, so closely intertwined that it was difficult to determine which was the cause and which was the effect.

Regardless of the cause of the separation of the races—buttressed throughout the Americas by law, custom, and often brutal, ugly, extra-legal force—racial segregation was nowhere fully successful in the New World. Miscegenation was common and persons of mixed ancestry gradually appeared in all the American colonies (Jones, 1986). This ongoing miscegenation took place against a backdrop of increased significance attached to race. Racism, a staple of nineteenth and post-nineteenth century thought, did not exist in the sixteenth and seventeenth centuries, but somewhere over the course of the eighteenth century, the races were constructed and given meaning so that the English settlers of North America, who at the end of the seventeenth century described themselves as Christians or English, were by the end of the eighteenth century describing themselves as whites. Slaves transported from Africa, who thought of themselves as Ewe, Ashanti, Ibo, or Yoruba, were thinking of themselves as black. When blacks in the United States began to construct their own independent institutions on the cusp of the nineteenth century they styled them as African, as in the African Methodist Episcopal Church, thereby adopting and affirming a racial identity for themselves. Similarly, the native peoples of the Americas changed the way in which they thought about themselves, so that they not only retained their sense of national identity — that is, they remained Cherokee, Seneca, and Narragansett — but also developed a sense of themselves as Indians. The terms "African" and "Indian" were themselves foreign to the people who adopted them as the slaves had no conception of themselves as Africans, a term they would have found meaningless, any more than the native peoples saw themselves as Indians. These labels were imposed on them by outsiders, but they were labels they eventually accepted and shaped their ideas about members of other races as well as about themselves.

The extent to which the terminology of race was accepted by Native Americans is demonstrated by the alteration of their creation myths. While every culture has creation myths, meant to explain the origin of its people, pre-contact Indian creation stories made no mention of race. There was no sense of race as a concept, and Amerindians had no systematic, continuous contact with persons from either Europe or Africa. By the 1820s, however, a Cherokee chief told a white man that the Great Spirit created three men, one white, one red, and one black, and after placing three closed boxes before them, spoke (McLoughlin, 1984: 257):

> "White man, you are pale and weak, but I made your first, and will give you first choice; go to the boxes, open them and look in, and chose which you will take for your portion." The white man [took the box that] was filled with pens, and ink, and paper, and compasses, and such things as [white] people now use. The Great Spirit spoke again and said, "Black man, I made you next, but I do not like you. You may stand aside. The Red man is my favourite, he shall come forward and take the next choice." [The red man chose] a box filled with tomahawks, knives, war clubs, traps, and such things as are "useful in war and hunting." The Great Spirit laughed when he saw how well his red son knew how to choose. Then he said to the negro, "You may have what is left, the third box is for you." That was filled with axes, and hoes, with buckets to carry

water in, and long whips for driving oxen, which meant the negro must work for both the red and white man, and it has been so ever since.

McLoughlin (1984) is among those scholars who argue that the Indians transformed their myths not only to account for the realities of the multiracial society in which they now lived, but to distance themselves from blacks and to convince whites and themselves that Indians were different from and superior to blacks. Ironically, the new creation myths they devised were influenced by the creation myths West Africans developed to account for slavery and the power of Europeans in their region.

Not only did Africans reconstruct their ideas about themselves to account for European hegemony, but African Americans also argued that blacks possessed certain characteristics distinct from those of other races. The best known proponent of this view was W.E.B. Du Bois, who in *The Souls of Black Folk* (1903) and other publications, claimed for blacks a certain genius, a set of gifts which they had to offer to the world in general, and the United States in particular. But Du Bois was not alone as other leading black social scientists, among them Kelly Miller, believed that Africans were gentle, kind, and biologically predisposed to be forgiving of their enemies and oppressors. As Fredrikson (1971) demonstrates, some blacks went so far as to argue that Africans were genetically inclined to be loving, community-oriented Christians, a point of view also held by white scholars. The fact that an entire race of people could be biologically inclined to accept a particular religious ideology seems absurd, but demonstrates the extent to which ideas about race were accepted.

Tension therefore existed between two opposing forces in the New World. On the one hand, miscegenation continued to take place. Not only did it continue among the three original racial stocks but among the offspring of these three racial groups and mixed bloods and between mixed bloods themselves. So, for example, not only did blacks and whites continue to mate, but their mulatto offspring then mated with both whites and blacks, other mulattos, and the mixed offspring of Indians and whites. A complex racial terminology emerged to make sense of this mixture and to not only place persons in different racial or sub-racial groups, but to rank them as well. On the other hand, although miscegenation continued, beliefs about the differences among the races became stronger. These differences also hardened into hierarchy so that it was not only believed that whites were different from blacks, but that they were physically, mentally, and morally superior to blacks. The exact ranking of the races varied over time and place, as did the placement of persons of mixed ancestry, but whites were always at the top of the system. Who ranked just beneath them was usually determined by political and demographic factors. So, for example, in the English-speaking Caribbean where the mass of black slaves represented the primary threat to white control, blacks were at the bottom of the system, mulattos just above them and persons of pure or mixed Amerindian ancestry were ranked above mulattos. In Spanish Peru, in contrast, the greatest threat to white rule were the masses of conquered Indians. As a consequence, Indians were at the bottom of the system, with mestizos and other persons of mixed Indian ancestry above them. Mulattos ranked beneath the Spaniards.

As slavery grew in importance in the New World, control of slaves became an increasing concern. Control was largely accomplished by brutality and cruelty and by stripping slaves of basic human rights to make it more difficult for them to free themselves and for others to emancipate them. In addition to physical brutality and legal restrictions, a psychological assault was launched on blacks with efforts made to prove that Africans were a backwards, brutish, ignorant, sub-human (if human at all) people destined by nature, or by God, to serve whites. This racist doctrine permeated virtually every aspect of Euro-American science and thought as blacks were found inferior by those knowledgeable of theology, philosophy, biology, history and the emergent social sciences. While most blacks rejected the idea of inherent racial inferiority, some accepted it, and still others were constrained to behave as if they accepted it. All persons of African descent had to cope with it. Blackness became a stigma, a sign that an individual was blighted. It became, in the title aptly selected by Abram Kardiner and Lionel Ovesey, two psychiatrists, for their (1951) book, *The Mark of Oppression*.

The tensions between these two forces, continued miscegenation and increased denigration of blackness placed persons with African physical features in an ever more difficult position. On the one hand, the mark of oppression was there, visible for all to see, at a time when it was viewed with hostility, contempt, and disgust. Africanity was different from ethnicity. For example, say a Serb who wished to be accepted as English need only learn to speak English, change his name, change his religion, change his style of dress, and move to a new area to be accepted as an Anglo-American. Moreover, what became increasingly important, for most purposes, was not whether one was of Serbian or English descent, but whether or not one was white (Davis, 1991). As racism became more prevalent, all Americans became increasingly attentive to skin color, lip shape, hair texture, and the physical characteristics that were considered the mark of Africanity. Changing a name and changing religion could not win acceptance for persons of African descent.

At least three strategies were adopted by those who sought to escape blackness. Some, despite clear physical evidence to the contrary, sought to be considered white, while others wanted to be regarded as Amerindians. Still others created entirely new groups, which, while they made diverse and original claims concerning racial identity, always denied they were black.

Seeking Whiteness: Differing Strategies for Changing Racial Contexts

Despite their physical appearance, some groups of African descent have regarded themselves and sought to have others regard them as white. In some cases, this decision to think of members of the group as white was made before race became both fixed and significant. The Cape Verdeans constitute such an example. The Cape Verde islands, located off the cost of West Africa and originally uninhabited, were gradually settled by persons from the Mid-East, Europe, and Africa (Coli and Lobban, 1990; Lobban, 1995). The islands were eventually colonized by the Portuguese who used them as a way station in the transatlantic slave trade (Halter, 1993). Gradually, a mixed race people developed on the islands, with lines drawn between Europeans and Africans, between persons of various religions, and a racial hierarchy was established. Social status in the Cape Verde islands was based on physical characteristics; persons of African appearance placed at the bottom of the system and those with European features were at the top. But the ranking was not, strictly speaking, based on color as one's social position was also influenced by culture (Lobban, 1995: 57). Those who practiced an African religion were ranked beneath those who were Catholics, while those who spoke Portuguese or Creole were elevated above those who spoke an African language. As the islands were subject to the Portuguese crown, most of their inhabitants thought of themselves as Portuguese.

Claiming Portuguese identity became problematic upon the nineteenth century migration of Cape Verdeans to the United States, where anyone of known African ancestry was considered black. The range of Cape Verdean phenotypes was much like that in the African American population, including persons who were very African in appearance, ranging from persons of obviously mixed race ancestry to persons who were quite European in appearance. As Europeans, however, the Portuguese were considered white, so that when they thought about race at all, most Cape Verdeans considered themselves white. Most Americans, however, whether white or black, did not. Black Americans resented attempts by Cape Verdeans to deny their blackness when they were obviously of African heritage, while white Americans treated them as they looked — like blacks. Further complicating the efforts of Cape Verdeans to be considered white was the rapid adoption of United States attitudes toward persons of African descent by immigrants from Portugal and from the Azores, a Portuguese colonial possession. These people, despite sharing a common language, religion, and culture, quickly distanced themselves from Cape Verdeans, excluding them for Portuguese Roman Catholic parishes, social clubs, and benevolent institutions (Halter, 1993: 7). In Providence, where a number of Cape Verdeans settled, conflict developed in Holy Rosary Church, whose parishioners were largely from the Azores. Cape Verdeans eventually stopped attending the church because they felt unwelcome, some saying the racial hostility they encountered there eventually led them to leave the Catholic Church entirely (Beck, 1992: 81). In New Bedford, Massachusetts, another center of Portuguese settlement, one Cape Verdean informant observed that while many older Cape Verdeans still claim to be Portuguese, New Bedford Portuguese "felt that [they] really weren't" (Halter, 1993: 171).

Cape Verdeans arrived in the United States with a racial identity formed outside America and then struggled to convince whites and blacks that they were white. In sharp contrast, the Freejacks, another group of persons of African descent who wanted to be considered white, formed their sense of identity in a time and place where blackness was regarded with contempt. The Freejack community, located not far from New Orleans, took shape in a period when race was considered important, but had not yet acquired a firm rigidity. Freejacks were the product of miscegenation among blacks, whites, Indians, and persons who were of mixed race ancestry. Under the laws of the colony of Louisiana, which was first French, then Spanish, then French again, Freejacks were classified as free people of color, and thereby regarded as neither black nor white. When the United States purchased Louisiana, efforts were made to eliminate all intermediate racial groups, and to follow Anglo-American conceptions of race which forced persons to be either black or white. After the Civil War, with the development of Jim Crow, these efforts were intensified and because Freejacks were known to have some African ancestry, they were classified as black. This they vigorously denied, but encountered some of the same problems faced by Cape Verdeans. First, some of them were clearly of African ancestry, and second, both blacks and whites refused to consider Freejacks as white. In a 1908 court case, two Freejack parents sued a railroad because their daughters, under Jim Crow laws, were pressured to leave the white railway car and move to the black one. The court traced the ancestry of the girls, and finding that their forefathers were free people of color, declared them, and by implication all Freejacks, to be black. The Freejack response to this ruling was to attempt to destroy all public records that documented their racial heritage (Posey, 1979: 185).

The Freejacks and other persons of African ancestry who attempted to present themselves as white tried to maintain a sense of whiteness by denying others the opportunity to treat them as if they were not. They avoided contact with whites who looked down on them as blacks, and with blacks who regarded them as equals. These communities became isolated with the result that intermarriage within them was quite high (Berry, 1963; Beale, 1972). In the south, where schools were either black or white, education became a problem. As whites refused to send their children to black schools, youngsters from such groups often had little education at all. Employment was also a problem as the Freejacks and other communities like them could not be hired for "white" jobs and refused to work at "black" ones. While Freejacks were not considered white by their neighbors, during the Second World War many of them were inducted into the armed services where, once they left the region, they were accepted as white. Based on this experience, many of the Freejacks returned home even more determined than ever to be treated as white (Posey, 1979: 187).

While seeking to be considered white, Freejacks and peoples like them sometimes willingly acknowledged Amerindian ancestry (Dane and Griessman, 1972; Blu, 1980; Sider, 1993). Indeed, it was common for them to attribute their darker skin color to Native American ancestry. At times, more exotic explanations were found by such people for their dark color by insisting they were of Turkish, Moorish, or Portuguese ancestry. They would not accept African ancestry. In his interview with a member of one of these groups, sociologist Berwyn Berry wrote (1963: 32):

> "Tell you the truth, Mr. Berry," said one old fellow whose confidence had been won through long hours of chitchat, *"we don't know what the hell we are.* Some folk say we is Indians. Well, maybe so and maybe not. My old man used to say we was part Cherokee and part Irish. I dunno. *But we know we ain't niggers.* We know that!" And he made the point emphatic by pounding his right fist into the palm of his left hand.

The issue here is not whiteness but blackness. Being white for these people is but one way of not being black. As their Africanity is obvious, they can sustain this position only by banding together, by supporting one another as a community united by agreeing on their whiteness. The refusal of outsiders to accept their whiteness turns them further in on themselves, forcing them to ever increasingly rely on one another in denial of blackness. Encounters with others are always dangerous; whites might treat them with the contempt reserved for blacks, while blacks may resume on their physical appearance to treat them as fellow blacks. Only with one another are they safe, secure in the knowledge that they will be accepted for what they claim to be — white.

Whiteness for such persons is therefore a communal activity based on the shared willingness to support one another in this claim. The psychological dynamics of denying blackness are therefore different from the individual who, knowing she is legally and socially black, decides to "pass" as white. There are degrees of passing. In the days of legal segregation, some persons passed as white only to use the restroom, sit in the front of the bus, or eat in a restaurant. Their passing was a temporary act, more a matter of convenience than anything else. Others might pass to obtain a job ordinarily closed to blacks, passing only at work and otherwise living their lives as black. Still others passed entirely, cutting all ties with their black past, including their families, and crossing over into the white world. These varied degrees of passing had two things in common. First, the person had to appear to be white. Even a hint of African ancestry was to invite the kind of scrutiny and attention the person passing could ill afford. Second, such a person sustained the fiction of whiteness entirely on her own. She was thrown on her own resources in presenting herself as white and relied entirely on her own talents for improvisation when challenges arose. Occasionally she might require the support of others to conceal her identity, or at the least not to give her away, but generally she relied on tactics she devised.

In both respects, such individual passing was different from the strategy adopted by mixed race groups claiming whiteness. Unlike those who passed as individuals, such groups often contained members who were obviously of African descent and when they moved among persons who did not know them — and even among many who did — were considered black. They were therefore not on their own in claiming whiteness, but rather operated as part of a group, sharing a history and a strategy that explained away their manifest blackness. But the two, those claiming whiteness as individuals and those demanding whiteness for their community, shared a consciousness of race. Those whose whiteness is unquestioned may devote some time to making certain that whites retrain power, and that people of color remain subordinate, but other than that do not have to devote much conscious energy to race, and virtually none at all to maintaining a sense of racial identity. Unlike individuals who are passing and persons of mixed race ancestry who claim whiteness, they do not have to be constantly on the alert, always prepared to defend their precarious, precious status as whites, ever watchful for slights real and imagined.

Seeking Indianness: Devising Tactics Before and After Racism

Other persons of African ancestry sought to escape blackness by claiming to be Native Americans. Seeking Indianess seeking whiteness paralleled in a number of ways. It could be attempted either by entire groups or by individuals and, as racism grew in strength, it became increasingly difficult to escape Africanity by claiming be Indian. Although Amerindians had no conception of race prior to contact with Europeans, and certainly no commitment to racism, most found it impossible to escape its impact. Because of this lack of Indian conceptions of race during the early years of contact, blacks as well as whites were sometimes adopted as members of a tribe. Most Indian nations had a procedure whereby persons who were not members could become members under the proper circumstances. Among the Cherokee, for example, a person captured in warfare could have one of three fates. He could be killed, enslaved, or adopted into the tribe, usually to replace a tribal member who had been killed in battle (Perdue, 1979). Other nations, such as the Creek, were even more flexible, sometimes adopting not only individuals but entire groups from other tribes. The Creek accepted into membership many of the remnants of coastal tribes who had been displaced and reduced in numbers by the colonists (Wright, 1986; Holland-Braund, 1991). If a person were willing to be adopted into the tribe and the tribe willing to accept him, then his previous tribal identity was forgotten. Persons so adopted often married into the nation, thereby establishing an entire network of kin.

Emphasis was placed on culture, or a willingness of the person adopted to accept the language, customs and beliefs of the nation, and to assume the rights and responsibilities of its adult members. Race played no role in whether or not persons were admitted to tribal membership. Whites and blacks were admitted, and both sometimes rose to positions of power, prestige, and influence within the nation. Chavez (1999) demonstrates that the leader of the 1680 Pueblo Indian revolt against the Spaniards in what is now New Mexico was of African descent. In his introductory note to Chavez's essay, Weber (1999: 82) writes:

> Chavez identifies one mixed-blood leader in particular, Domingo Naranjo, as the leader of the Pueblo Revolt. Described to Spaniards by Pueblo informants as a tall, black man with yellow eyes, Domingo Naranjo had posed as a representative from the god Pohe-yemo, directed operations from a *kiva* in Taos during the revolt and successfully concealed his identity from Spaniards during and after the revolt ... Domingo Naranjo, a man who lived as a Pueblo Indian at the Tewa-

speaking pueblo of Santa Clara, was actually the descendent of a black man who understood much about the beliefs of Indians in central Mexico as well as about Pueblo and Spanish ways and so successfully led the revolt in the guise of a representative of the god Pohe-yemo.

From the record, it is not possible to determine whether Naranjo merely "posed as a representative of the god Pohe-yemo," or whether as a member of the tribe he actually believed himself to be such a representative. In either case he was clearly accepted as a tribal member and obviously "understood much about the beliefs of Indians."

During the period before race became important, racial identity was more flexible and the line between the races much less firmly drawn by Indians. If the seventeenth century Naranjo described by Chavez was regarded by the Pueblo as one of themselves, the eighteenth century Sun Fish, also of African heritage, described by Hart (1994: 9) held a number of different racial identities:

> At one moment, Johnston [a British colonial official] defined the Sun Fish as Senecan; he called Addonogat and Squissahawe the Sun Fish's brothers and Chiefs. The next moment, however, he defined the Sun Fish as a mulatto and gave him the requisite pass that slaves needed when traveling alone. It is tempting to speculate whether Johnston gave the Sun Fish the Seneca identity publicly and the mulatto identity privately, but we have no way of knowing this was the case. It is reasonable to assume, however, that the Sun Fish employed his various identities—Seneca warrior and husband, free mulatto spy, informant, and cattle trader—to meet his specific needs as well as the needs of those with whom he was in contact at that particular moment. Who the Sun Fish was constantly changed.

The Sun Fish visited Johnston, whom he served as a spy in 1767. He was able, according to Hart, to hold these various identities, now an Indian, not a mulatto, now free, now regarded by most as a slave, because he lived on a frontier. This frontier region of New York, long contested by the Dutch, the French, the English, and a number of different Indian nations, was one in which no single group was able to exercise dominant power. The Sun Fish was able to shift racial identities as it suited him because none of these groups was able to fully enforce its idea of his racial identity on the others or on the Sun Fish himself. Although obviously of African ancestry, he was not always thought of as black. In order to shift back and forth, the Sun Fish had to be knowledgeable of both English and Seneca cultures, and able to speak the language of both. In this way he was able to validate his identity for both parties.

The attitude of the Indians toward race on New York's frontier is further demonstrated in the case of Eve Pickard, considered by the English to be a mulatto. Pickard, like the Sun Fish, was multi-lingual. She interacted regularly with the Mohawk and spoke their language. In a land dispute between the Canajoharie Indians and Pickard, she was denounced not as a mulatto, but as white (Hart, 1994: 24–26). These Mohawk apparently defined whiteness, as late as the 1760s, not in biological but rather in behavioral terms. In attempting to bilk Indians of their land, Pickard was behaving as white people did, and therefore, she was white. This reveals nothing of how Eve Pickard thought of herself any more that it is known whether the Sun Fish thought of himself as a Seneca or a mulatto. It only demonstrates that for the Indians of this time race was not yet fixed. What a person believed and how she behaved was much more important than her physical (racial) characteristics.

Amerindian attitudes changed toward blacks. Slavery itself had a powerful impact by degrading persons of African descent in the Indian mind. Indians came to appreciate the value colonists placed on slaves and though they initially had little use for them in their own economies, they entered into the slave trade. According to Halliburton (1977: 6), "The English urged the Cherokees to steal for them all the blacks whom they seized from Indians friendly to the French. The French in turn rewarded the Cherokees handsomely for blacks abducted from English plantations." Aside from the monies they earned in this slave trade—which they used to purchase guns, ammunition, tools, and other European goods—Indians were able to use the capture of blacks in playing the various European powers against one another. This was especially true in what is now the southeastern part of the United States where Indian nations shrewdly maneuvered to take advantage of the rivalry among the English, French, and Spanish (Unser, 1992). But as Indians became more knowledgeable of the Euro-American economic system, they began to see the value of owning slaves themselves and of working them much as the white slaveholders did. The Creek, for example, began to expand and improve their farms by use of slave labor. By the early years of the nineteenth century, their slavery resembled more and more that of the whites (Littlefield, 1977: 6). The Cherokee, writes Perdue (1979: 48), "came to see the subjugation of blacks to be in their own self-interest."

The ready acceptance of blacks into tribal membership, so characteristic of the era before race assumed central importance in the Americas, became increasingly rare. Blacks therefore found it increasingly difficult to escape blackness by becoming an Indian. This does not mean that all native peoples became racist; only as the power of Europeans in the New World increased, Indians became increasingly race conscious. Dowd (1992) argues that there were essentially two responses Indians made to the expanding power of whites. They could attempt to become like the settlers—that is, they could adopt white technology, become Christians, learn to read, shift from communal to individual land ownership. and make a number of other cultural changes. Or they could attempt to return to traditional ways, arguing that the decline in Indian power was the result of Indian rejection of the way of life intended for them. Virtually every Indian nation was divided into those who wished to return to tradition and those who wished to embrace Euro-American culture, so that whether to accept slavery, and the racist justifications for it, were part of the greater division over whether European civilization was suitable for Indians. For those who accepted, and indeed admired the ways of the white man, slavery was but another institution to be adopted. For those who rejected white customs as unsuitable, slavery was simply another aspect of white culture to be avoided. Many Indians were opposed to slavery then not so much because it was immoral, but because using forced labor to accumulate individual wealth was contrary to the traditional Amerindian way.

Complicating this debate was the fact that persons of mixed white and or Indian ancestry were coming to power in the tribes. Many of these men were the sons of white men who married Indian women, and because many nations were matrilineal, their children became tribal members. McLoughlin (1984, 1986) demonstrates that most of the large landowners, wealthy slaveholders, and political leaders behind the establishment of a Cherokee republic modeled on the United States were — to use the Spanish term — "mestizos." At the end of the eighteenth and the beginning of the nineteenth century, these men, like the Sun Fish, had the advantage of moving back and forth across the emergent racial line. Among the Cherokee they were regarded as Cherokee, while among the settlers they were considered white. They sent their sons to white schools and educated them in the ways of the white world, while at the same time encouraging them to participate in the public life, kinship networks, and political decisions of the Cherokee nation. Most of the slaveholding plantations among the Indians were controlled by this mestizo group, which, gradually, among most of the southeastern Indians, rose to wealth and power at the expense of full-blooded, tradition-oriented, non-English speaking, non–Christian Indians (Willis, 1970: 48). These mixed race Indians provided a direct channel through which anti-black thought made its way into Indian nations. At the end of the eighteenth and into the nineteenth century, they began to advocate not just the slavery practiced by their white neighbors, friends, and relatives, but the racist justifications for it. Like white slaveowners, they found in

Christianity a powerful rationale and justification for the subordination of persons of African descent.

As a result, even prior to the forced removal of southeastern Indians to Oklahoma along the Trail of Tears, many of these tribes passed laws that were little different from the anti-black laws passed by the southern states. For example, it was illegal to teach slaves to read, certain occupations were closed to free blacks, and a host of other regulations were passed by the nations' governments aimed and controlling slaves and limiting the opportunities of free blacks. Despite the efforts of some Indian leaders, Indian tribes were drawn into the Civil War. While most of the nations were divided with slaveholding, mixed-blood, Christian, English-speaking natives largely siding with the Confederacy, and non-slaveholding, full-blooded, non–Christian, non–English speaking natives generally remaining loyal to the Union, after the war the Federal government ignored these differences. The fact that some Indians in every nation had fought with the Confederate States of America provided the government with the excuse to declare all previous treaties with the tribes null and void on the grounds they had been in rebellion. The federal government then proceeded to impose on the nations much the same kind of directives imposed on the defeated South, insisting that all former slaves who had lived within the borders of an Indian nation at the outbreak of the war must be adopted into that nation as full members of the tribe. Some measure of the change in the attitude of Indians toward blacks may be found in the varied responses to these orders. According to Littlefield (1977: 203):

> The Seminoles, Creeks, and Cherokees adopted their blacks immediately, the Choctaws resisted adopting theirs until 1885. And the Chickasaw refused to adopt theirs at all. The rights enjoyed by the freedmen differed in extremes. The Chickasaw freedmen had no rights, except to occupy and improve small plots of land. Life was little better for Choctaw freedmen, and many of the Cherokee freedmen were excluded from rights because they had failed to return to the nation within the six-month limitation set by the Cherokee treaty. In contrast, the Creek freedmen were settled in three towns, and enjoyed full rights as citizens.

Native peoples had come to hold differing views toward blacks and blackness, but many persons of African descent who lived within these nations were of Indian ancestry and therefore blood relatives to those who sought to deny them membership in the tribe on the basis of race. As racism grew in strength, Indians moved a long way from the willingness of the Seneca to regard the Sun Fish as one of them. Escaping blackness by becoming an Indian became increasingly difficult.

Creating New Identities: Two Consequences

In addition to denying Africanity by considering oneself, and hoping to persuade others, that one was either white or Indian, some attempted to create an entirely new identity for themselves. A number of such groups sprang up in the southeastern part of the United States, where the three original races existed, but they also appeared in New Jersey, Delaware, New York and other areas where members of the three races were numerous (Gilbert, 1946; Berry, 1963; Griessman, 1972). Often, the history of these groups includes attempts to be recognized as either whites or as Indians, but when these attempts were rejected (often because of their African ancestry), they then turned to arguing that there were a unique group of people and, while neither Native American nor European in ancestry, were not African. The Lumbee of North Carolina, for example, were for a time successful in persuading the state of North Carolina that they were Indians—though the question what kind of Indians arose. They then persuaded the state legislature to designate them as Cherokee, but when the North Carolina Cherokee protested they were no such thing, they had to find another name for themselves (Sider, 1993). In effect, the Lumbee, and many other groups like them, created an original and separate status and identity for themselves.

These groups, notes Griessman (1972: 693), number 200 in the United States. He (Griessman, 1972: 693) notes that they go by various unflattering names, among them Red Bones, Brass Ankles, and Issues. A number of other scholars (Johnson, 1939; Gilbert, 1946; Beale, 1957: Berry, 1963; Beale, 1972; Dane and Griessman, 1972; Blu, 1980) who have written on these groups also note that the names by which they are known are often unflattering or insulting. Sometimes the group members themselves do not publicly accept these names, although they may privately use them and know that outsiders apply them to their group. They take this to mean that they are not black, but while the surrounding community identifies and recognizes them as a particular group, they are still regarded as black. It is important to them to have a name by which they are recognized—sometimes it is simply a number of family names—so that they can distinguish themselves from persons of African descent. Since the range of phenotypes within these groups often matches that within the larger African American population, family names become very important in drawing the line.

Such special groups exist throughout the Americas, but occupy a unique position in the United States where having white and Indian ancestry does not allow one to escape blackness. In Latin America, as a number of scholars (Harris, 1964; Degler, 1971: Mellafe, 1975; Davis, 1991) have demonstrated, multi-racial societies exist in which in addition to whites, Indians, and blacks there are also mestizos (persons of mixed European and Native American ancestry), mulattos (persons of mixed European and African ancestry), and zambos (persons of mixed Native American and African ancestry). In addition to these groups there is often a whole range of other racial classifications, assigning, for example, a specific name to a person of mixed mulatto and Indian heritage, or to one of mixed zambo and black ancestry (Morner, 1967; Olien, 1980). While distinct sub-groups may exist within this complex terminology it is culturally, and often legally, acceptable for such sub-groups to acknowledge some African ancestry. They separate themselves from blacks and are considered to be distinct from them, but this does not mean that they do not have African forefathers. The source of their physical characteristics is explained by their ancestry. But in the United States these groups want to be socially and historically distinct from black people — that is, they must show that they are not part of the black community and that they have a history separate from that of the black community. They must also show that they are racially distinct from black people and that their African physical features have nothing to do with blacks. In both cases then, a special identity emerges, but in the United States it is important that this identity deny Africa. In creating and claiming a new and special identity, problems exist in both regions. These strains in the United States have no counterpart elsewhere in the hemisphere,

There are two types of these new communities. One is here called "mosaic," the other "syncretic." Mosaic communities are those which, while they regard themselves and are regarded by others as a community, upon closer examination do not constitute a single community in which the various racial and cultural elements they are composed of have fully melded. Rather, they still consist of their component groups. Perhaps the best example of such a group are the Seminole Indians. Of all the Indians in the southeastern part of the United States, the Seminole, while they practiced slavery, appear to have been most resistant to the racist justifications white settlers developed for it. Some scholars find cultural reasons for this.

The Seminole were originally part of the Creek, who were not so much a tribe as they were a confederation, accepting not only individuals of varied racial backgrounds, but adopting entire communities of other Indians into the Creek nation (Wright, 1986; Holland-Braund, 1991). Just as they were not unified in their cultural components, the Creek were like most

Indians, divided over the acceptance of the white man's ways. This led to actual battles among the Creek, with some of those who wanted to maintain the traditional ways defeated and withdrawing into Spanish controlled Florida (Wright, 1986; Holland-Braund, 1991; Covington, 1993). Even though the Creek maintained that these people were part of the Creek nation and therefore subject to Creek laws, they called themselves Seminole and considered themselves a separate nation. The Spaniards welcomed the Seminole, viewing them as military allies against the expansionist English and their Indian supporters. After withdrawing to Florida, the Seminole continued to accept runaway slaves from the English colonies and to adopt some of them into the tribe. Once the United States assumed ownership of Florida in 1821, slaveholders insisted the Seminole should return these fugitives, and their descendants who, by the laws of the United States, remained their property. Most of the Seminole refused. The Second Seminole War, many historians believe, was fought because the Seminole refused to be removed to Oklahoma territory along with the other southern Indians. Many historians also believe that their refusal to leave was based on the fact that assembling the tribe to march along the Trail of Tears would enable slaveholders to identify those of African ancestry and take them back into slavery. The fact that some Seminole leaders were of obvious African ancestry provides support for this argument (Carlisle: 1972: 16).

The fact that some persons of African ancestry had rose to positions of power and prestige within the tribe, did, however, not mean that all blacks who lived within the boundary of the nation were Seminole (Willis, 1970: 47; Bateman, 1990: 6). To be sure, they acknowledged they lived in Seminole territory and generally cooperated with the Seminole, and often the Spaniards, in their battles against the English colonies of South Carolina and Georgia and later against the United States. There were, in fact, four distinct groups of persons of African ancestry living among the Seminole. The first group was Seminole. They had either been adopted into the nation or were the descendants of blacks who had been adopted. They spoke the language, dressed as Seminole, had Seminole relatives, and were therefore part of the Seminole clan system (Bateman, 1990: 13). There were also two groups of Seminole slaves. These men and women also spoke the language, sometimes dressed in Seminole fashion, but had no formally acknowledged kinship ties to their owners. They lived in Seminole communities, and provided a variety of services, some much like those of the slaves of white owners. Others performed more traditional tasks. The second group of Seminole slaves lived in their own communities. While they acknowledged that they were owned by Seminole and looked to the

Indians to protect them from the claims of Anglo-American slaveholders, they enjoyed considerable autonomy. Often they supplied their masters with an annual tribute, and were expected to join with them in wars against other Indians, English colonies and later the United States. Otherwise on their own. The fourth group of persons of African descent also lived in communities completely independent of the Seminole. These blacks, while they resided on land considered part of the Seminole nation, were regarded as free by both the Spaniards and the Seminole. They too fought against the enemies of the Seminole, though often in separate military units led by their own officers. They were thought of as black, and as allies of the Seminole — not as Seminole themselves.

Unfortunately, there is no record of relations among these black groups so it is not known, for example, how blacks in the independent communities interacted with slaves who lived within Seminole towns. Nor is there a clear idea of how racial identity was regarded. While some clearly saw themselves as black and others saw themselves as Seminole, there were many who obviously shifted identities as did the Sun Fish. Once the Seminole began to discuss with the United States government whether or not they would accept removal to Oklahoma, it became in the interest of persons of African descent to present themselves as Indians. When the government assembled all the Indians for the purpose of marching them west, slaveholders intended to be present to try to identify fugitive slaves (or their descendants) and take them back into slavery. One of the reasons these Indians took so long to accept removal was that many mixed-race Seminole feared just this possibility. In all probability, many of those who had not considered themselves or been considered by others as Seminole, now sought to claim an Indian identity, preferring removal to being enslaved. In sharp contrast, of course, slaveholders tried to identify as many Seminole as possible as black, so as to maximize the number of individuals who could be seized as slaves. So long as Seminole country was contested, first among the Seminole, Spaniards and English, and later among all these groups and the United States, it was possible for persons of African descent to change their identities and present themselves as Seminole, then as black slaves, and then as members of independent separate communities. The terms these independent groups applied to themselves are not known, though one scholar (Mulroy, 1993) considers all these groups who lived in Seminole space as maroons.

Whatever the name such groups gave to themselves, it is clear that while insisting on a separate racial identity for themselves, they were in fact composed of a number of different cultural groupings rather than a single culture. In writing of the Black Carib, another group, like some of the Seminole, composed of persons of mixed African and Indian ancestry, Taylor (1951: 144) found:

> The modal personality of he Black Carib of Belize is an African retention, encouraged rather than hindered by the years of sojourn among the Red Carib of St. Vincent, and reinforced by the adoption of a social system allowing greater freedom of emotional expression than did that of these Indians, whose language and culture they otherwise took-over.

As Taylor sees it, the Black Carib have not so much constructed a way of life that fully integrates two elements as they have constructed an African social order, which permits overt and public acknowledgement of emotion, within an Indian cultural and linguistic framework.

On the other hand, Bateman (1990), who has studied both the Black Carib and the Black Seminole, while agreeing that the Black Seminole constructed a mosaic society, believes that the Black Carib constructed a truly new, independent, and snycretic culture in the seventeenth century, fully blending African and Amerindian elements. She explains this by noting that those slaves who joined the Carib Indians on the island of St. Vincent generally arrived as individual males and from a variety of African nations. Some of them had also been born on other nearby Caribbean islands. Arriving on their own and hoping to win acceptance by the Indians, these fugitives had no choice but to adopt Carib ways, learn the Carib language, and practice Carib religion. As isolated individuals there was little chance that they could reconstruct the cultural lives they had enjoyed prior to joining the Indians. For their part, the Carib, as was true of so many Native Americans, adopted these runaways into their nation, provided they were willing to practice Carib ways. In sharp contrast, writes Bateman (1990: 10), the blacks who became associated with the Seminole shared a plantation slave culture, practiced an Afro-Christian Protestant-oriented common faith, and spoke an English based Creole. They arrived among the Seminole as people sharing a common culture, and whether they became Seminole slaves or lived in independent communities of their own, they continued this culture.

To be sure, the four black communities within the Seminole nation worked in harmony with the Seminole, but they had, according to Mulroy (1993), very different goals from the Indians. The Seminole wanted above all to retain their ancestral ways and keep tribal lands. They viewed persons of African descent who lived among them as allies who aided them in achieving these goals. The fact that these persons also thereby avoided enslavement or re-enslavement by Anglo-Americans was of secondary importance to these Indians. For persons of African descent, these goals were reversed. They were primarily interested in maintaining their freedom, and for them an independent Seminole nation, in control of tribal lands, was only a means whereby this goal could be achieved. The two groups, therefore, not only differed culturally, but had very different sociopolitical goals.

The second group of persons who sought to escape Africanity by creating entirely new racial identities created true syncretic cultures. Unlike the Seminole of African descent, they did not retain cultural elements, which made them distinct from persons of Indian descent. Instead they created completely new, syncretic cultures in which the African, Native American, and sometimes European cultural elements were blended. As noted above, Bateman (1990) concludes the Black Carib are such a group. Clearly, the Freejack, also discussed above, are also such a community, and Helms (1983) and Olien (1985) have concluded the Miskito Indians are also such a group. The Miskito, located on the eastern shores of Central America, have an African admixture dating back to the seventeenth century. They were important players in the struggle between the Spaniards and the English over Central America, and equally important players in the struggle between the United States and a number of European powers over who would control Central America and be able to build a canal linking the Atlantic and the Pacific. Whether the Miskito were Indians and therefore had to be treated as a people who had title to the land and must be consulted before a canal could be constructed (as the British maintained), or whether they were runaway black slaves and therefore had no meaningful title to the land and therefore need not be consulted (as the Americans maintained), was the subject of considerable debate in the late nineteenth and early twentieth centuries (Helms, 1985).

The Freejack, the Miskito, and a number of other mixed race groups have constructed identities that rest on their claims to have a history, a culture, and a biology distinct from that of the red, white, and black peoples who are their neighbors. It is important for the groups located in the United States that their culture be seen as a seamless one, and especially that it not be possible for outsiders to pry it apart and identify any of its elements as African in origin. For the Freejacks, a group identified as the "turpentine niggers" presented a problem. Like the Freejacks, members of this group, who arrived in the region to work in the turpentine industry, were the descendants of persons of mixed African and European ancestry and were so regarded by non–Freejacks. According to Posey (1979: 186):

> The Freejacks vehemently objected, however, because they feared any association with "turpentine niggers" might further jeopardize their

tenuous progress toward equality with Whites. Yet both the Black and White communities persisted in classifying them as Freejacks and in considering them residents of the Settlement ... both Freejacks and "turpentine niggers" worked side-by-side in the turpentine industry; eventually there was in-termarriage between families in both groups and the assimilation of the later arrived mixed-bloods into the Settlement. Thus, the two separate groups, with no similarity in historical or cultural traditions, having in common only an imposed categorical similarity of "mixed-blood" classification began to be formally constituted into a single ethnic group.

Freejacks, continues Posey (1979: 188), recognize "factions" within their community, and while these factions are derived from whether their ancestors were "turpentine niggers" or the original Freejacks, now all think of themselves as Freejack.

Among the Lumbee of North Carolina a similar syncretic identity has been constructed. Like the Freejack, the Lumbee are a group of people in flight from blackness who long struggled to be accepted as white. Failing this, they have argued for some time that they are Indians, and have convinced the state of North Carolina to define them as Indians (Sider, 1993). Like the Freejack and most other such communities, however, they clearly bear the marks of their Native American, European, and African ancestry. And like the Freejacks, it is the last of these that troubles them most. They have created a unique cultural identity, but cannot escape the physical realities of race. Johnson (1939: 523) found cleavages within this self-described Indian community:

> They are roughly correlated with physical traits.... At the bottom of the social scale are the darker Indians. They are on the whole poorer than the others, they are conscious of what others think of their appearance, and they are jealous of the lighter Indians. They are credited with a good deal of what is sometimes called "hell-raising." Next come the intermediate Indians. They are a little too dark to pass as white and they are especially sensitive to physical appearance. They envy the lighter ones and resent the darker ones, and they are inclined to be the militant, agitating type. Finally, there are the "white" Indians. They could pass for white almost anywhere. On the whole, they have a better economic status, a better education, and higher prestige. These color cleavages are a tabooed subject with the Indians, and yet they permeate the whole society.

Similarly, in her study of the Narragansett Indians of Rhode Island, Uy (1997) found that while the group was willing to publicly discuss its European ancestry and its struggle to have its tribal status recognized by government authorities, the Narragansett made virtually no public statements concerning their African ancestry. Their blackness was ignored despite the fact that many of them obviously had African ancestry. Tyre's (1989) study found that the Nanticoke of Delaware also vigorously deny any African ancestry. Hammond (1969: 287) found that internal stratification within such communities was based on economic standing and physical type, with those better off materially and more white in appearance at the top of the system and those who were poorer and darker skinned at the bottom.

In Cape Verde itself, a similar color hierarchy existed, complete with a complex terminology which labeled persons and placed them into groups (Lobban, 1995: 55–57). But among Cape Verdean Americans, according to one informant, "Visibly there are a lot of Cape Verdeans that have been accepted by society as whites and once that happens they don't want to have any black relatives. Both my mother and my stepfather were convinced in their own minds that they were white. This was not a question of passing. There was no need for them to masquerade" (Halter, 1993: 167). The fact that the parents of this informant were fully convinced that they were white demonstrates that their community had constructed a syncretic racial identity that contained no African elements. But, as was the case for every mixed race group, the fact that there were persons within this new group, often blood kin, who were African in appearance undercut the claim of whiteness. In general, such groups like the Lumbee and Narragansett Indians, handled persons of obvious African descent by ignoring their existence, and even relegating them to a lower position within the community. Despite, however, the presence of people who were manifestly black, such groups created a uniform culture in which they all agreed they were not black.

Conclusion

"Critical Afrocentrism is faithful to the context of African cultural experiences. It at the same time recognizes that all cultures influence and are influenced by other cultures. It is from this 'dialogue' between cultures that new cultural experiences and contexts arise and contribute to cultural identity and continuity" (Akinyela, 1992: 11). This dialogue between Afrocentric cultures and others is no where made more clear than the many and varied efforts of persons of African descent to escape blackness in the Americas. As this paper has attempted to demonstrate, these strategies vary. Because blackness has been so despised, persons have simply attempted to pass, usually as whites, but sometimes as Indians as well. The tactics these individuals adopt are quite different from those adopted by entire communities who try to present themselves as something other than black. The psychological consequences are also different for individuals than for communities. Whether these communities are located in the United States, or elsewhere in the hemisphere also makes a difference, as in Latin America where it is possible to acknowledge African ancestry without being considered black. But in the United States to admit to African ancestry, despite also having European and Native American foreparents, is to admit to being black. Strategies selected by those who want to escape blackness have also varied over time. In the earlier years of settlement, before racism triumphed, it was easier for blacks to pass into whiteness or Indianess than was later the case. For that matter, in Latin America, it was possible for persons of mixed-race to escape the oppression of being Indian by moving into one of the mixed race castes, even if this meant accepting a bogus African ancestry. Some Native Americans made just this choice, believing they thereby gained more independence, autonomy, and opportunity than by living the restricted lives Spanish colonists, state, and church were imposing on Indians.

If, as some scholars believe, an Afrocentric perspective is culturally, not biologically determined, then it is legitimate to ask what if this perspective finds its way into the lives of mixed race persons who, despite African physical ancestry, do not regard themselves as black? The best way to approach this question is to first acknowledge the dialogue Akinyela sees between Afrocentrism and other cultures, and then to suggest that this dialogue is sometimes conscious. In making choices as to racial identity, the mixed-race peoples discussed in this paper therefore reflect on the meaning of blackness. There have been literally millions of such people in the Americas, persons who have reflected on the meaning of blackness and decided to be black, but these people lie beyond the perimeters of this paper. Those who have reflected on blackness and decided not to be black are thereby linked to Afrocentricity through their reflectivity. Of course, all human beings are reflective, all have the capacity to take themselves as objects and look back on themselves and to think about the social context within which they find themselves. But the nature of slavery and the racist justifications for it in the New World forced on persons of African descent a special reflectivity so that they had no option but to reflect on the meaning of blackness (Jones, 1978).

That so many of them elected, given the racist denigration of blackness, to devise ways to escape from it should come as no surprise. In a sense, the Afrocentric perspective that was their African heritage manifested itself in the reflective and creative ways they developed to avoid blackness. These were above all pragmatic, adapting themselves to the restrictions placed on black people and the possibilities the restrictions created. So, for example, in much of Latin America, it was possible to escape blackness by being something other than black while still admitting to African ancestry. In the United States, where to admit to African ancestry was to accept being black, this option did not exist. What appeared to be African physical characteristics had to be explained away, accounted for in another way. These explanations, as this paper has demonstrated, were seldom persuasive, though they were often creative. It is tempting to suggest that they did not fully convince the people themselves. Certainly, tensions within mixed-race communities and their tendency to both be uncomfortable with, and to rank persons of obvious African ancestry at the bottom of their communities, suggest that they were not fully convinced themselves. Yet, it is clear that while individuals may have passed and were conscious of the fact that they were passing, entire communities were not passing. Despite their protestations to the contrary, many of these communities knew they were not white, nor were they Indian. After all, being white and being Indian meant being fully accepted as white or as Indian by whites and Indians. They seldom achieved this, but they were sometimes able to avoid being black.

So while the mixed-race people were not convinced they were not white or Indian, they were convinced they were not black. A perspective, rooted in reflective pragmatic Afrocentrism, enabled them to construct a worldview which did not see their Africanity. This was no small achievement. Not one of these communities was so backward that it did not have mirrors so that each day these people could see their despised African physical features reflected back at them. Yet they managed to together construct communities of denial in which, despite the mark of oppression, they were not black.

References

Akinyela, Makunga. (1992) "Critical Afrocentricity and the Politics of Culture." *Waso Weusi* 1: 11-18.

Bateman, Rebecca B. (1990) "Africans and Indians: A Comparative Study of the Black Carib and Black Seminole." *Ethnohistory* 37: 1-24.

Beale, Calvin L. (1957) "American Tri-Racial Isolates: Their Status and Pertinence to Genetic Research." *Eugenics Quarterly* 4: 187-196.

_____. (1972) "An Overview of the Phenomenon of Mixed Racial Isolates in the United States." *American Anthropologist* 74: 704-710.

Beck, Sam. (1992) *Manny Almeida's Ringside Lounge: The Cape Verdeans' Struggle for their Neighborhood*. Providence, RI: Goveia-Brown.
Berry, Brewton. (1963) *Almost White*. New York: Macmillan.
Blu, Karen. (1980) The Lumbee Problem: The Making of an American *Indian People*. New York: Cambridge University Press.
Brawley, Benjamin. (1970) *A Social History of the American Negro*. New York: Macmillan (1st published, 1921).
Bridges, George Wilson. (1828) *The Annals of Jamaica*. London: John Murray. 2 vols.
Campbell, Mavis. (1988) *The Maroons of Jamaica, 1655-1796: A History of Resistance, Collaboration and Betrayal*. Granby MA: Bergin and Garvey.
Carlisle, Rodney. (1970) *Prologue to Liberation: A History of Black People in America*. New York: Appleton-Century-Crofts.
Chavez, Angelico. (1999) "Pohe-yemo's Representative and the Pueblo Revolt of 1680," in David J. Weber (Ed.), *What Caused the Pueblo Revolt of 1680?* Boston: Bedford/St. Martin's (article 1st published, 1967).
Coli, Waltraud Berger and Richard A. Lobban. (1990) *Cape Verdeans of Rhode Island*. Providence, RI: The Rhode Island Heritage Commission and the Rhode Island Publication Society. Covington, J.W.
_____. (1993) *The Seminoles of Florida* Gainesville, FL: University Press of Florida.
Dane, J.K. and B.Eugene Griessman. (1972) "The Collective Identity of Marginal Peoples: The North Carolina Experience." *American Anthropologist* 74: 694-704.
Davis, F.James. (1991) *Who Is Black?* University Park, PA: Pennsylvania State University Press.
Degler, Carl N. *Neither Black Nor White: Slavery and Race Relations in the United States and Brazil*. New York: Macmillan.
Dowd, Gregory Evans. (1992) *A Spirited Resistance: The North American Indian Struggle for Unity, 1745-1815*. Baltimore: Johns Hopkins University Press.
DuBois, W.E.B. (1903) *The Souls of Black Folk*. Chicago: A.C. McClurg.
Fredrickson, George M. (1971) *The Black Image in the White Mind*. New York: Harper and Row.
Gilbert, W.H., Jr. (1946) "Memorandum Concerning the Characteristics of the Larger Mixed Blood Racial Islands of the Eastern United States." *Social Forces* 24: 438-447.
Griessman, B.Eugene. (1972) "The American Isolates." *American Anthropologist* 74: 693-694.
Halliburton, R., Jr. (1972) *Red over Black: Black Slavery Among the Cherokee Indians*. Westport, CT: Greenwood Press.
_____. (1977) *The Seminole Freedmen*. Westport, CT: Greenwood Press.
Halter, Marilyn. (1993) *Between Race and Ethnicity: Cape Verdean American Immigrants, 1860-1965*. Urbana, IL: University of Illinois Press.
Hammond, Peter B. (1969) "Afro-American Indians and Afro-Asians," in Gwendolan Carter and Ann Paden (Eds.), *Expanding Horizons in African Studies*. Evanston, IL: Northwestern University Press.
Harris, Marvin. (1964) *Patterns of Race in the Americas*. Westport, CT: Greenwood Press.
Hart, William B. (1994) "Black 'Go-betweens' and the Mutability of 'Race,' Status and Identity on New York's Frontier, 1750-1775." Paper presented at Crucibles of Cultures Conference, November 18-19.

Helms, Mary W. (1983) "Miskito Slaving and Culture Contact: Ethnicity and Opportunity in an Expanding Population." *Ethnohistory* 39: 179-197.

Holland-Braund, Kathryn E. (1991) "The Creek Indians, Blacks and Slavery." *Journal of Southern History* 57: 601-636.

Johnson, Guy B. (1939) "Personality in a White-Indian-Negro Community." *American Sociological Review* 4: 516-518.

Jones, Rhett S. (1977) "Black and Native American Relations before 1800." *Western Journal of Black Studies* 1: 151-163.

_____. (1978) "Structural Isolation, Race, and Cruelty in the New World." *Third World Review* 4: 34-43.

_____. (1981) "Identity, Self Concept, and Shifting Political Allegiances of Blacks in the Colonial Americas." *Western Journal of Black Studies* 5: 61-74.

_____. (1986) "The Foundations of Zambo Studies." *Hantu* 7: 3-4.

Jordan, Winthrop D. (1968) *White Over Black: American Attitudes Toward the Negro, 1558-1812*. Chapel Hill, NC: University of North Carolina Press.

Kardiner, Abram and Lionel Ovesey. (1951) *The Mark of Oppression: Explorations in the Personality of the American Negro*. Cleveland: The World Press.

Littlefield, Daniel H. (1977) *Africans and Seminoles*. Westport, CT: Greenwood Press.

_____. (1978) *The Cherokee Freedmen*. Westport, CT: Greenwood Press.

Lobban, Richard A., Jr. (1995) *Cape Verde: Crioulo Colony to Independent Nation*. Boulder, CO: Westview Press.

McConnell, R.C. (1968) *Negro Troops of Amtebellum Louisiana*. Baton Rouge, LA: Louisiana State University Press.

McLouglin, William G. (1984) *The Cherokee Ghost Dance*. Macon, GA: Mercer University Press. (1986) *Cherokee Renascence in the New Republic*. Princeton, NJ: Princeton University Press.

Mellafe, Rolando. (1975) *Negro Slavery in Latin America*. Berkeley, CA: University of California Press.

Morgan, Edmund. (1975) American Slavery—American Freedom: The Ordeal of Colonial Virginia. New York: Norton.

Morner, Magnus. (1967) *Race Mixture in the History of Latin America*. Boston: Little, Brown.

Mulroy, Kevin. (1993) *Freedom on the Border: The Seminole Maroons*. Lubbock, TX: Texas Tech University Press.

Olien, Michael D. (1985) "E.G. Squier and the Miskito: Anthropological Scholarship and Political Propaganda." *Ethnohistory* 111-133.

Palmer, Colin A. (1976) *Slaves of the White God*. Cambridge, MA: Harvard University Press.

Perdue, Theda. (1979) *Slavery and the Evolution of Cherokee Society, 1540-1866*. Knoxville, TN: University of Tennessee Press.

Pereira, Joe. (1994) "Maroon Heritage in Mexico." In E. Kofe Agorsah (Ed.), *Maroon Heritage: Archaeological Ethnographic and Historical Perspectives*. Kingston, Jamaica: Canoe Press.

Posey, Darrell A. (1979) "Origin, Development and Maintenance of a Louisiana Mixed-Blood Community: The Ethnohistory of the Freejacks of the First Ward Settlement." *Ethnohistory* 26: 177-192.

Rout, Leslie B. (1976) *The African Experience in Spanish America*. New York: Cambridge University Press.

Sider, Gerald M. (1993) *Lumbee Indian Histories: Race, Ethnicity, and Indian Identity in the Southern United States*. New York: Cambridge University Press.
Taylor, Douglas Macrae. (1951) *The Black Carib of British Honduras*. New York: Wenner-Gren Foundation.
Tyre, Kendal. (1989) "A Journey through Delaware's Past: The History of Colonial and Antebellum Free Blacks." Undergraduate History Honors Thesis, Brown University.
Unser, Daniel H., Jr. (1992) *Indians, Settlers, and Slaves in a Frontier Exchange Economy: The Lower Mississippi Valley Before 1783*. Chapel Hill, NC: University of North Carolina Press.
Uy, Mary Jean Sia. (1997) "The Narragansett Indians: Race and State, 1880-1993." Undergraduate History Honors Thesis, Brown University.
Weber, David J. (1999) "Did the Right Leader Make the Revolt Possible?" Introduction to Angelico Chavez, "Pohe-yemo's Representative and the Pueblo revolt of 1680." In David J. Weber (Ed.), *What Caused the Pueblo Revolt of 1680?* Boston: Bedford/St. Martin's.
Williams, Eric. (1944) *Capitalism and Slavery*. Chapel Hill, NC: University of North Carolina Press.
Willis, William S., Jr. (1970) "Anthropology and Negroes on the Southern Colonial Frontier." In James C. Curtis and Lewis L. Gould (Eds.). *The Black Experience in America*. Austin, TX: University of Texas Press.
Wood, Peter H. (1974) *Black Majority: Negroes in Colonial South Carolina from 1670 through the Stono Rebellion*. New York: Norton.
Wright, J.Leitch. (1986) *Creeks and Seminoles*. Lincoln, NB: University of Nebraska Press.

The Interaction Sphere of Nubia and Egypt: From the Old Kingdom to the Meroitic Period

Dr. Larry Ross

The ancient kingdom of the Nubians, located in the area of northern Africa known today as the nation-state Sudan, was called Kush (or Cush) by the ancient Egyptians; their paths crossed often. Through a mediation between the Egyptian dynastic chronology written by Manetho, a chronicler from the third century BC, and excerpts from more recent information on Nubia and Egypt in antiquity compiled by Steffen Wenig, William Yewdale Adams, Margaret Bunson, Regina Schulz & M. Seidel, Bruce Trigger, George G.M. James, Fritz & Ursula Hintze and other scholars, I intend to develop a contextualization of the relations between these ancient empires and their impact on the civilizations that followed.

Before the Early Dynastic Period (c. 2920 BC), the Scorpion King Zekhen ruled Egypt from the site of Abydos, where his tomb was recently discovered; Zekhen's tomb contained evidence of the world's first writing, thereby clarifying the often debated question of whether writing began in Egypt or Mesopotamia. The Scorpion King's ceremonial mace head contained representations of the crowns of Upper Egypt and Lower Egypt, suggesting that the two regions were united by 3200 BC, well before the First Dynasty. Thus, the 0 Dynasty precedes the First Dynasty. Though cuneiform writing became a *lingua franca* in the ancient world and persisted into the first millennium AD, it was preceded by Egyptian hieroglyphic writing, now dated at 3200 BC.

The importance of the Old Kingdom in the relations between Nubia and Egypt is noteworthy, because prior to that, relations may have been few:

> It is significant that prior to the invasion of Egypt by the Dynastic Race (c. 3400 BC), Nubia was very thinly populated and only showed connection with the northern Nile valley by a few cemeteries located in the area immediately to the south of the First Cataract. Then suddenly we have a big increase in population, and the advent of a new culture as far as Nubia is concerned. The only possible explanation is the incursion of large numbers of Predynastic people in retreat from the pressure caused further north by the invasion of the forerunners of the pharaonic Egyptians. Be that as it may, the archaeological remains of the A-Group people show that at the time Lower Nubia, at any rate, enjoyed a period of comparative prosperity; of conditions beyond the Second Cataract we have as yet little evidence [Emery 1965:124].

The convention of using the term "race" up and to during the Victorian Era and well into the twentieth century to describe a population is extremely problematic in the case of Egypt: the modern meaning of the term does not correspond with ancient Egyptian color symbolism. (The dismemberment of ancient populations into "races" has been used as a scheme for discussing their interaction. However, the unscientific basis of these arbitrary categories undermines the research. When we refer to groups of people as populations, since there is more genetic diversity within populations than there is between them, we may avoid making untenable statements about people.)

The Egyptian rulers were of African descent, and the boundaries of Egypt and Nubia shifted dramatically over time, to the point that no specific population and skin color can be associated with specific geographic coordinates. Yellow (*ketj*) represented female skin color; red (*desher*) represented male skin color; and black (*kem*) represented ritual death or mummification, Nubians, the mud of the Nile, fertility, or even the god Osiris. In general, white was not used to represent the skin color of a population; it was "used to represent limestone, sandstone, silver, milk, fat, honey, vegetables, teeth, bones, the crown of Upper Egypt, the baboon associated with Thoth, and white bread in offering to the dead" (Bunson 1991: 55). In view of the fact that Nubians were at times the rulers of Egypt, the existing literature that is based on the division of ancient African populations into clearly or loosely demarcated "races" must be critically re-examined.

In ancient Egypt, records of each king's activities were kept on what has been termed "The Palermo Stone," which affords us a year-by-year accounting for the First through the Fifth Dynasties. The Palermo Stone reports that:

> Sneferu, the first king of the Fourth [dynasty] carried out a raid in Nubia that resulted in the capture of 7,000 people and 200,000 domesticated animals. It has been argued that the high proportion of beasts to humans indicates that he was attacking pastoralists. Nubians who are attested as titled servants of Fifth Dynasty officials may have been the descendants of captives taken by Sneferu, although Nubians continued to enter Egypt throughout the Old Kingdom as prisoners, slaves, or bowman recruits for the Egyptian army and police force [Trigger 1976: 47].

The geographic area controlled by the Old Kingdom possessed relatively few naturally occurring gold deposits, however, metals were abundant in Nubia. The word "*Nub*" is the Egyptian word for gold, thus to the Egyptians Nubia was literally the "land of gold." One of the largest gold mines in Africa was located at Buhen, near the First Cataract of the Nile. This was squarely in Nubian territory, before the Egyptian army's invasion. Gold mines were found all over Nubia, and Egyptian armies continued to raid Nubia in order to seize its wealth for nearly 3,000 years. "The name of one of the statelets of Predynastic Egypt, Nubt 'Gold town,' suggests that its prosperity was based at least partly on the exploitation of this metal. Mines had their own wells and were operated by a labor force supervised by the military. Especially during the New Kingdom, gold was mined in the Eastern desert and Nubia" (Silverman 1997: 64). East of Buhen, there were two huge gold mines in Nubia, just south of Wadi Allakai, both made accessible by dried out river bed routes. (Egypt had a few copper and tin mines, from which bronze could be fashioned, and only one or two iron mines. Thus, the bulk of their metals came from sites that lay outside the boundaries of the Old Kingdom.) Sneferu was also carrying on diorite quarrying in the Nubian desert, and it had apparently been a common practice for Egyptian kings since Engelbach investigated these quarries in 1933, he found there the names of Khufu, Redjedef, Sahure, and Djedkare-Isesi — all kings of the Fourth and Fifth Dynasties — as well as the names of rulers of the Middle Kingdom" (Trigger 1976:48).

Eventually, the Egyptians began to use alabaster as a replacement for diorite. They abandoned the diorite quarries, since alabaster was available locally:

> No royal names from later in the Old Kingdom are recorded in the Toshka quarries. This suggests that by the beginning of the Sixth [dynasty] c.2340 BC, Nubia was free from Egyptian occupation. The relaxation of Egyptian control seems to have come about as a result of the

growing independence of Upper Egypt, which was apparent by the reign of Teti I, the first king of the Sixth [dynasty]. The decline of Egyptian control in Nubia seems related to a general decline in royal power [Trigger 1976:48].

Centralized power was probably declining in Egypt if the scale of royal tombs is taken into account; their size was steadily declining, and noble tombs were no longer located in the same place as the reigning monarch's tomb. The absence of Egyptian domination in Lower Nubia during the Sixth Dynasty may have contributed to the reappearance of the indigenous populations. These populations, designated as C-Group culture by their burials in round or oval graves, are also known to have built stone dwellings and made incised black pottery with white encrustation.

> At present it is impossible to accept as certain any proposed ethnic identification for the C-Group of Lower Nubia. It appears from rock inscriptions that the Egyptians of this period called the northern part on Lower Nubia Wawat; the Tomas area Irtje; and the third district, between there and the Second Cataract, Satju. These toponyms may, however, have been old ones that lacked any ethnographic meaning after the disappearance of the A-Group [Trigger, 1967:54].

The Egyptians did abandon their settlements in Lower Nubia at the onset of the Sixth Dynasty, but they continued river traffic to obtain raw materials for luxury goods and also continued recruiting efforts in the region. They maintained a settlement at the site of Buhen in order to trade directly with Dongola, a wealthy Nubian site near the Land of Iam:

> The principal concern of the Egyptians was to continue their trade with Dongola. In the course of the Sixth Dynasty, control of this trade fell into the hands of the Governors of Aswan who assumed special powers as the Keeper of the Door to the South. On his tomb, opposite Aswan, Harkhuf records that, beginning in the reign of Merenre, he personally led four expeditions to the land of Iam to recruit troops and to barter for goods there. On the first of these journeys he was accompanied by his father Iri. It is likely that Iri was making his last visit to Iam and was familiarizing his son and successor with the route and introducing him to his Nubian trading partners. Harkhuf returned from his third journey with 300 donkeys laden with incense, ebony, oil, leopard skins, elephant tusks, throwing sticks, and other products. He was guarded by a contingent of Iamite recruits who were returning with him for service in the Egyptian army. The Harkhuf inscriptions suggest that by the Sixth Dynasty, Iam was a prosperous chiefdom whose ruler dealt with Egyptian officials on equal terms [Trigger 1967:56–57].

This rapport between the ruler of Iam and the Egyptians was somewhat unusual, because "while his subjects were recruited as mercenaries for the Egyptian army, the ruler of Iam was not counted among the Nubian 'chiefs' who owed allegiance to the King of Egypt" (Trigger 1967:58). However, the relations between Lower Nubia and Egypt began to deteriorate when Prince Mekhu either died or was killed on a trading expedition to Nubia, and the Egyptians sent a punitive expedition under Prince Pepinakht, who recorded that he "hacked up Wawat and Irtje, slaying prominent people and carrying off many prisoners." And then, "On a second expedition, Pepinakht was able to persuade two chiefs to visit the Egyptian court and to present some cattle as tribute" (Trigger 1967:59). Thus the Egyptians used intimidation to keep Nubia's trade routes open for themselves, especially routes to the Kerma Basin, even though they abandoned their settlement at Buhen. Evidence of continued trade relations can be found in the C-Group graves of this period where Egyptian goods are plentiful. They actually increased in frequency at the beginning of the First Intermediate Period (c. 2181–2040 BC). During the First Intermediate Period, the incipient states of Nubia became organized into Kush and Early Kerma in upper Nubia, and Wawat in lower Nubia. As Nubia grew and became stronger, the Egyptian Seventh Dynasty was experiencing the breakdown of their centralized rule (c. 2181–2140 BC) from the capital at Memphis. Fierce fighting among regional Egyptian warlords over territory resulted and Egypt was destabilized. In ancient Egypt, land was the most valued commodity; one's wealth, even that of the pharaohs, was determined by how much land one controlled.

Pepi II ruled Egypt for about 90 years of the First Intermediate Period, and contemporary accounts suggest that the Nile River may have had a number of uncharacteristically low periods from 2180–2130 BC, and "a period of anarchy and bloodshed followed the collapse of the central government, after which Upper Egypt was dominated by two rival royal families" (Trigger 1967:60).

Two separate kingdoms resulted, one ruled by the Ninth and Tenth Dynasties from Heracleopolis, and one by the Eleventh Dynasty from Thebes. The cult of Amen/Amen-Ra was established, and the term Amen remains sacred to this day, though few are aware of its Egyptian origin:

> The gods Seth and Horus represent the legacy of prehistoric periods when respectively Naqada and Hierakonpolis were in turn center of importance in Upper Egypt. Thebes was to fill this role from the Eleventh Dynasty onwards, with its temple eventually becoming the principal cult center in Upper Egypt and its god Amen/Amen-Ra, gaining a dominant position in the theology of kingship [Trigger, Kemp, O'Connor, Lloyd 1998: 178].

Prosperity returned to Egypt after the rivalries were subsumed by Mentuhotep II at the onset of the Middle Kingdom (c.2040–1786 BC) when the Egyptians occupied Lower Nubia. Once the Egyptian states of Heracleopolis and Thebes were united by Nebhepetre Mentuhotep II into a centralized monarchy, the Egyptians invaded northern Nubia and the Sinai buffer zones and set up fortifications in an effort to secure its territorial boundaries. This strategy worked from about 1991 BC until the invasions of the Second Intermediate Period (c. 1786–1767 BC). These dynasties remained insecure and unstable, evidenced by the coup which ended the Eleventh Dynasty that put Sehetepibre Amenemhet I on the throne. When Nebtawyre Mentuhotep IV died, "his line came to and end and the throne was mounted by Amenemhet I, founder of the Twelfth Dynasty (c. 1991–1786 BC). An inscription at Korosko records that in the penultimate year of his reign he arrived to "overthrow Wawat." He is said to have waged war against the Medjay of the Eastern Desert and the Toshka diorite quarries may have been worked again by the end of his reign" (Trigger 1967:64).

Amenemhet I was a usurper, and he was not of royal birth. His mother, Nefret, was a Nubian, thus it is certain that in 1991 BC, the king of Egypt was Nubian which further undermines claims that Egyptians and Nubians were somehow separate "races" as opposed to integrated populations. Amenemhet I was assassinated around 1962 BC, and his son Kheperkare Senwosret I succeeded him as king of Egypt. Nubian mercenaries took advantage of Egypt's instability:

> Although Nubian and other foreign mercenaries plundered native Egyptians during the initial period of anarchy, many Nubians as well as Medjay from the eastern desert were recruited during the civil wars that followed and some of these men achieved prominent positions in Egyptian society. A model of a troop of Nubian bowmen found in a tomb at Assiut in central Egypt and a reference to Wawat Nubians and Medjay as followers of the ruler of Hermopolis indicate that Nubian contingents fought for the Herakleopolitan coalition, while a large colony at Gebelien, near Luxor, was no doubt in the service of the rival Theban dynasts [Trigger 1967:61].

These Nubians who held prominent positions in Egypt had became a part of the fabric of Egyptian society, just as their predecessors who had served in the Egyptian army had. Raids into Nubia by the Egyptians and raids into Egypt by the Nubian mercenaries created a great deal of instability in both regions, and there are many reports of famine in Nubia; some famines may have been artificially created. Senwosret I built a number of forts in Lower Nubia and used Egyptian soldiers: "This was the first settlement in Nubia by Egyptians since the end of the Fifth Dynasty and it marked the beginning of a new phase in relations between Egypt and the southern hinterland" (Trigger 1967:64). Buhen was reoccupied and staffed with soldiers; the town of Kor was also occupied and Nubia was placed under the control of Serenput, the Prince of Aswan. "In his tomb he describes himself as 'Great Controller of Nubia' and 'Overseer of all Foreign Lands'" (Trigger 1967:65). Senwosret's expedition was recorded:

> A magnificent sandstone stela erected at Buhen by General Mentupotep appears to record an expedition into Upper Nubia in the eighteenth regnal year of Senwosret I; it describes warlike activity: tents set on fire and grain hurled into the Nile. On the stela the god Mentu is shown presenting Senwosret I a line of bound captives inscribed with the names of Nubian peoples and places. The latter include Ashmeik and Sai Island. At the head of the list is Kush, which hereafter features prominently in Nubian history. Senwosret may have been accompanied on this campaign by Ameni; in his tomb, Ameni recounts that, while his father was still alive, he and his soldiers had accompanied Senwosret I when the king overthrew his enemies in Kush. Ameni claimed to have traveled south of Kush to the "borders of the earth" and to have returned bearing tribute for the king [Trigger 1967:65].

These tomb inscriptions are clear evidence of the rising trend of Egyptian imperialism during the Middle Kingdom, while "until the day when they became outright subjects of the pharaoh, the outlook of the Lower Nubians remained essentially democratic and tribal" (Adams 1977:162). In conjunction, the Egyptians berated Kush in an attempt to justify their aggressive actions:

> "Miserable Kush," the oft-repeated epithet of Egyptian conquest texts, expresses succinctly the disdain which civilized peoples have often felt towards their barbarian neighbors. Something of this same attitude is conveyed in the nineteenth-century term "Darkest Africa." African darkness, as the Victorians conceived it, was more than a matter of skin color; it was a darkness of the mind as well. Implicit therein was the justification for Europe's "civilizing mission"—in part genuine, in part an excuse for colonial exploitation. Repeated and gratuitous allusion to Nubian backwardness evidently provided the ancient Egyptians too with a sense of moral justification for the exploitation of their African neighbors. At first glance the Egyptians' belief in their superiority seems warranted by their material accomplishments. Nevertheless the attitude of the Egyptians smacks to some extent of the haughtiness of the *nouveau-riche*, for their own rise from savagery to civilization had been recent and rapid [Adams 1977:163].

The Egyptians escalated their fort building activities, and their periodic raids, in an attempt at totally subjugating the native populations of Nubia and interrupting their trade routes.

Further insight into the nature of Egypt's interest in the Second Cataract region is provided by the "boundary" stele which was erected a Semna in the name of Senusret III. In translation it reads, "Southern boundary, made in the year 8, under the majesty of the King of Upper and Lower Egypt, Khakaura Senusret III who is given life forever and ever; in order to prevent that any [Nubian] should cross it, by water or by land, with a ship, or any herds of the [Nubians]; except a [Nubian] who shall come to do trading in Iken [Mirgissa], or with a commission. Every good thing shall be done with them, but without allowing a ship of the [Nubians] to pass by Heh, going downstream, forever" [Adams 1977:185].

This would suggest a bleak outlook for Nubia, but rivalries in the Thirteenth Dynasty led to a downfall of the Egyptian forts in Nubia and Kush reached its peak between 1750–1500 BC. (The Twelfth Dynasty ended with the first known female pharaoh, Sebekkare Nefrusobek [c. 1787–1783 BC], who appears to have been the legitimate heir; the lack of a male heir to the throne often lead to instability.)

The end of unified Egyptian rule allowed traders known as the Hyksos, thought to be from Asia, to pass through Nubia. Later, the Hyksos and the Kushites would unify against their common enemy, Egypt. The name "Hyksos" was contrived by Manehto, a historian who compiled a kings list around 280 BC. Manetho was working centuries after the fact, so the precise origin of this population remains in question:

> These Asiatics, called Hikau-Khoswet, Amu, A'am, or Setetyu by generations of people on the Nile, were recorded by Manetho as having suddenly appeared in Egypt. He wrote that they raced on horse-drawn chariots to establish tyranny over the land. The did enter Egypt, but they did not appear there suddenly, with what Manetho termed "a blast of God." If there was a single factor that increased the Asiatic population in Egypt, it was slavery, introduced as an institution in the Middle Kingdom. Asiatics came to Egypt either as captives or immigrants eager for employment. As workers they were assimilated into Egyptian society [Bunson 1991: 119].

There were other groups in Egypt as well, groups who did not submit altogether to Egyptian rule, especially during the Intermediate Periods, called *nomes*. Nomes were kinship-based groups; they were relatively autonomous, and they asserted themselves in the absence of unified Egyptian rule:

> Unified rule came to an end in the Thirteenth [Dynasty]; during the Second Intermediate Period [Dynasties 13–17] the country was once again divided among warring factions. The shadowy 13th and 14th Dynasties together lasted just over a century. In the meantime intruders from Asia

> (the Hyksos) entered the delta region and set up a kingdom of their own. They reigned as the pharaohs of the 15th and 16th Dynasties. Quasi-independent Egyptian rule was maintained at Thebes in the south, but the Theban dynast was obliged to pay tribute to his stronger neighbor and to allow Hyksos trade to pass through his territory. While Egypt was thus divided, the power and wealth of Nubia increased apace. By 1700 BC there were three major powers on the Nile in place of the former one, prompting the Theban ruler to complain: "a chieftan is in Avaris [in the Delta] and another in Kush: I sit united with an Asiatic and a Nubian, each man in possession of his slice of Egypt." By the time that Hyksos rule was firmly established in the north, it seems certain that Egyptian political control in Nubia had come to an end [Adams 1977:189].

Though there was a considerably reduced Egyptian presence in Nubia between the Middle Kingdom and the New Kingdom, as well as a major change in the political relations between Kush and Egypt, some of the inscriptions found at Buhen are quite illustrative:

> Much more suggestive, though enigmatic, is a group of hieroglyphic stelae found at Buhen, which seem to indicate that at some time during the Second Intermediate Period the one-time Egyptian stronghold was governed by an Egyptian family on behalf of the ruler of Nubia. The Stele of Sepedher, the longest of the group, reads in part: "I was a valiant commandant of Buhen, and never did any commandant do what I did: I built the temple of Horus, Lord of Buhen, to the satisfaction of the ruler of Cush.' Another stele gives the Nubian king a name, making it plain that it is indeed a native ruler and not the pharaoh who is designated by the term 'ruler of Cush'" [Adams 1977:191].

Thus, fighting among officials over the royal succession within the Thirteenth Dynasty, and more assassinations, weakened the buffer zones. These events provided the Kushites and the Syro-Palestinians easier access to Egypt's territories, and the Kushites of upper Nubia seized lower Nubia while the Syro-Palestinians [Hyksos] seized Egypt, thereby establishing what came to be known as the Fifteenth Dynasty as the Kingdom of Kerma flourished in Nubia:

> The flowering of the Kingdom of Kerma was during the Second Intermediate Period, that is, after the end of the Middle Kingdom. During the domination of Egypt (1730–1580 BC) by the Hyksos who came from Western Asia, close diplomatic and trade relations existed between the Hyksos rulers and the princes of Kerma, and these relations occasionally led to alliances against the Theban princes. The contents of a letter written by the Hyksos king Apophis to the ruler of Kush is known from a stela of Kamose, for Kamose was able to capture the messenger with the letter: "Aaweser-Re, son of Re, Apophis, greets the son of the ruler

of Kush. Why have you not informed me that you have become ruler of Kush? Its ruler Kamose has attacked me in my own territory. I have not attacked him as he did you. He intends harming both our lands.... Come north without fear, see, he is here with me; no one will offer you resistance in Egypt and I will keep him until you have arrived. Then we will divide the towns of Egypt between us and both our lands will live in joy" [Hintze 1968:15].

Kerma culture reached its peak between 1785–1554 BC, though its origins stretch back to the Sixth Dynasty around 2300 BC; it is characterized and differentiated by the recurring pattern of grave-goods and the positioning of the dead in their tombs. "The most typical vessel form in Kerma, black-topped ware, is a round-bottomed, wide-mouthed beaker which has no parallel in Lower Nubia" (Adams 1977:196). Bronze daggers were also a common grave item. We now know, from recent excavations, that pottery was being made in Nubia as early as 8,000 BC, long before pottery occurred in Egypt. Adams points out:

> The best of the Kerma black-topped pottery has extremely thin walls and sharp rims, recalling those of the "variegated hematitic" ware of the A Horizon. The vessels have a glossy, jet-black interior and rim, the black band usually extending downwards for about an inch over the vessel exterior. The lower exterior is deep red. In most cases the black upper body and the red lower body are separated by a narrow, irregular strip of a whitish metallic color. This feature is not found in any of the other black-topped wares of Nubia, and its origin and purpose have been the subject of much discussion [Adams 1977:196].

In these tombs, mortuary items abound, especially toilet items which are laid close to the body, and sacrificed rams. Adams also notes that there are five particular burial traditions that occur only at Kerma tombs:

> Five characteristics distinguish the Kerma burials from those of the Lower Nubian peoples: bed burial, Kerma pottery, domed tumuli, ram sacrifices, and human sacrifices [Adams 1977:198].

All burials from the Kerma period that have been found before they were looted had what the Nubians called an *angareeb*, which is a bed upon which the body was laid; the *angareeb* is still used today in Sudan. Curiously, it is very rare in C-Group graves, and this remains a mystery. The domed tumuli are grave mounds that are common in burials in Upper and Lower Nubia:

> However, the typical C-Group tumulus is cylindrical in shape, being built within a vertical retaining wall of masonry. The Kerma tumulus is dome-shaped, sloping downwards from a low crown to the level of the

> ground in all directions. The ring of stones delimiting the tumulus is only a few inches high; it is primarily decorative and perhaps to protect the edges of the mound from erosion. In many Kerma graves the encircling ring of stones is dark in color, while the surface of the mound within the ring is covered with white of yellow pebbles. Kerma tumuli are even more variable in size than those of the C Horizon; the largest of them are far larger than anything found in Lower Nubia [Adams 1977:198].

Sacrificial rams and goats were generally placed in front of the *angareeb*, and some graves contained up to six sacrificed animals. These animals are also found in separate pits at some sites. Arguably, the most astonishing feature of the Kerma graves is the high frequency of human sacrifices during the period that the culture flourished:

> A surprisingly large number of Kerma graves—at least those dating from the heydey of the kingdom—contain the bodies of one or more sacrificial victims who were buried at the same time as the "owner" of the grave. They were found even in the small unimposing cemetery of Mirgissa, but much more consistently and abundantly at Kerma itself. Many relatively small and humble graves contained one or two sacrificed retainers, while the largest of the royal tombs may have had four hundred. From the positions of the bodies, Reisner concluded that they had been buried alive and had died of suffocation [Adams 1977:199].

Human sacrifice was a common practice in Egypt as far back as the Old Kingdom. The close relations between Nubia and Egypt most often resulted in a subordinate position for the Nubians, thus they were acculturated by the Egyptians over time. Egyptian art, religion, and writing were common in Nubia, so human sacrifice was not really foreign. The site of Kerma was excavated by George A. Reisner during the Harvard-Boston Expedition in the Sudan, which took place between the years 1913 and 1916. Reisner was especially interested in a building constructed of mud brick known as the Western
Deffufa:

> The Western *Deffufa*, which first claimed Reisner's attention, is one of the most extraordinary structures in Nubia, and the only one of its kind in existence. As originally constructed it was a solid rectangular mass of mud brick more than 150 feet long and 75 feet wide, and probably stood to a height considerably greater than the 60 feet which is still preserved [Adams 1977:200].

An even more remarkable find was the eight "Great Tumuli" which actually exceeded some of the specifications of the famous Egyptian tombs, and at the same time, the assemblages of grave goods. The manner in which the main body was buried clearly diverged from Egyptian practices:

> These structures are without parallel among the funerary monuments of Nubia. The largest of them is nearly 300 feet in diameter, and the interior chambers are far more extensive than are those of any Egyptian pyramid. To complete the picture of barbarian magnificence it may be added that the number of human sacrifices in Tumulus X at Kerma — 322 by actual count, and perhaps as many as 400 before plundering — is larger than in any other known tomb of any civilization. The chief body appears always to have been covered with a hide, usually an ox-hide, and in some cases at least the hide covered the sacrifices as well. It will be recalled by Egyptologists that in the letter of Amenemhat III to Sinuhe, the king, after promising Sinuhe a princely Egyptian burial, goes on to say: "Let not thy death take place in a foreign land, let not the Bedouin make thy funeral procession, let thyself not be placed in the hide of a ram" [Adams 1977:204].

The cultural developments at Kerma represent the transition from a tribal-oriented society to a dynastic-oriented society; the transition helped the Nubians resist Egyptian imperialism for some time. The Egyptians, however, were able to regain their power in Nubia, and even increase it beyond any previous levels:

> As it turned out, the indigenous development of an imperial system in Sudan was forestalled by the Egyptians. Thrusting aside the native rulers, they established their own hegemony from the First to the Fourth Cataract. The full complex of civilization thus arrived in Nubia not as the outcome of local developments, but as a transplant from Egypt. It was many centuries later before a genuinely Nubian empire was achieved, but when it came, it owed much of the legacy to Kerma [Adams 1977:216].

The Egyptians also pushed aside the Hyksos; they had termed the Hyksos' occupation of Egypt "the Great Humiliation." The Theban kings had retained power, and Wadjkheperre Kamose is the king who is credited with starting the downfall of the Hyksos in Egypt. Kamose was the last ruler of the Seventeenth Dynasty; his father was Sekenenre Ta'o II and his mother was Queen Ahhotep.

Kamose resolved that he would oust the Hyksos and the Nubians from Egypt, however, he employed Nubian fighters known as the Medjay in his campaign. The Medjay were an integral part of Egyptian society during the dynastic periods. "The Medjay, famed as warriors of cunning and stamina, served as scouts for the Egyptians on the marches or at the oases of the Lybian Desert. In actual battle, they formed light infantry units and rushed to the front lines, delighting in hand-to-hand combat and in slaughter of the enemy. The Medjay became the backbone of the newly formed state police" (Bunson 1991: 159). By the reign of his successor, Nebpehtire Ahmose of the Eighteenth Dynasty, the Hyksos had been dispatched and Egypt entered what is arguably its most glorious period during the New Kingdom (1570–1085 BC). The rulers of the Eighteenth Dynasty include the most well-known pharaohs: Ma'atkare Hatshepsut, Menkheperre Thutmose III, the religious reformer Akhenaten Amenhotep IV, Mema'atre Seti I, and the infamous Userma'atre'setepenre Ramesses II, known for the excessive number of monuments that he made to himself. (This may have been an attempt by Ramesses II to insure his immortality, in conjunction with the estimated 250 children that he is said to have fathered; in ancient Egypt, ones name must be kept alive by their children. If the person's name is forgotten, then he or she cannot achieve immortality). According to Wilson,

> Although the memory of a name was enough to confer immortality, names recorded in their written forms or spoken by priests or well-wishers were considered to be more secure than trusting to the fickle memories of one's family. Egyptian society was based on family life and the people fervently hoped that all members of their families would be reunited after death. So it was essential that the necessary rituals were carried out by the surviving relatives who, in their turn, would receive the same duty from their heirs. No one wished to face great-grandpa in the next world and have to explain why his mortuary offerings had been allowed to lapse [Wilson 1995: 21].

The Eighteenth Dynasty was the most imperialistic of Egypt's previous dynasties; it successfully conquered southern Nubia, and went on to take Palestine. It instituted a tribute system in Nubia whereby viceroys controlled vassals who extorted tribute from Nubians for the pharaoh. The kings were absolute rulers during this period, and their filial resentments continued as royal successions took place. For example, Thutmose III, the nephew of Hatshesut; resented the idea of a woman as pharaoh (Hatshesut wore a false beard and dressed as a man during her reign; she is also pictured as a man in her tomb) so much that he had almost all of her monuments destroyed after she died. Hatshepsut was a usurper because Akheperenre Thutmose II had appointed his son, Thutmose III, king before he died.

The next major development in Egypt occurred with the ascension of Akhenaten Amenhotep IV (1379–1362 BC), who used his unabated powers to change Egypt's religious practice of polytheism to monotheism, essentially declared himself a god, and moved the capital of Egypt to Tell-el-Amarna. Nubia did not suffer any major expansion of Egyptian rule during Akhenaten's reign, and "the Amarna period was not a time of growth for the Egyptian empire. Egypt's southern dominions, which fell under the direct supervision of the Nubian viceroy, the king's son of Kush, seem to have suffered least, remaining relatively — if not totally — stable" (Reeves 2001: 152).

Notably, Akhenaten may have seen the people in the conquered territories as one, in conjunction with being the world's first known monotheists. From the sacred writings of ancient Egypt that Dr. Maulana Karenga compiled in *The Husia*, we find that one praise of the Pharaoh Akhenaten said: "O' Sole God besides whom there is none. You set every person in his [her] place and satisfy their needs. Their tongues differ in speech and so do their characters. The color of their skins are different also. For you distinguished the people How excellent are your ways O' Lord of eternity" (Karenga 1989: 22). Most of the Eighteenth Dynasty's expansion is attributed to the raids of Thutmose II:

> The last major campaign of conquest and annexation was undertaken in the reign of Thutmose II. Slave-raids, disguised as punitive expeditions, are occasionally reported until the end of the New Kingdom. For all practical purposes Nubia was Egyptian territory, and its people were Egyptian subjects. Having acquired this vast and lucrative domain — equal in size to Egypt itself, and far exceeding in size the domains of Asia — the Pharaoh set out to govern and exploit it, and ultimately to Egyptianize it. In the end these efforts succeeded beyond expectation, and the effect was to be felt in Egypt for centuries to come [Adams 1977:218].

As the Egyptians dominated the whole of Nubia, they repaired the forts that had been abandoned at sites like Buhen, even though they served no military purpose, per se; for the most part, they made new walls on the forts called "skin walls" in order to beautify the facades. These facades served as testaments of Egyptian rule in Nubia that could not be mistaken. Thutmose II built large temples in Nubia, and Rameses II continued to do so on an even more monumental scale. Rameses II was somewhat iconoclastic in that he built grandiose monuments that had no connection with a city. His most noteworthy temple is the well-known one at Abu Simbel: "Abu Simbel has been described as everything from a masterpiece to a 'gigantic abomination.' Its uniqueness, however, is beyond dispute" (Adams 1977:222).

During this period, "the area of Napata, just below the Fourth Cataract, emerged as the great political and religious center of Nubia under the empire of Kush, but its foundation goes back to the period of New Kingdom colonization. Conspicuously missing from the list of New Kingdom 'urban' centers in Nubia is Kerma. The kingdom evidently went under in the first rush of reconquest, and we never hear of it again" (Adams 1977:229). With the viceregnal regime in place in Nubia, Kush became more of a focus:

> Thuwre, the Commandant of Buhen appointed by Ahmose, was given the title "King's Son of Kush" in the reign of Amenhotep I. He was the first of a line of twenty-five or more officials who bore that tile, and who governed both Nubia and the southernmost district of Egypt as deputies of the pharaoh. They are usually designated as Viceroys of Kush, although strictly speaking their mandate included both Kush [Upper Nubia] and Wawat [Lower Nubia] as well as the region from Aswan to El Kab in Egypt. The Viceroy was responsible for the punctual payment of the tribute of Nubia [both from Wawat and Kush] [Adams 1977:229].

Slaves were given as tribute to the viceroys, as it is recorded in the *Annals of Thutmose III*:

> Tribute of Wawat (Adams 1977:232; his translation of the word "Negro" is erroneous)
> Year 31. 92 cattle, 1 harvest
> Year 33. 20 slaves, 104 cattle, 1 harvest
> Year 34. 254 deben of gold, 10 slaves, and an unknown number of cattle
> Year 35. 34 slaves, 94 cattle, 1 harvest
> Year 38. 2844 deben of gold, 16 slaves, 77 cattle
> Year 39. 89 cattle, ivory and ebony
> Year 41. 3144 deben of gold and 3 kidet of gold, 114 cattle, and an unknown quantity of ivory
> Year 42. 2374 deben of gold and 1 kidet of gold, 1 harvest
>
> Tribute of Kush
> Year 34. 300 deben of gold, 60 Negro slaves, 275 cattle, ivory and ebony
> Year 35. 70 deben of gold and 1 kidet of gold, an unknown quantity of slaves, cattle, ivory and ebony, 1 harvest
> Year 38. 100 deben of gold and 6 kidet of gold, 36 Negro slaves, 306 cattle, ivory and ebony, 1 harvest
> Year 39. 144 deben of gold and 2 kidet of gold, 101 Negro slaves, and an unknown quantity of cattle
> Year 41. 94 deben of gold and 2 kidet of gold, 21 Negro slaves, and an unknown quantity of cattle

According to Adams, a deben of gold is equivalent to 20 pounds of gold; however, a recently published article provides evidence that the deben varied in weight over time:

> The Egyptian weight system appears to have been founded on a unit called the kite, with a decimal ratio, 10 kites equaling 1 deben, and 10

debens equaling 1 sep. Over the long span of Egyptian history, the weight of the kite varied from period to period, ranging all the way from 4.5 to 29.9 grams (0.16 to 1.05 ounces). About 3,400 different weights have been recovered from ancient Egypt, some in basic geometric shapes, others in human and animal forms [Britannica 2002].

Based on this updated scale, the Tribute from Wawat from years 31 to 42 would range from approximately 807 to 5,654 pounds, not including kidets of gold; the Tribute from Kush would range from approximately 63 to 464 pounds of gold, not including kidets of gold. At this level of tribute, I estimate that the Egyptians may have taken about 1,870 to 61,180 pounds of gold from Nubia over a 100-year period; over a 1,000-year period, the Egyptians may have taken about 18,700 to 611,800 pounds of gold from Nubia, which is about 9 to 305 tons of gold (excluding kidets of gold). Thus, the lucrative colony of Nubia contributed the wealth upon which the Eighteenth Dynasty flourished, and we see just a hint of what was accumulated in Egypt from the tomb of the boy king Tutankhamun. Many Egyptologists believe that his short reign does not equal what the other pharaohs of his time may have been buried with, their tombs having been robbed in antiquity.

By the end of the Eighteenth Dynasty, the Nubians had become acculturated to the point that there was little or no discernible difference between Egyptian or Nubian cultural practices:

> By the late XVIII [Dynasty] the ascendancy of Egyptian burial rites and burial furniture was complete, and a distinct Nubian population can no longer be identified either by graves or pottery [Adams 1977:235].

During the Nineteenth Dynasty, the Nile is thought to have declined since a great deal of emigration from Lower Nubia took place. The trend continued throughout the Twentieth Dynasty and weakened Egypt's stronghold on Nubia:

> A declining Nile and a crumbling empire forced the Egyptians out of Nubia in the XX [Dynasty], but the Nubians were not immediately able to exploit their new strength or Egypt's weakness. It took some time for the lesson of the pharaohs to sink in. When it did, however, an Egyptianized, politically aroused Nubia, with its enormous resources of gold, was to emerge as a major force on the Nile. For two thousand years the shadow of Egypt had lain upon Nubia; at the end of the New Kingdom the shadow of Nubia was beginning to be visible in Egypt [Adams 1977: 24].

The period between the end of the Eighteenth Dynasty and the beginning of the Twenty-Fifth Dynasty spanned some six hundred years, and relevant hieroglyphic inscriptions from the period are virtually unknown. However, according to Basil Davidson, "Late in the first half of the eighth century BC, the kings of Kush invaded and conquered Egypt" (Davidson 1993: 58). This is the time span during which the indigenous rulers of Nubia developed the areas of Napata and Dongola.

> At Kurru near Napata there is the oldest cemetery of the ruling house which was able to extend its sphere of influence over an increasing area until the king called Kashta succeeded in conquering Upper Egypt before 750 BC. He forced the "Consort of the god Amon," Shepenupet I, who resided at Thebes and was a daughter of Osorkon III, King of Libya, to adopt his own daughter Amenirdis. In this way, the influence of the Kingdom of Napata was ensured over the divine state of Amon of Thebes and, consequently, over Upper Egypt, while Osorkon III ruled only over Lower Egypt. Piankhy (751–716 BC), son and successor of Kashta, completed the work of conquest begun by his father. A large stela, which he had erected on the Gebel Barkal near Napata, records his campaigns against Egypt. After his victory, Piankhy returned to Napata; and it was not until the reign of his brother and successor Shabako (716–701 BC) that the capital was moved to Thebes so that Shabako could have firmer control over the administration of Egypt. The kings considered themselves true Egyptian Pharaohs: the language of their inscriptions and the style of their buildings and memorials were purely Egyptian, and in many details consciously resumed the language and artistic style of the Old and Middle Kingdom [Hintze 1968:17].

Questions have arisen regarding the exact origin of the Nubians who conquered Egypt in the eighth century BC, and the level of acculturation that Nubians had experienced makes such a determination difficult, though some claims, like Reisner's Libyan origin theory, are no longer accepted by archaeologists. According to Welsby:

> The territorial expansion of the early Kushite state is shrouded in mystery. The excavations of a cemetery of 105 tumuli at Debeira East, north of the Second Cataract, may shed some light on this problem. Much of this material consists of Egyptian imports which, as with the similar material from the el Kurru tumulus, can be dated to the late New Kingdom. A close relationship between the two sites, which lie several hundred kilometers apart, seems likely although its significance is unclear. Some scholars have suggested that the ruling clan buried at Kurru came from the Meroe region, others that they were the descendants of one of the princely families who governed the area on behalf of the Egyptian administration during the New Kingdom. Reisner's view that the earliest Kushite rulers were of Libyan origin is now totally discarded [Welsby 1998: 14–15].

This information brings up an important question. The "Kushite domination of Egypt" is a generally accepted concept in the literature, but if the so-called Nubian pharaohs considered themselves Egyptian, wrote in the Egyptian language, worshipped the Egyptian deity, and were considered legitimate Egyptian pharaohs by the so-called Egyptians themselves, how valid are the distinctions between these groups, and on what basis have they been made? The mural from the Tomb of Huy clearly shows that there was a continuum of phenotypic characteristics in Nubia even during the Eighteenth Dynasty. Was this reversed somehow? I think not. Dr. Bruce Trigger emphasizes that the research in this area as it pertains to the populations in question exhibits some major theoretical shortcomings:

> Nowhere has the confusion of culturally acquired characteristics and biologically inherited ones produced more bizarre and dangerous myths than in respect to northeastern Africa. In the nineteenth century, scholars, who lacked reliable historical information for many parts of the world, sought to utilize contemporary variations in physical types as a means of reconstructing important aspects of human history. They assumed that as a general rule the more similar two groups of people were physically, the more closely they were related historically and culturally. Early human history was seen as a process of dispersal and differentiation which occurred at the same time and along similar lines in terms of race, language, and culture. These early racial studies embodied contemporary nationalistic and racial prejudices. While the scientific basis for these studies has long been discredited, specific ideas and much of the terminology survive and continue to influence interpretations of African prehistory. All of these people are Africans. To proceed further and divide them into Caucasoid and Negroid stocks is to perform an act that is arbitrary and wholly devoid of historical or biological significance [Trigger 1978:27].

These Nubian pharaohs worshipped Amon, the ancient god of the Egyptian empire, and "the Egyptians also considered them to be legitimate Pharaohs who had reunited Egypt and abolished Libyan foreign rule" (Hintze 1968:18). The Nubians were even using the *Book of the Day*, which explained the sky's topography and the sun's movements, that dated back to the Middle Kingdom as late as during the reign of Taharqa, providing another example of the level of restoration to the old ways that the Twenty-Fifth Dynasty brought:

> The only New Kingdom tomb in which the Book of the Day has been found to date is that of Ramesses VI. It reappears in the royal necropolis at Tanis; there are selections in the tomb of Osorkon II, and a nearly complete version exists in that of Shoshenq III. The latest versions occur in the tomb of the scribe Ramose from the reign of Taharqa of Dynasty 25 [Hornung 1999: 114].

In conjunction, Deiter Kessler makes it clear that the Twenty-Fifth Dynasty was not made up of "outsiders" who were held in the esteem of the Hyksos by the indigenous Egyptian population: "The Kushite chieftans continued to use the Egyptian temple buildings on their lands to legitimize their position, and they eventually succeeded in gaining control of Lower Nubia. It was only a matter of time before the Kushite ruler was accepted by the ruling families of Thebes as the new pharaoh by decree of Amun, thus initiating the Twenty-Fifth Dynasty" (Schulz and Seidel 1998: 273).

Therefore, I believe that a review of the underlying assumptions that are frequently brought up, even in the research contained herein, is warranted. There are strictly delineated boundaries, supposedly, of Egyptian or Nubian rule in Egypt and Nubia, but as we have seen, by the end of the Eighteenth Dynasty, the so-called Nubians could not be differentiated on any discernible basis. By Kashta's reign, he was recognized as the legitimate pharaoh in both Egypt, which is quite a feat in itself and Nubia. The Twenty-Fifth Dynasty has also been erroneously referred to as "The Ethiopian Dynasty" by a number of scholars who have conducted research on Egypt; this dynasty has nothing whatsoever to do with Ethiopia, and the two would actually be military adversaries during the Meroitic period and beyond. Shortly after the fall of the Twenty-Fifth Dynasty, African civilization began to shape what would later be termed "Western" civilization, once the proscriptions against allowing the Greeks to have intimate knowledge of its closely guarded philosophies and practices were lifted:

> Owing to the practice of piracy, in which the Ionians and Carians were active, the Egyptians were forced to make immigration laws restricting the immigration of the Greeks and punishing their infringement by capital punishment, i.e. the sacrifice of the victim. Before the time of Psammitichus, the Greeks were not allowed to go beyond the coast of Lower Egypt, but during the reign of Amasis, those conditions were modified. For the first time in Egyptian history Ionians and Carians were employed as Mercenaries in the Egyptian Army [670 BC], interpretation was organized through a body of interpreters, and the Greeks began to gain useful information concerning the culture of the Egyptians. Their contact with Egypt resulted in the genesis of their enlightenment [James 1992: 41].

Around 671 BC, the Assyrians attacked Egypt, took Memphis and went on to destroy Thebes; their reign lasted until 654 BC when Psammitichus I defeated them with the help of Ionian mercenaries and the king of Lydia:

> The last king of the Twenty-Fifth Dynasty, Tanwetamani, thereupon withdrew to Napata. Thus ended a period of 75 years in which Egypt and Kush formed a united empire. Tanwetamani's successors ruled a further

thousand years in northern Sudan; their capital was first Napata again and then Meroe, farther south and about 144 miles north of present day Khartoum. According to the location of the royal tombs, the history of the Kingdom of Kush can be divided into two great periods: the Napata, until 295 BC, and the Meroitic, until about AD 350. The relationship between the Kingdom of Kush and her neighbor Egypt and the various Egyptian rulers was a very changeable one and was often of a military nature. Psammitichus II undertook a campaign against Napata in 591 BC with the help of Greek and Carian mercenaries. The ensuing destruction of Napata was perhaps one of the reasons for the transfer of the capital to Meroe, which consequently may already have taken place under Aspelta 592–568 BC [Hintze 1968:19].

Archaeological excavations in the Sudan have provided evidence that the Nubian kings moved their capital to Meroe where they ruled for a millennium, and where there were numerous strategic benefits:

> Following the expulsion from Egypt of the kings of Kush after the Assyrian invasion of 671 BC, the Kushites retreated to their former homeland. Their rule in the Sudan continued for another thousand tears with the capital initially at Napata neat the Fourth Cataract, moving about 600 bc upstream to Meroe. The move of the state capital was of threefold importance. It marked the effective break from dependence upon Egypt, it brought the capital within reach of the fuel that was need to maintain the iron-smelting industry which soon arose, and it provided the town with surroundings that enabled crops and hers to be raised a the scale sufficient to feed its growing population [Phillipson 1994: 166–167].

The Kingdom of Kush suffered from the invasion of the Persians, and ultimately, the Kushites were paying tribute to and visiting the Persian courts of Darius and Xerxes in the sixth century BC: Meroe was plundered by a desert tribe known as the Rehrehes after King Talakhamani died in 431 BC, but the new king of Kush eventually repelled the invaders after his speedy coronation.

Meroe persisted, becoming a major iron-smelting center, and is credited with spreading the techniques for iron-casting throughout ancient Africa. The 'Great Stele' of Amaninenas and Akinidad from Meroe is somewhat perplexing, though, and it really brings to the forefront the ideas about "stocks" expressed by Trigger:

> The phonetic values of most of the characters are known, yet the language expressed in this long-forgotten alphabet continues to baffle scholars despite fifty years intensive study. It may belong, as does modern Nubian, to the general Sudanic family of African languages, but it shows no close affinity to any known speech of today. Thus, as Shinnie remarks:

"Meroitic has, with Etruscan, the distinction of being one of the two ancient languages the phonetic values of whose signs can be read with reasonable certainty, but the meaning of whose words cannot be understood. This is a great barrier to a complete understanding of Meroitic history and culture, and until the language has been successfully read and the inscriptions translated, much of the story of Meroe will remain unknown" [Adams 1977:298].

Thus, what ultimately happened to Meroe and its population remains unclear, though there is evidence that the Ethiopians did invade Meroe in the fourth century AD. Most sources simply say that Meroe was inhabited by what has been termed the "X-Group" from AD 250–550.

I believe that from this contextualization, a different picture emerges with regard to the events of northeastern Africa from the terminal fourth millennium BC to the Meroitic Period. The indigenous populations should no longer, in my opinion, be viewed as monolithic, discrete groups. Rather, we should now take a more objective approach, leaving behind the nationalistic and "racial" biases of the past that have led many scholars to unscientific conclusions.

References

Adams, William Y. *Nubia: Corridor to Africa*. Princeton: Princeton University Press, 1977.
Bunson, Margaret. *The Encyclopedia of Ancient Egypt*. New York: Gramercy Books, 1991.
Davidson, Basil. *African Civilization Revisited*. Trenton: Africa World Press, 1993.
Emery, Walter B. *Egypt in Nubia*. London: Hutchison & Co. 1965.
Hintze, Fritz and Ursula Hintze. *Civilizations of the Old Sudan*. Liepzig: German Democratic Republic, 1968.
Hornung, Erik. *The Ancient Egyptian Books of the Afterlife*. Ithica: Cornell University Press, 1999.
James, George G.M. *Stolen Legacy: Greek Philosophy Is Stolen Egyptian Philosophy*. Trenton: Africa World Press, 1992.
Karenga, Maulana. *The Husia*. Los Angeles: University of Sankore Press, 1989.
Pappas, Theodore, ed. *Britannica 2002 Standard Edition*. CD-ROM.
Phillipson, David W. *African Archaeology*. Cambridge: Cambridge University Press, 1994.
Reeves, Nicholas. *Akhenaten: Egypt's False Prophet*. London: Thames & Hudson: New York, 2001.
Save-Soderberg, Torgny. *Temples and Tombs of Ancient Nubia*. London: Thames and Hudson, 1987.
Schulz, Regine and Matthias Seidel, eds. *Egypt: The World of the Pharaohs*. Cologne: Konemann Verlagsgesellschaft, 1998.

Silverman, David P., ed. *Ancient Egypt.* New York: Oxford University Press, 1997.
Trigger, Bruce. *Nubia Under the Pharaohs.* London: Thames and Hudson, 1976.
_____. *Africa in Antiquity: The Arts of Ancient Nubia and the Sudan.* New York: The Brooklyn Museum, 1978.
_____, B.J. Kemp, D. O'Connor, and A.B. Lloyd. *Ancient Egypt: A Social History.* Cambridge: Cambridge University Press, 1998.
Welsby, Derek A. *The Kingdom of Kush: The Napatan and Meroitic Empires.* Princeton: Markus Weiner Publishers, 1998.
Wenig, Steffen. *Africa in Antiquity: The Arts of Ancient Nubia and the Sudan.* New York: The Brooklyn Museum, 1978.
Wilson, Hilary. *Understanding Hieroglyphs.* Lincolnwood: Passport Books, 1995.

About the Contributors

Reynaldo Anderson is a doctoral candidate in Communications at the University of Nebraska at Lincoln and an adjunct instructor in African American Studies at St. Louis University.

Molefi Kete Asante, Ph.D., is Professor of African American Studies at Temple University.

Kathleen E. Bethel is Senior Reference Librarian for Africana Studies at Northwestern University.

Kevin Cokely, Ph.D., is an Assistant Professor in Counseling Psychology at Southern Illinois University at Carbondale.

James L. Conyers, Jr., Ph.D., is Director of African American Studies and University Professor of African American Studies at the University of Houston.

Malachi Crawford, is a doctoral student in History at the University of Missouri at Columbia.

George J. Sefa Dei, Ph.D., is Professor of Sociology at the University of Toronto.

Paul Easterling, is a graduate student in Africana Studies at the State University of New York at Albany.

Rhett Jones, Ph.D., is Professor of History and Africana Studies at Brown University.

Terry Kershaw, Ph.D., is an Associate Professor of Sociology and African American Studies and Director of the Black Studies Program and Center of Ethnic Studies at Virginia Tech.

Carol Lloyd, Ph.D., is Professor of Teacher Education at the University of Nebraska at Omaha.

Miriam Ma'at-Ka-Re Monges, Ph.D., is an Associate Professor of Social Work and African American Studies at California State University at Chico.

Tanya Y. Price, Ph.D., is an Assistant Professor of Anthropology and African American Studies at the University of Missouri at Kansas City.

Reiland Rabaka, Ph.D., is an Assistant Professor of Black Studies at California State University at Long Beach.

Larry Ross, Ph.D., is an Assistant Professor of Black Studies at the University of Nebraska at Omaha.

Jason J. Thompson, is a doctoral student in Communications at Northwestern University.

Ahati N.N. Toure, is the Assistant Director of African American Studies at the University of Houston and a doctoral candidate in Africana and U.S. History at the University of Nebraska at Lincoln.

Sandy Van Dyk, Ph.D., is an Associate Professor and Chair of the Humanities Department at Bloomfield College of New Jersey.

Index

academic achievement 5–6; assessment 15–18
Adams, Barbara 164, 169–170
administrators, role of 22
advanced placement classes 19
African American Achievement Plan 5–9
African American male narrative 163–174
African Diaspora 176, 187–197
African holocaust 67; *see also* slavery
African psychology 141–158
afrocentric critical analysis 176–184
afrocentric discourse 216–219
afrocentric knowledge 215–219
afrocentricity in education: African psychology 141–158; benefits of 47–48; Black Studies and 31–33; challenge of 40–41; critical theory and *see* critical theory; defined 37–39, 50–51; Eurocentricity compared 39, 52–53, 213–215; history and 43–47; libraries and librarians 55–62; multiculturalism 39–43; resistance to 41–42; theory of 51–55; *see also* specific listings
American colonial period 258–259
American Indian identity claims 268–280
American Indians, role of 258–262
anti-colonialist discourse 211–228
Ark of the Covenant 204
Asante, Molefi K. 31, 32, 142–144, 153–154, 176–184
assessment 15–18
Azibo, D. 32

Baldwin, J. 32
Banks, Curtis 152–153
Bartolome, L. I. 14
behavior styles 13
Bennett, Lerone, Jr. 177–184
bias: cultural 7–8, 12–14, 18–21; standardized tests 15–18
Black Caribs 276–277
Black male narrative 163–174
Black nationalism 131–132
Black Panther Party 125–126
Black Power Movement 123–128
Black Seminole Indians 274–280
Black Studies, university level: afrocentricity and *see* afrocentricity in education; critical analysis 33; empowerment 33; first department of 27–28; focus of 30; interdisciplinarity 28–30; multiculturalism 39–43; positivism and 30–31; research 29–30, 33; sociology and 30–32; theoretical framework 33–34 *see also* critical theory; values 33–34
Brown, John 170–171
budget issues 18
Busby, Margaret 199–200

California Achievement Tests 10–11, 17–18, 20
Canada, African experience in 218, 224–228
Cape Verde Island 264–265, 280
Carmichael, Stokely 123–126
Casey, Bernie 163
"castles" of slavery 187–197
The Challenge of Blackness 177–184

311

Cherokee Indians 268, 270
Chickasaw Indians 272
Choctaw Indians 272
Civil Rights Movement 12–13
Clack, Doris 59
Clarke, John Henrik 169–170
classical education 27
college prep classes 11, 19, 21
Committee for the Defense of History 41
community, role of 14, 27, 219–222
Conyers, James L., Jr. 163–174
Creek Indians 268
Creole identity 264
critical analysis: Asante, Molefi K. 31–32, 142–144, 153–154, 176–184; critical pedagogy 5–22; literary criticism 176–184
critical pedagogy 5–22
critical theory 67–69; anti-colonialist discourse 211–228; Asante, Molefi K. 31–32, 142–144, 153–154, 176–184; Douglas, Frederick 113–122; Du Bois, W. E. B. 69–94, 170–171; literary criticism 176–184; Woodson, Carter G. 165–169
Crummel, Alexander 130–139
cultural bias 7–8, 12–14, 18–21
cultural capital 7

decolonization of knowledge 211–228
deficit model in education 6, 14
demographics 9–12
Diaspora, African 176, 187–197
discipline policies 13
discriminatory practices 14, 18–21
disparities in student achievement 5–22
dominance, institutionalization of 213–215
double consciousness 191
Douglas, Frederick 113–122, 130–133, 135–139
Du Bois, W. E. B. 27, 69–94, 130–131, 133–139, 163, 170–171, 191, 262
dungeons of slavery 187–197
Dutton, Charles 163

education defined 38
educational outcomes 5–6
Egypt, historical view of 286–306

essentialism 191–192, 219–220
Ethiopia 201–204
Eurocentric education 42–43, 213–215
Eurocentricity 39, 52, 213–215

Fanon, Franz 217
fiction, analysis of 176–184
Foucault, M. 218
Freejacks 265–267, 278–279
Freire, Paulo 6, 14
funding issues 18

Gates, Henry Louis, Jr. 113, 118
Ghana 187–189, 192–194
Gilroy, Paul 191
Gordon, Lewis 173–174

Hamilton, Charles V. 126–127
Henry, Charles P. 164, 171–172
Henslin, James 31–32
high schools 5–22
history 12–13 27–28; afrocentricity and 43–46; American colonial period 258–259; American West 231–245; corrections needed 46–47; Douglas, Frederick 113–122; Egypt 286–306; historiography applied 237–245; intellectual history 129–139; Native Americans, role of 258–262; Nubia 286–306; protest literature and 177; Spanish American colonies 258–260
honors classes 19
Howe, Stephen 152–153
Hurston, Zora Neal 172

identity issues 43–44 124, 174, 176, 189, 196–197, 222–224; Indianness, claims of 268–280; mestizo identity 274; mixed-race identities 257–282; multiracial identities 262–282; whiteness, claims of 264–282
institutionalized racism 14–15 20–21, 211–228
intellectual history 129–139
interdisciplinarity 28–30

Jahn, Janheinz 123, 129–130
Jim Crow laws 265–266

Kambon, Kobi 146–147, 149–151, 157–158

Kardiner, Abram 263
Kebra Nagast 201–202
King, Martin Luther, Jr. 172
King Solomon 199–209

language as decolonizing tool 211–213
language style 13
liberal arts 27
libraries and librarians 55–62
literary criticism 176–184
Lumbee people 273

Makeda, Queen 199–209
Malcolm X 164, 172–173
math proficiency 11–12
mathematics issues 19–20
Menelik 203–204
mestizo identity 274
Middle Passage 44–45, 188–197
middle schools 5–22
Miller, Kelly 262
Million Man March 163
miscegenation 260–282
Mis-Education of the Negro 27, 37, 164–167
mixed-blood Indians 271–272
mixed-race identities 257–282
Mudimbe, V. Y. 145
multiculturalism 8, 39–42
Muntu 123–124, 129–130
Myers, Linda James 149

Naranjo, Domingo 268–269
Narragansett Indians 279–280
nationalisms 131–139
Native American identity claims 268–280
Native Americans, role of 258–262
Newton, Huey P. 125
non-fiction, analysis of 176–184
North Africa, ancient history and 286–306
Ntu 123, 127–128
Nubia 286–306

Ogbu, J. 13
Oklahoma Territory 272
Ovesey, Lionel 263

parents, role of 27
pedagogy, critical 5–22

Pickard, Eve 270
politics of education 6, 21–22, 211–228
positivism 30–31
poverty 14, 18
protest literature 177
psychology, African 141–158
Pueblo Indian Revolt 268–269

Queen Makeda 199–209
Queen of Sheba 199–209

race, teacher response to 14–15, 20–21
race ignored in school 15
racial bias in testing 16–18
racial segregation 260
racism in classrooms 8–9, 13–15
Ravitch, D. 42
reading proficiency 11–12
reform of system 9, 12, 20–22, 211–228
religious practice as factor 264
remediation model in education 14, 20–21
respect for students 7, 21
Robinson, Nana Okofo 188–189
Robinson, Sister Imahkus Ninzinga 188–189
Rushton, J. Philippe 145, 154–155

San Francisco State University 27
Schlesinger, Arthur 41
science proficiency 11–12
Seale, Bobby 124
secondary schools 5–22
Seminole Indians 274–280
Seneca Indians 269–270
Sheba, Queen of 199–209
"Shebanization" of knowledge 199–209
Shorty, Bongo 188–189, 196
slave trade *see* slavery
slavery 27, 44–45, 44–46
social mobility 27
social support structures 12
sociology 30–32
Solomon, King 199–209
Spanish American colonies 258–260
standardized tests 6, 15–18, 20
Sun Fish 270

Taylor, Quintard 231–245
teachable moments 9

teacher response to race 14–15, 21
teaching methods 9, 14, 21
Toure, Kwame 123–126
tracking in education 19–20
Trail of Tears 272
Turner, Nat 170–171

urban communities 27

vocational education 27

Walker, S. Jay 164, 170–171
Washington, Booker T. 27, 163

Weldon, Jacob and Ruth 44
West, American 231–245
West as region 231–245
white culture 7–8, 213–215
white supremism 41
white teachers, attitudes of 14–15, 21
whiteness as identity 264–282
wholism, African 204–206
wisdom, quest for 199–209
womanism 208–209
Woodson, Carter G. 27, 37, 164–169
Wright, Bobby 155–156
writing proficiency 11–12

www.ingramcontent.com/pod-product-compliance
Ingram Content Group UK Ltd.
Pitfield, Milton Keynes, MK11 3LW, UK
UKHW041924140426
5217IPUK00014B/303